Cultural Rights of Third-Country Nationals in EU Law

Anna Magdalena Kosińska

Cultural Rights of Third-Country Nationals in EU Law

Translated by Adam Kunysz

palgrave
macmillan

Anna Magdalena Kosińska
John Paul II Catholic University of Lublin
Lublin, Poland

Translated by
Adam Kunysz
Tarnobrzeg, Poland

ISBN 978-3-030-30153-8   ISBN 978-3-030-30154-5 (eBook)
https://doi.org/10.1007/978-3-030-30154-5

This Palgrave Macmillan imprint is published by the registered company Springer Nature Switzerland AG.
The registered company address is: Gewerbestrasse 11, 6330 Cham, Switzerland

To Karolina and Milena with love

Contents

Abbreviations

AFSJ	Area of Freedom, Security and Justice
AMIF	Asylum, Migration and Integration Fund
CEAS	Common European Asylum System
CFR	Charter of Fundamental Rights
CJEU	Court of Justice of the European Union
EASO	European Asylum Support Office
ECHR	European Convention on Human Rights
ECtHR	European Court of Human Rights
EMN	European Migration Network
ERF	European Return Fund
EU	European Union
IOM	International Organization for Migration
TEU	Treaty on European Union
TFEU	Treaty on the Functioning of the European Union
UNESCO	United Nations Educational, Scientific and Cultural Organization
UNHCR	United Nations High Commissioner for Refugees

CHAPTER 1

Introduction

1.1 Justification for Undertaking Research

The subject undertaken in the current work, that is the guarantees of the cultural rights of third-country nationals and of their functioning in the legal system of the European Union, seems to be of particular significance and is worthy of an in-depth analysis for several reasons.

First of all, the European Union is experiencing the migration crisis, which consists in an intensive influx of third-country nationals to EU Member States. Only in 2016 almost 1.3 million persons coming originally from countries that are culturally distant from the orbit of the European culture, such as Syria, Afghanistan, Iran, Pakistan and Nigeria, applied for international protection in the European Union.[1] As a result, the questions of effective cultural integration of immigrants and potential activities with a view of increasing the European identity have become widely debated issues. On the other hand, it turns out it is necessary to clearly define the ways in which third-country nationals might exercise their cultural rights, including the right to express their own cultural identity and cultivate their unique customs and traditions. It is also justifiable to define the scope of protection granted to foreign nationals in the case of persecution on cultural grounds that they might experience in their countries of origin.

[1] Key findings of the European Asylum Support Office (EASO) annual accounts on the situation in the area of asylum in the EU in 2016. The European Asylum Support Office. Data available at: https://www.easo.europa.eu/news-events/easo-annual-report-situation-asylum-eu-and-latest-asylum-figures-0. Accessed 12.09.2017.

A. M. Kosińska, *Cultural Rights of Third-Country Nationals in EU Law*,
https://doi.org/10.1007/978-3-030-30154-5_1

It seems vital to analyse the problem of the guarantees of cultural rights from the perspective of the European Union, as it appears to be a common perception that the EU is not particularly involved in the issues of cultural policy, focusing rather on the issues of economic integration or security. However, in the legal system of the EU there are instruments, which, on the one hand, facilitate the exercise of cultural guarantees, and, on the other, which are conducive to the protection of European identity and culture.

In order to preserve European identity and culture, as well as diversity within geographically distant regions, it is necessary to undertake mindful activities at the European level. These activities should not only include the integration policies directed at third-country nationals but also clearly delineate the cultural responsibilities in terms of integration, which should be exercised by foreign nationals willing to reside within the territory of the EU.

1.2 Research Theses

The main research thesis of the current study assumes that there exists a catalogue of the cultural rights of third-country nationals in the legal system of the European Union. In accordance with the catalogue, the rights are protected in a sufficient way. At the same time, the catalogue allows for the possibility of defining the limits of exercising the above rights.

The cultural rights of foreign nationals in European Union law may be reconstructed on the grounds of the provisions of EU primary and secondary law, the case-law of the Court of Justice of the European Union (CJEU) and the guarantees of the European Convention on Human Rights (ECHR),[2] and the case-law of the European Court of Human Rights (ECtHR).[3] The cultural rights of foreign nationals include specific rights and powers, guaranteed in different legal acts. Thus, the catalogue consists of a divergent collection of rights and it has an essentially open character.

[2] Convention for the protection of human rights and fundamental freedoms of 4 November 1950.

[3] In accordance with Art. 52 of the Charter of Fundamental Rights: "In so far as this Charter contains rights which correspond to rights guaranteed by the Convention for the Protection of Human Rights and Fundamental Freedoms, the meaning and scope of those rights shall be the same as those laid down by the said Convention. This provision shall not prevent Union law providing more extensive protection." Charter of Fundamental Rights, *Official Journal of the European Union*, OJ C 202 of 07.06.2016, 389.

The so-called fundamental rights of a cultural nature are guaranteed in the provisions of primary law (Charter of Fundamental Rights) and constitute a specific type of metalaw. On the other hand, specific rights are guaranteed in the acts of secondary law and they most often concern a particular group of foreign nationals, for example, only persons seeking international protection. This allows for the adoption of a specific methodology, according to which within primary law, metalaws constitute the source and basis for interpretation of particular rights, guaranteed in secondary law.

Apart from the main thesis, the current study requires the formulation of the following supporting theses.

In accordance with the first supporting thesis, one of the values lying at the foundations and identity of the European Union is European culture. Despite the fact that the Union's competence to support, coordinate or supplement the actions of Member States in the area of culture might be often viewed as a weak competence,[4] in the system of EU primary and secondary law there exist instruments which facilitate policy-making in the area of culture and allow Member States to exert a real influence on the condition of European culture.

European migrations after World War II had a real impact on the sphere of culture. Due to globalization and uncritical support for the doctrine of multiculturalism, as well as increased migration influxes, the European culture is experiencing a phase of crisis and is in need of special protection and strengthening measures at the level of the EU. Along the lines of the second supporting thesis, the cultural responsibilities of foreign nationals in the sphere of integration, which can be implemented under the legal norms currently in force, allow for the real protection and strengthening of European identity and culture.[5] They also contribute to the real participation of third-country nationals in cultural life.

[4] P. Saganek, "Komentarz do artykułu 6," in *Traktat o funkcjonowaniu Unii Europejskiej. Komentarz. Tom I (art. 1–89)*, eds. D. Miąsik, N. Półtorak, A. Wróbel, published: WKP 2012, electronic version, available in the lex system.

[5] Integrative cultural responsibilities are defined neither by the key acts of EU law nor by the national law. However, for the purposes of the current study they might be understood as the responsibility of third-country nationals to undertake specific activities with regard to learning about and respecting the fundamental social and cultural norms of the host country.

In accordance with the third supporting thesis, the cultural rights of foreign nationals[6] are, as a rule, of a derogable nature. In the case of a conflict of values, the protection of public order, public security and the rule of *living together*[7] have key priority. By examining the provisions which might facilitate the derogation of the cultural rights of foreign nationals, it is also possible to define the extent of their application.

As for the fourth supporting thesis, it argues that there exists the right to protection against the culture of the country of origin. This right entitles a foreign national to protection against the oppressive culture of the country of origin, which prevents the said foreign national from the full exercise of their full cultural identity.[8] In the case when a foreign national, as a result of exercising broadly understood cultural rights (including artistic expression, customs, rituals, as well as issues relating to religious practices), were to experience persecution within the meaning of the provisions of the asylum law, or were to be exposed to inhuman treatment if expelled to their country of origin, such foreign national has the right to stay in the receiving country and protection against the oppressive elements of the culture of the country of origin.

1.3 The Scope of Research

Along the lines of the title, the academic purpose of the current study is to provide an in-depth analysis and the evaluation of legal instruments relating to the guarantees of the cultural rights of third-country nationals in the legal system of the European Union. The research result of the study

[6] Cultural rights as the so-called second-generation rights are laid down as derogable rights, that is, it is possible to repeal their effect, contrary to non-derogable rights, such as the prohibition of inhuman treatment. See: W. Burek, "Prawa niederogowalne a zagadnienie hierarchii praw człowieka. Perspektywa Prawnomiędzynarodowa," *Przegląd Sejmowy*, no. 4 (2015): 59–60.

[7] The "living together" principle, as relied on by the European Court of Human Rights in its famous ruling in case S.A.S, entails restrictions to the rights of a person as an element of protection of the rights and freedoms of others, thus facilitating a harmonious social coexistence as part of civil society. See: I. Trispiotis, "*Two Interpretations of 'Living Together' in European Human Rights Law*," *The Cambridge Law Journal*, vol. 75 issue 3/2016. Ruling of the ECtHR of 01.07.2014 in case S.A.S. v. France, Application no. 43835/11.

[8] For the sake of the coherence of the conducted study, the term "protection against the culture of the country of origin" has been adopted. However, the protection a person generally entitled to is based on specific elements of culture of an oppressive character—such as social behaviours or rituals.

consists in a formulation of and presentation of a catalogue of cultural rights of third-country nationals, which at the same time entails the delineation of their limits.

The subject matter of the present study concerns third-country nationals, that is persons who come from the countries which are not EU Member States, and who are not the citizens of the Union within the meaning of Art. 20 of the Treaty on the Functioning of the European Union.[9] For the purposes of the current study, third-country nationals are also referred to as "foreign nationals" or "immigrants."[10] They include both regular immigrants, who enter the EU territory legally, and involuntary immigrants—persons seeking international protection, as well as undocumented migrants—persons whose residence in the territory of Member States is of an irregular character.

The system of European Union law is understood in the current study as a legal system, including both primary law of the Union (Charter of Fundamental Rights with reference to protection standards afforded by the European Convention on Human Rights and the treaties in force—the Treaty on the Functioning of the European Union and the Treaty on European Union) and secondary law and the case-law of the CJEU, as part of *acquis communautaire*.[11] For comparative and illustrative purposes, the study also describes specific incidental solutions implemented by Member States within their margin of discretion, entailed in the implementation of the provisions of the migration law directives. For the purpose of analysis of the particular areas of migration law, the current work

[9] Treaty on the Functioning of the European Union, consolidated version, OJ C 202 of 07.06.2016, p. 47. An extended definition of a third-country national can be found in the glossary prepared by the European Migration Network (EMN), available at: https://ec.europa.eu/home-affairs/what-we-do/networks/european_migration_network/glossary/t_en. Accessed 12.09.2017.

[10] For the purpose of the current study it is also justifiable to refer to the terms: emigration, immigration and migration. The term migration entails the movement of a person across the borders of states. Immigration means, according to the EMN glossary, the act of arriving in a state with the intention to remain for a period exceeding one year. Finally, emigration denotes the act of departing or exiting from one state with the intention to remain abroad for a period exceeding one year. See: Asylum and Migration Glossary 3.0. a tool for better comparability produced by the European Migration Network October 2014, available at: https://ec.europa.eu/home-affairs/what-we-do/networks/european_migration_network/glossary/index_a_en. Accessed 31.12.2017.

[11] A. Szachoń-Pszenny, "Źródła prawa Unii Europejskiej," in *Prawo instytucjonalne Unii Europejskiej w zarysie*, ed. A. Kuś (Lublin, 2012), 209.

also examines selected political documents of the EU from the Area of Freedom, Security and Justice.

The scope of the current study includes the concept of cultural rights and the limits of their execution. Defining the rights of such nature does not belong to the easiest of tasks, as they are not comprised in a finite catalogue. Moving further, the very concept of culture is such a multifaceted term that defining even its artefacts raises multiple obstacles. However, at this point it is worth quoting the definition of F. Znaniecki, which served as a basis for numerous research on the phenomenon of culture. In accordance with the philosopher's definition, culture "includes religion, language, literature, art, customs, traditions, laws, social organisation, production techniques, economic exchange, as well as philosophy and science."[12]

While defining cultural rights it was helpful to refer to the post-modern definition of the very culture and the accompanying phenomena. The classical definition of cultural rights includes the freedom of artistic expression, the right to have access to cultural goods and the right to participate in cultural life.[13]

Due to the multiplicity of identified and described rights, the current study proposes the terminology: "rights of a cultural character." This is motivated by the fact that not all of the analysed rights of third-country nationals are cultural rights in the classical meaning of the term, for example, not all of them are listed in the International Covenant on Economic, Social and Cultural Rights[14] or at the constitutional level. However, they refer to the broadly understood sphere of a person's rights to exercise their needs in the area of culture—for instance the right of an individual to cultural identity.

It is equally difficult to define the concept of the limits of exercising one's cultural rights, as most certainly due to the multifarious character of the discussed issue, it is again insufficient to resort to only the classical understanding of limitation and derogation clauses in the international law. The limits of cultural rights of third-country nationals are described

[12] F. Znaniecki, *Nauki o kulturze. Narodziny i rozwój*, trans. J. Szacki (Warszawa, 1971), 22.

[13] Cultural rights are guaranteed in Art. 15 of the International Covenant on Economic, Social and Cultural Rights—International Covenant on Economic, Social and Cultural Rights, opened for signature in New York on 19 December 1966, Journal of Laws of 1977, no. 38, it. 169.

[14] See: International Covenant on Economic, Social and Cultural Rights, Journal of Laws of 1977, no. 38, it. 169.

both on the basis of the analysis of universal provisions pertaining to cultural rights *in se* and on the basis of the analysis of specific provisions of the acts of secondary EU law, which provide a person's specific rights of a cultural character.

The territorial and jurisdictional scope of the subject matter concerns, as a matter of fact, the territory of the European Union. However, in the case of the analysed case-law of the European Court of Human Rights, the jurisdictional range is based on the analysis of Strasbourg standards, relating to the guarantees of particular rights of a cultural character, which find their reference to the rights guaranteed in the Charter.

1.4 Sources and Literature

The study relies on multiple legal sources—primarily EU primary law (Treaty on European Union, Treaty on the Functioning of the European Union, Charter of Fundamental Rights) and secondary law (mainly regulations and directives adopted within the Area of Freedom, Security and Justice), acts of international public law from the area of the protection of human rights and national law, in so far as it relates to the implementation of secondary law and Union immigration policies. Moreover, the study makes use of a broad selection of the case-law of the Court of Justice of the European Union (with regard to both the cases concerning third-country nationals, and broadly understood cultural issues) and the case-law of the European Court of Human Rights.

As far as the literature on the subject is concerned, the issues concerning strictly the cultural rights and obligations of third-country nationals have not been analysed in a comprehensive and detailed way yet. The available legal studies either concern third-country nationals' fundamental rights or are selective publications concerning very specific cultural entitlements.[15] However, the evolution and legal instruments regarding

[15] One should mention here, for instance: M.B. Dembour, *When Humans Become Migrants. Study of the European Court of Human Rights with an Inter-American Counterpoint* (Oxford, 2015); J. Balicki, *Imigranci i uchodźcy w Unii Europejskiej. Humanizacja polityki imigracyjnej i azylowej* (Warszawa, 2012); B. Mikołajczyk, *Osoby ubiegające się o status uchodźcy. Ich prawa i standardy traktowania* (Katowice, 2004); *Are human rights for migrants? Critical reflections on the status of irregular migrants in Europe and the United States*, eds. M.B. Dembour, T. Kelly (Routledge, 2011); *Human Rights and the Refugee Definition. Comparative Legal Practice and Theory*, eds. B. Burson, D.J. Cantor (Brill/Nijhoff, 2016); *Human Rights and Immigration*, eds. R. Rubio-Marin (Oxford, 2014);

the Area of Freedom, Security and Justice have been analysed in depth in the subject literature,[16] as has been the development of the very cultural rights in the system of national and international law.[17] Numerous publications relating to the subject of culture and migration are publications from the field of sociology, political studies or cultural studies. Nevertheless, due to the adopted methodology and an interdisciplinary character of the

C. Costello, *The Human Rights of Migrants and Refugees in European Law*, Oxford 2016. The studies concerning fundamental rights in the EU system are also valuable for the doctrine: *Ochrona praw podstawowych w Unii Europejskiej*, ed. J. Barcz (Warszawa, 2008); *Karta Praw Podstawowych Unii Europejskiej. Komentarz*, ed. A. Wróbel (Warszawa, 2013). It is also worth mentioning the following studies: *Integracja kulturowa migrantów. Wyzwania i dylematy*, ed. J. Balicki, (Warszawa, 2007); A. Śledzińska-Simon, "Is there a place for the Islamic veil in the workplace? Managerial prerogatives and the duty of reasonable accommodation in the EU anti discrimination governance," *Era FORUM*, vol. 17, issue 2 (2016); A.M. Abramowicz, "Uzewnętrznianie symboli religijnych w miejscu pracy w świetle orzeczenia Europejskiego Trybunału Praw Człowieka z dnia 15 stycznia 2013 r. w sprawie Eweida i inni v Zjednoczone Królestwo," in *Aktualne problemy wolności myśli, sumienia i wyznania*, eds. P. Stanisz, A.M. Abramowicz, M. Czelny (Lublin, 2015); D. Ferenc-Kopeć, "The limitation of religious freedom in regard to national security—deliberations on Shaminder Puri v Border Guard case," in *Human Rights between War and Peace*, eds. M. Sitek, G. Dammacco, M. Wójcicka (Olsztyn, 2014); K. Groenendijk, "Pre-departure Integration Strategies in the European Union: Integration or Immigration Policy?" *European Journal of Migration and Law*, vol. 13, issue 1 (2011); W. Kalin, "Troubled Communication: Cross Cultural Misunderstandings in the Asylum Hearing," in *Human Rights and Refugee Law*, vol. II, eds. J.C. Hathaway (Edward Elgar Publishing, 2013); *Cultural Integration of Immigrants in Europe*, eds. Y. Algan, A. Bisin, A. Manning, T. Verdier (Oxford, 2012); A. Bocker, T. Strik, "Language and Knowledge Tests for Permanent Residence Rights: Help or Hindrance for Integration?" *European Journal of Migration and Law*, vol. 13, issue 2 (2011).

[16]Amongst others, see publications from the Brill's "International Refugee Law Series" cited in the current study. See also: *EU Immigration and Asylum Law (Text and Commentary): Second Revised Edition*, vol. 1, *Visas and Borders Controls*, eds. S. Peers, E. Guild, J. Tomkin (Leiden/Boston: Martinus Nijhoff Publishers, 2012); *EU Immigration and Asylum Law (Text and Commentary): Second Revised Edition*, vol. 2, *EU Immigration Law*, ed. S. Peers, E. Guild, D. Costa et al. (Leiden/Boston: Martinus Nijhoff Publishers, 2012); A. Szachoń-Pszenny, *Acquis Schengen a granice wewnętrzne i zewnętrzne w Unii Europejskiej* (Poznań, 2011).

[17] *Cultural Rights as Collective Rights An International Law Perspective*, ed. A. Jakubowski (Leiden/Boston, 2016); P.Ł.J. Andrzejewski, "Prawo człowieka do tożsamości kulturowej w Polsce," in *Prawa człowieka w społeczeństwie obywatelskim*, ed. A. Rzepliński (Warszawa, 1993); *Realizacja i ochrona konstytucyjnych wolności i praw jednostki w polskim porządku prawnym*, ed. M. Jabłoński (Wrocław, 2014); A. Frankiewicz, "Konstytucyjna regulacja dostępu do dóbr kultury i wolności korzystania z kultury," *Przegląd Prawa Konstytucyjnego*, no. 3 (2013); *The Cultural Dimension of Human Rights*, ed. A.F. Vrdoljak (Oxford, 2013).

phenomenon of migrations, they proved to be not only a useful but an indispensable source of reference.

The issues concerning both culture and fundamental rights of migrants featured in the studies I carried out in my previous research on the Area of Freedom, Security and Justice. Hence, some selected issues which were touched upon in previous publications (none of which de facto concerned migrants' cultural rights in a direct way) were revisited in a more extensive analysis.

1.5 Methodology

The methodology adopted for the purposes of the present study assumed resorting to the methods typical of legal sciences. They included the historical-legal method, the analytical method (legal-dogmatic) and the legal comparative-method.

The historical-legal method was used for analysing the development of the protection of cultural rights, as well as the evolution of EU law and migration policy. It was also used for examining the influence of migration on culture and EU law in the historical perspective (the post-war period).[18]

The legal-dogmatic method was one of the main methods applied in the current study for the examination of legal norms of the acts of primary and secondary law, as well as of the case-law of the CJEU, with a view to establishing model solutions and defining the cultural rights of third-country nationals.

After the legal-dogmatic approach, the legal-comparative method was applied in the selected sections of the current study in order to analyse a selection of legal models adopted by the Member States as a result of the implementation of the EU migration law at the national level. It is also worth pointing out to the possibility of a broader application of the legal-comparative method, not only for the purpose of comparing legal principles but also for a legal approach to "certain common problems."[19] Such

[18] On the subject of the special role of the historical-legal method in facilitating the understanding of the origins and development trends of social phenomena and in facilitating the contextualization of specific phenomena in the contemporary social reality, see: P. Dobosz, "Problemy metodologii współczesnej nauki prawa administracyjnego na tle metody historyczno-prawnej," *Kwartalnik Prawa Publicznego*, no. 1 (2001): 31–32.

[19] See: P. du Plessis, "Historia prawa a metodologia nauk prawnych," *Czasopismo Prawno-Historyczne*, vol. LXII, no. 2 (2010): 23.

problems most certainly include the range of acceptable guarantees of the cultural rights of third-country nationals in specific Member States.

Due to a multifaceted nature of the subject under discussion, a certain methodological pluralism[20] had to be adopted in the current study. For the analysis of the legal norms guaranteeing the rights of a cultural character, the method of hermeneutical analysis was adopted. This approach entails the examination of the texts of legal provisions at the grammatical as well as historical or psychological level. One of the notions behind the research onto the provisions of the Union's law in the area of the cultural rights as guaranteed to third-country nationals was the assumption that law is a cultural construct "being continually constituted in the process of social communication."[21]

The norms of EU law regarding migrants' cultural rights were examined in a hierarchical order, beginning with the provisions of primary law, through secondary law and its implementation in the provisions at the level of national law. For the purposes of the analysis, the adopted categorization and division of migration law included the following: the laws with regard to the entry into the territory of the Union, returns of third-country nationals to their countries of origin, asylum law (Common European Asylum System) and the law concerning the residence of third-country nationals legally staying in the territory of the Union.

1.6 Structure of the Work

The research conducted as part of the current study on the basis of the above-mentioned theses and methodology is comprised in the seven chapters. Chapter 1 is of introductory character.

Chapter 2 ("Migration and Culture Within the European Union Framework") discusses the development of the European migration law, with a special focus on the development of the Area of Freedom, Security and Justice and the impact of the migration crisis on the evolution of the existing legal instruments. This section of the work provides a description of the instruments guaranteeing the protection of fundamental rights in the European Union and the limits for exercising the protection of those

[20] The term methodological pluralism has been used in the current text within the meaning presented by T. Barankiewicz, "Współczesne metody badania prawa," *Studia Prawnicze KUL*, no. 1/41 (2010): 117.

[21] Ibidem, 121.

rights. This chapter is also dedicated to the issues pertaining to the possibility of protecting cultural rights in the legal system of the European Union.

In Chap. 3 ("Guarantees of the Cultural Rights of Third-Country Nationals in European Union Primary Law") the analysis concerns the provisions of the Charter of Fundamental Rights from the perspective of defining and delineating the guarantees of the cultural rights of third-country nationals. This section contains an analysis with regard to cultural divergence, the freedom of art and scientific research, the right to respect for family life, the right to education and religious freedom. Additionally, the right to protection against the culture of the country of origin is defined and described.

Chapter 4 ("Cultural Rights of Third-Country Nationals in the Migration Process: Entry and Return") includes an analysis of the provisions of secondary EU law with regard to the entry into the territory of the European Union and the execution of returns of foreign nationals to the countries of origin under the existing guarantees of cultural rights. The analysis includes both the procedure of border control and the issue of visa law, as well as exceptionally significant instruments with regard to the procedure of family reunification and the possibility of implementing integration tests for foreign nationals by Member States, together with more restrictive criteria of entry conditioned by cultural factors. The second section of the chapter contains an analysis of the guarantees of the rights of a cultural character transpiring from the provisions of the return law—both at the level of executing the return and the organization of return and stay in detention. The chapter also includes characteristics of the possibility of exercising rights of a cultural character by foreign nationals illegally staying in the territory of Member States and the limits of exercising such rights.

Chapter 5 ("Possibilities of Protection and Exercise of the Cultural Rights of Third-Country Nationals Within the Framework of the Common European Asylum System") is devoted to an analysis of the legal norms of the Common European Asylum System pertaining to the guarantees of the rights of a cultural character, which both persons seeking international protection and beneficiaries of this protection are entitled to. This part of the study examines the guarantees resulting from the Union law both at the stage of qualification and in the course of the procedure for granting protection and reception of foreign nationals, granting international protection and organization of the system of reception of persons seeking protection. A special attention has been paid to the issue of the choice of the place of stay by a foreign national with regard to the guarantees of the rights of a cultural character.

Chapter 6 ("Cultural Rights of Third-Country Nationals: Regular Migrants") concentrates on an examination of the guarantees of cultural rights resulting from the acts of secondary law relating to the status of specific groups of regular immigrants, such as long-term residents or EU Blue Card holders, as well as students and academics. The chapter also includes an analysis of the functioning of legal guarantees, that is of the so-called integrative cultural rights as the third-generation rights in the legal system of the EU. The chapter also contains an analysis of the most important political documents from the field of integration policies with regard to third-country nationals.

Chapter 7 consists of concluding remarks.

The current study presents the state of the legislation as at 1 July 2019.

The English edition of the book is a shortened version of the original monographic study.

CHAPTER 2

Migration and Culture Within the European Union Framework

2.1 Introductory Remarks

The aim of the present chapter is to demonstrate the impact of migration on the culture of the receiving country, including also the European culture as a whole. Europe seemed not to have appreciated the significance of migration and its influence not only in the area of security and economy of the Union but also in the sphere of culture and cultural life of the receiving states.

The European Union's migration policy is often described with the term "Fortress Europe," which can be entered only after meeting the requirements defined by applicable laws.[1] "Fortress Europe" is a term

[1] *Labour migration to western Europe after 1945*, in *The Cambridge Survey of World Migration*, ed. R. Cohen (Cambridge, 2010), 271. As described by A. Bysiecka-Maciaszek: "the term *Fortress Europe* in its legal aspect refers to the restrictive migration and asylum policy of EU states (Europe as a fortress as opposed to a Europe without borders), whereas in its social aspect it points to the negative attitude of the inhabitants of the receiving countries," A. Bysiecka-Maciaszek, "Rasizm i fundamentalizm kulturowy w 'Fortecy Europa,'" in *Acquis Return. Doświadczenia implementacji i rozwój polityki powrotowej Unii Europejskiej*, eds. A.M. Kosińska, P. Wojtasik (Lublin, 2015), 118. On the practical application of the term see: L. Block, S. Bonjour, "Fortress Europe or Europe of Rights? The Europeanisation of Family Migration Policies in France, Germany and Netherlands," *European Journal of Migration and Law*, vol. 15, issue 2 (2013): 203; A. Geddes, *Immigration and European Integration. Beyond the Fortress Europe?*, second edition, European Policy Research Unit Series, Manchester University Press 2008, 29. See also: K. Romaniszyn, *Migracje polityczno-ekonomiczne jako fenomen współczesności*, in *Migracje polityczne w XX wieku. Migracje i*

A. M. Kosińska, *Cultural Rights of Third-Country Nationals in EU Law*,
https://doi.org/10.1007/978-3-030-30154-5_2

which in particular refers to the restrictions regarding the possibility of entering into the territory of the Schengen states. It seems that at the level of migration policy-making, one should consider not only the responsibilities of third-country nationals with regard to entry but also those regarding the whole of their stay within the territory of the EU. Recommendations pertaining to policy-making in the area of shaping integration policy and introducing a broader catalogue of cultural responsibilities can be found further in the present work. However, at this stage I would like to suggest that it might be worthwhile to propose—*per analogiam* to the concept of *Fortress Europe*—the concept of *Demanding Europe*. The term *Demanding Europe* encompasses the features of effective integration policy—imposing on third-country nationals specific responsibilities in the area of learning and implementing the existing cultural patterns and, as a consequence, guaranteeing also cultural rights, whose implementation is conditional upon respect for the principles of the legal system and the cultural sphere of the host country.

As it transpires from the analysis of the development of migration law, the adoption of new legal norms was seemingly forced by the development of migration processes. A legal issue which has not yet been fully analysed in the context of EU legislation is that concerning the cultural rights of third-country nationals. On the one hand, it might be assumed that such a law should be regulated under national constitutional law—in this way the national law will guarantee access to culture and cultural freedoms. On the other hand, there is a need for a uniform regulation concerning cultural rights, even to a minimum degree, at the European level, which, as a matter of fact, has already been partly achieved, for example, in the framework of the Common European Asylum System. Another issue calling for a discussion is the problem of the subject of protection and the decision of the legislator whether European law (and national law of Member States) should solely and exclusively protect European culture (and national cultures), or also other cultures, whose manifestations arrive in the Member States together with the influx of migrants.[2]

społeczeństwo, ed. J.E. Zamojski (Warszawa, 2000), 92 et seq. As K. Romaniszyn observes: "The restrictive immigration policy adopted by Western countries in the current situation is merely a half-measure and simultaneously an attempt to transfer the burden onto the 'buffer' states," ibidem, 97.

[2] See also: S. Castles, M.J. Miller, *Migracje we współczesnym świecie*, trans. A. Gąsior-Niemiec (Warszawa, 2011), 31.

The present chapter will also address the evolution of the European migration law and will present an analytical characterization of the European Union system of fundamental rights. The aim of the chapter is to indicate an increasing interest in the problem of migration within the EU and to describe the stages of integrating migration policy in the *acquis communautaire*. Further, the chapter will focus on the instruments of protecting fundamental rights in EU law, whose aim is also to guarantee the protection of migrants' rights[3] as a group especially prone to exclusion and violations.[4] The very idea of protecting migrants' rights has its roots in international law and its basis can be found, as mentioned above, in the Geneva Convention.[5] In the regional system of the Council of Europe there also exist special guarantees of protecting human rights with regard to migrants.[6] The chapter ends with considerations concerning the concept of cultural rights and the place of culture in the policies and law of the European Union.

[3] The Charter of Fundamental Rights of the European Union guarantees protection of third-country nationals especially under Art. 18 regarding the right to seek asylum and Art. 19 ensuring the protection of the non-refoulement principle and prohibition of collective expulsions. Charter of Fundamental Rights of the European Union, OJ C 202 of 07.06.2016, 389, further also as CFR.

[4] On the subject of inequalities in managing migration, see: C. Grey, *Justice and Authority in Immigration Law* (Oxford and Portland, Oregon 2017), 51 et seq. See also: M. Gijsberts, P. Scheepers, M. Coenders, "Exclusion of Legal Migrants in Western Europe," in *Nationalism and Exclusion of Migrants. Cross—-National Comparisons*, eds. M. Gijsberts, L. Hagendoorn, P. Scheepers (London and New York: Routledge, 2017), 121 et seq.

[5] At the level of United Nations, migrants' rights are protected also by the International Covenant on Civil and Political Rights—for example, Art. 13 of the Covenant guarantees protection against expulsion, whereas the UN gave a mandate in 1999 to the Special Rapporteur on the human rights of migrants, see: http://www.ohchr.org/EN/Issues/Migration/SRMigrants/Pages/SRMigrantsIndex.aspx. Accessed 30.12.2017. The International Covenant on Civil and Political Rights opened for signature on 16 December 1966, further also as ICCPR.

[6] The guarantees are provided primarily in the European Convention on Human Rights (e.g. Art. 4 of the Additional Protocol no. 4 introduces the prohibition of collective expulsions). The Convention for the Protection of Human Rights and Fundamental Freedoms adopted in Rome on 4 November 1950, further also as ECHR, European Convention on Human Rights. Actions with a view to strengthening the protection of migrants' rights and their promotion are also undertaken by the Council of Europe's Commissioner for Human Rights. See: https://www.coe.int/en/web/commissioner/thematic-work/migration. Accessed 30.12.2017.

2.2 Foreign Nationals in the European Union: Statistics and an Attempt at Interpretation

For the purposes of the present study a foreign national is understood as a third-country national, that is, a citizen of a state which is not a Member State of the European Union. The data on the number of foreign nationals in the EU should be divided, in accordance with the systematics adopted above relating to the types of migration, into data relating to legal migration (regular, documented), asylum migration (i.e., including persons seeking international protection) and undocumented migration (the so-called grey area), which is the hardest to approach from the statistical perspective and more often than not with regard to irregular migrants one can provide only approximate figures (more on this topic below).

In accordance with the data made available by the Eurostat[7] in 2017, the number of persons who arrived to EU Member States was 4.4 million. Immigrants from third countries accounted for 2.0 million.

From the Eurostat data it also transpires that as of 1 January 2018 the European Union was inhabited by 22.3 million of third-country nationals—which made up 4.4% of all the inhabitants of the EU.[8]

With regard to the countries of origin of regular migrants, in accordance with the data presented by the Directorate General of the European Commission for Migration and Home Affairs, the persons residing in the EU came from Turkey (over 1.6 million), Morocco, China, India, Ukraine, Russia, Albania, Pakistan, the United States and Ecuador.[9] From among the residence permits issued in 2013 (over 2.3 million), it is estimated that 28% was issued on account of family reasons, 23% on account of undertaking work, whereas 20% for educational purposes.

In the context of the issue of the protection of cultural rights, as discussed in the present study, the acquisition of citizenship by third-country nationals is an interesting phenomenon. Even though this problem will be analysed only marginally, as pertaining to the systems of constitutional law, it is worth remembering that foreign nationals applying for citizenship of

[7] Migration and migrant population statistics, Statistics Explained, Data extracted in March 2019, https://ec.europa.eu/eurostat/statistics-explained/index.php/Migration_and_migrant_population_statistics. Accessed 20.06.2019.

[8] Ibidem.

[9] Data for 2014 available on the website: https://ec.europa.eu/home-affairs/sites/home-affairs/files/e-library/docs/infographics/immigration/migration-in-eu-infographic_en.pdf. Accessed 12.09.2017.

a given country are usually required, at least in theory, to be acquainted with the culture of the host country. Therefore, the acquisition of citizenship by such foreign nationals should be accompanied by the full acculturation of such persons. Nonetheless, it is difficult to estimate what this process looks like in practical terms as in Member States; for example, in Poland there is no obligation to take an exam on Polish culture and history. A project initiated by Malta seems particularly controversial as it facilitates the acquisition of the citizenship of this state, and thus EU citizenship, through making a financial contribution to the National Development and Social Fund and meeting other financial requirements provided for by law.[10] The creators of the programme inform that it is the first project of its kind accepted by the European Commission. However, considering the traditional understanding of citizenship as a deep relation with the state and peoples of the given country, it is hard to refrain from voicing concern about the idea proposed by Malta. It seems that it degrades the concept of citizenship to the category of residence permit, not dependent on the existence of a real spiritual relation with the receiving country.

As reported by the Eurostat, in 2017 a combined 673,000 non-EU citizens residing in one of the EU Member States acquired EU citizenship which denotes a decrease by 22% in comparison with 2016.[11]

In the context of the discussed problem, what is especially interesting is the phenomenon of citizenship acquisition by third-country nationals coming from Africa, where most countries are culturally different from European countries. Citizens of a third country acquiring the citizenship of an EU Member State may exercise their cultural rights on the basis of the constitutional provisions of a Member State. It remains an open question how to reconcile citizenship as a collection of rights of a political character (first-generation) with the so-called cultural citizenship, that is cultural identity of a given person and his ingrained cultural needs, often learned in the country of origin.[12] In such a case, it seems difficult to differentiate the responsibilities of the new home country at the legal

[10] See: Individual Investor Programme of the Republic of Malta, available on the website: http://iip.gov.mt/. Accessed 30.12.2017.

[11] Migration and migrant population statistics, Statistics Explained, Data extracted in March 2019.

[12] B. Svensson gives an interesting opinion on this: "culture and cultural policy provide a basis for understanding what citizenship means in practical terms and how it functions. In fact, citizenship is what constitutes cultural policy," B. Svensson, *Kulturowe granice obywa-*

level in providing the possibility of exercising migrants' cultural rights. The crux of the matter is the differentiation between the so-called traditional cultural rights—relating to the values commonly cultivated in European culture and the rights to preserve the cultural identity of a new citizen, whose identity often has little in common with European tradition and culture.

It often happens that the second and subsequent generations of migrants already have the citizenship of the receiving country, but still they do not feel culturally integrated with their new homeland. For the purposes of the present work, the case-law relating to the above category of legal entities will be discussed, as the issues analysed in those cases directly concern the possibilities of exercising cultural rights by third-country nationals and guaranteed protection standards with regard to culturally divergent groups.

On the other hand, in practical terms, in the Member States there are groups of migrants whose stay is that of an irregular character, but due to extended residence or through their education in a Member State they feel very strong ties with the receiving country despite the lack of political citizenship. In the case of expulsion of such persons, as a result, they are deprived of their cultural citizenship and the ties with the country which they identify themselves with are severed.

Statistics concerning persons applying for international protection in the territory of the EU are provided by the European Asylum Support Office (EASO). The year 2015 as the first year of the migration crisis was a record year from the perspective of submitted applications for international protection. In accordance with the EASO annual report, the number of submitted applications for international protection was 1,392,155, which indicated an 110% increase in comparison with 2014.[13] It had also been the highest indicator since 2008, that is the time when such data started to be collected at the European level.

The main countries of origin of persons seeking protection included Syria (383,710), Western Balkans (Albania, Kosovo, 201,405),

telstwa, in *Tożsamość i obywatelstwo w społeczeństwie wielokulturowym*, ed. E.H. Oleksy (Warszawa, 2008), 197.

[13] *Annual Report on the Situation of Asylum in the European Union 2015*, European Asylum Support Office, 2016, 5. Report available on the website: https://www.easo.europa.eu/sites/default/files/public/EN_%20Annual%20Report%202015_1.pdf. Accessed 12.09.2017.

Afghanistan, Iraq and Pakistan.[14] Among the receiving countries there were primarily Germany (34% of asylum applications), next Hungary, Austria and Italy. In comparison with previous years, Austria was a *novum*, as it had never appeared among the first five countries receiving persons seeking protection since 2011.

The data for 2018 states that in the EU there was a total of 664,480 submitted applications for protection, which comprised a 10% decrease in comparison with 2017.[15] Syria still remained the first country of origin of the applicants, next was Afghanistan Iraq, Pakistan and Nigeria.

Irregular migration in contrast to legal and asylum migration is very difficult to present in the statistics. It is usually assumed that the number of undocumented third-country nationals can be assessed on the basis of declared amnesties (regularization campaigns) and estimated on the basis of the number of illegal border crossings or the number of issued and executed return decisions, as well as the number of refusals of entry.[16]

In accordance with the research results of the project CLANDESTINO, it was estimated that in 2011 in the European Union there were 1.9–3.8 million of irregular migrants.[17]

The Frontex report (Risk analysis for 2017) indicates that the year 2016 was a record one from the perspective of migrants' arrivals in Italy through the Mediterranean. It is estimated that it was 182,000 persons mostly from Nigeria, Eritrea and Guinea.[18] The year 2016 was also a record one in terms of detection of illegal crossings of the EU's external borders—there were 511,371 recorded instances of such cases. What is interesting is that an increase was noted in the crossings in the Central-Mediterranean region (181,459, i.e., 18% increase in comparison with 2015). As far as the declared country of origin of persons trying to illegally

[14] *Annual Report on the Situation of Asylum in the European Union 2015*, 11. In the years 2011, 2012 and 2013 also Russia appeared among the first five countries of origin.

[15] International protection in the EU+: 2018 overview, https://www.easo.europa.eu/asylum-trends-annual-report-2018. Accessed 3.07.2019.

[16] See also: E. Guild, "Who is an irregular migrant?" in *Irregular Migration and Human Rights: Theoretical, European and International Perspectives*, eds. B. Bogusz, R. Cholewiński, A. Cygan, E. Szyszczak (Leiden: Brill/Nijhoff, 2004), 3.

[17] C. Morehouse, M. Blomfield, *Irregular migration in Europe*, Migration Policy Institute, December 2011, 1. Publication available on the website: www.migrationpolicy.org/pubs/TCMirregularmigration.pdf. Accessed 12.09.2017.

[18] *Risk analysis for 2017*, European Border and Coast Guard Agency 2017, 18. Report available on the website: http://frontex.europa.eu/assets/Publications/Risk_Analysis/Annual_Risk_Analysis_2017.pdf. Accessed 12.09.2017.

cross EU borders is concerned, it was mostly Syrians (17%), Afghans (11%) and Iraqis (6%).[19]

With regard to the number of effective return decisions (ending with a return to the country of origin), their number was 176,223 in 2016 and 148,121 in 2018.[20] The main issue reported by the Frontex, but also well known from the practical side to national border guards, was the difficulty in obtaining documents from the country of origin—especially from the countries of Western Africa.[21]

In 2018, the number of persons estimated to be staying illegally was 361,366, which was a decrease in comparison with 2016. Irregular migrants stayed most of all in Germany and France.[22] As it transpires from the above data, foreign nationals in the European Union make up a multicultural mosaic and even though their presence is not always very conspicuous and obvious in terms of their impact on the culture of the receiving countries, they find support in the diasporas and culturally close national and ethnic minorities or the subsequent generations of migrants who already possess citizenship of Member States, but continually cultivate the traditions of their ancestors' countries. Hence it is crucial for the Member States, which for the most part are responsible for managing migrations, to know both the social situation in migrants' countries of origin and the customs and cultural traditions which are often transferred to the hosting countries.

2.3 European Migration Law: Development and Current Challenges

2.3.1 *Law on Migration Before the Treaty of Amsterdam*

At the initial stages of European integration, the management of migrations did not lie in the competence of the European Community—the freedoms resulting from the treaties related only to migrating workers (freedom of movement). As a result, the right to free movement extended over members of families of migrating workers who were not citizens of

[19] *Risk analysis for 2017*, 9.

[20] Ibidem, 30; https://frontex.europa.eu/media-centre/news-release/frontex-publishes-risk-analysis-for-2019-Dh6Wkf. Accessed 3.07.2019.

[21] Ibidem, 9.

[22] *Risk analysis for 2019*, European Border and Coast Guard Agency 2019, 24.

the Member States.[23] A bigger interest in immigration at the level of creating the Community's policy might be observed in the 1980s[24]—this is the time when the ad hoc Group on Immigration (1986) and the Coordinators group on the free movement of persons (1988)[25] were established. The ad hoc Group on Immigration prepared the Dublin convention determining the Member State responsible for examining applications for asylum (1990).[26] Moreover, in the Maastricht Treaty (1992), migration and asylum issues were determined as cooperation in the area of justice and interior affairs and classified within the so-called III pillar of the EU where decisions were taken within an intergovernmental framework.[27]

Simultaneously, a non-Community agreement was signed on the gradual abolition of checks at the common borders—the Schengen Agreement,[28] which was expanded in 1990 by the Convention Implementing the Schengen Agreement.[29] The whole Schengen *acquis* at the beginning was not part of EU law and was later incorporated under the Treaty of Amsterdam.[30] Thus, the Schengen *acquis* became part of EU

[23] E. Borawska-Kędzierska, K. Strąk, *Polityka wizowa, azylowa i imigracyjna, Przestrzeń Wolności, Bezpieczeństwa i Sprawiedliwości Unii Europejskiej*, vol. XI, part 2, (Warszawa, 2009), XI, 2–1. See also: M. Horspool, M. Humphreys, *European Union Law* (Oxford, 2010), 386.

[24] In fact, already in 1975, the so-called TREVI group was established with a view of co-ordinating activities in the area of fighting against terrorism and drug trafficking. See: A. Szachoń-Pszenny, *Acquis Schengen a granice wewnętrzne i zewnętrzne w Unii Europejskiej*, (Poznań, 2011), 61.

[25] E. Borawska-Kędzierska, K. Strąk, *Polityka wizowa, azylowa*, XI, 2–2.

[26] D. Joly, "Whose protection? European harmonisation," in *The Cambridge Survey of World Migration*, ed. R. Cohen (Cambridge, 2010), 496.

[27] J. Balicki, *Imigranci i uchodźcy w Unii Europejskiej. Humanizacja polityki imigracyjnej i azylowej* (Warszawa, 2012), 38.

[28] The Agreement between the Governments of the States of the Benelux Economic Union, the Federal Republic of Germany and the French Republic on the gradual abolition of checks at their common borders, OJ L 239 of 22.09.2000, 13. The Schengen Agreement was preceded by the Franco-German agreement on the gradual abolition of border checks, signed in Saarbrucken.

[29] The Convention Implementing the Schengen Agreement of 14 June 1985 between the Governments of the States of the Benelux Economic Union, the Federal Republic of Germany and the French Republic on the gradual abolition of checks at their common borders, OJ L 239 of 22.09.2000, 19.

[30] See: Protocol integrating the Schengen *acquis* into the framework of the European Union; Amsterdam Treaty amending the Treaty on the European Union, the Treaties establishing the European Communities and certain related acts, OJ C 340 of 10.11.1997, 1.

law as of 1 May 1999, that is the day of the Treaty of Amsterdam entering into force.[31]

2.3.2 *The Creation and Development of the Area of Freedom, Security and Justice*

The Area of Freedom, Security and Justice (AFSJ) was created on the basis of the Schengen *acquis* under the Amsterdam Treaty, whose provisions entered into force in 1999. The Area constitutes a significant part of the EU's legal system and is still being developed.[32] The Area uses legal instruments, such as regulations, directives, decisions, as well as implementing and delegated acts.[33] The relevant treaty provisions provide the basis for the functioning of the AFSJ—currently it is Title V of the Treaty on the Functioning of the European Union (TFEU). In accordance with its Art. 67:

1. The Union shall constitute an area of freedom, security and justice with respect for fundamental rights and the different legal systems and traditions of the Member States.
2. It shall ensure the absence of internal border controls for persons and shall frame a common policy on asylum, immigration and external border control, based on solidarity between Member States, which is fair towards third-country nationals.

[31] *EU Immigration and Asylum Law (Text and Commentary): Second Revised Edition, vol. 2: EU Immigration Law*, eds. S. Peers, E. Guild, D. Costa et al. (Leiden/Boston: Martinus Nijhoff Publishers, 2012), 23.

[32] It is worth adding that under the Lisbon Treaty, a change of the legal instruments of the AFSJ occurred—after a transitional period (which remained effective until 30 November 2004, the so-called five-year transitional period), the old legal instruments of the III pillar were transformed into new legal acts. See: A. Szachoń-Pszenny, "Istota swobodnego przepływu osob w Unii Europejskiej," in *Transgraniczny przepływ towarów i osob w Unii Europejskiej*, S. Dubaj, P. Sawczuk, A. Szachoń-Pszenny, P. Witkowski, eds. A. Kuś, M. Kowerski (Lublin–Zamość, 2011), 71. See also: D. Kostakopoulou, "The Area of Freedom, Security and Justice and the Political Morality of Migration and Integration," in *A right to inclusion or exclusion? Normative fault lines of the EU's Area of freedom, security and justice*, ed. H. Lindahl (Hart Publishing, 2009), 185 et seq.; I. Wróbel, *Wspólnotowe prawo imigracyjne* (Warszawa, 2008), 35 et seq.; A. Geddes, *Immigration and European Integration*, 111 et seq.

[33] On the sources of law, see: A. Szachoń-Pszenny, "Źrodła prawa Unii Europejskiej," in *Prawo instytucjonalne Unii Europejskiej w zarysie*, ed. A. Kuś (Lublin, 2012), 205 et seq. See also: https://eur-lex.europa.eu/legal-content/EN/TXT/?uri=LEGISSUM%3Al14534. Accessed 3.07.2019.

Apart from that, treaty provisions became the basis for the development of European policies and law in the areas of border management and the development of the Schengen Area, as well as the visa policy (Art. 77 TFEU) granting international protection (Art. 78 TFEU), development of the Union's immigration policy, including the fight against trafficking in people and prevention against irregular migration (Art. 79 TFEU).

In accordance with the Lisbon Treaty, the issues related to migration are considered as competences divided between the Union and individual Member States (Art. 4(2)(j) TFEU).[34] As A. Balch and A. Geddes emphasize, this area is exceptionally difficult to manage by the Union as Member States, traditionally, jealously guarded their competence, while the area of migration was dominated by the executive authority of national governments, which cautiously approached the idea of integration or harmonization.[35]

As far as the jurisdiction of the Court of Justice (CJ) over migration issues is concerned, it was implemented under the Amsterdam Treaty.[36] Developing its case-law in this area the CJ confirmed, amongst others, the direct effect of the norms of migration law.[37]

The guidelines with regard to the development of the Area of Freedom, Security and Justice were adopted by the European Council[38] in the so-

[34] Art. 4(2)(j) Treaty on the Functioning of the European Union, consolidated version, OJ C 202 of 7.06.2016 47, further also as TFEU.

[35] A. Balch, A. Geddes, "The Development of the EU Migration and Asylum Regime," in *Migration and the new technological borders*, eds. H. Dijstelbloem, A. Meijer (Palgrave Macmillan, 2011), 23.

[36] *EU Immigration and Asylum Law (Text and Commentary): Second Revised Edition*, vol. 2, 24. In accordance with Article 13(1) of the Treaty on European Union, the full name of the institution is the Court of Justice of the European Union, further also as CJEU. In accordance with Art. 19 of the Treaty on European Union, the structure of the CJEU comprises the Court of Justice (CJ), the General Court and specialized courts. Before the Lisbon Treaty entered into force, the acronym ECJ was used—the European Court of Justice. Those acronyms are used according to the circumstances in the present work. Treaty on European Union. OJ C 202 of 7.06.2016, 13, further also as TEU.

[37] This is laid down in the judgement Kadzoev (Judgement of the CJEU of 30.11.2009 in the case Said Shamilovich Kadzoev (Huchbarov), C 357/09 PPU, ECLI:EU:C:2009:741) and El Dridi (Judgement of the CJEU of 28.04.2011 in the case Hassen El Dridi, alias Soufi Karim, C 61/11 PPU, ECLI:EU:C:2011:268) on the interpretation of the Directive 2008/115. It is worth adding that the Court in its case-law decided that EU contracts of association also create an integral part of EU law (Judgement of the CJEU of 30.04.1974 in the case R. & V. Haegeman v Belgian State, C 181/73, ECLI:EU:C:1974:41). See: *EU Immigration and Asylum Law (Text and Commentary): Second Revised Edition,* vol. 2, 35.

[38] In accordance with Art. 68 TFEU: "The European Council shall define the strategic guidelines for legislative and operational planning within the area of freedom, security and justice."

called multiannual programmes: the Tampere Programme (1999–2004),[39] the Hague Programme (2005–2009)[40] and the Stockholm Programme (2010–2014).[41]

For the analysis of the European migration law (which will be the subject of the following sections of the book), it will be useful to adopt a systematics which transpires from Art. 77–79 TFEU. Therefore, the term "EU migration law" will encompass the following: law on the management of external borders (including *acquis Schengen* and visa law), strictly migration law regarding the management of regular migration, as well as irregular migration (including the fight against irregular migration and trafficking in human beings and return law) and asylum law with regard to granting international protection on the territory of the European Union.[42]

In giving brief characteristics of the sources of European law in the area of managing external borders, it should be once again emphasized that by virtue of the Treaty of Amsterdam *acquis Schengen* was incorporated into the system of EU law on 1 May 1999. What is more, until 2011, as a rule, all the then existing legal tools were replaced by the sources of EU law.[43] The main sources of law in this field include: the Schengen Borders Code[44] and the regulation establishing the Frontex Agency, together with amend-

[39] Tampere European Council 15 and 16 October 1999 Presidency Conclusions, available on the website: http://www.europarl.europa.eu/summits/tam_en.htm. Accessed 12.09.2017.

[40] The Hague Programme: strengthening freedom, security and justice in the European Union, OJ C 53, 3.03.2005, 1.

[41] The Stockholm Programme: An open and secure Europe serving and protecting the citizens, OJ C 115, 4.5.2010, 1. Moreover, the issues concerning migrants' rights were discussed on the European Commission summits, amongst others in Nice (2000), Laeken (2001), and Sevilla (2002). See: J. Balicki, *Imigranci i uchodźcy w Unii Europejskiej*, 42–43.

[42] This categorization can find its justification in the documents drafted by DG Home Affairs, summarizing the 20 years EU migration policy, see: Timeline—response to migratory pressures, http://www.consilium.europa.eu/en/policies/migratory-pressures/history-migratory-pressures/. Accessed 12.09.2017. On the subject of the shaping of the European migration policy, see: A. Geddes, "Borders, Territory, and Migration in the European Union: From the Politics of Migration in Europe to the European Politics of Migration," in *Of States, Rights, and Social Closure*, eds. O. Schmidtke, S. Ozcurumez (New York: Palgrave Macmillan, 2008), 205 et seq.

[43] *EU Immigration and Asylum Law (Text and Commentary): Second Revised Edition, vol. 1: Visas and Borders Controls*, eds. S. Peers, E. Guild, J. Tomkin (Leiden/Boston: Martinus Nijhoff Publishers, 2012), 18.

[44] Regulation (EU) 2016/399 of the European Parliament and of the Council of 9 March 2016 on a Union Code on the rules governing the movement of persons across borders (Schengen Borders Code), OJ L 77, 23.03.2016, 1, which replaced Regulation (EC) no. 562/2006 of the European Parliament and of the Council of 15 March 2006 establishing a Community Code on

ing regulations,[45] regulation on the Second Generation Schengen Information System (SIS II)[46] and the regulation establishing the eu-LISA agency and the Eurosur system.[47]

At the same time, for the purpose of strengthening the realization of EU policies in the discussed area, the following instruments were established: External Borders Fund (2007–2013)[48] and the Internal Security Fund (2014–2020).

The EU visa law consists primarily in: Regulation (EU) 2018/1806 listing the third countries whose nationals must be in possession of visas

the rules governing the movement of persons across borders (Schengen Borders Code), OJ L 105, 13.04.2006, 1, further also as Regulation 2016/399 or Schengen Border Code.

[45] Regulation (EU) 2016/1624 of the European Parliament and of the Council of 14 September 2016 on the European Border and Coast Guard and amending Regulation (EU) 2016/399 of the European Parliament and of the Council and repealing Regulation (EC) no. 863/2007 of the European Parliament and of the Council, Council Regulation (EC) no. 2007/2004 and Council Decision 2005/267/EC, OJ L 251, 16.09.2016, 1, further also as Regulation 2016/1624. The Agency was established on the basis of Council Regulation (EC) no. 2007/2004 of 26 October 2004 establishing a European Agency for the Management of Operational Cooperation at the External Borders of the Member States of the European Union, OJ L 349, 25.11.2004, 1. Moreover, the source of law in this area was the regulation establishing a mechanism for the creation of Rapid Border Intervention Teams—Regulation (EC) no. 863/2007 of the European Parliament and of the Council of 11 July 2007 establishing a mechanism for the creation of Rapid Border Intervention Teams and amending Council Regulation (EC) no. 2007/2004 as regards that mechanism and regulating the tasks and powers of guest officers, OJ L 199, 31.07.2007, 30.

[46] Regulation (EC) no. 1987/2006 of the European Parliament and of the Council of 20 December 2006 on the establishment, operation and use of the Second Generation Schengen Information System (SIS II), OJ L 381, 28.12.2006, 4, further also as Regulation 1987/2006. It is also worth mentioning the decision establishing the Task Force Mediterranean—see: Communication from the Commission to the European Parliament and the Council on the Work of the Task Force Mediterranean, Brussels, 4.12.2013, COM(2013) 869 final. In accordance with the text: "The Task Force Mediterranean (TFM) was set up following the JHA Council of 7–8 October 2013."

[47] eu-LISA was established by Regulation (EU) no. 1077/2011 of the European Parliament and of the Council of 25 October 2011 establishing a European Agency for the operational management of large-scale IT systems in the area of freedom, security and justice, OJ L 286, 1.11.2011, 1, repealed by Regulation (EU) 2018/1726 of the European Parliament and of the Council of 14 November 2018 on the European Union Agency for the Operational Management of Large-Scale IT Systems in the Area of Freedom, Security and Justice (eu-LISA), and amending Regulation (EC) no. 1987/2006 and Council Decision 2007/533/JHA and repealing Regulation (EU) no. 1077/2011, OJ L 295, 21.11.2018, 99.

[48] Decision no. 574/2007/EC of the European Parliament and of the Council of 23 May 2007 establishing the External Borders Fund for the period 2007–2013 as part of the General programme "Solidarity and Management of Migration Flows," OJ L 144, 6.06.2007, 22.

when crossing the external borders and those whose nationals are exempt from that requirement,[49] Community Code on Visas[50] and Regulation concerning the Visa Information System.[51]

At present, we can already speak of the functioning of the new generation borders (intelligent borders),[52] which are managed by the Eurosur system[53] and through access to the data of large-scale IT systems—SIS,[54] VIS and Eurodac.[55] The key role is also played by EU Agencies: Frontex[56]

[49] Regulation (EU) 2018/1806 of the European Parliament and of the Council of 14 November 2018 listing the third countries whose nationals must be in possession of visas when crossing the external borders and those whose nationals are exempt from that requirement, OJ L 303, 28.11.2018, 39.

[50] Regulation (EC) no. 810/2009 of the European Parliament and of the Council of 13 July 2009 establishing a Community Code on Visas (Visa Code), OJ L 243 of 15.09.2009, 1, further also as Regulation 810/2009, Visa Code. See: *EU Immigration and Asylum Law (Text and Commentary): Second Revised Edition*, vol. 1, 251–314.

[51] Regulation (EC) no. 767/2008 of the European Parliament and of the Council of 9 July 2008 concerning the Visa Information System (VIS) and the exchange of data between Member States on short-stay visas (VIS Regulation), OJ L 218 of 13.08.2008, 60.

[52] B. Mikołajczyk, "Granice nowej generacji," in *Państwo i terytorium w prawie międzynarodowym*, eds. J. Menkes, E. Cała-Wacinkiewicz (Warszawa, 2015), 168. See: C. Goodes, "Smart Borders and Security," in *Immigration and Security*, ed. K. Iglicka (Warszawa: Centrum Stosunków Międzynarodowych, 2006), 33.

[53] Regulation (EU) no. 1052/2013 of the European Parliament and of the Council of 22 October 2013 establishing the European Border Surveillance System (EUROSUR), OJ L 295 of 6.11.2013, 11.

[54] Regulation 1987/2006.

[55] Regulation (EU) no. 603/2013 of the European Parliament and of the Council of 26 June 2013 on the establishment of "Eurodac" for the comparison of fingerprints for the effective application of Regulation (EU) no. 604/2013 establishing the criteria and mechanisms for determining the Member State responsible for examining an application for international protection lodged in one of the Member States by a third-country national or a stateless person and on requests for the comparison with Eurodac data by Member States' law enforcement authorities and Europol for law enforcement purposes, and amending Regulation (EU) no. 1077/2011 establishing a European Agency for the operational management of large-scale IT systems in the area of freedom, security and justice (recast version), OJ L 180, 29.06.2013, 1. See also: *Fundamental rights and the interoperability of EU information systems: borders and security*, FRA 2017. Report available on the website: www.fra.europa.eu. Accessed 12.09.2017.

[56] Since 14 October 2016 the Frontex Agency is referred to as the European Border and Coast Guard Agency. The proposal to change the range of the mandate of the Agency was presented on 10 March 2016, while the EU Council adopted its position on 6 April 2016. On 21 April the project of the regulation was presented, to be finally adopted on 14 September 2016. See: Regulation 2016/1624. Initially, the Agency was established on the basis of Regulation of the Council (EC) no. 2007/2004 of 26 October 2004 establishing a

and eu-LISA (managing the large-scale IT systems). It remains a priority of the European Union to provide the highest standard of security[57] and the highest quality of control of third-country nationals entering the European Union. Within the system of EU law, the *stricte* immigration law can be divided into two areas—regulations concerning regular migration (that is, occurring in accordance with the existing regulations) and irregular migration (in other words, non-documented or illegal).[58]

The basic legal acts adopted in the area of regular migration include the directive on long-term residents,[59] directive on family reunification,[60] the so-called new student directive and directive on academics,[61] directive on

European Agency for the Management of Operational Cooperation at the External Borders of the Member States of the European Union, OJ L 349, 25.11.2004, 1, which was amended several times (see: Regulation no. 1168/2011 and Regulation no. 656/2014). On the subject of the Agency's activities in the area of managing migrations, see: L. den Hertog, "Fundamental Rights and the Extra-territorialization of EU Border Policy: A Contradiction in Terms?" in *Foreigners, refugees or minorities? Rethinking people in the context of border controls and visas*, eds. D. Bigo, S. Carrera, E. Guild (Ashgate, 2013), 206–226; R. Mungianu, Frontex: "Towards a Common Policy on External Border Control," *European Journal of Migration and Law*, vol. 15, no. 4 (2013): 359–387.

[57] See: A. Dudzic, "Polska w drodze do Schengen oraz kierunki rozwoju obszaru wolności, bezpieczeństwa i sprawiedliwości w Unii Europejskiej," in *Bezpieczni w Europie. Materiały z konferencji organizowanej przez Urząd Komitetu Integracji Europejskiej oraz Wydział Prawa Uniwersytetu w Białymstoku*, ed. M. Zdanowicz (Warszawa, 2007), 38 et seq. See also: M. Arden, *Human Rights and European Law. Building New Legal Orders* (Oxford, 2015), 148 et seq.; M.A. Alexseev, *Immigration Phobia and the Security Dilemma. Russia, Europa and the United States* (Cambridge, 2006), 33 et seq.

[58] On the subject of terminology and definitions of illegal migration, see: C. Dauvergne, *Making people illegal. What globalization means for migration and law* (Cambridge University Press, 2011), 11. In accordance with the definition proposed by the author, any person in breach of legal provisions regulating entry and stay on a given territory should be considered an irregular migrant.

[59] Council Directive 2003/109/EC of 25 November 2003 concerning the status of third-country nationals who are long-term residents, OJ L 16 of 23.1.2004, 44, further also as Directive 2003/109.

[60] Council Directive 2003/86/EC of 22 September 2003 on the right to family reunification, OJ L 251 of 3.10.2003, 12, further also as Directive 2003/86.

[61] Directive (EU) 2016/801 of the European Parliament and of The Council of 11 May 2016 on the conditions of entry and residence of third-country nationals for the purposes of research, studies, training, voluntary service, pupil exchange schemes or educational projects and au pairing, OJ L 132, 21.5.2016, 21, further also as Directive 2016/801. It replaced Council Directive 2004/114/EC of 13 December 2004 on the conditions of admission of third-country nationals for the purposes of studies, pupil exchange, unremunerated training

the EU Blue Card,[62] directive on a single application procedure[63] and directive on seasonal workers.[64]

At the same time, funds supporting integration of immigrant were created: the European Fund for the Integration of Third-Country Nationals (2008–2013)[65] and the Asylum, Migration and Integration Fund (2014–2020).[66]

The rules of managing irregular migration were regulated primarily on the grounds of directives: initially, it was the directive on the mutual recognition of decisions on the expulsion of third-country nationals,[67]

or voluntary service, OJ L 375, 23.12.2004, 12, and Council Directive 2005/71/EC of 12 October 2005 on a specific procedure for admitting third-country nationals for the purposes of scientific research, OJ L 289, 3.11.2005, 15.

[62] Council Directive 2009/50/EC of 25 May 2009 on the conditions of entry and residence of third-country nationals for the purposes of highly qualified employment, OJ L 155, 18.06.2009, 17, further also as Directive 2009/50.

[63] Directive 2011/98/EU of the European Parliament and of the Council of 13 December 2011 on a single application procedure for a single permit for third-country nationals to reside and work in the territory of a Member State and on a common set of rights for third-country workers legally residing in a Member State, OJ L 343, 23.12.2011, 1, further also as Directive 2011/98.

[64] Directive 2014/36/EU of the European Parliament and of the Council of 26 February 2014 on the conditions of entry and stay of third-country nationals for the purpose of employment as seasonal workers, OJ L 94, 28.3.2014, 375, further also as Directive 2014/36.

[65] Council Decision of 25 June 2007 establishing the European Fund for the Integration of third-country nationals for the period 2007–2013 as part of the General programme "Solidarity and Management of Migration Flows," 2007/435/EC, OJ L 168, 28.6.2007, 19.

[66] Regulation (EU) no. 516/2014 of the European Parliament and of the Council of 16 April 2014 establishing the Asylum, Migration and Integration Fund, amending Council Decision 2008/381/EC and repealing Decisions no. 573/2007/EC and no. 575/2007/EC of the European Parliament and of the Council and Council Decision 2007/435/EC, OJ L 150, 20.05.2014, 168, further as Regulation 516/2014.

[67] Council Directive 2001/40/EC of 28 May 2001 on the mutual recognition of decisions on the expulsion of third-country nationals, OJ L 149, 2.06.2001, 34. It was followed by: Council Decision of 29 April 2004 on the organization of joint flights for removals from the territory of two or more Member States, of third-country nationals who are subjects of individual removal orders, OJ L 261, 6.08.2004, 28 and Regulation (EU) no. 493/2011 of the European Parliament and of the Council of 5 April 2011 amending Council Regulation (EC) no. 377/2004 on the creation of an immigration liaison officers network, OJ L 141, 27.05.2011, 13. Also: Council Decision of 16 March 2005 establishing a secure web-based Information and Coordination Network for Member States' Migration Management Services, OJ L 83, 1.04.2005, 48.

followed by the return directive[68] and directive providing for minimum standards on sanctions and measures against employers of illegally staying third-country nationals.[69] The European Return Fund[70] was established with a view to supporting the activities of the Member States for the return of non-documented third-country nationals to their countries of origin. It is currently replaced by the Asylum, Migration and Integration Fund (AMIF). A part of the so-called *acquis* in the area of returns includes readmission agreements with third countries, that is, agreements providing for simplified procedures for returning irregular migrants as part of cooperation between EU migration services and partner countries.[71] As part of counteracting irregular migration, the European Union is also making attempts aiming at combating trafficking in human beings—the basic legal act in this area includes the directive on preventing and combating trafficking in human beings.[72]

The European Union law in the area of asylum and granting international protection has been put within the framework of the so-called Common European Asylum System (CEAS). The idea of the CEAS has

[68] Directive 2008/115/EC of the European Parliament and of the Council of 16 December 2008 on common standards and procedures in Member States for returning illegally staying third-country nationals, OJ L 348, 24.12.2008, 98, further also as Directive 2008/115, Return Directive.

[69] Directive 2009/52/EC of the European Parliament and of the Council of 18 June 2009 providing for minimum standards on sanctions and measures against employers of illegally staying third-country nationals, OJ L 168, 30.06.2009, 24.

[70] Decision no. 575/2007/EC of the European Parliament and of the Council of 23 May 2007 establishing the European Return Fund for the period 2008–2013 as part of the General Programme Solidarity and Management of Migration Flows, OJ L 144, 6.06.2007, 45, further also as Decision 575/2007.

[71] See a list of agreements signed by the EU with third countries: https://ec.europa.eu/home-affairs/what-we-do/policies/irregular-migration-return-policy/return-readmission_en. Accessed 04.07.2019. The agreements are available in their full text in the EUR-Lex service. See also: Communication from the Commission to the European Parliament and the Council. Evaluation of EU Readmission Agreements, Brussels, 23.2.2011, COM(2011) 76 final.

[72] Directive 2011/36/EU of the European Parliament and of the Council of 5 April 2011 on preventing and combating trafficking in human beings and protecting its victims, and replacing Council Framework Decision 2002/629/JHA, OJ L 101, 15.04.2011, 1; Directive 2011/92/EU of the European Parliament and of the Council of 13 December 2011 on combating the sexual abuse and sexual exploitation of children and child pornography, and replacing Council Framework Decision 2004/68/JHA, OJ L 335, 17.12.2011, 1; Directive 2012/29/EU of the European Parliament and of the Council of 25 October 2012 establishing minimum standards on the rights, support and protection of victims of crime, and replacing Council Framework Decision 2001/220/JHA, OJ L 315, 14.11.2012, 57.

been confirmed in the Presidency Conclusions adopted in Tampere in 1999,[73] whereas its fundamental aim was to work out a common procedure and a uniform status of refugee for all EU Member States.[74] The development of the CEAS included the so-called I phase, which was to conclude in 2004—until 2004 the following instruments were adopted: Procedures Directive,[75] Reception Directive,[76] Qualification Directive,[77] the Dublin Regulation[78] and the regulation concerning the Eurodac system.[79] In 2008, the European Commission decided that a further harmonization of asylum policies is needed,[80] which was confirmed in the Stockholm Programme. At the same time, in the following years, the amended texts of the Procedures Directive,[81] Reception Directive,[82]

[73] Tampere European Council 15 and 16 October 1999 Presidency Conclusions, http://www.europarl.europa.eu/summits/tam_en.htm. Accessed 12.09.2017.

[74] E. Tsourdi, "Qualifying for International Protection in the EU: New Understanding of the 1951 Convention and Beyond," in *Exploring Boundaries of Refugee Law. Current Protection Challenges*, eds. J.P. Gauci, M. Giuffré, E. Tsourdi (Brill/Nijhoff, 2015), 240. See also: R. Bank, "Forced Migration in Europe," in *The Oxford Handbook of Refugee and Forced Migration Studies*, eds. E. Fiddian-Qasmiyeh, G. Loescher, K. Long, N. Sigona (Oxford, 2014), 692.

[75] Council Directive 2005/85/EC of 1 December 2005 on minimum standards on procedures in Member States for granting and withdrawing refugee status, as of 21 July 2005, OJ L 326, 13.12.2005, 13.

[76] Council Directive 2003/9/EC of 27 January 2003 laying down minimum standards for the reception of asylum seekers, OJ L 31, 6.02.2003, 18.

[77] Council Directive 2004/83/EC of 29 April 2004 on minimum standards for the qualification and status of third-country nationals or stateless persons as refugees or as persons who otherwise need international protection and the content of the protection granted, OJ L 304, 30.09.2004, 12.

[78] Council Regulation (EC) no. 343/2003 of 18 February 2003 establishing the criteria and mechanisms for determining the Member State responsible for examining an asylum application lodged in one of the Member States by a third-country national, OJ L 50, 25.02.2003, 1.

[79] Council Regulation (EC) no. 2725/2000 of 11 December 2000 concerning the establishment of "Eurodac" for the comparison of fingerprints for the effective application of the Dublin Convention, OJ L 316, 15.12.2000, 1.

[80] See: Communication from the Commission to the European Parliament, the Council, the European Economic and Social Committee and the Committee of Regions—Policy plan on asylum—An integrated approach to protection across the EU, Brussels, 17.06.2008, COM/2008/ final, 5.

[81] Directive 2013/32/EU of the European Parliament and of the Council of 26 June 2013 on common procedures for granting and withdrawing international protection, OJ L 180, 29.06.2013, 60, further also as Directive 2013/32, Procedures Directive.

[82] Directive 2013/33/EU of the European Parliament and Council of 26 June 2013 laying down standards for the reception of applicants for international protection (recast), OJ L 180, 29.6.2013, 96, further also as Directive 2013/33, Receptions Directive.

Qualification Directive[83] as well as the above-mentioned regulations[84] were adopted. In order to strengthen the EU's activities in the area of international protection a decentralized agency was also established—the European Asylum Support Office (EASO), with a seat in Valletta on Malta.[85]

As can be seen from the above legislation, the EU migration *acquis* should be understood in a wide sense, as community *acquis* encompassing several spheres: the regulations regarding the functioning of the Schengen area and border management, the management of regular migrations (as well as the integration of third-country nationals) and irregular migrations (including the return law), finally, the Common European Asylum System. The above regulations will come under scrutiny from the perspective of the guarantees of cultural rights for third-country nationals.

2.3.3 *Migration Crisis and the Changes in European Union Migration Law*

The migration crisis which started in 2015 entirely changed the perspective of perceiving immigrants and migrations in Europe and, what followed, had an impact on decreasing the level of acceptance and absorption

[83] Directive 2011/95/EU of the European Parliament and of the Council of 13 December 2011 on standards for the qualification of third-country nationals or stateless persons as beneficiaries of international protection, for a uniform status for refugees or for persons eligible for subsidiary protection, and for the content of the protection granted (recast version, in force since 21 December 2013), OJ L 337, 20.12.2011, 9, further also as Directive 2011/95, Qualification Directive.

[84] Regulation (EU) no. 604/2013 of the European Parliament and of the Council of 26 June 2013 establishing the criteria and mechanisms for determining the Member State responsible for examining an application for international protection lodged in one of the Member States by a third-country national or a stateless person, OJ L 180, 29.06.2013, 31, further also as Regulation 604/2013, the Dublin III Regulation, Regulation (EU) no. 603/2013 of the European Parliament and of the Council of 26 June 2013 on the establishment of "Eurodac" for the comparison of fingerprints for the effective application of Regulation (EU) no. 604/2013 establishing the criteria and mechanisms for determining the Member State responsible for examining an application for international protection lodged in one of the Member States by a third-country national or a stateless person and on requests for the comparison with Eurodac data by Member States' law enforcement authorities and Europol for law enforcement purposes, and amending Regulation (EU) no. 1077/2011 establishing a European Agency for the operational management of large-scale IT systems in the area of freedom, security and justice, OJ L 180, 29.06.2013, 1, further also as Regulation 603/2013.

[85] The EASO was established under Regulation (EU) no. 439/2010 of the European Parliament and of the Council of 19 May 2010 establishing a European Asylum Support Office, OJ L 132, 29.05.2010, 11.

of the cultural patterns characteristic of the countries of origin of migrants.[86]

The beginning of the migration crisis is seen in the events off the coast of Lampedusa of 19 April 2015, which cost the lives of about 700 people.[87] However, it was not the first accident of its kind on the Mediterranean Sea, whereas the roots of the migration crisis could be traced back to 2011, which witnessed subsequent groups of Tunisians escaping from Africa in connection with the events of the Arab Spring (it is estimated that in 2015 as many as 55,000 persons arrived at the Italian coasts).[88]

As a result of the crisis of 2015, the European Commission adopted the so-called Ten Action Plan, followed by the European Agenda on Migration.[89] The Agenda included ad hoc plans of activities with a view to

[86] It is worth noting and remembering that Europe as widely understood North is not usually the final destination of persons seeking international protection and most of the refugees live in the so-called South. In accordance with the data presented by the IOM and World Bank in 2010, so before the Arab Spring, four out of five refugees remained in the South (about 81% of the world's population). See: *World Migration Report 2013. Migrant well-being and development*, IOM 2013, 68.

[87] "700 migrants feared dead in Mediterranean shipwreck," http://www.theguardian.com/world/2015/apr/19/700-migrants-feared-dead-mediterranean-shipwreck-worst-yet. Accessed 12.09.2017. Announcement of the UNHCR on the accident: http://www.unhcr.org/news/press/2015/4/5533c2406/unhcr-new-mediterranean-boat-tragedy-biggest-urgent-action-needed.html. Accessed 12.09.2017. Previous accidents at the coast of Lampedusa occurred in 2012 r. (4 November) and 2013 (on the night of 3–4 October). On the subject of the crisis see: Z. Mach, N. Styczyńska, "Kwestia uchodźców w kontekście wyzwań dla Unii Europejskiej," *Studia Migracyjne—Przegląd Polonijny*, no. 4 (2016): 26 et seq; M. Takle, "Is the Migration Crisis a Solidarity Crisis?" in *The Crisis of the European Union*, ed. A. Grimmel (London, 2018), 116–129.

[88] See: Judgement of the ECtHR of 15.12.2016 in the case Khlaifia and others v. Republic of Italy, complaint no. 16483/12, para. 49. See: P. Fargues, Ch. Fandrich, *Migration after the Arab Spring*, Migration Policy Centre Research Report; 2012/09, http://cadmus.eui.eu/handle/1814/23504. Accessed 12.09.2017; G. Campesi, "The Arab Spring and the Crisis of the European Border Regime: Manufacturing Emergency in the Lampedusa Crisis" (November 1, 2011), Robert Schuman Centre for Advanced Studies Research Paper no. 2011/59; "Criminal Justice," Borders and Citizenship Research Paper no. 2481918, publication available on the websites: https://ssrn.com/abstract=2481918 and https://doi.org/10.2139/ssrn.2481918. Accessed 12.09.2017; H. Boubakri, *Revolution and international migration in Tunisia*, Migration Policy Centre; MPC Research Report; 2013/04, publication available on the websites: http://hdl.handle.net/1814/29454 and http://www.migrationpolicycentre.eu/. Accessed 12.09.2017.

[89] What is also significant, already on 18 May 2015 a new sea operation EUNAVFOR Med was established, whose aim was to neutralize the refugee smuggling routes in the Mediterranean. See: https://eeas.europa.eu/csdp-missions-operations/eunavfor-

neutralizing the situation in the Mediterranean and increasing the actual migration security. However, as was emphasized in the document: "While the migration crisis in the Mediterranean has put the spotlight on immediate needs, it has also revealed much about the structural limitations of EU migration policy and the tools at its disposal. This is an opportunity for the EU to strike the right balance in its migration policy and send a clear message to citizens that migration can be better managed collectively by all EU actors."

The four pillars of improving migration management include the following: reducing the incentives for irregular migration, border management (saving lives and securing external borders), Europe's duty to protect: a strong common asylum policy and a new policy on legal migration.[90]

The key instruments in managing migration flows were to involve relocation[91] and resettlements.[92] The first proposition concerning the so-called relocation quotas, that is, the number of migrants—persons seeking international protection who might be received by the Member States was presented by the European Commission on 27 May 2015[93] and then

med/12353/background-documents-and-legal-basis-eunavfor-med-operation-sophia_en. Accessed 12.09.2017.

[90] Communication from the Commission to the European Parliament, the Council, the European Economic and Social Committee and the Committee of the Regions. A European Agenda on Migration, Brussels, 13.05.2015, COM(2015) 240 final, http://ec.europa.eu/dgs/home-affairs/what-we-do/policies/european-agenda-migration/background-information/docs/communication_on_the_european_agenda_on_migration_pl.pdf. Accessed 10.09.2016. See: S.K. Mazur, "Polityka imigracyjna Unii Europejskiej," in *W pułapce wielokulturowości*, ed. A. Siewierska-Chmaj (Rzeszow, 2016), 77.

[91] In accordance with the European Agenda on Migration, "'relocation' means the distribution among Member States of persons in clear need of international protection" (see: European Agenda on Migration, 22).

[92] In accordance with the European Agenda on Migration, "'resettlement' means the transfer of individual displaced persons in clear need of international protection, on submission of the United Nations High Commissioner for Refugees and in agreement with the country of resettlement, from a third country to a Member State, where they will be admitted and granted the right to stay and any other rights comparable to those granted to a beneficiary of international protection" (see: European Agenda on Migration, 22).

[93] Proposal for a Council Decision establishing provisional measures in the area of international protection for the benefit of Italy and Greece, Brussels, 27.05.2015 COM(2015) 286 final 2015/125 (NLE), https://ec.europa.eu/home-affairs/sites/homeaffairs/files/elibrary/documents/policies/asylum/general/docs/proposal_for_a_council_decision_on_provisional_relocation_measures_for_italy_and_greece_en.pdf. Accessed 12.09.2017.

adopted by the European Council on 25–26 June 2015.[94] The programme for relocation was initially designed for 40,000 persons, but in September 2015 a proposal of a mechanism increasing the number of persons to be received by the Member States to 120,000 was made and adopted by decision of the Council of the European Union of 22 September 2015.[95] The concept of relocation was met with criticism from the Member States and as it transpired, for instance, from the Ninth Report on Relocation and Resettlement prepared by the Commission in February 2017,[96] it was possible to effectively relocate 8766 persons out of the target of 63,302 persons from Greece, 3200 persons were relocated from Italy, out of the targeted 34,953, whereas it was possible to resettle 13,968 out of the planned 22,504 persons.[97] The discussion on the subject of relocation had intensified to such an extent that Hungary and Slovakia decided to file a complaint with the Court of Justice of the European Union (CJEU) against the existing mechanism of relocation. The CJEU, however, dismissed the complaint as a whole by the judgement of 6 September 2017.[98]

The complaint under discussion was a proof of a solidarity crisis among the Member States in the area of managing migrations. This crisis was very accurately diagnosed by the Advocate General Y. Bot in his opinion, emphasizing that solidarity is a value which lies at the foundation of the European Union and that "more specifically, solidarity is both a pillar and at the same time a guiding principle of the European Union's policies on border checks, asylum and immigration, which form the subject matter of

[94] European Council meeting (25 and 26 June 2015)—Conclusions, Brussels, 26 June 2015 (OR. en) EUCO 22/15 CO EUR 8 CONCL 3, http://www.consilium.europa.eu/en/press/press-releases/2015/06/26-euco-conclusions/. Accessed 12.09.2017.

[95] Council Decision establishing provisional measures in the area of international protection for the benefit of Italy and Greece, Brussels, 22 September 2015 (OR. en) 12098/15 ASIM 87 Interinstitutional File: 2015/0209 (NLE), legislative acts and other instruments.

[96] Report from the Commission to the European Parliament, the European Council and the Council. Ninth report on relocation and resettlement, Brussels, 8.02.2017 COM(2017) 74 final.

[97] See: Annexes to the Interim Report https://ec.europa.eu/home-affairs/what-we-do/policies/european-agenda-migration/proposal-implementation-package_en. Accessed 12.09.2017.

[98] Judgement of the CJEU of 6.9.2017 in the case Slovak Republic (C-643/15) and Hungary (C-647/15) v. Council of the European Union, C-643/15 and C-647/15, ECLI:EU:C:2017:631.

Chapter 2 of Title V of the FEU Treaty, devoted to the area of freedom, security and justice."[99]

In accordance with the opinion of the Advocate General, the very decision in the case of relocation contributed to the protection of migrants' fundamental rights, especially to the realization of the guarantees under Art. 18 of the Charter of Fundamental Rights.[100] Undoubtedly, as part of developing the migration *acquis*, it is necessary to rely on the said solidarity principle, which is grounded in Art. 78 and 80[101] TFEU.

The summary of the activities for the purpose of implementing the European Agenda on Migration is to be found in the Communication of the Commission published in September 2017.[102] In accordance with Communication of the Commission "Delivery of the European Agenda on Migration," as of 20 September it was possible to relocate more than 28,500 persons, which constituted over 90% of the cases in which requests concerning relocation had been sent out.[103]

An important moment in developing the strategy for combating the migration crisis was the European Council summit on the subject of migration held in Valetta in Malta in November 2015.[104] A political decla-

[99] Opinion of Advocate General Y. Bot delivered on 26 July 2017 in case Slovak Republic, Hungary v. Council of the European Union, C 643/15 and C 647/15, ECLI:EU:C:2017:618, para. 20. A similar opinion on the subject of the meaning of the solidarity principle for dealing with the migration crisis was presented by Advocate General E. Sharpston in her opinion: "The progressive creation of an area without internal frontiers in which free movement of persons is guaranteed in accordance with the TFEU and the establishment of Union policies regarding the conditions of entry and stay of third-country nationals, including common efforts towards the management of external borders, makes it necessary to strike a balance between responsibility criteria in a spirit of solidarity." See: Opinion of Advocate General E. Sharpston in the case A.S. v. Republic of Slovenia, C 490/16, para. 139.

[100] Paragraph 335 of the Opinion of Advocate General in the case C 643/15.

[101] In accordance with Art. 80 TFEU: "The policies of the Union set out in this Chapter and their implementation shall be governed by the principle of solidarity and fair sharing of responsibility, including its financial implications, between the Member States. Whenever necessary, the Union acts adopted pursuant to this Chapter shall contain appropriate measures to give effect to this principle."

[102] Communication from the Commission to the European Parliament, the Council, the European Economic and Social Committee and the Committee of the Regions, on the Delivery of the European Agenda on Migration, Brussels, 27.09.2017, COM(2017) 558 final.

[103] Ibidem, 5.

[104] Valletta Summit, 11–12 November 2015 Action Plan, Valletta Summit, 11–12 November 2015 Political Declaration. The adopted documents are available on the website: http://www.consilium.europa.eu/en/policies/migratory-pressures/history-migratory-pressures/. Accessed 12.09.2017.

ration and an action plan were then accepted, the latter of which entailed undertaking actions in the areas of developing benefits of migration, actions addressing root causes of irregular migration and forced displacement, actions for the benefit of regular migration, international protection and asylum, actions for the prevention of and fight against migrant smuggling and trafficking in human beings, actions to facilitate return, readmission and reintegration.

What is significant, the migration crisis forced some Member States to temporarily reintroduce border controls at the selected internal borders[105] and to strengthen cooperation with third countries (especially with Turkey[106]). Taking into account the necessity of adjusting legal norms to the current challenges of the difficult migration reality and aiming at a full realization of the principle of effectiveness of law, the EU institutions also presented proposals of changes in the CEAS[107] and the Dublin system.[108]

[105] Such a mechanism is provided for in the Schengen Borders Code: Chapter II: "General framework for the temporary reintroduction of border control at internal borders," Art. 25 et seq. Regulation 2016/399.

[106] See: Conclusions of the European Council of 17–18 March 2016. The agreement with Turkey was signed on 18 March 2016. See also: A. Adamczyk, G. Ilik, *Greek-Turkish Relations, UE and Migration Problem*, "Yearbook of Polish European Studies" 2016, vol. 19, 198.

[107] The proposed changes included, amongst others, replacing directives with regulations in the area of common procedures and qualifications. See: Proposal of the European Commission of 13 June 2016. "Completing the reform of the Common European Asylum System: towards an efficient, fair and humane asylum policy," Brussels, 13 July 2016; http://europa.eu/rapid/press-release_IP-16-2433_en.htm. See also: proposal for a regulation on adopting a list of safe countries of origin: Proposal for a Regulation of the European Parliament and of the Council establishing an EU common list of safe countries of origin for the purposes of Directive 2013/32/EU of the European Parliament and of the Council on common procedures for granting and withdrawing international protection, and amending Directive 2013/32/EU, Brussels, 9.09.2015, COM(2015) 452 final 2015/0211 (COD). See also: P. Van de Peer, "Negotiating the Second Generation of the Common European Asylum System Instruments: A Chronicle," in *Reforming the Common European Asylum System. The New European Refugee Law*, eds. V. Chetail, P. De Bruycker, F. Maiani (Brill, 2016), 55 et seq.

[108] See proposal for a regulation: Proposal for a Regulation of the European Parliament and of the Council establishing the criteria and mechanisms for determining the Member State responsible for examining an application for international protection lodged in one of the Member States by a third-country national or a stateless person (recast), Brussels, 4.05.2016 COM(2016) 270 final 2016/0133 (COD), http://eur-lex.europa.eu/procedure/EN/2016_133. Accessed 12.09.2017. See also: F. Maiani, "The Dublin III Regulation: A New Legal Framework for a More Human System?" in *Reforming the Common European Asylum System. The New*

The migration crisis has contributed not only to the implementation of the necessary changes in EU legal system. It also resulted in negatively changing the attitude of the receiving societies towards migrants. On the one hand, such a change was influenced by the media reports and problems encountered by the Member States in managing the increasing number of migrants. What is perhaps even more important, an increase in negative attitudes was also caused by the tragic events which occurred in 2015–2016. One should mention here primarily the attack on the offices of satirical magazine *Charlie Hebdo* in Paris (7 January 2015)[109] and terrorist attacks in Paris (13 November 2015)[110] and Brussels (22 March 2016).[111]

Consequently, it seems that the migration crisis not only introduced changes in the EU migration policy but also initiated a new chapter in the understanding of cultural identity of the inhabitants of European countries, an increase in the awareness of cultural differences and a discussion on the subject of tolerance and possibilities for integration of third-country nationals in the countries in which they reside. The ongoing debate at the EU level is bound to assess the effectiveness of the existing integration systems, the need for changes and work towards creating an effective concept of exercising cultural rights, in full respect for all the sides of cultural exchange and cultural processes. The activities of the Member States with a view to respecting native culture and regional values, as well as common roots of the European culture, should be accompanied by an actual inclusion of third-country nationals living in specific Member States in culture-making processes.

European Refugee Law, eds. V. Chetail, P. De Bruycker, F. Maiani (Brill, 2016), 101 et seq. See: ECRE Comments on the Commission Proposal for an Asylum Procedures Regulation COM(2016) 467, November 2016, http://www.ecre.org/wp-content/uploads/2016/11/ECRE-Comments-APR-November-2016-final.pdf. Accessed 12.09.2017. See: Policy Note: The Road out of Dublin: reform of the Dublin Regulation. ECRE's overview of the main changes in the proposal to recast the Dublin Regulation, and its recommendations for the Council and European Parliament, ECRE Policy note 2/2016, http://www.ecre.org/wp-content/uploads/2016/10/Policy-Note-02.pdf. Accessed 12.09.2017.

[109] "Charlie Hebdo attack: France's worst terrorist attack in a generation leaves 12 dead," *The Telegraph*, http://www.telegraph.co.uk/news/worldnews/europe/france/11331902/Charlie-Hebdo-attack-Frances-worst-terrorist-attack-in-a-generation-leaves-12-dead.html. Accessed 11.09.2017.

[110] *2015 Paris Terror Attacks Fast Facts*, CNN Library, http://edition.cnn.com/2015/12/08/europe/2015-paris-terror-attacks-fast-facts/. Accessed 11.09.2017.

[111] "Brussels Attacks," *Mirror*, http://www.mirror.co.uk/all-about/brussels-terror-attack. Accessed 11.09.2017.

2.4 Protection of Fundamental Rights in the Legal Order of the European Union

2.4.1 Shaping of the Protection of Fundamental Rights in the European Union: A Historical Perspective

The aim of the European Community was primarily economic integration; hence, the issues of the protection of human rights were not of a particular interest to the states establishing the EEC. In accordance with the Schuman Declaration, the aim of the newly created Community was to be economic cooperation[112] and not the issues of protecting human rights, which was to become the domain of the Council of Europe.[113]

In general, the founding treaties did not include the norms facilitating the protection of human rights, with one exception, that is the prohibition of discrimination on grounds of sex under Art. 119 Treaty establishing the European Community.[114]

The emergence of the protection of fundamental rights in the EU's legal system was caused by the decision-making activities of the European Court of Justice (ECJ). The evolution the ECJ's line of jurisprudence is also noted by J. Menkes, who outlines its subsequent stages.[115] In the first stage the Court admitted to its lack of competence to rule in cases concerning the range of human rights (at the turn of the 1950s and 1960s). However, already in 1969 the fundamental rights were accepted as general principles of the Community's legal system[116] (rulings Stauder,[117] Internationale[118]).

[112] https://europa.eu/european-union/about-eu/symbols/europe-day/schuman-declaration_pl. Accessed 12.09.2017.

[113] In his speech in Zurich in 1946 Churchill emphasized that the first step to the rebuilding of Europe after World War II was to be the creation of the Council of Europe; http://www.churchill-society-london.org.uk/astonish.html. Accessed 12.09.2017.

[114] J. Menkes, "Karta Praw Podstawowych a konstytucja Europy," *Studia Europejskie*, no. 2 (2011): 31.

[115] J. Menkes, "Karta Praw Podstawowych," 32.

[116] See: A. Florczak, "Ochrona praw człowieka w systemie prawa wspólnotowego," in *Prawa Człowieka. Wybrane zagadnienia i problemy*, eds. L. Koba, W. Wacławczyk (Warszawa, 2009), 101.

[117] Judgement of the Court of Justice of 12.11.1969 in the case Stauder, C 29/69, ECLI:EU:C:1969:57; see also: Judgement of the Court of Justice of 21.09.1988 in the case Pascal Van Eycke v. ASPA NV, C 267/86; ECLI:EU:C:1988:427.

[118] Judgement of Court of Justice of 17.12.1970 in the case Internationale Handelsgesellschaft mbH v. Einfuhr- und Vorratsstelle fur Getreide und Futtermittel, C 11/70, ECLI:EU:C:1970:114. At that time, the Court ruled that "respect for fundamental

Finally, the Court recognized that international agreements regarding the protection of human rights complement the Community's legal system (cases Ruttili, Hauer).[119] It is also worth pointing out that due to the pressure exerted by the constitutional courts of Germany and Italy, the Court recognized the existence of an unwritten catalogue of fundamental rights as a component of the Union's legal system. In 1989, Judge J. Mancini declared that "the inclusion of the unwritten Charter of Rights in the Union's law system is in its essence the most significant contribution which the Court has made for the development of the Constitution of Europe."[120]

2.4.2 General Principles of the Functioning of the System for the Protection of Fundamental Rights in the European Union

The system for the protection of fundamental rights[121] in the European Union was finally regulated by the Treaty of Lisbon. As was mentioned above, the fact that fundamental rights began to be treated as a general principle of the Community law was the result of the line of decision-making of the Court of Justice.[122] Due to the Court's special role in the

rights forms an integral part of the general principles of law protected by the Court of Justice. The protection of such rights, whilst inspired by the constitutional traditions common to the Member States, must be ensured within the framework of the structure and objectives of the community." See also: I. Justyńska, *Zasada poszanowania praw człowieka w europejskim prawie wspólnotowym* (Toruń, 2009), 121.

[119] Judgement of the Court of Justice of 28.10.1975 in the case Roland Rutili v. Ministre de l'interieur, C 36/75, ECLI:EU:C:1975:137; Judgement of the Court of Justice of 13.12.1979 in the case Liselotte Hauer v. Land Rheinland-Pfalz, C 44/79, ECLI:EU:C:1979:290. For instance, the Court referred to the ICCPR in the case 374/87 *Orkem* (Judgement of the Court of Justice of 18.10.1989 in the case Orkem v. Commission of the European Communities, ECLI:EU:C:1989:387). Moreover, the subject of the existence of fundamental rights in the Community's legal system was referred to by national courts, whereas the most important evidence lies in the rulings of the German Constitutional Court in the cases Solange I (1974) and Solange II (1986). See: D. Chalmerd, G. Davies, G. Monti, *European Union Law*, Second Edition (Cambridge, 2011), 235. See also: F. Fabbrini, *Fundamental Rights in Europe. Challenges and Transformations in Comparative Perspective* (Oxford, 2014), 10.

[120] See: M. Horspool, M. Humphreys, *European Union Law*, 158.

[121] On the differences in terminology, see: M. Jabłoński, S. Jarosz-Żukowska, *Prawa człowieka i systemy ich ochrony. Zarys wykładu* (Wrocław, 2010), 279.

[122] A. Bodnar, "Karta Praw Podstawowych: zrożnicowany charakter prawny postanowień Karty i ich skutki dla jednostek, sądow oraz ustawodawcy," in *Ochrona praw podstawowych w*

protection of fundamental rights, it is worth stressing that fundamental rights as general principles of the Community law had a dynamic structure because the range of their protection was being defined and shaped in the process of applying legal norms.[123] As C. Mik observes, before the Treaty of Lisbon entered into force, "fundamental rights were accepted as general principles of the Community law and were not categorized from the normative point of view."[124] On the other hand, the Charter of Fundamental Rights brought with itself a differentiation into rights, freedoms and principles. The categorization of the Charter will be discussed in greater detail in the following section of the book—it is merely signalled here. The basic normative difference between the rights and principles lies, as C. Mik observes, in the possibility of taking judicial action to assert one's rights, which are, contrary to the principles, individual claims.[125] The author also emphasizes that the European Convention on Human Rights (ECHR) and constitutional traditions common to all Member States were accepted as the material sources of the general principles of law.[126]

Unii Europejskiej, ed. J. Barcz (Warszawa, 2008), 144. As for the existence of the catalogue of fundamental rights, it is worth noticing that due to the genesis and the initial character of the protection (through the ECJ's case-law), there was no formal catalogue of fundamental rights. It was believed, though, that the character of protection should be no smaller than the one guaranteed under the ECHR and constitutions of the Member States. See: M. Jaśkowski, "Sądowa ochrona praw podstawowych w Unii Europejskiej i Wspolnocie Europejskiej," in *Prawa podstawowe w prawie i praktyce Unii Europejskiej*, eds. C. Mik, K. Gałka (Toruń, 2009), 116.

[123] E. Morawska, "Konstrukcja normatywna praw podstawowych Unii Europejskiej w Karcie praw podstawowych Unii Europejskiej," in *Prawa podstawowe w prawie i praktyce Unii Europejskiej*, eds. C. Mik, K. Gałka (Toruń, 2009), 44. See also: V. Bazzocchi, "The European Charter of Fundamental Rights and the Area of Freedom, Security and Justice," in *The EU Charter of Fundamental Rights. From Declaration to Binding Instrument*, ed. F. Giacomo (Springer, Dordrecht 2011), 177–197.

[124] C. Mik, "Karta Praw Podstawowych: wyznaczniki standardow ochronnych," in *Ochrona praw podstawowych w Unii Europejskiej*, ed. J. Barcz (Warszawa, 2008), 65.

[125] C. Mik, "Karta Praw Podstawowych: wyznaczniki standardow ochronnych," 67.

[126] T. Jurczyk, "Trzy źrodła praw podstawowych Unii Europejskiej," in *Aktualne wyzwania ochrony wolności i praw jednostki. Prace uczniów i współpracowników dedykowane Profesorowi Bogusławowi Banaszakowi*, eds. M. Jabłoński, S. Jarosz-Żukowska (Wrocław, 2014), 286. See: Art. 52(5) Charter of Fundamental Rights.

The key factors for the understanding of the functioning of the system of protection are the treaty provisions.[127] Already Art. 2 of the Treaty on European Union (TEU) states that:

> The Union is founded on the values of respect for human dignity, freedom, democracy, equality, the rule of law and respect for human rights, including the rights of persons belonging to minorities. These values are common to the Member States in a society in which pluralism, non-discrimination, tolerance, justice, solidarity and equality between women and men prevail.[128]

What is significant for the current analysis is that the Union's obligation to promote the idea of the protection of human rights is also to be found in Art. 3(5) TEU concerning the external relations of the Union. In accordance with the Article:

> In its relations with the wider world. ... It shall contribute to ... the protection of human rights, in particular the rights of the child, as well as to the strict observance and the development of international law, including respect for the principles of the United Nations Charter.[129]

However, what is significant here, the realization of the aims of the Union is possible only within the competences provided for in the Treaties.[130] Article 6 of the Treaty on European Union concerns the con-

[127] It is also significant that the Preamble to TEU includes a reference to the category of human rights: "CONFIRMING their attachment to the principles of liberty, democracy and respect for human rights and fundamental freedoms and of the rule of law, CONFIRMING their attachment to fundamental social rights as defined in the European Social Charter signed at Turin on 18 October 1961 and in the 1989 Community Charter of the Fundamental Social Rights of Workers."

[128] Also Art. 3 TEU defining the objectives of the Union states that: "It shall combat social exclusion and discrimination, and shall promote social justice and protection, equality between women and men, solidarity between generations and protection of the rights of the child."

[129] Moreover, in accordance with Art 21 TEU: "The Union's action on the international scene shall be guided by the principles which have inspired its own creation, development and enlargement, and which it seeks to advance in the wider world: democracy, the rule of law, the universality and indivisibility of human rights and fundamental freedoms, respect for human dignity, the principles of equality and solidarity, and respect for the principles of the United Nations Charter and international law."

[130] Art. 3(6) TEU.

firmation of the status of the Charter of Fundamental Rights as a normative source of rights and constitutes grounds for the Union's joining of the European Convention on Human Rights. Additionally, it contains the articulated sources of fundamental rights:

> Fundamental rights, as guaranteed by the European Convention for the Protection of Human Rights and Fundamental Freedoms and as they result from the constitutional traditions common to the Member States, shall constitute general principles of the Union's law.[131]

It is commonly accepted in the doctrine that the sources of fundamental rights in the EU's system of law are the Charter of Fundamental Rights, the European Convention on Human Rights (as external sources of fundamental rights)[132] and constitutional traditions common to the Member States. The general principles of law (resulting also from international law) are commonly believed to include, amongst others, the principle of proportionality, equality and non-discrimination, legal certainty, non-retroaction, transparency or the principle of *non-refoulement*.[133] Fundamental rights, in accordance with Art. 6(3) TEU, constitute a part of the Union's law as general principles of law. Non-normative sources of fundamental rights include the inherent and inalienable dignity of man.[134]

The three categories of fundamental rights are distinguished, in turn, on the grounds of the normative source in which they are originated. Thus, in the EU's system of law one can distinguish the so-called treaty rights (e.g., the right to good administration), convention rights (the rights guaranteed in the ECHR) and the rights resulting from the common constitutional traditions of the Member States.[135]

In the very Charter of Fundamental Rights there appear three other sources, but they are related only to the rights and principles included in the Charter and they are the following: the treaty rights, the rights recognized by the constitutions of the Member States and the rights originating in the international treaties with regard to human rights, which are binding for the Member States.[136] In fact, international law constituted a guideline for the Court in the shaping of the protection of fundamental

[131] Art. 6(3) TEU.
[132] See: T. Jurczyk, "Trzy źrodła praw," 282.
[133] On this subject see also: M. Horspool, M. Humphreys, *European Union Law*, 137.
[134] E. Morawska, "Konstrukcja normatywna praw," 47.
[135] More on this subject, see: ibidem, 43.
[136] D. Chalmerd, G. Davies, G. Monti, *European Union Law*, 239.

rights in its case-law—not only the area of the treaty law (such as, e.g., the Convention on the Rights of the Child[137]) but also customary law.[138] Thus, international law is a mark for the minimum level of protection for the EU's system.[139]

Art. 7 TEU is also of significant importance as it regulates the functioning of the mechanism of control of the rule of law in the Member States and allows the EU Council to suspend certain treaty rights, including the right to vote in the EU Council with regard to a Member State, whose actions pose a serious risk of violating the values under Art. 2 TEU.[140]

Title II TEU concerns the so-called democratic principles and already Art. 9 TEU states that: "In all its activities, the Union shall observe the principle of the equality of its citizens" and defines the citizen of the EU.[141] The duty to apply the principle of non-discrimination is also articulated in the Treaty on the Functioning of the European Union and in accordance with its Art. 18 any discrimination on grounds of nationality is prohibited. Moreover, in accordance with Art. 19 TFEU:

[137] Judgement of the CJEU of 27.06.2003 in the case the European Parliament v the European Council C 540/03, ECLI:EU:C:2006:429. See item 37 of the judgement: "The Court has already had occasion to point out that the International Covenant on Civil and Political Rights is one of the international instruments for the protection of human rights of which it takes account in applying the general principles of Community law" (see, inter alia, Case 374/87 *Orkem* v *Commission* [1989] ECR 3283, para. 31; Joined Cases C-297/88 and C-197/89 *Dzodzi* [1990] ECR I-3763, para. 68; and Case C-249/96 *Grant* [1998] ECR I-621, para. 44). That is also true of the Convention on the Rights of the Child referred to above which, like the Covenant, binds each of the Member States.

[138] Judgement of the Court of Justice of 16.06.1996 in the case A. Racke GmbH & Co. v. Hauptzollamt Mainz C 162/96, ECLI:EU:C:1998:293. The question referred for a preliminary ruling concerning the validity of the regulation no. 547/92 of 3.02.1992 in light of the principles of international customary law.

[139] M. Jaśkowski, "Sądowa ochrona praw podstawowych," 129. Moreover, in the doctrine there are voices that the Union's law might be recognized as part of international public law. M. Jarmoszka also points out that the EU's legal system recognizes the rules of interpretation of EU law in accordance with international law. See: M. Jarmoszka, "Reguły wykładni karty Praw Podstawowych Unii Europejskiej," in *Prawa podstawowe w prawie i praktyce Unii Europejskiej*, eds. C. Mik, K. Gałka (Toruń, 2009), 64.

[140] See: K. Woch, "Podstawy prawne Unii Europejskiej," in *Prawo instytucjonalne Unii Europejskiej w zarysie*, ed. A. Kuś (Lublin, 2012), 99. See also: *EU Law Foundations, The Institutional Functioning of the EU, Volume II 2011–2012, Maastricht Centre for European Law Faculty of Law*, Maastricht University, https://www.maastrichtuniversity.nl/sites/default/files/obs_8811_law_foundations.pdf. Accessed 12.07.2019.

[141] In accordance with Art. 9 TEU: "Every national of a Member State shall be a citizen of the Union. Citizenship of the Union shall be additional to national citizenship and shall not replace it."

> Without prejudice to the other provisions of the Treaties and within the limits of the powers conferred by them upon the Union, the Council, acting unanimously in accordance with a special legislative procedure and after obtaining the consent of the European Parliament, may take appropriate action to combat discrimination based on sex, racial or ethnic origin, religion or belief, disability, age or sexual orientation.[142]

The subsequent articles[143] of part II TFEU (Non-discrimination and citizenship) regulate citizens' rights, such as the right of free movement (Art. 21), election rights (Art. 22), the right to consular protection (Art. 23) and the right to petition the European Parliament and the right to apply to the Ombudsman (Art. 24).[144] However, it is worth emphasizing that also third-country nationals living in the territory of the EU are entitled to exercise the right to petition, as well as the right to apply to the Ombudsman.

To sum up the above analysis, one should point out that the European Union has created an effective system for the protection of fundamental rights. The effectiveness of the Union's system transpires primarily from the definitive delineation of the sources of fundamental rights, which are pointed out in Art. 6 TEU. This approach allows for the realization of the protection at the level of the Union, but with reference to the national systems of the Member States and in conjunction with the commonly accepted values protected by international law.[145]

[142] A. Pacześniak, "Zakaz dyskryminacji w systemie prawnym Unii Europejskiej," in *Ochrona praw podstawowych w Unii Europejskiej*, ed. A. Florczak (Warszawa, 2009), 162–176; G. Michałowska, *Ochrona praw człowieka w Radzie Europy i w Unii Europejskiej* (Warszawa, 2007), 183–195. See also: Handbook on European non-discrimination law—2018 edition, European Union Agency for Fundamental Rights, www.fra.europa.eu. Accessed 12.07.2019.

[143] Art. 20 et seq. TFEU.

[144] For more on the subject of the complaint rights, see: R. Kołatek, "Pozasądowa ochrona praw podstawowych podstawowych Unii Europejskiej," in *Aktualne wyzwania ochrony wolności i praw jednostki. Prace uczniów i współpracowników dedykowane Profesorowi Bogusławowi Banaszakowi*, eds. M. Jabłoński, S. Jarosz-Żukowska (Wrocław, 2014), 177. See also: https://www.ombudsman.europa.eu/pl/make-a-complaint. Accessed 12.07.2019.

[145] R. Grzeszczak claims that "the Union possesses a complete and effective system of instrument ensuring the protection of fundamental rights, which determines not only the relations with regard to the Member States but also with regard to international law," R. Grzeszczak, "Zupełny i efektywny system ochrony praw podstawowych w Unii Europejskiej," in *Unia Europejska w roli gwaranta i promotora praw podstawowych*, ed. D. Kornobis-Romanowska (Sopot, 2016), 79.

2.4.3 *Significance of the European Convention on Human Rights for the EU System of Protection*

In accordance with Art. 6 TEU the European Convention on Human Rights is considered to be the external source of fundamental rights. More so, in accordance with Art. 6(2) TEU, it is possible for the Union to accede as a party to the ECHR[146]:

> The Union shall accede to the European Convention for the Protection of Human Rights and Fundamental Freedoms. Such accession shall not affect the Union's competences as defined in the Treaties.

As D. Kornobis-Romanowska observes, the Union's purpose in acceding to the ECHR is to formally combine the Union's *acquis* with the Convention's *acquis* in order to increase the effectiveness as well as homogeneity in the respect for human rights in Europe.[147]

At present the Union is not party to the ECHR and therefore it cannot bear responsibility for its own actions which might violate the ECHR. The European Court of Human Rights (ECtHR) is in a position to examine the acts of national law (States—parties to the Convention), also those implementing EU law.[148]

The Court of Justice also referred in its case-law to the ECHR,[149] whereas the ECtHR worked out its case-law with regard to EU law.[150]

[146] See also: L.F.M. Besselink, *Should the European Union ratify the European Convention on Human Rights? Some remarks on the relations between the European Court of Human Rights and the European Court of Justice* in *Constituting Europe. The European Court of Human Rights in a National, European and Global Context*, eds. A. Follesdal, B. Peters, G. Ulfstein (Cambridge, 2013), 301 et seq.

[147] D. Kornobis-Romanowska, "Prawa podstawowe w orzecznictwie TSUE jako czynnik konstytucjonalizacji czy umiędzynarodowienia UE?" in *Unia Europejska w roli gwaranta i promotora praw podstawowych*, ed. D. Kornobis—Romanowska (Sopot, 2016), 35.

[148] Ibidem. On the subject of the principle of "equivalent protection" see: A. Bodnar, "Standard 'równoważnej ochrony' w odniesieniu do ochrony praw człowieka po opinii Trybunału Sprawiedliwości 2/13," *Europejski Przegląd Sądowy*, no. 12, (2015): 45 et seq.

[149] As A. Wróbel observes: "the European Court of Human Rights is treated here as an authority of persuasion strengthening the legitimacy of those courts (Union courts—footnote A.M.K), especially from the perspective of insufficient or lack of protection of fundamental rights in EU/EC law," A. Wróbel, "Konsekwencje przystąpienia UE do EKPCz dla umocnienia ochrony jednostki w UE i dla umocnienia europejskiego systemu ochrony praw człowieka. Wprowadzenie," in *Ochrona praw podstawowych w Unii Europejskiej*, ed. J. Barcz (Warszawa, 2008), 193. On the subject of the case-law of the CJEU with reference to the ECHR, see: M. Jaśkowski, "Sądowa ochrona praw podstawowych," 126.

[150] See, for instance, judgement of the ECtHR of 18.02.1999 in the case Matthews v. the United Kingdom, complaint no. 24833/94; judgement of the ECtHR of 30.06.2005 in the

In the doctrine of human rights in the system of the Community and then in the EU system it was accepted that the Union is obliged to protect fundamental rights at the level no weaker than the one described by the ECHR.[151] The ECHR is thus a benchmark for the minimum level of protection of the individual's rights.

The EU's accession to the ECHR seems to be the consequence of the dualism in the system of the protection of human rights at the European level. As A. Bisztyga observes, the creators of the Treaty of Lisbon and the new legal order of the EU decided that the doubletrack character of the protection of fundamental rights in Europe (EU, CoE) would be an added value.[152]

The process of the EU's accessing the ECHR has its roots in the 1970s. It was at that time that the European Commission declared in a report published in 1979 that the Union should formally become party to the Convention. The proposal was resubmitted in 1990.[153] The Maastricht Treaty also referred to the issue of respecting the rights guaranteed in the ECHR by the Union.[154] The Union's attempts of acceding to the ECHR failed after the Court of Justice issued an opinion 2/94 of 28 March 1996 declaring that the Community had no competence to accede to the ECHR.[155]

case Bosphorus v. Ireland, complaint no. 45036/98; judgement of the CJEU of 21.01.2011 in the case M.S.S. v. Belgium and Greece, complaint no. 30696/09. See also: R. Grzeszczak, "Zupełny i efektywny system ochrony," 87 et seq.

[151] M. Jaśkowski, "Sądowa ochrona praw podstawowych," 116.

[152] A. Bisztyga, "Europejska Konwencja Praw Człowieka a Karta Praw Podstawowych Unii Europejskiej—stan kompatybilności czy konkurencyjności?" *Przegląd Prawa Konstytucyjnego*, no. 3, (2011): 186. However, the author remains sceptical about the concept of the double-track protection, pointing out to its lack of clarity and complexity.

[153] T.C. Hartley, *The Foundations of European Union Law* (Oxford, 2010), 151.

[154] A. Bisztyga, "Europejska Konwencja Praw Człowieka," 181.

[155] Opinion 2/94 of the European Court of Justice of 28 March 1996, I-1759, ECLI:EU:C:1996:140. The Court in paragraphs 34 and 35 of the opinion stated: "Respect for human rights is therefore a condition of the lawfulness of Community acts. Accession to the Convention would, however, entail a substantial change in the present Community system for the protection of human rights in that it would entail the entry of the Community into a distinct international institutional system as well as integration of all the provisions of the Convention into the Community legal order. Such a modification of the system for the protection of human rights in the Community, with equally fundamental institutional implications for the Community and for the Member States, would be of constitutional significance and would therefore be such as to go beyond the scope of Article 235. It could be brought about only by way of Treaty amendment."

Another possibility for the Union's accession to the ECHR appeared together with the Treaty of Lisbon entering into force under Art. 6 TEU[156] and the ratification of Protocol No 14 to the ECHR, which entered into force on 1 June 2014. In 2012, the accession negotiations started, which resulted in the preparation of the agreement on the accession during one of the last negotiation meetings (2–5 April 2013).[157] Next, the agreement was referred to the CJEU, where the full Court delivered its opinion on the matter in question. In its opinion 2/13 delivered on 18 December 2014,[158] the Court stated that it was impossible for the Union to accede to the ECHR on the grounds of the proposed agreement due to the risk of adversely affecting the specific characteristics and the autonomy of the EU as a result of the lack of coordination between Art. 53 of the ECHR and Art. 53 of the Charter and the risk that the principles of mutual trust between the Member States under EU law may be undermined. Moreover, according to the Court, the proposed agreement did not determine the relations between the mechanism established by Protocol No 16[159] and the preliminary ruling procedure and, more so, did not preclude "the possibility of disputes between Member States or between Member States and the EU concerning the application of the ECHR within the scope *ratione materiae* of EU law being brought before the ECtHR."[160]

[156] Before, in 2001, a working group was established to prepare a legal and technical study specifying the Union's accession to the ECHR.

[157] Fifth negotiation meeting between the Steering Committee for Human Rights (CDDH) ad hoc negotiation group and the European Commission on the accession of the European Union to the European Convention on Human Rights, Final report, http://www.echr.coe.int/Documents/UE_Report_CDDH_ENG.pdf. Accessed 12.09.2017. See also: http://www.echr.coe.int/Pages/home.aspx?p=basictexts/accessionEU&c=. Accessed 12.09.2017.

[158] Opinion of the Court of Justice 2/13 of 18.12.2014, ECLI:EU:C:2014:2454, further also as Opinion 2/13.

[159] As was emphasized in the opinion 2/13: it "provides, in Article 1(1), for the highest courts and tribunals of the Contracting Parties to be able to request the ECtHR to give advisory opinions on questions of principle relating to the interpretation or application of the rights and freedoms defined in the ECHR or the protocols thereto" (para. 36). See also: M. Balcerzak, "Kompetencja doradcza Europejskiego Trybunału Praw Człowieka—status quo a Protokół nr 16 do Europejskiej Konwencji Praw Człowieka," *Polski Rocznik Praw Człowieka i Prawa Humanitarnego* (2015): 5–27.

[160] The Court pointed out that the proposed agreement: "does not lay down arrangements for the operation of the co-respondent mechanism and the procedure for the prior involvement of the Court of Justice that enable the specific characteristics of the EU and EU law to

In consequence, at present, the Union's admission to the ECHR on the grounds of the agreement prepared so far is not possible in light of EU law. However, as is emphasized in the doctrine, accession to the ECHR would strengthen the European system of protection by submitting the actions of the Union's institutions to external control.[161]

2.4.4 *Charter of Fundamental Rights of the European Union*

The Charter of Fundamental Rights constitutes one of the three pillars for the protection of fundamental rights in the EU, as laid down in Art. 6 TEU, next to the accession to the ECHR and fundamental rights as the general principles of law.[162] At the moment of the Treaty of Lisbon entering into force, the Charter became a part of primary law and is legally binding in the same way as the treaties, which is confirmed in Art. 6(1) TEU:

> The Union recognises the rights, freedoms and principles set out in the Charter of Fundamental Rights of the European Union of 7 December 2000, as adapted at Strasbourg, on 12 December 2007, which shall have the same legal value as the Treaties.

The beginnings of the work on the Charter date back to the summit of the European Council in Cologne in June 1999, where the Convent

be preserved," and it "fails to have regard to the specific characteristics of EU law with regard to the judicial review of acts, actions or omissions on the part of the EU in CFSP matters in that it entrusts the judicial review of some of those acts, actions or omissions exclusively to a non-EU body" (para. 258 of the opinion).

[161] A. Gajda, "Przystąpienie Unii Europejskiej do Europejskiej Konwencji Praw Człowieka i Podstawowych Wolności," *Kwartalnik Kolegium Ekonomiczno-Społecznego. Studia i Prace*, no. 1 (2013): 34. As the author observes, "Until the EU does not accede to the Convention, individuals will not have a possibility to file a complaint against the Union's institutions directly before the ECtHR. As of now, the European Union remains the only legal system, in which its legal acts are not subject to the external control of this Court. Accession to the ECHR would fill the gap in the protection of fundamental rights in the EU and its institutions will become subject to the same external control as the legal acts of the EU's Member States. Therefore, accession will strengthen both Courts." See also: A. Gajda, "Przystąpienie UE do EKPCz i inkorporacja Karty Praw Podstawowych do prawa UE a umocnienie ochrony praw podstawowych w III filarze UE," in *Ochrona praw podstawowych w Unii Europejskiej*, ed. J. Barcz (Warszawa, 2008): 264–289.

[162] A. Wróbel, "Wprowadzenie," in *Karta Praw Podstawowych Unii Europejskiej. Komentarz*, ed. A. Wróbel (Warszawa, 2013), 3.

responsible for drafting the text of the Charter was appointed.[163] On 7 December 2000 at the summit of the European Council in Nice the text of the Charter was solemnly proclaimed and received the status of an "interinstitutional agreement."[164] Next, the Charter of Fundamental Rights formed part of the European Constitution. Finally, the Charter was included within the Treaty of Lisbon and became legally binding on the day of the Treaty entering into force, that is, on 1 December 2009. However, already before that date, that is after 2000 in the preambles of the Union's legal acts there appeared references to the Charter. The Charter was also cited in the opinions of Advocates General,[165] and also by the Court of First Instance. Finally, also the Court of Justice referred to the Charter in its reasonings.[166]

In accordance with Art. 51 of the Charter, the addressees of the Charter, that is the bodies obligated to the protection of fundamental rights, are the institutions and organs of the Union as well as the Member States, but only within the limits within which they apply the Union's law. Moreover, the Charter does not extend in any way the Union's competences as provided for in the treaties; neither does it establish any new powers.[167] This regulation constitutes a certain alteration with regard to the international

[163] J. Menkes, "Karta Praw Podstawowych," 35. K. Cymerys, "Aksjologia, idee i zasady ogólne Karty Praw Podstawowych Unii Europejskiej," in *Efektywność europejskiego systemu ochrony praw człowieka. Efektywność mechanizmów ochrony praw człowieka Rady Europy, Unii Europejskiej i OBWE*, ed. J. Jaskiernia (Toruń, 2012), 493.

[164] A. Banaszkiewicz, "Karta Praw Podstawowych jako 'uwieńczenie' unijnego systemu ochrony praw człowieka," *Studia Erasmiana Wratislaviensia*, vol. IV (2010): 183. See also: A. Jackiewicz, "Problematyka praw człowieka w świetle Karty Praw Podstawowych w aspekcie integracji Polski z Unią Europejską," *Studia Europejskie*, no. 2, (2003): 53.

[165] See: Opinion of the Advocate General A. Tizzano of 8.02.2001 in the case Broadcasting, Entertainment, Cinematographic and Theatre Union (BECTU) v. Secretary of State for Trade and Industry, C 173/99, ECLI:EU:C:2001:81 (para. 26–28). See: M. Jarmoszka, *Reguły wykładni*, 89.

[166] See: Judgement of the Court of Justice of 27.06.2003 in the case European Parliament v. the European Council, C 540/03, ECLI:EU:C:2006:429, then Judgement of the Court of Justice of 13.03.2007 in the case Unibet (London) Ltd. and Unibet (International) Ltd. v. Justitiekanslern, C 432/05, ECLI:EU:C:2007:163, Judgement of the Court of Justice of 29.01.2008 in the case Productores de Musica de Espana (Promusicae) v. Telefonica de Espana SAU, C 275/06, ECLI:EU:C:2008:54. See also: F. Jasiński, "Karta Praw Podstawowych: struktura, zakres regulacyjny i dotychczasowe znaczenie w praktyce," in *Ochrona praw podstawowych w Unii Europejskiej*, ed. J. Barcz (Warszawa, 2008), 55.

[167] Art. 51 CFR. See also: D. Kornobis-Romanowska, "Prawa podstawowe w orzecznictwie TSUE," 28.

system for the protection of fundamental rights, where the entities are empowered in a general sense. The Charter limits those empowerments to the application of EU law.[168]

In literature, it also pointed out to the existence of the so-called doctrine *Reverse Solange*, in accordance with which in the case when a Member State seriously and persistently breaches the essence of fundamental rights, the Charter of Fundamental Rights finds its application towards this Member State outside the jurisdiction of EU law, which is justified by the essence of EU citizenship and under Art. 2 TEU.[169] However, as was stressed by the Advocate General E. Sharpston, the protection of fundamental rights cannot lead to the usurping of competences by the EU.[170]

E. Morawska characterizes fundamental rights in an exceptionally accurate way, pointing out that from the perspective of the theory of law they belong to general clauses. Thus, they do not contain "rigid content"—the content is determined in the process of applying the law. The consequence of such an approach lies in the flexibility of interpretation of fundamental rights.[171] The Charter is also described in the legal science as the so-called evolutionary instrument (work in progress), whose interpretation will be shaped by the case-law of the European courts.[172]

The Charter of Fundamental Rights consists of the Preamble and VIII titles (Dignity, Freedoms, Equality, Solidarity, Citizens' Rights, Justice, General provisions governing the interpretation and application of the Charter).[173]

In accordance with Art. 52(5) CFR its provisions are divided in the rights (which may provide grounds for an individual's claims) and into the principles, which:

> may be implemented by legislative and executive acts taken by institutions, bodies, offices and agencies of the Union, and by acts of Member States

[168] C. Mik, "Karta Praw Podstawowych: wyznaczniki standardów," 69.

[169] See: D. Kornobis-Romanowska, "Prawa podstawowe w orzecznictwie TSUE," 32.

[170] Opinion 2/13, para. 162.

[171] E. Morawska, "Konstrukcja normatywna praw," 53.

[172] On this subject, see: H. Izdebski, "Rola i miejsce Karty Praw Podstawowych w Unii Europejskiej w europejskiej filozofii praw człowieka," in *5 lat Karty Praw Podstawowych UE*, ed. A. Gubrynowicz (Warszawa, 2006), 19.

[173] On this subject, see: R. Mazur, "Karta Praw Podstawowych UE," in *Ochrona praw podstawowych w Unii Europejskiej. Wybrane zagadnienia*, ed. A. Florczak (Warszawa, 2009), 45–50.

when they are implementing Union law, in the exercise of their respective powers. They shall be judicially cognisable only in the interpretation of such acts and in the ruling on their legality.

However, the Charter does not include a clear, separate catalogue of principles.[174] The principles of EU law were identified by the Court of Justice in its case-law, including among them the principles originally included in the Community law (e.g., the principle of subsidiarity) and the principles whose content was established by the Court (such as the principle of the right to protection or the principle of the protection of acquired rights).[175]

The Charter does not include a substance classification of human rights based on the universal system of the covenant on Human Rights. Therefore, the Charter does not contain hierarchy and division into the sections grouping the rights of first and second generation.[176] As J. Menkes observes, the placing of the rights of first, second and third generation[177] next to one another constitutes a new solution in the European legislative tradition,[178] whereas "the Creators of the Charter decided that combining the rights of different generations in a single document reflects the inseparability of human rights."[179] Undoubtedly, this solution is not in line with the existing legislative traditions within the area of human rights and the structure of the Charter might initially seem to be unclear, especially that the traditional division into the generations of human rights can be found also in the constitutional law.

The rights enshrined in the Charter are not new rights but merely a catalogue of the already functioning and protected fundamental rights (hence in legal acts the term "recognition of the rights" is used), having their source in the ECHR and other acts of international law, such as the Council of Europe Convention on Human Rights and Biomedicine, the European Social Charter or the UN Convention on the Rights of the Child.[180]

[174] T. Jurczyk, "Trzy źrodła praw," 286.

[175] M. Jarmoszka, "Reguły wykładni," 70.

[176] E. Morawska, "Konstrukcja normatywna praw," 53.

[177] It is worth pointing out that the Charter identifies the rights of third-generation, the so-called solidarity rights—already in the Preamble it is written that "Enjoyment of these rights entails responsibilities and duties with regard to other persons, to the human community and to future generations." See: H. Izdebski, "Rola i miejsce Karty," 15.

[178] J. Menkes, "Karta Praw Podstawowych," 38.

[179] Ibidem, 39.

[180] Ibidem, 39–42. The table presents the normative sources of the rights included in the Charter of Fundamental Rights.

To a large degree, the Charter contains the rights which were already known in the case-law of the CJEU. However, the rights such as freedom of the arts and sciences are a *novum* for the Union's system of protection and in this sense the Charter goes beyond the general principles of law, that is the understanding of protection which had been shaped before the Treaty of Lisbon entered into force.[181]

The provisions for the interpretation and application of the Charter[182] are laid down in its Art. 52–54, some of which have been already cited in the present subchapter.[183] These Articles also include the four rules regarding the standards for the protection of fundamental rights in the EU's system. Firstly, in accordance with Art. 53 of the Charter, none of the provisions from that Charter might be interpreted as restricting the protection that had already been recognized in international law (especially by the ECHR), Union law or the Member States' constitutions. Secondly, in accordance with Art. 52(7), the courts referring to the Charter are obliged to give due regard in their interpretation to the explanations drawn up as providing guidance to the Charter. Thirdly, in accordance with Art. 52(3) CFR:

> In so far as this Charter contains rights which correspond to rights guaranteed by the Convention for the Protection of Human Rights and Fundamental Freedoms, the meaning and scope of those rights shall be the same as those laid down by the said Convention. This provision shall not prevent Union law providing more extensive protection.

The fourth rule is included in Art. 52(4) CFR, which states that the interpretation of the Charter should be conducted in harmony with the common constitutional traditions of the Member States in so far as the Charter recognizes those rights. These Articles provide a specific guarantee for the Member States, so that as a result of introducing the catalogue

[181] K. Orzeszyna, "Karta Praw Podstawowych w Unii Europejskiej w Traktacie Lizbońskim," Roczniki Nauk Prawnych, vol. XIX, no. 2 (2009): 53.

[182] On the subject of the interpretation of EU law, see: M. Jarmoszka, "Reguły wykładni," 71 et seq. As M. Jarmoszka emphasizes, on the basis of the Preamble to the CFR, C. Mik pointed out to the following methods of its interpretation: pro homine, legal, flexible, evolutionary and the interpretation for the responsible exercize of rights, see: M. Jarmoszka, "Reguły wykładni," 77 (footnote 48).

[183] See: C. Mik, "Karta Praw Podstawowych: wyznaczniki standardów," 75.

of the protected fundamental rights into EU law, the competences of the Member States will not be infringed.[184]

The proof of the Member States' concern regarding the possible infringements of their constitutional competences was the adoption of the so-called British Protocol by Poland and Great Britain, which was attached to the Treaty of Lisbon and which restricted the possibility of applying the Charter with regard to these states.[185] The aim of the Protocol was to indicate that the Charter does not create a new catalogue of human rights and to preclude an extensive interpretation of the CFR by the CJEU and national courts with regard to Poland and the United Kingdom.[186] Moreover, the Protocol deprived the provisions of the Charter of the principle of the primacy of EU law over national law and partly ruled out the direct effectiveness of the Charter's norms (included in Title IV and referring to national law).[187]

2.5 Cultural Rights in the System of the Protection of Fundamental Rights in the European Union

2.5.1 Introductory Remarks

Within the framework of the competence conferred by the Treaties, the European Union does not have a common cultural policy but supports the actions of the Member States. The aim of this subchapter is to identify the place of culture in the EU's policies and law. Despite few legal provisions and restricted competence, the Union is involved in numerous activities for the protection of culture, albeit not of a systemic character, which will be described in the present subchapter. The said activities stem from,

[184] K. Orzeszyna, "Karta Praw Podstawowych," 46.

[185] Protocol (no. 30) on the application of the Charter of Fundamental Rights of the European Union to Poland and to the United Kingdom. OJ C 202 of 7.06.2016, 312. See also: P. Kułak, J. Hołub, "Mechanizm ochronny praw podstawowych w obrębie Unii Europejskiej—rola i znaczenie Karty Praw Podstawowych," in *Efektywność europejskiego systemu ochrony praw człowieka. Efektywność mechanizmów ochrony praw człowieka rady Europy, Unii Europejskiej i OBWE*, ed. J. Jaskiernia (Toruń, 2012), 516.

[186] K. Kowalik-Bańczyk, "Protokoł w sprawie stosowania Karty Praw Podstawowych Unii Europejskiej do Polski i Zjednoczonego Krolestwa. Komentarz," in *Karta Praw Podstawowych Unii Europejskiej. Komentarz*, ed. A. Wróbel (Warszawa, 2013), 1419.

[187] Ibidem, 1420.

amongst others, provisions included in the Treaties and the Charter of Fundamental Rights. A special role in the globalized reality is played by cultural exchange and the developing sectors of the cultural industry and cultural services. The protection of cultural identity of the whole Europe is certainly bound to be gaining in importance in confrontation with the influx of persons culturally different from the Europeans, coming from dynamically developing regions of the world.

The subchapter will include a characteristic of the EU's activities in the area of culture. The cultural rights in the contemporary European reality will also be redefined with a view to indicating and analysing the possibilities of the Union to protect broadly understood cultural rights.

In accordance with the thesis proposed in this text, there is a need for a redefinition of cultural rights and their broader, interdisciplinary perspective, which will correspond to the actual possibilities of their realization in the contemporary, globalized society. In accordance with the thesis adopted in the current work, in the EU there exist legal instruments facilitating the protection of broadly understood cultural rights. Simultaneously, due to the dominant globalization trends in culture, unifying cultural patterns, the Union should embark on more intensive policy-making that would protect the European cultural identity.

On the basis of the characterized policies and redefined cultural entitlements, it will be possible to reconstruct the catalogue of cultural rights which the third-country nationals may enjoy on the grounds of EU law. The classical understanding of the cultural right as the right to participate in cultural life is a subject right, whereas problems arise with defining the range of exercising of this right. In different legal systems, there are different guarantees of its realization. Thus, for instance, in Polish law there are no regulations with regard to participation in cultural life and citizens' access to cultural goods in chapter II of the Constitution concerning the rights and freedoms, but the creation of conditions for the "dissemination and equal access to cultural goods" appears as a programmatic norm in chapter I.[188] A similar situation occurs in EU law—the Union creates the conditions for the realization of this cultural right by carrying out cultural policies, which in a real way extend the cultural offer and contribute to

[188] See: art. 6 of the Constitution of the Republic of Poland. Constitution of the Republic of Poland adopted on 2 April 1997 and adopted by the National Assembly of Poland on 2 April 1997, approved by a national referendum on 25 May 1997, and signed by the President of Poland on 16 July 1997. Journal of Laws of 1997 no. 79, item 483, as amended.

citizens' participation in culture. These actions are addressed at all the inhabitants of the Union, including also the categories of foreign nationals.

On the basis of the said conclusions, it seems justifiable to claim that the Union's cultural policies, even though not directly guaranteeing subjective (individual) cultural rights, have a real impact on the possibilities of exercising one's cultural rights and it is necessary to analyse them with regard to the possibilities of participating of third-country nationals in the Union's cultural life.

2.5.2 *Concept of Cultural Rights*

Among the generations of human rights already listed in this work, cultural rights were usually classified as second-generation rights, next to the rights of economic and social character.[189] However, a full definition of cultural rights is extremely difficult to formulate, if not straight impossible, due to the complex nature of the very culture (depending on the adopted definition—whether it concerns merely symbolic culture, or also social culture or even material one), as well as its dynamic character—it would suffice to take into account the development of cultural media at the turn of the twentieth and twenty-first centuries.

In the doctrine, cultural rights are often defined on the basis of the guarantees of the International Covenant on Economic, Social and Cultural Rights (ICESCR). In this case, cultural rights are understood as "the need to provide the rights to participate in cultural life, to access scientific achievements and their applications and to protect the interests resulting from scientific, literary and artistic activity."[190] Moreover, as M. Barczewski points out, cultural rights also include the rights serving to preserve and develop ethnic, religious, linguistic and national identity.[191]

[189] See: The International Covenant on Economic, Social and Cultural Rights, Journal of Laws of 1997 no. 38 item 169, further also as ICESCR.

[190] M. Barczewski, "Prawa kulturalne," in *Leksykon ochrony praw człowieka. 100 podstawowych pojęć*, eds. M. Balcerzak, S. Sykuna (Warszawa, 2010), 353.

[191] It is also worth mentioning here the Fribourg Declaration, which is not a legally binding document but presents an interesting concept of the catalogue of cultural rights. The Declaration lists cultural rights understood as an individual's right to respect their cultural identity (protected with regard to freedom of opinion, religion and expression), one's right to know and to have one's own culture respected (as well as those cultures that make up the common heritage of humanity), one's right to have access to cultural heritage (also through the rights to education and information) understood as a resource for future generations. The declaration also lists, amongst others, the right to have access to and participate in cul-

Cultural rights were also referred to by the International Convention on the Elimination of all Forms of Racial Discrimination (amongst others, the right to equal participation in cultural activity).[192]

The ICESCR was widely interpreted within the framework of the adopted resolutions[193] and in the General Comment No. 21 adopted on 21 December 2009 by the Committee on Economic, Social and Cultural Rights[194] on everybody's right to take part in cultural life, guaranteed under Art. 15 of the Pact.[195] The remaining cultural rights guaranteed in Art. 15 of the Covenant include the right to build on the scientific progress and its application and the right to the protection of copyright of culture creators. Art. 15 also guarantees the freedom of artistic expression, while the obligation of protection, development and dissemination of culture was imposed upon the signatory states, together with activities for the development of international cooperation.

tural life—individually or together with others—through the rights to freedom of expression in public or in private, the right to exercise one's own cultural practices, the right to the protection of the moral and material interests linked to the works that result from one's cultural activity (Art. 5). Additionally, the Declaration guarantees the right to education and information, as rights connected with participation in cultural life, as well as the right to cultural cooperation. Art. 3. The Fribourg Declaration. The Fribourg Declaration on Cultural Rights of 7 May 2007. The Declaration is available on the website: www.culturalrights.net, www1.umn.edu. Accessed 12.09.2017.

[192] The International Convention on the Elimination of all Forms of Racial Discrimination, opened for signature in New York on 7 March 1966, Journal of Laws of 1969 no. 25, item 187.

[193] Intellectual property rights and human rights, Sub-Commission on Human Rights resolution 2000/7, 17/08/2000, E/CN.4/SUB.2/RES/2000/7, http://ap.ohchr.org/documents/alldocs.aspx?doc_id=8200. Accessed 12.09.2017; Resolution of the Sub-Commission on the Promotion and Protection of Human Rights 2001/21 on Intellectual property and human rights (E/CN.4/Sub.2/RES/2001/21).

[194] General Comment no. 21—Right of everyone to take part in cultural right, Committee on Economic, Social and Cultural Rights, 21 December 2009, Economic and Social Council. Document available on the website: http://www.refworld.org/docid/4ed35bae2.html. Accessed 12.09.2017.

[195] Guarantees of cultural rights in the UN's system might be found in Art. 27 of the Universal Declaration of Human Rights. The Universal Declaration of Human Rights (UDHR) is a declaration adopted by the United Nations General Assembly on 10 December 1948 in Paris, 10.12.1948, text available on the website: http://libr.sejm.gov.pl/tek01/txt/onz/1948.html. Accessed 12.09.2017. See: E. Stamatopoulou, *Cultural Rights in International Law, Article 27 of the Universal Declaration of Human Rights and Beyond* (Brill/Nijhoff, 2007); A.M. Kosińska, *Kulturalne prawa człowieka. Regulacje normatywne i ich realizacja* (Lublin, 2014), 88.

Moreover, the guarantees for the protection of the right to cultural identity are included in the International Covenant on Civil and Political Rights, which in its Art. 27 prohibits that ethnic, religious or linguistic minorities be denied the right, "in community with the other members of their group, to enjoy their own culture, to profess and practise their own religion, or to use their own language."

As was mentioned above, generally cultural rights are classified as second-generation rights (i.e., the rights requiring the activity of the state for the realization of the guarantees for an individual, understood as the rights which are not the rights of immediate effect) and the rights of a derogable character. Nevertheless, taking into account the entirety of cultural life and the guarantees functioning in the legal circulation concerning a broadly understood participation in culture, it should be stated that the rights of a cultural character are first-generation rights (freedom of artistic expression),[196] second-generation rights (the right to participate in cultural life, the right of access to cultural goods—whose realization creates positive obligations on the side of the state,[197] the right to cultural identity[198]), third-generation rights, that is solidarity rights, encompassing the right to participate in the common cultural heritage[199] and fourth-generation rights concerning

[196] See: D. Bychawska-Siniarska, D. Głowacka, *Wolność artystyczna. Praktyczny przewodnik*, Helsińska Fundacja Praw Człowieka 2014, publication available on the website: http://www.hfhr.pl/wolnosc-artystyczna-praktyczny-przewodnik-nowa-publikacja-hfpc/. Accessed 12.09.2017.

[197] On the subject of the protection of cultural heritage, see: K. Zeidler, "Przestrzenie badawcze prawa ochrony dziedzictwa kultury," *Gdańskie Studia Prawnicze*, vol. XXXIII (2015): 492.

[198] See more on this subject: P.Ł.J. Andrzejewski, "Prawo człowieka do tożsamości kulturowej w Polsce," in *Prawa człowieka w społeczeństwie obywatelskim*, ed. A. Rzepliński (Warszawa, 1993), 142 et seq.

[199] More on this subject, see: M. Jovanović, "Cultural Rights as Collective Rights," in *Cultural Rights as Collective Rights. An International Law Perspective*, ed. A. Jakubowski (Leiden/Boston, 2016), 15 et seq. In accordance with the UNESCO Universal Declaration on Cultural Diversity adopted in November 2001, cultural diversity is the common heritage of humanity and should be preserved for future generations. See: UNESCO Universal Declaration on Cultural Diversity, the document is available on the website: http://portal.unesco.org/en/ev.php-URL_ID=13179&URL_DO=DO_TOPIC&URL_SECTION=201.html. Accessed 12.09.2017.

the protection of the cultural rights of minority groups (primarily national and ethnic minorities, but also, e.g., linguistic minorities).[200]

In accordance with the principle of subsidiarity of the international system of human rights,[201] cultural rights are protected primarily at the national level and guaranteed in the constitutional provisions. In the Constitution of Poland, cultural rights are guaranteed in an incomplete way—in chapter II of the basic law (The freedoms, rights and obligations of persons and citizens) there is only Art. 73 on the freedoms of artistic creation and the freedom to enjoy cultural goods.[202] Art. 5 and 6 in chapter I of the Constitution are considered to be merely programmatic norms and do not entitle an individual with the possibility of executing them.[203]

However, it is worth pointing out that with time, the international system for the protection of cultural rights is increasingly gaining in importance.[204] In addition to the guarantees under the ICESCR within the framework of the UN's system there are international agreements adopted within the activities of the United Nations Educational, Scientific and

[200] See: S. Wiessner, "Culture and the Rights of Indigenous People," in *The Cultural Dimension of Human Rights*, ed. A.F. Vrdoljak (Oxford, 2013), 119–124. See: J. Symonides, "The OSCE Normative Regulations of the Minorities Protection," in *OSCE and Minorities. Assessment and Prospects*, ed. S. Parzymies (Warszawa, 2007), 149; K. Drzewiecki, "The OSCE High Commissioner on National Minorities—Confronting Traditional and Emerging Challenge," in *OSCE and Minorities. Assessment and Prospects*, ed. S. Parzymies (Warszawa, 2007), 14.

[201] T. Jasudowicz, *Zasady ogólne prawa międzynarodowego*, 207. On the subject of international instruments of protection and constitutional traditions, see: A. Młynarska-Sobaczewska, "Prawo do kultury w katalogu praw człowieka," *Przegląd Prawa Konstytucyjnego*, no. 3 (2013): 27–56.

[202] M. Jabłoński, J. Węgrzyn, "Wolność twórczości artystycznej i naukowej oraz dostępu do dóbr kultury," in *Realizacja i ochrona konstytucyjnych wolności i praw jednostki w polskim porządku prawnym*, ed. M. Jabłoński (Wrocław, 2014), 699 et seq.

[203] A. Frankiewicz, *Konstytucyjna regulacja dostępu do dóbr kultury i wolności korzystania z kultury*, "Przegląd Prawa Konstytucyjnego" 2013, no. 3, 58.

[204] As Z. Kulińska-Kępa emphasizes, attempts to unify the catalogue of economic, social and cultural rights were raised at the international forum much earlier than the discussion on the subject of civic and political rights, see: Z. Kulińska-Kępa, *Prawa obywatelskie i polityczne a prawa gospodarcze, społeczne i kulturalne. Porównanie systemów ochrony* (Warszawa, 2017), 47.

Cultural Organization (UNESCO)[205] and concerning cultural cooperation and the protection of cultural heritage.[206]

At the European regional level cultural rights are protected also within the framework of the Council of Europe, but the system of this protection is incomplete in as much as the very ECHR[207] does not include the norms on cultural life (the right to education was guaranteed only in the Additional Protocol No 1[208]). However, the ECtHR in its case-law extensively addressed the possibility of protecting cultural rights indirectly by referring to Art. 8 (the right to the protection of private and family life),[209] Art. 9 (freedom of thought, conscience and religion),[210] Art. 10 (freedom

[205] On the subject of internationalization of cultural rights in the UNESCO system, see: J. Symonides, "UNESCO a prawa kulturalne—ich treść i implementacja w nowym kontekście międzynarodowym," in *O prawach człowieka w podwójną rocznicę Paktów. Księga pamiątkowa w hołdzie profesor Annie Michalskiej*, eds. T. Jasudowicz, C. Mik (Toruń, 1996), 171. Cf.: A. Przyborowska-Klimczak, *Rozwój ochrony dziedzictwa kulturalnego w prawie międzynarodowym na przełomie XX i XXI wieku* (Lublin, 2011).

[206] The UNESCO Convention for the Protection of the World Cultural and Natural Heritage of 16 November 1972, Journal of Laws of 1976 no. 32, item 190; the UNESCO Convention for the Safeguarding of the Intangible Cultural Heritage, Paris, 17 October 2003, Journal of Laws of 2011 no. 172, item 1018; The UNESCO Convention on the Protection and Promotion of the Diversity of Cultural Expressions of 21 October 2005, Journal of Laws of 2007 no. 215, item 1585. See: *Ochrona niematerialnego dziedzictwa kulturalnego*, eds. A. Niewęgłowski, M. Poźniak-Niedzielska, A. Przyborowska-Klimczak (Warszawa, 2015). Cf.: W. Kowalski, K. Piotrowska-Nosek, H. Schreiber, K. Zalasińska, *Konwencje UNESCO w dziedzinie kultury. Komentarz* (Warszawa, 2014). On the subject of crimes against culture, see: F. Lenzerini, "Suppressing and Remedying Offences against Culture," in *The Cultural Dimension of Human Rights*, ed. A.F. Vrdoljak (Oxford, 2013), 241 et seq.

[207] It is also worth adding that in the system of the Council of Europe in May 2007 a text of a new convention was adopted on offences against cultural goods (Council of Europe Convention on Offences relating to Cultural Property), information available on the website: http://www.coe.int/en/web/conventions/full-list/-/conventions/treaty/221. Accessed 12.09.2017.

[208] Protocol no. 1 to the Convention for the Protection of Human Rights and Fundamental Freedoms of 20 March 1952, Journal of Laws of 1995 no. 36, item 175.

[209] See: judgement of the ECtHR of 18.01.2001 in the case Chapman v. the United Kingdom, complaint no. 27238/95.

[210] See: judgement of the ECtHR of 4.12.2008 in the case Dogru v. France, complaint no. 27058/05; judgement of the ECtHR of 23.02.2010 in the case Ahmet Arslan and others v. Turkey, complaint no. 41135/98.

of expression)[211] and the above-mentioned Protocol No 1.[212] The proof of the Council of Europe's interest in the issues of the protection of the right to culture is the European Cultural Convention[213] adopted on 19 December 1954 in Paris, which obligated the signatory States to protect and develop culture in the European perspective.

The possibilities for the protection of cultural rights in the Union are, in turn, restricted due to the division of competences, resulting from the treaties, between the EU and the Member States. An in-depth analysis of the possibilities and effects of the Union's activities in support of culture will be presented in the following subchapter.

Cultural rights have been defined in the present subchapter in the most universal way.[214] However, it should be observed with full responsibility that a universal and classical definition of the rights of cultural character requires a redefinition primarily due to the dynamic transformations, which have been observed in the cultural sector over the period of the last several decades.

At present, access to cultural goods is more and more often analysed at a global level. Moreover, it is often accompanied by increasingly broader use of new technologies, including digitization of cultural goods, facilitating their indirect reception. M. Jabłoński and J. Węgrzyn observe that "The use of new technologies in a significant way broadens the existing understanding of the freedom of access to cultural goods."[215] New

[211] See: judgement of the ECtHR of 16.02.2010 in the case Akdas v. Turkey, complaint no. 41056/04; judgement of the ECtHR of 25.01.2007 in the case Kunstler v. Austria, complaint no. 68354/01; judgement of the ECtHR of 29.03.2005 in the case Alinak v. Turkey, complaint no. 40287/98.

[212] See report: Cultural Rights in the case-law of European Court of Human Rights, Council of Europe. European Court of Human Rights 2011, report available on the website: www.echr.coe.int. Accessed 12.09.2017; M. Wólkowska, "Prawa kulturalne w Europejskiej Konwencji Praw Człowieka," *Studia Iuridica Toruniensia*, vol. XIII (2013): 241–260. See: Recommendation 1990 (2012) The right of everyone to take part in cultural life, Author(s): Parliamentary Assembly Origin: Assembly debate on 24 January 2012 (4th Sitting) (see Doc. 12815, report of the Committee on Culture, Science, Education and Media, rapporteur: Ms Marland-Militello). Text adopted by the Assembly on 24 January 2012 (4th Sitting), document available on the website: http://assembly.coe.int/nw/xml/XRef/Xref-XML2HTML-en.asp?fileid=18058&lang=en. Accessed 12.09.2017.

[213] The European Cultural Convention adopted in Paris on 19 December 1954, Journal of Laws of 1990 no. 8, item 44.

[214] More on the subject of the definition of cultural rights, see: A.M. Kosińska, *Kulturalne prawa człowieka*, 76–84.

[215] M. Jabłoński, J. Węgrzyn, "Wolność twórczości artystycznej i naukowej," 702.

technologies include, amongst others, digitization of cultural goods and their dissemination through electronic means.[216]

Cultural rights are becoming an increasingly global issue, whereas the supranational communities act in favour of facilitating access to cultural goods in transnational dimensions, which also has an impact on the possibilities of a wider access to cultural goods in connection with the guarantees of third-generation rights. The freedom of artistic expression is becoming increasingly part of intercultural conflicts, which are accompanied by a discussion on the relation between the freedom of speech and the freedom of artistic expression.[217]

Simultaneously, cultural life is increasingly intertwined with the service sector (the economic side of culture is openly talked about) and as a consequence, access to culture means at the same time access to consumer goods, such as books or pop-culture objects.

The rights of a cultural character at present denote a wide collection of rights connected with access to cultural goods, participation in cultural life and freedom of artistic expression, which also include the rights of individuals and communities to preserve their cultural identity and cultivate local traditions. At the same time, cultural rights are often connected with the duties of the state's institutions and owners of cultural goods to preserve monuments in the right state, so as to guarantee individuals and communities the possibilities of enjoying cultural goods of the region. Cultural obligations are most commonly associated with the state bodies having supervision over monuments, but it seems that cultural duties are the responsibility of all persons enjoying cultural goods—this duty includes primarily keeping cultural goods in the right condition.

A significant proposition includes a promotion of cultural responsibilities of an educational character—due to a civilizational crisis it should be a

[216]The widespread circulation of cultural goods is also indirectly assisted by the functioning of a public domain, such as the National Digital Archive (NDA). See: B. Bednarek-Michalska, A. Tarkowski, B. Szczepańska, "Domena publiczna—co to takiego?" *Biuletyn EBIB*, no. 1 (2009), electronic version of the magazine available at: http://www.ebib.pl/2009/101/a.php?bednarek_tarkowski_szczepanska. Accessed 12.09.2017. The NDA was created pursuant to the regulation of the Minister of Culture and National Heritage of 6 February 2008 concerning the change of name and the range of activity of the National Digital Archive in Warsaw, Journal of Laws of 2008 no. 28, item 167. Internet website: www.nac.gov.pl. Accessed 12.09.2017.

[217]See, for instance, the case of Dorota Nieznalska in connection with the installation "Passion." The case is discussed in: D. Bychawska-Siniarska, D. Głowacka, *Wolność artystyczna*, 17.

cultural duty for EU citizens to know native culture—which is, perhaps in an imperfect way, but still, verified at the level of school education. With regard to the integration issues, another proposition worth considering is to obligate third-country nationals to learn about the culture of the receiving countries and respect for the culture of the host country. This issue will be discussed in greater detail in further sections of the book—it is, however, worth observing here that numerous Member States introduce regulations aimed at verifying the level of migrants' knowledge of the cultural aspects of the receiving country, which should be perceived as an exceptionally valuable solution.

At the beginning of the twenty-first century, cultural rights entail a clash between tradition and modernity—they are a melting pot reflecting the changes in cultural life, but also potential conflicts. Hence, guaranteeing the realization of cultural rights at both the national and supranational level at present requires of the decision-making bodies to demonstrate a high level of sensitivity concerning cultural identities. On the other hand, it is necessary to set clear priorities which will allow for the protection and promotion of the values common for the European civilization and will curb the creeping civilizational and cultural crisis.

2.6 Culture in European Union Law and the Possibility of Protection of Cultural Rights in the EU Legal System

2.6.1 Preliminary Observations

In accordance with the theses proposed in the present work, one of the European values lying at the foundation of the EU and constituting its identity is European culture. The European Union and European Union law are based on European values, including European culture. In the Union's system of law, culture is not protected in a comprehensive way but only in a selective way, due to the fact that the Treaty indicates only the competence of support as relevant for the action sector in the area of culture. What is more, it should be remembered that as a result of globalization and giving voice to the doctrine of multiculturalism, as well as strong migration influxes, European culture is experiencing a crisis and is in need of special protection at the level of the EU. The Union primarily protects European identity and further other cultural rights. It should be borne in mind while analysing the actual legal protection provided by the EU. In the policies and law of the Union there exists the right to the protection of European heritage and the common cultural values are protected in a spirit of solidarity. Other cultural rights might be protected provided that the guarantees of the protection of treaty priority—European identity—are ensured. This value cannot be subject to derogation in favour of other values characteristic of other cultures, which means that full protection should be ensured in the first place to European culture. If the protection of the above values is collision-free, it is possible to protect other cultural values. At present, the role of the Union in the sphere of culture cannot be undervalued—within its structure it facilitates cultural actions of an integrated nature, strengthened at the level of several Member States.

The protection of cultural rights in the EU's law system is not only possible—it is real. However, it is a system of special protection, as EU law protects certain areas of cultural rights in a particular way. This protection finds its grounds primarily in the provisions of the Charter of Fundamental Rights, but it also finds its justification in an analysis of the whole system of actions undertaken by the EU in the field of culture.

The lack of appropriate interest in the issues of culture and its significance for the process of integration was criticized in the doctrine.[218] As part of preliminary remarks, it should be emphasized that at present the Union's competences in the area of culture are provided for in the TFEU in Art. 6 as supportive competences,[219] which means that the Member States have autonomy in the shaping of their cultural policy. However, as W. Sobczak observes, the Union realizes the task of supporting the cultural development of the Member States,[220] which characteristically dis-

[218] K. Krzysztofek, "Integracja Polski z Unią Europejską jako przestrzenią kulturową," *Studia Europejskie*, no. 1 (2000): 90. J. Monnet, undertaking a reflection at the slowly progressing integration within the EU stated that if he were to undertake the task of uniting Europe one more time, he would start with culture. See also: D. Jurkiewicz-Eckert, "Od Traktatu o Unii Europejskiej do Europejskiej Agendy dla Kultury—narodziny i rozwój polityki kulturalnej UE," *Studia Europejskie*, no. 1 (2015): 82. According to the author, "it is not without reason that over the course of the last several years, both in the series of the most important legal acts and community documents, as well as in public debate on the future of the Union, a duty of taking into account cultural aspects in all actions undertaken by the Community have been emphasized."

[219] See: M. Cesarz, "Porządek prawny Unii Europejskiej," in *Procesy integracyjne i dezintegracyjnew Europie*, eds. A. Pacześniak, M. Klimowicz (Wrocław, 2014), 183.

[220] W. Sobczak, "Ochrona dziedzictwa kultury w systemie prawnym Unii Europejskiej," *Środkowoeuropejskie Studia Polityczne*, no. 3 (2009): 105. As the author emphasizes,

play great diversity, which is accurately conveyed in the official motto of the Union: "United in diversity."[221]

The Union is realizing its cultural policy, even though the EU's legal acts do not define the concept of culture. Obviously, various sociological definitions which are referred to in the present work might be helpful in defining the content of this concept. Nevertheless, it seems also beneficial to refer to the UNESCO Convention on the Protection and Promotion of the Diversity of Cultural Expressions of 2005.[222] The Convention does not directly define the concept of culture but determines the meaning of concepts, such as "cultural content" ("refers to the symbolic meaning, artistic dimension and cultural values that originate from or express cultural identities"—Art. 4 paragraph 2) and forms of cultural expression ("are those expressions that result from the creativity of individuals, groups and societies, and that have cultural content"—Art. 4 paragraph 3). In the Union's documents and legal acts there are also to be found terms, such as common cultural heritage (the term used since the 1970s)[223] or the "cultural area common to all inhabitants of Europe"[224] (further as "European cultural area").

"Accentuating the common cultural heritage seems to be though a task that is bit 'overwhelming,' given the fact that the differences between various regions of Europe are exceptionally deep. However, it is an interesting and puzzling thing that the Treaty does not attempt to define the concept of 'culture,' leaving this issue, as a matter of fact, to the doctrine."

[221] D. Jurkiewicz-Eckert, "Od Traktatu o Unii Europejskiej," 65.

[222] Council Decision 2006/515/EC of 18 May 2006 on the conclusion of the Convention on the Protection and Promotion of the Diversity of Cultural Expressions, OJ L 201, 25.7.2006, 15; the state of implementation is analysed in the document: http://www.diversitystudy.eu/es/esstudyunescoconventionpl.pdf. Accessed 12.09.2017.

[223] D. Jurkiewicz-Eckert, "Od 'wspólnego dziedzictwa kulturowego' do 'wspólnego obszaru kulturowego.' O nowych kierunkach debaty wokół przyszłości kultury w Unii Europejskiej," *Studia Europejskie*, no. 3 (2003): 83.

[224] Used for the first time in the Communication of the Commission of 1998—then in the decision establishing the programme Culture 2000. See: D. Jurkiewicz-Eckert, "Od 'wspólnego dziedzictwa kulturowego,'" 84. As the author observes, "the present discussion over the concept of the "common cultural heritage" and "European cultural area" entails at the same time that culture will play an increasingly vital role in the integration processes and because of that the EU's cultural policy should be thoroughly reformulated and strengthened by legislative and financial support," ibidem, 87. First European Community Framework Programme in Support of Culture (2000–2004). Proposal for a European Parliament and Council Decision establishing a single and programming instrument for cultural cooperation (Culture 2000 programme), COM(1998) 266 final.

After A Kuś, the EU's cultural policy can be described as "conscious influence on the Union's institutions on cultural processes, in accordance with the assumptions, purposes and values lying at the foundation of the functioning of the EU, with a view to inciting citizens' participation in culture."[225] In turn, Sobczak emphasizes that in the EU's cultural policy one can distinguish three areas: the protection of common European heritage, development of European culture and its promotion.[226]

The addressees of the Union's cultural policy are also third-country nationals residing in the territory of the Member States. As E. Psychogiopoulou emphasizes, the Union's competences in the area of culture, even though restricted, allow indirectly, through the development of cultural policy, to contribute to the protection and promotion of cultural rights.[227] It is beyond doubt that the Union's cultural policy is most beneficial to foreign nationals with a regular status who have long-term residence permits, such as long-term residents or students. As a rule, each of the groups of third-country nationals might be a beneficiary of cultural activities, while they also indirectly contribute to the effective integration with the receiving society.

2.6.2 *Current Regulatory Framework with Regard to Culture in European Union Law*

At present, the issues concerning the EU's cultural policy and the place of culture in the Union's law were regulated in the Treaty on the Functioning of the European Union and the Treaty on European Union.

The key importance for the analysed issue lies in Art. 6 TFEU, which lays down the so-called competences aimed to support, coordinate or complement the activities of the Member States and lists culture among them. This type of competence (previously referred to in the literature as parallel competences) was introduced in the Treaty of Lisbon. Taking into account the fact that the treaty introduces the division into the exclusive, shared and supporting competences, one can, in a sense, speak of their gradation, whereas the competences under Art. 6 might be described as

[225] A. Kuś, "Polityka kulturalna Unii Europejskiej," in *Ochrona dziedzictwa kulturowego i materialnego pogranicza*, eds. A. Dębiński, L. Pietraszko (Lublin, 2011), 272.

[226] W. Sobczak, "Ochrona dziedzictwa kultury," 113.

[227] E. Psychogiopoulou, "The European Union and Cultural Rights," in *The Cultural Dimension of Human Rights* (Oxford, 2013), 170.

the so-called weak competences.[228] These competences can also be described as soft competences. At this stage, at the beginning of the discussion on the place of culture in the contemporary EU law, it is worth emphasizing that what is typical of soft competences is that, first of all, they do not replace the competences of the Member States and, secondly, harmonization of the national legislative and executive provisions in the areas listed under Art. 6 TFEU is not permissible. Thus, it is the Member States that bear the primary responsibility for managing culture and for guaranteeing cultural rights. Due to the adopted solution, cultural rights in the EU are not autonomous but merely complement the national system. However, even particular rights may be of significant importance, as it transpires from the case-law presented below.

In providing a characteristic of treaty provisions, one should first of all refer to Art. 167 TFEU, which is in a sense a provision of a fundamental character for all activities of the EU in the area of culture, and then point out the other provisions, which are significant from the perspective of the realization of the guarantees of cultural entitlements. In accordance with the said Art. 167 TFEU:

1. The Union shall contribute to the flowering of the cultures of the Member States, while respecting their national and regional diversity and at the same time bringing the common cultural heritage to the fore.
2. Action by the Union shall be aimed at encouraging cooperation between Member States and, if necessary, supporting and supplementing their action in the following areas:
   - improvement of the knowledge and dissemination of the culture and history of the European peoples,
   - conservation and safeguarding of cultural heritage of European significance,
   - non-commercial cultural exchanges,
   - artistic and literary creation, including in the audiovisual sector.

[228] P. Saganek, "Komentarz do artykułu 6," in *Traktat o funkcjonowaniu Unii Europejskiej. Komentarz*, vol. I, (art. 1–89), eds. D. Miąsik, N. Półtorak, A. Wróbel, published: WKP, 2012, electronic version available in the system of electronic legal information Lex.

The said Article does not have a direct effect, as it contains both competency and action standards. As was already highlighted above, the Court of Justice in its case-law decided that cultural goods are subject to treaty freedoms. However, those freedoms may be subject to restrictions, on account of the need for their protection, which was recognized by the Court to represent an overriding public interest.[229]

Moreover, in accordance with paragraph 3 Art. 167 TFEU, the Union and the Member States are fostering cooperation with third countries and international organizations in the sphere of culture (in particular with the Council of Europe). What is significant, under Art 167 paragraph 4 TFEU, is that the EU should take cultural aspects into account in its actions in order to respect and to promote the diversity of its cultures. In paragraph 4 Art. 167 TFEU, the wording "diversity of 'its' cultures" implies the EU's interest in the domestic, original cultures, not the diversity of cultures in the sense of immigration multiculturalism. This focus on the promotion and support of one's own, European identity can be seen in other treaty provisions, which will be cited below.

In accordance with paragraph 5 Art. 167 TFEU, the realization of the EU's cultural policy is guaranteed by the European Council and the European Parliament, which adopt legal instruments in accordance with the ordinary legislative procedure and after consulting the Committee of the Regions.[230]

The essence of culture and its significance for European integration finds its confirmation in the Preamble to the Treaty on European Union, in accordance with which the signatories of the treaty are "drawing inspiration from the cultural, religious and humanist inheritance of Europe, from which have developed the universal values of the inviolable and

[229] See: A. Siwek-Ślusarek, "Komentarz do art. 167 TFUE," in *Traktat o funkcjonowaniu Unii Europejskiej. Komentarz*, vol. II, Art. 90–222, eds. A. Kowalik-Bańczyk, M. Szwarc-Kuczer, A. Wróbel, published: WKP, 2012, electronic version available in the system of electronic legal information Lex. See: Directive 2006/123/EC of the European Parliament and of the Council of 12 December 2006 on services in the internal market, OJ L 376, 27.12.2006, 36. In accordance with Art. 36 TFEU: "The provisions of Articles 34 and 35 shall not preclude prohibitions or restrictions on imports, exports or goods in transit justified on grounds of public morality, public policy or public security; the protection of health and life of humans, animals or plants; the protection of national treasures possessing artistic, historic or archaeological value; or the protection of industrial and commercial property," Treaty on the Functioning of the European Union, consolidated version, OJ C 202 of 7.06.2016, 47.

[230] A. Siwek-Ślusarek, *Komentarz do art. 167 TFUE.*

inalienable rights of the human person, freedom, democracy, equality and the rule of law."[231]

Moreover, the Preamble expresses the intention of deepening solidarity between the nations of the Member States in respect for their history, culture and traditions. A specific type of guarantee for the protection of cultural rights can also be found in Art. 3 TEU, describing the aims of the Union, in accordance with which (paragraph 3, last sentence) the Union "shall respect its rich cultural and linguistic diversity, and shall ensure that Europe's cultural heritage is safeguarded and enhanced."

Regulations concerning respect for cultural diversity in the realization of the Union's policies are also to be found in the provisions of the TFEU regarding the common agricultural policy, fisheries and transport (Art. 13 TFEU). Finally, in accordance with Art. 107 paragraph 3 item d TFEU it is possible to provide public aid (whose general prohibition is laid down in Art. 107 TFEU in case it threatened to distort competition on the external market) in order to "promote culture and heritage conservation where such aid does not affect trading conditions and competition in the Union to an extent that is contrary to the common interest."[232]

As was also indicated in the preceding subchapter on the essence of cultural rights—they are of a hybrid character and in the present discussion, it is impossible to disregard the educational issues, concerning the fact that the right to education can be perceived as a right of social and cultural nature. The frameworks for the EU's educational policy are laid down in Art. 165 TFEU, in accordance with which:

> The Union shall contribute to the development of quality education by encouraging cooperation between Member States and, if necessary, by supporting and supplementing their action, while fully respecting the responsibility of the Member States for the content of teaching and the organisation of education systems and their cultural and linguistic diversity.

[231] See: Preamble TEU. Treaty on European Union, OJ C 202 of 7.06.2016, 13.

[232] Moreover, in accordance with Protocol no. 29 to the Treaty of Lisbon, "The provisions of the Treaties shall be without prejudice to the competence of Member States to provide for the funding of public service broadcasting and in so far as such funding is granted to broadcasting organisations for the fulfilment of the public service remit as conferred, defined and organized by each Member State, and in so far as such funding does not affect trading conditions and competition in the Union to an extent which would be contrary to the common interest, while the realisation of the remit of that public service shall be taken into account," Protocol no. 29 to the treaty of Lisbon on the system of public broadcasting in the Member States, OJ C 202 of 7.06.2016, 311.

The actions undertaken by the Union in the above-mentioned area are listed under paragraph 2 Art. 165 TFEU.[233] This Article is also not of direct effect, as it includes a competence norm. However, the relevant acts of secondary law were adopted for the realization of the educational policy.[234] The CJEU also interpreted educational issues in the cases submitted to the Court, contributing to the strengthening of the guarantees of the right to education for both migrant workers,[235] as well as EU citizens undertaking studies.[236]

[233] They include: developing the European dimension in education, particularly through the teaching and dissemination of the languages of the Member States, encouraging mobility of students and teachers, promoting cooperation between educational establishments, developing exchanges of information and experience on issues common to the education systems of the Member States, encouraging the development of youth exchanges and of exchanges of socio-educational instructors, and encouraging the participation of young people in democratic life in Europe, encouraging the development of distance education and also developing the European dimension in sport.

[234] Among them, the following might be mentioned: Art. 7 and 12 Regulation (EEC) no. 1612/68 of the Council of 15 October 1968 on freedom of movement for workers within the Community, replaced by Regulation (EU) no. 492/2011 of the European Parliament and of the Council of 5 April 2011 on freedom of movement for workers within the Union, OJ L 141, 27.5.2011, 1; regulation concerning the right of residence included in the so-called Citizenship Directive 2004/38. See also: Regulation (EC) no. 883/2004 of the European Parliament and of the Council of 29 April 2004 on the coordination of social security systems, OJ L 166 of 30.4.2004, 1.

[235] Judgement of the Court of Justice of 21.06.1988 in the case Sylvie Lair v. Universität Hannover, C 39/86, ECLI:EU:C:1988:322; Judgement of the Court of Justice of 26.02.1992 in the case V.J.M. Raulin v. Minister van Onderwijs en Wetenschappen, C 357/89, ECLI:EU:C:1992:87; Judgement of the Court of Justice of 3.07.1986 in the case Deborah Lawrie-Blum v. Land Baden-Württemberg, C 66/85, ECLI:EU:C:1986:284; Judgement of the Court of Justice of 26.02.1992 in the case M.J.E. Bernini v. Minister van Onderwijs en Wetenschappen, C 3/90, ECLI:EU:C:1992:89; Judgement of the Court of Justice of 21.06.1988 in the case Steven Malcolm Brown v. The Secretary of State for Scotland, C 197/86, ECLI:EU:C:1988:323; Judgement of the Court of Justice of 2.07.1974 in the case Donato Casagrande v. Landeshauptstadt München, C 9/74, ECLI:EU:C:1974:74. See: A. Siwek-Ślusarek, "Komentarz do art. 165 TFUE," in *Traktat o funkcjonowaniu Unii Europejskiej. Komentarz*, vol. II, Art. 90–222, eds. A. Kowalik-Bańczyk, M. Szwarc-Kuczer, A. Wróbel, published: WKP, 2012, electronic version available in the system of electronic legal information Lex.

[236] Judgement of the Court of Justice of 13.02.1985 in the case Françoise Gravier v. Ville de Liège, C 293/83, ECLI:EU:C:1985:69. Judgement of the Court of Justice of 13.07.1983 in the Sandro Forcheri and his wife Marisa Forcheri, née Marino, v Belgian State and asbl Institut Supérieur de Sciences Humaines Appliquées—Ecole Ouvrière Supérieure, C 152/82, ECLI:EU:C:1983:205.

Direct guarantees of cultural rights were included in Art. 13 of the Charter of Fundamental Rights, entitled "Freedom of the arts and sciences," in accordance with which "The arts and scientific research shall be free of constraint. Academic freedom shall be respected." Indirect guarantees of the rights of cultural character are to be found in the following Articles: 7 (regarding respect for private and family life), 9 (regarding the right to marry and right to found a family), 10 (guaranteeing freedom of thought, conscience and religion),[237] 14 (guaranteeing the right to education), 22 (guaranteeing the right to cultural, religious and linguistic diversity in the EU)[238] and 25 (ensuring that the elderly have access to cultural life). Due to the abundance of content and problems with regard to the guarantees of the rights of cultural character (such terms seem to reflect more the nature of the guarantees in the area of culture in the EU than the term "cultural rights"), the relevant provisions will be analysed in the following chapter.

The guarantees of the freedoms of the internal market have an influence on the possibility of exercising cultural rights, including the right to participate in cultural life and having access to cultural goods. The prohibition of quantitative restrictions as regards with exports and imports under Art. 34 and 35 TFEU also concerns the trade in cultural goods and guarantees the freedom of imports and exports of cultural goods.[239] On the other hand, the freedom of movement for workers within the Union also refers to the workers of the culture sector.[240]

[237] See: J. Krukowski, *Państwo a kultura i religia w Unii Europejskiej* in *Kultura i Prawo V. Tożsamość kulturowa Unii Europejskiej a pluralizm religijny*, eds. J. Krukowski, J. Isensee, M. Sitarz (Lublin, 2007), 39–54.

[238] See also: K. Krzysztofek, "Pogranicza i multikulturalizm w rozszerzonej Unii," *Studia Europejskie* vol. 2003, no. 1, 77 et seq.

[239] E. Psychogiopoulou, "The European Union and Cultural Rights," 163. As the author points out, Art. 36 TFEU directly enumerates the possibilities for restricting the freedoms under Art. 34 and 35 TFEU on account of the need for "the protection of national treasures possessing artistic, historic or archaeological value." Art. 36 TFEU provides thus for the special protection of national cultural goods.

[240] *Per analogiam*, the right to freedom of establishment guaranteed under Art. 49 TFEU can be exercised by entrepreneurs in culture sectors, whereas the freedom to provide services (guaranteed under Art. 56 TFEU) can be exercised by service providers in the area of culture—E. Psychogiopoulou, "The European Union and Cultural Rights," 163.

It also seems appropriate to highlight at this stage the involvement of the Union in the preparation of the UNESCO Convention on the Protection and Promotion of the Diversity of Cultural Expressions of 2005.[241] Ten Union is party to the Convention,[242] which indicates that it is interested in the issues regarding the protection of cultural rights—within the Conventions adopted so far, the UNESCO has created a specific system of protection within the Framework of the UN, which develops the guarantees of the Covenants on Human Rights and creates possibilities for the protection of cultural rights—also those of the third generation, such as the right of access to the common heritage of mankind. Suffice it to mention the key conventions in this respect, such as the Convention Concerning the Protection of the World Cultural and Natural Heritage[243] or Convention for the Safeguarding of the Intangible Cultural Heritage.[244]

The fact that the EU joined this system of protection testifies, in my opinion, to the EU's good intentions and real interest in the protection of the rights of cultural character within the possibilities established by the treaty system of the EU. Despite the fact that the Union is not party to the other UNESCO conventions, they may still exert an actual influence on

[241] UNESCO Convention on the Protection and Promotion of the Diversity of Cultural Expressions, drafted in Paris on 20 October 2005, Journal of Laws of 2007 no. 215, item 1585. As Młynarska-Sobaczewska observes, the second half of the twentieth century was a period of an increased interest in the issues regarding cultural diversity—it resulted in the UNESCO activities and the adoption, apart from the Convention of 2005, a UNESCO Convention for the Safeguarding of the Intangible Cultural Heritage. See: A. Młynarska-Sobaczewska, "Utopian Concept, Mixed Structure, Digital Extent and New Claims How to Take Seriously the Right to (Artistic) Culture?" *International Human Rights Law Review*, vol. 6, issue 2 (2017): 180.

[242] Council Decision 2006/515/EC of 18 May 2006 on the conclusion of the Convention on the Protection and Promotion of the Diversity of Cultural Expressions OJ L 201 of 25.07.2006, 15, further also as the UNESCO Convention on the Protection and Promotion of Diversity. See: W. Sobczak, "Ochrona dziedzictwa kultury," 121.

[243] The Convention concerning the Protection of the World Cultural and Natural Heritage adopted in Paris on 16 November 1972 by the United Nations Educational, Scientific and Cultural Organization (UNESCO) General Conference at its 17th session. Journal of Laws of 1976 no. 32, item 190.

[244] The Convention for the Safeguarding of the Intangible Cultural Heritage adopted by the UNESCO General Conference in Paris on 17 October 2003, Journal of Laws of 2011 no. 172, item 1018.

the Union's cultural policy and the guarantees of the rights of cultural character due to the fact that the Court of Justice accepted international agreements in the area of human rights, in which the Member States are parties, as a source of useful guidance for the protection of fundamental rights.[245]

2.7 Concluding Remarks

As it transpires from the analysis of the European migration law, the European Union has demonstrated active interest in the area of managing migrations, practically from the moment when the Treaty of Amsterdam entered into force. As a result, during the last 20 years, a large *acquis* has been created, which encompasses practically all the stages of managing immigration at the level of the Union. As a consequence of the functioning of migration *acquis*, there are also various regulations determining the status of a third-country national residing in the territory of the Union. As presented in this chapter, the legal provisions determining the legal and administrative status of foreign nationals reflect the variety of the phenomenon of immigration to the Union and thus the variety of the migrant groups. As a result, it is difficult to treat third-country nationals residing in the Member States of the Union as a homogeneous group and as consequence, this non-homogeneity has an important impact on the possibility of defining the cultural rights that would be guaranteed to third-country nationals by EU law. As it happens, persons remaining in the reception centres will require an entirely different set of measures for the realization of their rights than legally working highly specialized professionals or persons under custody in detention centres awaiting expulsion. Hence, defining the range of protection of the rights of a cultural character should occur through defining the universal standards and then the standards to which the specific groups of migrants are entitled to by virtue of law.

Firstly, what is significant for the purpose of the present work is the character of fundamental rights as the general principles of the

[245] Judgement of the Court of Justice of 14.05.1974 in the case J. Nold, Kohlen- und Baustoffgroßhandlung v. Commission of the European Communities, C 4/73, ECLI:EU:C:1974:51, para. 13. Thus, the provisions of the ICCPR might provide a useful guidance in the area of the definition of cultural rights. See: E. Psychogiopoulou, "The European Union and Cultural Rights," 162.

Community's law, described in the doctrine as "dynamic." This dynamics was manifested by defining specific fundamental rights in the process of applying law—a similar situation may also be occurring currently, when specific cultural rights, regulated in various legal acts, will build up a new dynamic catalogue. The said catalogue, additionally, is in the process of continual evolution due to the Union's large interest in migration matters and changes occurring within the framework of migration law—such as the planned (yet another) reform within the framework of the CEAS. Cultural rights are guaranteed partly in the Charter itself and that is why they well correspond with the concept of the Charter as an evolving instrument, interpretable in the process of applying the law.

It is also worth emphasizing the special importance of the European Convention on Human Rights for the shaping of the standards for the protection of fundamental rights, including those of third-country nationals. Even though in the very ECHR there are no guarantees of classically understood cultural rights, The European Court of Human Rights accumulated an extensive case-law in the area of "cultural rights," on the grounds of the guarantees of other rights and freedoms of man, such as freedom of speech or freedom of religion.[246] Thus, the Strasbourg case-law defines by virtue of Art. 6 TEU the standards for the protection of fundamental rights in the Union, including cultural rights. These issues will be discussed in the following sections of the book.

However, what is crucial is that the universal principles for the protection of cultural rights at the level of the Union also concern third-country nationals residing in the territory of the Member States. As was mentioned above, the fullest participation in cultural life is available to legal migrants, who have a regulated residence status. This group includes primarily long-term residents and persons who were granted international protection, but also persons pursuing employment on the basis of the single permit and members of their families. The opportunity to participate in cultural life can also be used by, for example, seasonal workers, delegated workers, as well as academics, students and highly qualified workers. Third-country nationals can be both recipients of culture and providers of services in the sector of culture. Certain difficulties in the realization of cultural rights can be encountered by persons remaining in reception centres or in spe-

[246] Cultural Rights in the case-law of European Court of Human Rights, Council of Europe. European Court of Human Rights 2011.

cialized facilities with a view to removal—in such circumstances the possibility of having contact with mediated culture is of particular significance (this trend finds its reflection in the current case-law of the CJEU with regard to cultural matters, as was demonstrated earlier in this chapter).

The involvement of third-country nationals in local and regional cultural life will always constitute an added value for both—on the one hand for migrants themselves, by increasing the possibility of exercising their cultural life, but on the other hand also for the receiving society. The active involvement of foreign nationals in the area of cultural life may provide an effective tool for integration, cultural education and an exchange of cultural experiences, which might be an inspiration for the development and creative interpretation of European culture.

CHAPTER 3

Guarantees of the Cultural Rights of Third-Country Nationals in European Union Primary Law

3.1 Cultural Rights of Third-Country Nationals Within the EU Legal System: The Question of the Existence of the Legal Catalogue

Cultural rights belong to the rights of a specific nature, encompassing primarily the right of access to cultural goods, the right to participate in cultural life, the right to freedom of artistic expression and the right to one's own cultural identity. While writing generally about the cultural right of foreign nationals, it is worth referring to the concept of *paideia*, which entails upbringing aimed at an ideal of humanity.[1] In this way, cultural rights may become an effective integration tool, facilitating the acquisition of culture and therefore the implementation of European values. Respect for the European values which are characteristic for the continental culture should become one of the main objectives of integration policies pursued by the Member States. The rights of a cultural character in themselves consist of a mosaic of very divergent rights. Simultaneously, they pertain to a very divergent group, such as third-country nationals residing in the territory of the European Union. They include, on the one hand, economic migrants (including long-term residents), and on the other hand, forced migrants, such as refugees and persons of an undocumented status. As such, both their needs and the

[1] See: W. Jaeger, *Paideia*, trans. M. Plezia, H. Bednarek (Warszawa, 2001), 29. See: A.M. Kosińska, *Kulturalne prawa człowieka* (Lublin, 2014), 19.

A. M. Kosińska, *Cultural Rights of Third-Country Nationals in EU Law*,
https://doi.org/10.1007/978-3-030-30154-5_3

possibilities of participating in culture will be diametrically different during their stay in the territory of the Union.

As it transpires from the analysis of the Union's law in the area of culture, the competences of the Union are restricted in this respect and cultural rights are guaranteed primarily at the national level through the provisions of a constitutional character. The Union's law complements this system in a selective way, touching upon the essential issues regarding the cultural rights of foreign nationals by including certain legal regulations in the acts of migration law, which constitute the *acquis* of the Area of Freedom, Security and Justice. They will be the subject of the analysis in the following chapters.

While analysing the cultural rights of third-country nationals, a broader picture should be taken into account, that is Europe's cultural foundations and the need for their protection, as well as the protection of European identity. It seems that as a result of the implementation of the multiculturalism doctrine (which *nota bene* in itself did not imply eradicating European values), European culture entered a period of crisis and this is why it requires a special protection precisely at the level of the Union. This protection is viable through the implementation of integrative cultural responsibilities.

The basis for the functioning of the guarantees of the cultural rights of foreign nationals in the law of the Union is Art. 21 CFR, which introduces the prohibition of discrimination on account of, amongst others, race, skin colour, language, religion and beliefs. Consequently, the provision lists the prohibited differentiating criteria relating to the ethnic background and cultural identity of the entities under protection.[2] An indirect impact on the strengthening of equal participation in cultural life can also be seen in other legal acts regarding equal treatment, such as, for example, Council Directive 2000/43/EC of 29 June 2000 implementing the principle of equal treatment between persons irrespective of racial or ethnic origin.[3] Truth be told,

[2] Art. 21 CFR can be found in its Title III, Equality, where there are also guarantees of respect for cultural diversity (Ar. 22 CFR), the principle of equality between women and men (Art. 23 CFR), the rights of the child (Art. 24 CFR), the rights of the elderly (Art. 25 CFR) and the rights of persons with disabilities (Art. 26 CFR). All the above guarantees, except for the prohibition of discrimination on grounds of nationality under Art. 21(2) CFR, are applicable not only to the citizens of the Union but also to all persons subject to EU law, therefore also foreign nationals. See: A. Wróbel, "Wprowadzenie," in *Karta Praw Podstawowych Unii Europejskiej. Komentarz*, ed. A. Wróbel (Warszawa, 2013), 693.

[3] Council Directive 2000/43/EC of 29 June 2000 implementing the principle of equal treatment between persons irrespective of racial or ethnic origin, OJ L 180, 19.07.2000, 22, further also as Directive 2000/43.

the range of the application of the directive does not list cultural life in a direct way, but equal treatment should be provided in the area of employment (therefore, including the creative industries), as well as in access to goods and services (therefore, the range of services may include cultural services).[4]

Immigration also has a real, often positive impact on the picture of the Union's cultural life, contributing to its openness to new trends and patterns. In the globalized reality, it is difficult to completely ignore the questions of the right to cultural identity of the representatives of different cultures (even more so due to the fact that those cultures are not essentially far in their identity from the European civilization). It is worth quoting here, for instance, Art. 4 of the Fribourg Declaration, in accordance with which everybody has the right to choose one's own identity and to modify it (identity regarding a community or cultural communities) irrespective of the state borders.[5] Moreover, nobody can have their identity imposed on them or become assimilated against their will. Also the Convention on the protection of the rights of all migrant workers and members of their families in its Art. 31 confirms the right to respect for cultural identity of migrant workers, while in its Art. 43 guarantees the right of access to and participation in cultural life.[6]

In accordance with the commentary No. 21 to Art. 15 ICCPR the States Parties should pay particular attention to the protection of migrants' cultural identity, as well as their language, religion and local culture, and protect their right to the organization of cultural, artistic and intercultural events.[7] The States Parties to the Pact also should not prevent migrants

[4] Art. 3(1) Directive 2000/43. Among the so-called equality directives, one should also mention the Council Directive 2000/78/EC of 27 November 2000 establishing a general framework for equal treatment in employment and occupation, OJ L 303, 2.12.2000, 16, further also as directive on equal treatment, Directive 2000/78. As is emphasized in the Preamble of the Directive: "9. Employment and occupation are key elements in guaranteeing equal opportunities for all and contribute strongly to the full participation of citizens in economic, cultural and social life and to realising their potential." Having unrestricted access to the job market also counteracts exclusion from cultural life.

[5] Fribourg Declaration on Cultural Rights of 7 May 2007, available on the website: www.culturalrights.net, www1.umn.edu. Accessed 12.09.2017.

[6] Art. 43(1)(G) International Convention on the protection of the rights of all migrant workers and members of their families adopted on 18 December 1990 by resolution 45/158 of the UN General Assembly.

[7] General Comment no. 21—Right of everyone to take part in cultural right, Committee on Economic, Social and Cultural Rights, 21 December 2009, Economic and Social Council. Document available on the website: http://www.refworld.org/docid/4ed35bae2.html Accessed 12.09.2017.

from maintaining cultural links with their countries of origin. Additionally, in the commentary it is stated that due to the fact that culture is closely linked to education, the States Parties should implement appropriate measures in order to make it possible for migrants' children to attend state schools,[8] in accordance with the equality principle. The right to education is a right of a partly cultural character and is guaranteed under Art. 14 CFR. Foreign nationals residing in the territory of the Union, as a rule, are guaranteed the right to have access to the system of education under the provisions which regulate their status in detail. These guarantees will be analysed in greater detail in further sections of the present study, also in the fragment on the freedom of religion.

A significant role in the shaping of the guarantees of the rights of a cultural character of third-country nationals is played by the Union's courts, which encounter real and concrete problems of migrants in their everyday functioning. Hence, an analysis of cultural rights will consist in a kaleidoscopic synthesis, being in itself a resultant of the functioning of the Area of Freedom, Security and Justice. The cultural rights of third-country nationals in the EU's system consist of a specific mosaic of rights and freedoms, but also of responsibilities, which find their common denominator with the classically understood cultural rights that have been shaped at the level of international and national protection.

The standards for the protection provided for in the Charter of Fundamental Rights correspond, in accordance with the explanations to the Charter and its Preamble, to the standards laid down in the European Convention on Human Rights. Hence, it was justified and necessary to refer in the present chapter to the case-law of the ECtHR relating, on the one hand, to third-country nationals and their rights of a cultural character and, on the other hand, to issues pertaining to phenomena and behaviours typical of the representatives of the non-European cultural circles.

3.2 Cultural Rights in the Charter of Fundamental Rights and the Cultural Rights of Third-Country Nationals

Cultural rights of foreign nationals cannot be interpreted in a direct way on grounds of treaty provisions. However, there exists a possibility of reinterpreting them out of the provisions of the Charter of Fundamental

[8] See also: Convention against Discrimination in Education, adopted in Paris on 15 December 1960, Journal of Laws of 1964 no. 40, item 268.

Rights. It is a key to the understanding of the importance of the CFR in the development of the standards for the protection in the EU to refer to the description of the Charter as the so-called evolutionary instrument, whose interpretation is shaped by the case-law.[9]

As was mentioned in the previous chapter, the rights under the CFR which correspond to the rights under the European Convention on Human Rights (ECHR) are protected in the same degree as guaranteed by the Convention, whereas none of the provisions from the Charter can be interpreted as restricting the protection provided for under international law, EU law or the constitutional law of the Member States.[10] The present chapter will present the case-law of the ECtHR with regard to the rights guaranteed by the ECHR, which find their equivalents in the Charter of Fundamental Rights, such as, for example, freedom of religion. To a large degree the case-law will concern third-country nationals and the specific issues with regard to the problem of migration and cultural integration in the host country. Due to the fact that the case-law of the Court of Justice of the European Union (CJEU) is not rich in this area as of yet, the Strasburg standards of case-law will complement the characteristic of the range of protection of the cultural rights of foreign nationals. The basis for this methodology can be found under Art. 6(3) TEU and Art. 53 CFR.

Some of the rulings under analysis in the present chapter do not concern third-country nationals in a direct way, that is, third-country nationals are not party to the proceedings at the national level. However, they will be presented as factor in the shaping of the standards for the protection of the cultural rights of third-country nationals due to the fact that they entail the protection of broadly understood cultural values, such as the freedom to express one's religious beliefs. The adopted methodology finds its justification also in the fact that the rulings referred to in the present chapter concern the issues of cultural identity or cultural expression which are separate from the tradition of European culture as defined in the present study and encompass the cultural identity of migrant groups arriving in the Member States (as, e.g., in the case of the Sikhs).

[9] On this subject see: H. Izdebski, "Rola i miejsce Karty Praw Podstawowych," in *5 lat Karty Praw Podstawowych UE*, ed. A. Gubrynowicz (Warszawa, 2006), 19.

[10] See: Art. 53 CFR.

3.2.1 Protection of Cultural Diversity

An especially important provision of the CFR which allows for the understanding of the place of culture in the EU's policies is its Art. 22.[11] In accordance with the above provision: "The Union shall respect cultural, religious and linguistic diversity." As A. Wróbel observes, the Union's responsibility to respect diversity corresponds to "the fundamental right to respect cultural, religious and linguistic diversity, which, in accordance with its analytical structure has the character of a principle" and is a private right of an individual.[12] What is important, the Union is obliged to respect cultural diversity and not cultural identity within the Member States. Art. 22 CFR refers thus to the cultural diversity of the Union as a whole and not to the separate Member States.[13] The responsibility of the Union is to preserve diversity[14] (undermining of which might, possibly, lead to cultural unification of the European regions). Art. 22 CFR concerns, in principle, the diversity within the Union, therefore it is the diversity that is already there, resulting from Europe's cultural heritage. With regard to the fact of placing this provision in the chapter "Equality," the provision also introduces the obligation of equal treatment of cultures and cultural heritage within the European Union.[15] However, it does not refer to the issues relating to the shaping of multicultural policies but to the cultural divisions so characteristic of the continent. Therefore, Art. 22 CFR endorses the EU's cultural policy in actions which are focused on the promotion of the diversity of European culture, but leaves aside the issues with regard to the arrival of third-country nationals in Europe and consequently, the emergence of new

[11] In accordance with the explanations to the Charter: "This Article has been based on Article 6 of the Treaty on European Union and on Article 151(1) and (4) of the EC Treaty, now replaced by Article 167(1) and (4) of the Treaty on the Functioning of the European Union, concerning culture. Respect for cultural and linguistic diversity is now also laid down in Article 3(3) of the Treaty on European Union. The Article is also inspired by Declaration no. 11 to the Final Act of the Amsterdam Treaty on the status of churches and non-confessional organisations, now taken over in Article 17 of the Treaty on the Functioning of the European Union." See: Explanations relating to the Charter of Fundamental Rights, OJ C 303, 14.12.2007, 17.

[12] A. Wróbel, "Komentarz do art. 22 Karty Praw Podstawowych," in *Karta Praw Podstawowych Unii Europejskiej. Komentarz*, ed. A. Wróbel (Warszawa, 2013), 770, 765.

[13] Ibidem, 767.

[14] Ibidem, 770.

[15] As E. Psychogiopoulou emphasizes, Art. 22 CFR imposes a negative responsibility of the Union, consisting of non-intervention into diversity, so as to avoid its violation, E. Psychogiopoulou, "The European Union and Cultural Rights," in *The Cultural Dimension of Human Rights*, (Oxford, 2013), 169.

cultural trends. The intention of the Union's legislators was to primarily turn attention to the essence of European culture, which is not homogeneous and, as such, requires appreciation, respect and promotion. This is also the culture that third-country nationals who concentrate their life interests in the EU's Member States should learn about. With regard to third-country nationals, the individual right for the respect of diversity is thus of a passive character. It transpires from the fact that foreign nationals have the right to integration with the divergent culture of the Member States. Nevertheless, the very Art. 22 does not entail in its interpretation that the Union has a responsibility—in the sense of undertaking positive actions—to respect cultural diversity resulting from immigration. Still, such responsibilities transpire, for instance, from Art. 21 CFR cited above, which prohibits discrimination or from international law, which, on the basis of its case-law, having its beginnings in the case Nold, might provide guidelines for the protection of fundamental rights.[16] What may have a special importance with regard to the protection of diversity is the above-mentioned Art. 27 ICCPR, which guarantees minorities the right to their own cultural life. The General Comment No. 23 includes an interpretation of the word "exist" with regard to the wording "In those States in which ethnic, religious or linguistic minorities exist." In accordance with the commentary, for the functioning of the guarantees under Art. 27, the length of residence of a given person within the territory of a State Party is of no importance. Such persons do not have to be permanent residents. They might even be migrant workers or visitors to a given Member State if they belong to minorities.[17]

Art. 22 CFR was very often referred to by the CJEU in its case-law—especially in cases regarding linguistic diversity.[18] However, a case that was interesting for the present analysis was the case Loutfi Management

[16] See, for instance: Judgement of the Court of Justice of 14.05.1974 in the case J. Nold, Kohlen- und Baustoffgroßhandlung v. Commission of the European Communities, C 4/73, ECLI:EU:C:1974:51, para. 13.

[17] UN Human Rights Committee (HRC), CCPR General Comment no. 23: Article 27 (Rights of Minorities), 8 April 1994, CCPR/C/21/Rev.1/Add.5, item 5.2. Comment available on the website: http://www.refworld.org/docid/453883fc0.html. Accessed 30.12.2017.

[18] See, for example, Judgement of the Court of Justice of 16.04.2013 in the case Anton Las v. PSA Antwerp NV, C 202/11, ECLI:EU:C:2013:239; Judgement of the Court of Justice of 12.05.2011 in the case Malgožata Runevič-Vardyn and Łukasz Paweł Wardyn v. Vilniaus miesto savivaldybės administracija and others, C 391/09, ECLI:EU:C:2011:291; Judgement of the Court of Justice of 12.09.2013 in the case Italian republic v. the European Commission and the European Personnel Selection Office (EPSO), T 164/08, ECLI:EU:T:2013:417.

Propriété intellectuelle SARL v. AMJ Meatproducts NV, Halalsupply NV,[19] which concerned the registration of a community trade mark. The company Loutfi was the proprietor of two community trade marks (*El Benna*, *El Bnina*—they are Arabic terms transcribed into the Latin alphabet) and decided that the trade mark *El Baina* registered by the company Meatproducts was detrimental to their essential business interests. What is interesting in the given case is that the trade marks concerned food products marketed as *halal*—that is, prepared in accordance with the rituals prescribed by the Muslim religion and aimed primarily at Muslim consumers. The trade marks also had words written in the Arabic alphabet and, according to the national court: "the relevant public must, in the present case, be defined as being the public composed of Muslim consumers of Arab origin who consume 'halal' food products in the European Union and who have at least a basic knowledge of written Arabic." While examining whether a confusion might indeed occur in that case, the national court analysed, on the one hand, how the three words in the three trade marks look like (they are similar words: *Benna, Bnina, Baina*), and on the other hand, their pronunciation (they sound different in Arabic), as well as their denotation (their meaning is also different: taste, sweetness, sight).

Finally, before the national court decided whether the trade mark *El Baina* might be a source of confusion, it decided to stay the proceedings and refer a question for a preliminary ruling, asking the CJEU for a decision in light of Art. 21 and 22 CFR. The national court asked the CJEU whether in the assessment of the likelihood of confusion between community trade marks, the competent Court of the Member State should take into account the fact of the differences in the pronunciation and meaning of Arabic words (despite their visual similarity when transcribed into the Latin alphabet) even in a situation when Arabic is not an official language of the European Union. The Court of Justice answered the question for preliminary ruling in the positive, justifying its ruling by stating that

> It follows from the above that those phonetic and conceptual differences should be taken into account because, if they are not, the assessment of the likelihood of confusion could be made only partially and, as a result, without taking into account the overall impression made by the Community trade marks and the sign considered on the relevant public.[20]

[19] Judgement of the Court of Justice of 25.06.2015 in the case Loutfi Management Propriété Intellectuelle SARL v. AMJ Meatproducts NV i Halalsupply NV, C 147/14, ECLI:EU:C:2015:420, further also as judgement in the case C 147/14.

[20] Para. 25 of the judgement in the case C 147/14.

What is interesting, however, the Court did not refer in any way to the Charter of Fundamental Rights, deciding that there was no such need, as the answer to the question referred to for a preliminary ruling was possible on the grounds of the very Regulation 207/2009 on the community trade mark. Such line of thought may seem to be, in a sense, on the cautious side, as reference to Art. 22 CFR would require the Court to provide its interpretation in light of the functioning of a multicultural society. However, even despite the lack of references to the CFR, the ruling remains of a significant importance, as it highlights a very real problem of a side-by-side functioning of multiple cultures, which necessarily affects consumers rooted in those cultures.

3.2.2 *Freedom of the Arts and Sciences*

The Article guaranteeing cultural freedom is Art. 13 of the Charter of Fundamental Rights, in accordance with which "The arts and scientific research shall be free of constraint. Academic freedom shall be respected."[21] Article 13 introduces the freedom of the arts which is not directly guaranteed in the ECHR—thus, the CFR introduces as if a broader regulation, even though the ECtHR often interpreted the existence of the protection of artistic freedom in relation to Art. 10 ECHR, guaranteeing the freedom of expressing opinions.[22] The freedom of the arts is a freedom of an active character and consists in creation.[23] The freedom of artistic expression is guaranteed to all entities being subject to EU law, therefore also including third-country nationals. Third-country nationals may exercise the guarantees under Art. 13 as creators of culture, but also as researchers and scientists, arriving in the territory of the Union.

The freedom of the arts is not the only *stricte* cultural freedom that is guaranteed in the Charter. Article 13 has not been subject to an in-depth analysis so far. EU law does not provide direct protection for the classical right to participate in cultural life or the right of access to cultural goods.

However, at this stage it is worth quoting the ruling of the ECtHR with regard to precisely the freedom of speech in the case of Khurshid

[21] In accordance with the explanations to the CFR: "This right is deduced primarily from the right to freedom of thought and expression. It is to be exercised having regard to Article 1 and may be subject to the limitations authorised by Article 10 of the ECHR."

[22] J. Sobczak, "Komentarz do artykułu 13 Karty Praw Podstawowych," in *Karta Praw Podstawowych Unii Europejskiej. Komentarz*, ed. A. Wróbel (Warszawa, 2013), 507.

[23] Ibidem, 511.

Mustafa and Tarzibachi v. Sweden,[24] which directly refers to participation in cultural life and having access to mediated culture. The applicants were Swedish nationals of Iraqi origins living with their three children in Stockholm. The couple rented a flat and in the agreement between the landlord and the tenants it was stipulated that they were not allowed to install an external TV antenna or any other such installations and that it was their responsibility to maintain order. After moving in, the tenants started using a satellite antenna which was installed in the flat in order to receive television programmes in Arabic and Farsi. After the change of the building administration, the tenants were asked to remove the antenna and when they refused to do it, they were asked to move out. The applicants decided that the order to remove the antenna violated their freedom to receive information under Art. 10 ECHR. The Court ruled that even though the tenancy agreement was signed between two entities of private law, during the proceedings at the national level the Court applied and interpreted national provisions and the Constitution and as a result the complaint was admissible. While examining the case the Court assessed whether the restriction of Art. 10 was justifiable and necessary in a democratic society. The satellite dish allowed the applicants and their children to watch programmes from the country and region of their origin. The programmes included political, social and, what is significant, cultural content, which was especially valuable for the applicants as an immigrant family trying to maintain contact with the culture and language of their country of origin. The Court observed that the content of television programmes could not be simply replaced by newspapers and radio programmes and the very installation of a satellite dish did not pose a threat to public safety. As a result, the Court found that a violation of Art. 10 ECHR occurred. The judgement in the case of Mustafa and Tarzibachi is exceptionally interesting and significant due to the fact that the Charter provides protection at the level at least comparable to that provided for under the Convention, whereas the rights guaranteed under the ECHR are perceived as the EU's general rights under Art. 6(3) TEU. It must be therefore concluded that the interpretation applied to Art. 10 of the

[24] Judgement of the Court of Human Rights of 16.12.2008 in the case Khurshid Mustafa and Tarzibachi v. Sweden, complaint no. 23883/06. See also: A. Młynarska-Sobaczewska, "Utopian Concept, Mixed Structure, Digital Extent and New Claims How to Take Seriously the Right to (Artistic) Culture?" *International Human Rights Law Review*, vol. 6, issue 2/2017, 181.

Convention provides a guideline for the Union's standards for protection. In the judgement, the ECtHR emphasized the importance of maintaining cultural ties with the migrants' country of origin and the role of the new media in maintaining the said ties. An interesting conclusion concerned the gradation of the mass media—in the opinion of the Court, television offers a wider and richer access to native culture than, for example, the printed media.

3.2.3 *Right to Private and Family Life and the Right to Found a Family in View of the Cultural Rights of Third-Country Nationals*

Respect for the cultural identity of an individual is based on the freedoms under Art. 7 (respect for private and family life) and Art. 9 (the right to marry and the right to found a family) of the Charter of Fundamental Rights.

In accordance with Art. 7 CFR: "Everyone has the right to respect for his or her private and family life, home and communications."[25] As J. Sobczak emphasizes, the identity of an individual constitutes a factor in the private life (the right to identity). It consists of the right to have a surname, family, biological and gender identity.[26] The issues concerning a change of names, their transliteration or the collision between the national

[25] In accordance with the explanations to the CFR: "The rights guaranteed in Article 7 correspond to those guaranteed by Article 8 of the ECHR."

[26] J. Sobczak, "Komentarz do art. 7 Karty Praw Podstawowych," in *Karta Praw Podstawowych Unii Europejskiej. Komentarz*, ed. A. Wróbel (Warszawa, 2013), 239. An interesting issue raised in the case-law of the ECtHR was the problem of a polygamic marriage contracted outside Europe (Decision of the European Commission of Human Rights of 17.12.1968 in the case Alam and Khan v. the United Kingdom, complaint no. 2991/66). The applicants in this case were father Mohamed Alma and his son from the second marriage Mohamed Khan. Mr Alam was a Pakistani working in the United Kingdom and wanted to enter the United Kingdom with his sons. Mr Alam had two wives—with the first one he had two sons and a daughter and with the second, a widow after his deceased brother, a daughter and two sons. Mr Alam married both wives in accordance with the religious law of Islam. Mr Alam's son, the applicant Mohamed Khan, was refused entry into the territory of the United Kingdom. During the examination at the airport, Mr Alam did not reveal that he had a second wife and that Mr Khan was his son from that marriage. The applicants decided that their right under Art. 8 ECHR was violated due to the lack of the possibility of reuniting the son with his father residing abroad. The case was eventually settled amicably. See: Alam and Khan v. United Kingdom, Report on the submission 17.12.1968, Strasbourg; M.B. Dembour, *When Humans Become Migrants. Study of the European Court of Human Rights with an Inter-American Counterpoint* (Oxford, 2015), 99 et seq.

systems are directly related to the right to identity and were the subject of the rulings of the CJEU.[27] Despite the fact that the existing case-law of the Court of Justice in this matter concerned citizens of the Union, what is exceptionally valuable from the perspective of the present study is the interpretation carried out in those cases by the Court. The right to cultural identity may be classified as one of the second-generation rights, applicable also in the same degree to third-country nationals, whereas the established standards for protection may turn out to be equally valuable in the case of foreign nationals.

What is significant from the perspective of the issues under discussion, the right to family life consists of the right of an individual to live with his or her relatives. Thus, the Member States have an obligation not to expel such persons (being citizens of third countries) or allow them to enter into the territory of the Union.[28] In migration law, the basic legal act on the reunification of family is the Council directive on the right to family reunification.[29] Art. 3 of the directive lists the family members of a foreign national who have the right to reunite with him. The case-law of the CJEU in the area of family reunification is extensive.[30] However, with regard to the analysis of the cultural rights of third-country nationals within the EU's legal system, it seems worth referring to an interesting case of a cultural background—that of K v. Bundesasylamt.[31] While it is true that the question referred for preliminary ruling concerned the interpretation of the Dublin Regulation on the Member State responsible for examining an application and in the present case the CJEU did not refer to Art. 7 CFR, still, the ruling in an interesting way illustrates the problem of the reconstruction of the family on the basis of the cultural background. At the national level, the case concerned a foreign national K, who entered into

[27] Here in reference to the EU's citizens; see: Judgement of the Court of Justice of 17.12.1992 in the case Heinz-Jörg Moritz v. the Commission of the European Communities, C 68/91, ECLI:EU:C:1992:531; Judgement of the Court of Justice of 2.10.2003 in the case Carlos Garcia Avello v. The Belgian State, C 148/02, ECLI:EU:C:2003:539; Judgement of the Court of Justice of 27.04.2006 in the case Standesamt Stadt Niebüll, C 96/04, ECLI:EU:C:2006:254; Judgement of the Court of Justice of 12.05.2011 in the case Malgožata Runevič-Vardyn and Łukasz Paweł Wardyn v. Vilniaus miesto savivaldybės administracija and others, C 391/09, ECLI:EU:C:2011:291.

[28] J. Sobczak, "Komentarz do art. 7 Karty Praw Podstawowych," 248.

[29] Directive 2003/86.

[30] The case-law will be subject to a selective analysis in the further sections of the work.

[31] Judgement of the Court of Justice of 6.11.2012 in the case K v. Bundesasylamt, C 245/11, ECLI:EU:C:2012:685, further as judgement in the case C 245/11.

the territory of Poland, filed an application for international protection and next illegally entered Austria in order to reunite with her son and his family—wife and children. During the proceedings at the national level, Mrs K proved that she maintained strong ties with her daughter-in-law (supporting her in child care), who had experienced traumatic events in her country of origin and as a result was seriously ill. As was emphasized in the ruling: "If what happened were to become known, the daughter-in-law would risk violent treatment at the hands of male members of the family, on account of cultural traditions seeking to re-establish family honour."[32] Mrs K was her daughter-in-law's closest confidante and supporter.

However, in accordance with the law in force, Mrs K should have been returned to Poland under the provisions of the Dublin regulation and made to wait there for the assessment of her application for refugee status. Mrs K filed a complaint against the return decision and eventually the proceedings resulted in referring a question for a preliminary ruling to the CJEU. While examining the provisions concerning the Member State that would be responsible to assess the application, the CJEU held that a non-responsible Member State becomes enabled to be identified as responsible for the examination of the asylum application under specific circumstances. Such specific circumstances were met in the case of Mrs K, whose ill daughter-in-law, with children requiring care and herself being culturally at risk, resided in a non-responsible Member State. Thus, the reunification of family members on account of the cultural background was deemed as having priority in the given case.

Another interesting case concerning respect for family life was the case proceeded before the ECtHR: Z.H. and R.H. v. Switzerland.[33] The proceeding concerned two foreign nationals, citizens of Afghanistan, who entered Switzerland illegally through Italy. They told the Swiss authorities that they were married (they were then 15 and 19 years of age) and that they had got married a year before in Iran during a religious ceremony. The Swiss authorities decided that such a marriage could not be recognized in Switzerland, even more so in view of the fact that in Afghanistan it is prohibited to marry a woman who is below 15 years of

[32] Para. 16 of the judgement in the case C 245/11.

[33] Judgement of the European Court of Human Rights of 8.12.2015 in the case Z.H. and R.H. v. Switzerland, complaint no. 60119/12, further as the case of Z.H. and R.H. v. Switzerland.

age. Additionally, in Switzerland, having sexual contacts with an underaged girl below 16 years old is a crime. Therefore, Mr R.H. was not recognized as a family member of Z.H. and, as an adult, was expelled to Italy. R.H. filed a complaint against the return decision claiming that it violated Art. 8 ECHR. The Court ruled that Art. 8 does not impose on the States Parties the obligation to determine the existence of marriage (whether religious or of some other character), concluded with a 14 year old, whereas it is the responsibility of the Member State authorities to protect morality and the rights of the child. What is interesting, Mr R.H. returned to Switzerland a few days later after his expulsion and his application for refugee status was examined with a positive result. The case is an interesting illustration of the way in which national courts have to deal with the range of cultural differences, which occur in the so-called foreigners' cases. The decisions of the national courts provide in this case a good example of how to set protection priorities, such as the protection of minors. In the case of cultural differences, there is often a good chance that conflicts between legal orders will occur—between the written laws, customary laws or religious laws, which migrants often abide by. A clear delineation of the position of national courts following the rules of the written laws and European standards for protection offers an effective solution to the cases, in which there might have appeared interpretative doubts regarding cultural differences. Not all cultural rights of foreign nationals can be respected and be subject to protection in Europe, especially if they result from customary laws of the countries of origin, not having equivalents in the European tradition.

An interesting case with regard to the right of a uniform name, based on the plea of the infringement of Art. 8 ECHR, was the case of Henry Kismoun v. France.[34] The applicant in the case was a national of France and Algeria, who was raised by his father in Algeria (where he left with his siblings in 1961) and did not maintain any contact with his mother (a French citizen) living in France. In Algeria the applicant was using the name Kismoun. When Mr Kismoun tried to contact his mother, he was informed that in France his personal data is kept under his mother's name. Thus, in Algeria Mr Kismoun was named Cherif Kismoun, but in France he was registered as Christian Henry. The applicant filed an application to change his name in the French system, but his application was refused. He then accused the French authorities of infringing Art. 8

[34] Judgement of the European Court of Human Rights of 5.12.2013 in the case Henry Kismoun v. France, complaint no. 32265/10.

ECHR. The applicant emphasized that he wanted to have only one name that would express his origins. Eventually, the Court ruled that a violation of Art. 8 ECHR occurred, acknowledging thus Mr Kismoun's right to have only one name.

Moving further, in the case B.A.C. v. Greece,[35] the Court found that there occurred a breach of Art. 8 ECHR, which resulted in the lack of possibility of continuing education by the applicant. The proceeding concerned a national of Turkey who left the country in 2002 and applied for refugee status in Greece and was granted a positive opinion from the Consultative Asylum Committee. Unfortunately, during the course of the next 12 years, the case of Mr B.A.C was not finally concluded. The Court held that the lack of a final decision in the proceedings for granting a refugee status meant a violation of Art. 8 ECHR. In the context of the possibility of exercising one's rights of a cultural character, the Court pointed out that due to his uncertain residence status in Greece, the applicant had no possibility to begin his studies, also due to the fact that he did not have the card confirming his refugee status.[36]

Art. 9 CFR concerns the right to marry and the right to found a family[37] and corresponds to the guarantees under Art. 12 ECHR. The basis for interpretation of Art. 9 of the Charter is at present the rich case-law of the ECtHR, also in the issues regarding foreign nationals. Such issues as, for example, the above-mentioned right of the Member States Parties to establish the minimal age for getting married,[38] the duty of conducting marriage in accordance with the legal rules[39] or the problem of fictitious marriages contracted by migrants with a view to entering European countries.[40]

[35] Judgement of the European Court of Human Rights of 13.10.2016 in the case B.A.C. v Greece, complaint no. 11981/15, further also as judgement in the case of B.A.C.

[36] Para. 43 of the judgement in the case B.A.C.

[37] The right to marry and the right to found the family are guaranteed in accordance with national acts guaranteeing the exercise of those rights.

[38] Decision of the European Commission of Human Rights of 7.07.1986 in the case Janis Khan v. the United Kingdom, complaint no. 11579/85, further as the case of Janis Khan v. the United Kingdom; I.C. Kamiński, "Komentarz do art. 9 Karty Praw Podstawowych," in *Karta Praw Podstawowych Unii Europejskiej. Komentarz*, ed. A. Wróbel (Warszawa, 2013), 311.

[39] Decision of the European Commission of Human Rights of 18.12.1974 in the case X v. Federal Republic of Germany, complaint no. 6167/73.

[40] Decision of the European Commission of Human Rights of 16.10.1996 in the case Sanders v. France, complaint no. 31401/96; Decision of the European Commission of Human Rights of 3.12.1997 in the case Klip and Kruger v. the Netherlands, complaint no. 33257/96.

In an interesting case Khan v. the United Kingdom, the applicant was a citizen of the United Kingdom of the Muslim faith.[41] He married his girlfriend without the consent of her parents during a religious ceremony—the bride was 14 years old on the day of the wedding and the groom was 21. The religious law allowed girls who were above 12 years of age to be married without their parents' consent. After 14 months of marriage the father of the girl took her to their family home by force. Mr Khan was sentenced to 9 months of prison on account of having sexual contacts with a minor under 16 years of age on the grounds of the national criminal law. The applicant decided that the national law penalizing his conduct regarding a minor restricted his possibility of manifesting his faith (Art. 10 ECHR) through a marriage in accordance with the rules of Islam. Moreover, the applicant claimed that an infringement of Art. 12 ECHR occurred, as due to the conviction, he could not consummate his marriage and found a family. However, the Commission ruled that no violation of Art. 12 occurred on account of the fact that the regulations concerning marriage are subject to national law and it is the Member States Parties that decide about the legal age of the bride and groom in their legal acts. Further, in the case X v. the Federal Republic of Germany, the Commission decided that the obligation of contracting marriage in the form provided for by the law instead of the religious form is not an infringement of the right to marry.[42]

The rulings analysed above in the present subchapter concern in part not only third-country nationals but also citizens of the Member States. However, on account of cultural specificities, the rulings reflect the character of the culture of the migrants arriving in the Member States from Muslim countries and may be helpful in the interpretation of the setting of the boundaries for the cultural rights of third-country nationals.

3.2.4 *Freedom of Religion and the Cultural Rights of Third-Country Nationals*

The freedom of conscience and religion is guaranteed under Art. 10 of the Charter of Fundamental Rights.[43] As I.C. Kamiński emphasizes, the exis-

[41] The case of Janis Khan v. The United Kingdom.

[42] Decision of the European Commission of Human Rights on the inadmissibility of the complaint of 18.12.1974 in the case X v. Federal Republic of Germany, complaint no. 6167/73.

[43] In accordance with the explanations to the CFR: "The right guaranteed in para. 1 corresponds to the right guaranteed in Article 9 of the ECHR and, in accordance with Article 52(3) of the Charter, has the same meaning and scope. Limitations must therefore respect

tence of guarantees under Art. 10 CFR is significant due to the differences in the models of the functioning of religious communities in public life,[44] as adopted by the Member States. Art. 10 CFR should be interpreted in connection with Art. 22 of the Charter and Art. 17 TFEU, in accordance with which the Union respects the legal status of religious communities. The freedom of religion has its external and internal dimension. On the so-called *forum externum*, it may be subject to restrictions.[45] Both the case-law of the CJEU as well as of the ECtHR concerns to some degree the rights of foreign nationals and the rights of persons belonging to non-European cultures. Religion constitutes an important and sometimes the most important element of cultural identity of third-country nationals and thus the guarantee of the freedom of religion for the representatives of the said group is equivalent at the same time with the guarantee of the right to cultural identity.

The interpretation of Art. 10 CFR was carried out by the Court in its ruling in the case of Y and Z (C 71/11).[46] The proceedings at the national level concerned two foreign nationals who arrived in Germany and filed an application for international protection, justifying it with their membership in the *Ahmadiyya* group, which is a reformed version of Islam. The foreign nationals claimed that due to their membership in *Ahmadiyya*, they were persecuted in their country of origin—Pakistan. Simultaneously, the Pakistani criminal code provided for a penalty of imprisonment if a

Article 9(2) of the Convention, which reads as follows: 'Freedom to manifest one's religion or beliefs shall be subject only to such limitations as are prescribed by law and are necessary in a democratic society in the interests of public safety, for the protection of public order, health or morals, or for the protection of the rights and freedoms of others.'"

[44] I.C. Kamiński, "Komentarz do art. 10 Karty Praw Podstawowych," in *Karta Praw Podstawowych Unii Europejskiej. Komentarz*, ed. A. Wróbel (Warszawa, 2013), 331.

[45] Ibidem, 339. This is what may happen when, for example, the public authorities exclude religious entities from the possibility of gaining broadcasting concessions or broadcasting advertisements of a religious character. See: Decision of the European Court of Human Rights on the inadmissibility of the complaint of 7.11.2000 in the case United Christian Broadcasters Ltd. v. the United Kingdom, complaint no. 44802/98; Judgement of the European Court of Human Rights of 10.07.2003 in the case Murphy v. Ireland, complaint no. 44179/98.

[46] Judgement of the Court of Justice of 5.09.2012 in the case Bundesrepublik Deutschland v. Y and Z, C 71/11 and C 99/11, ECLI:EU:C:2012:518, further as judgement in the case C 71/11. On this subject see also: A.M. Kosińska, "Wolność myśli, sumienia i religii migrantów w prawie Unii Europejskiej i w prawie krajowym—wybrane problem," in *Aktualne problemy wolności myśli, sumienia i religii*, eds. P. Stanisz, A.M. Abramowicz, M. Czelny (Lublin, 2015), 145–147.

member of the Ahmadiyya group were to pretend that he was a Muslim. What is more, as the national court found, "under Article 295 C of that code, any person who defiles the name of the Prophet Mohammed may be punished by death or life imprisonment and a fine."[47] In the proceedings of first instance, the national bodies refused to grant the foreign nationals refugee status; however, on appeal, the courts decided that they deserve to be granted refugee status as they belonged to the *Ahmadiyya* community and were threatened by collective persecution. Both foreign nationals were very much devoted to their faith and believed that a public professing of faith would help them keep their religious identity, which was virtually impossible in Pakistan.

The national bodies responsible for granting international protection challenged the verdicts of the courts of appeal before the federal administrative court raising that the interpretation carried out by the Court of Appeal was too general, whereas the restrictions imposed on the group in Pakistan do not concern the fundamental sphere of faith but merely its public practicing. The national court decided to refer a question for preliminary ruling to the CJEU, asking for the interpretation of Art. 9 of the qualification directive[48] in light of Art. 9 ECHR (whose subject corresponds to Art. 10 CFR).

[47] Para. 31 of the judgement in the case C 71/11.
[48] In accordance with Art. 9 of the Directive 2004/83:

1. Acts of persecution within the meaning of article 1 A of the Geneva Convention must:
   (a) be sufficiently serious by their nature or repetition as to constitute a severe violation of basic human rights, in particular the rights from which derogation cannot be made under Article 15(2) of the European Convention for the Protection of Human Rights and Fundamental Freedoms; or
   (b) be an accumulation of various measures, including violations of human rights which is sufficiently severe as to affect an individual in a similar manner as mentioned in (a).
2. Acts of persecution as qualified in para. 1, can, inter alia, take the form of:
   (a) acts of physical or mental violence …;
   (b) legal, administrative, police, and/or judicial measures which are in themselves discriminatory or which are implemented in a discriminatory manner;
   (c) prosecution or punishment, which is disproportionate or discriminatory.

Council Directive 2004/83/EC of 29 April 2004 on minimum standards for the qualification and status of third-country nationals or stateless persons as refugees or as persons who otherwise need international protection and the content of the protection granted, OJ L 304, 30.09.2004, 12.

The Court decided to jointly examine the first two questions for a preliminary ruling and reformulated them in order to eventually examine the cases whether Art. 9 of the qualification directive "is to be interpreted as meaning that any interference with the right to religious freedom that infringes Article 10(1) of the Charter may constitute an 'act of persecution' within the meaning of that provision of the Directive and whether a distinction must be made between the 'core areas' of religious freedom and its external manifestation."

The Court emphasized that the freedom of religion constitutes a foundation of human rights; however, not every breach of the guarantees under Art. 10 CFR will constitute an act of persecution within the meaning of the Geneva Convention and the Charter of Fundamental Rights.[49] The formation of the Court emphasized, nevertheless, that the differentiation into the external and internal spheres (*forum externum* and *internum*) within the freedom of religion is not appropriate for an unequivocal interpretation whether a breach in fact occurred. Whether or not persecutions exist within the meaning of the qualification directive will be decided by the character and the consequences of the repressions which might be inflicted upon a foreign national.[50] If an applicant for international protection is subject to "inhuman or degrading treatment or punishment,"[51] then we are dealing, according to the Court, with persecution within the meaning of the qualification directive. The lack of the possibility of demonstrating one's faith by means of religious practices and a risk of being punished for such behaviour are an expression of persecution. By defining the concept of religion, the qualification directive encompasses with this term, amongst others, participation in public practices either alone or in community with other persons.[52] The Court also observed that the agencies qualifying a foreign national for international protection should pay heed to such subjective factors as the importance of the possibility of demonstrating one's faith as declared by a foreign national, which for him is a condition of maintaining one's religious integrity.

The third question referred for a preliminary ruling concerned a very specific matter, that is, the question whether it is permissible to interpret

[49] Para. 58 and 59 of the judgement in the case C 71/11.
[50] Para. 65 of the judgement in the case C 71/11.
[51] Para. 67 of the judgement in the case C 71/11.
[52] Para. 69 of the judgement in the case C 71/11.

the directive in such a way so as to justify a foreign national's fear of persecution in his country of origin even in a situation where he could avoid exposure to persecution by abstaining from performing certain religious practices.[53]

The Court emphasized that as a matter of fact the applicants had not experienced persecution in Pakistan and they would only be exposed to it in the event of coming back to their country of origin. However, they distinctly declared the need to perform religious practices. The Court decided that if such practices were to indeed expose them to persecution, it would be justifiable to grant them refugee status. In paragraph 2 of the judgement the Court observed that "In assessing an application for refugee status on an individual basis, those authorities cannot reasonably expect the applicant to abstain from those religious practices."

The ruling presents the stance of the Court with regard to the problem of the lack of possibility for a foreign national to exercise his broadly understood cultural identity in the country of origin. Exposure to the risk of persecution on account of an active professing of one's faith was in the assessment of the Court a circumstance that would justify granting him international protection and, in this way, make it possible for a foreign national to exercise his right to cultural and religious identity.

As was emphasized above, the standards for the protection of the cultural rights of foreign nationals are also formed through the case-law not necessarily directly regarding third-country nationals but also other entities, belonging to a culturally different group of countries than those within the European culture. Hence, in the context of the cultural rights of third-country nationals originating in the Arabic countries, there are two rulings of 14 March 2017 which deserve special attention (case C 157/15 Achbita, C 188/15 Bougnaoui). They concerned the issue of wearing clothing of a religious character in the workplace.[54]

In the case C 157/15[55] the Court interpreted the Council Directive 2000/78/EC of 27 November 2000 establishing a general framework for

[53] Para. 73 of the judgement in the case C 71/11.

[54] See also: A. Śledzińska-Simon, "Is there a place for the Islamic veil in the workplace? Managerial prerogatives and the duty of reasonable accommodation in the EU antidiscrimination governance," *Era FORUM*, vol. 17, issue 2 (2016): 203–220.

[55] Judgement of the Court of Justice of 14.03.2017 in the case Samira Achbita and Centrum voor gelijkheid van kansen en voor racismebestrijding v. G4S Secure Solutions, NV, C 157/15, ECLI:EU:C:2017:203, further as judgement in the case C 157/15.

equal treatment in employment and occupation.[56] The national proceedings concerned an employee Ms S. Achbita and her employer, a private entrepreneur G4S providing reception services for the clients from the public and private sectors. Ms Achbita worked as a receptionist and in the company there was an unwritten rule prohibiting workers from wearing symbols of a religious character. Ms Achbita was a Muslim and informed her employer that she intended to wear an Islamic headscarf during working hours. The employer informed her that the wearing of a headscarf would not be tolerated. Next, he introduced the amendments to the company regulations, in accordance with which "employees are prohibited, in the workplace, from wearing any visible signs of their political, philosophical or religious beliefs and/or from engaging in any observance of such beliefs."[57]

Since Ms Achbita still insisted on wearing a headscarf in the workplace, she was dismissed from her duties. After her dismissal she brought an action to Court, which she followed by an appeal and next resorted to an appeal for a judicial review against the unfavourable judgement of the Appeal Court. Finally, the Belgian Court of Cassation decided to refer a question for a preliminary ruling to the CJEU. The national court asked the Court of Justice to interpret Art. 2(2)(a) of Directive 2000/78, asking a question whether it is possible to interpret it as meaning that the prohibition on wearing a headscarf in the workplace regulations of a private entrepreneur (where the employer's rule prohibits all employees from wearing outward signs of political, philosophical and religious beliefs at the workplace) constitutes direct discrimination.

On examining the case, the Court observed that the term "religion" was not defined in the directive itself. However, in its Preamble there is a reference to Art. 9 ECHR, which, in a similar way as in the Charter, adopts a broad definition of religion—both *forum internum* and *forum externum*. The Court also observed that the company's regulation referred in the same degree to all workers, obligating them to wear neutral clothing in the workplace. The Court held that the regulation in question did not discriminate against Ms Achbita in any way. Consequently, the regulation did not introduce a different standard of treatment that would be directly based on religion or on the beliefs contrary to the directive.

[56] Directive 2000/78.

[57] Para. 15 of the judgement in the case C 157/15.

However, the Court did not exclude the possibility that the regulation may in an indirect way introduce a different standard of treatment based on religion or beliefs and it should be the responsibility of the national court to determine whether "the apparently neutral obligation it encompasses results, in fact, in persons adhering to a particular religion or belief being put at a particular disadvantage."[58] However, even such an unequal treatment does not constitute indirect discrimination, provided that it is objectively justified by a legal purpose and the measures serving for the realization of that purpose are adequate and necessary. According to the Court, the objective set by the company, that is the policy of neutrality, is legally justified and finds its confirmation in the case-law of the ECtHR (for instance, in the case of Eweida[59]). The prohibition of wearing religious symbols is in the opinion of the Court an adequate measure for reaching a coherent and systematically implemented policy of neutrality and finds its reflection in the case-law of the ECHR.[60] Finally, the Court emphasized that it should be examined whether the prohibition applied with regard to Ms Achbita was necessary and whether it was limited only to the minimum of the possible situations, that is, whether it exclusively concerned the workers dealing with customers. In such a case, in the opinion of the Court, the implemented prohibition was necessary for the realization of the employer's objective, which was a coherent policy of neutrality. The Court ruled that the Belgian Court should investigate whether the employer could have proposed Ms Achbita a different working position, instead of ending her employment, where she would not have to deal with customers.

Therefore, in the sentence of the said ruling, the Court held that in the case of Ms Achbita there was no occurrence of direct discrimination and the examination whether indirect discrimination occurred is the responsibility of the national court.

The Court also conducted the interpretation of Directive 2007/78 in the case of Asma Bougnaoui (C 188/15),[61] in which a question for a preliminary ruling was filed by the French Court. Ms Bougnaoui started working in the Micropole company. At the beginning she was doing a

[58] Para. 34 of the judgement in the case C 157/15.

[59] See: para. 39 of the judgement in the case C 157/15.

[60] Para. 40 of the judgement in the case C 157/15.

[61] Judgement of the Court of Justice of 14.03.2017 in the case Asma Bougnaoui and Association de défense des droits de l'homme (ADDH) v. Micropole SA, C 188/15, ECLI:EU:C:2017:204, further as judgement in the case C 188/15.

student internship there and she was informed that wearing an Islamic headscarf might pose a problem with regard to the relations with the company's customers. During the internship Ms Bougnaoui wore a simple scarf. When her internship ended, she was employed by Micropole as a design engineer. At that time, she was informed that on account of her contacts with the company's customers, the wearing of an Islamic headscarf would not always be possible. Due to the fact that Ms Asma did not abide by the policy of ideological neutrality and wore an Islamic headscarf during meetings with the company's customer (which, in his opinion, upset a number of employees), she was dismissed of her duties and her contract was terminated.

Ms Bougnaoui considered that dismissal to be discriminatory and brought an action against it to the Court. After an unfavourable judgement from the labour court, she appealed against that decision and further she filed a cassation complaint. Justifying her stance, Ms Bougnaoui argued that

> the wearing of the Islamic headscarf by an employee of a private undertaking when in contact with customers does not prejudice the rights or beliefs of others, and that the embarrassment or sensitivity of the customers of a commercial company, at the mere sight, allegedly, of a sign of religious affiliation, is neither a relevant nor legitimate criterion, free from any discrimination, that might justify the company's economic or commercial interests being allowed to prevail over the fundamental freedom of religion of an employee.[62]

The cassation court decided to stay the proceedings and referred a question for a preliminary ruling to the CJEU, asking for the interpretation of Art. 4 of the directive on equal treatment.[63] The national court wanted to clarify the admissibility of the interpretation in accordance with which a wish of a customer not to have the services of the company provided by an employee wearing an Islamic headscarf might provide a "genuine and determining occupational requirement."[64]

In its answer to the question for a preliminary ruling, the Court referred to the definition of religion and religious freedom, which has not been included by the Union's legislator in the directive itself (which, *nota bene*, forbids discrimination on the grounds of religion) but finds its ground in

[62] Para. 17 of the judgement in the case C 188/15.
[63] Directive 2000/78.
[64] Para. 25 of the judgement in the case C 188/15.

Art. 10 CFR, being correspondent to Art. 9 ECHR. As the Court emphasized in its ruling, the right to the freedom of conscience and religion entails: "freedom to change religion or belief and freedom, either alone or in community with others and in public or in private, to manifest religion or belief, in worship, teaching, practice and observance."[65] In a similar way as in the case of Achbita, the Court ruled that the freedom of religion covers both *forum internum*, as well as *forum externum*. The Court also emphasized that the Member States may decide that a difference in treatment on the grounds of religion (or any other grounds referred to in Art. 1 of the directive on equal treatment) does not constitute discrimination provided that religion (or any other characteristic) constitutes a genuine and determining occupational requirement by reason of the nature of the particular occupational activities concerned or of the context in which they are carried out. The condition for accepting religion as such a characteristic is that the objective is legitimate and the requirement is proportionate.[66] The Court distinctly emphasized that the characteristic related to religion may constitute a "genuine and determining occupational requirement" in only very limited number of circumstances.[67] Moreover, such circumstances should be based on objective factors, and not subjective ones, as in the case under discussion. The Court decided that such a subjective circumstance was the willingness to realize the customer's wish that the services would not be provided by a worker wearing an Islamic headscarf.

The Court finally ruled that the situation in which the employer fulfils the customer's wish that the services would not be provided by a worker wearing an Islamic headscarf did not constitute a genuine and determining occupational requirement within the meaning of Art. 4 Directive 2000/78.

The above rulings concerning the admissibility of the wearing of an Islamic headscarf constitute a *novum* in the line of the jurisprudence of the Court of Justice. They are also useful for delineating the boundaries between the possibility of exercising cultural rights by persons belonging to non-European cultural circles and for establishing the rules of their equal treatment in social life. Of course, in their policies, the Member States have the right to provide for and implement the principles of religious and ideological neutrality, which contributes to the maintaining of proper relations between

[65] Para. 29 of the judgement in the case C 188/15.
[66] Para. 35 of the judgement in the case C 188/15.
[67] Para. 38 of the judgement in the case C 188/15.

persons originating in different cultures, without favouring the representatives of any of them. Nevertheless, it is hard to resist the feeling that such actions simultaneously lead to the deprivation of social life of the cultural markers, including also the markers characteristic of European culture.[68] Also the case-law of the ECHR is rich in the judgements regarding the issues of wearing religious clothing and a broadly understood religious freedom.[69] Due to the connection between the Charter and ECHR and the correspondence between Art. 10 CFR and Art. 9 ECHR one should bring up the cases that fit in with the issues of the protection of migrants' rights. Naturally, it very often happened that the cases referred to the Court concerned not only foreign nationals but also the Union's citizens of the Muslim religion. It is a denomination which is characteristic of a considerably large group of migrants who have been arriving in the Community at first as economic migrants and with time as refugees since the 1960s. Thus, the Islamic culture is close to many immigrant diasporas in the United Kingdom, France, Benelux and even in Poland, where the Chechens escaping the war have been arriving since the 1990s.

The case regarding the wearing of an Islamic headscarf was that of Dahlab v. Switzerland,[70] concerning a primary school teacher who converted to Islam, married a citizen of Algeria and wore an Islamic headscarf in the workplace. The school authorities requested that Ms Dahlab stop wearing an Islamic headscarf but, on account of her refusal, the case was brought before the national courts and finally before the ECtHR. The applicant claimed that there occurred a violation of Art. 9 ECHR. While presenting its stance, the government of Switzerland observed that preserving ideological neutrality was a necessary action in a pluralistic society

[68] See: ruling in the case Eweida and others v. the United Kingdom, Judgement of the European Court of Human Rights of 15.01.2013, complaint no. 48420/10, 59842/10, 51671/10 and 36516/10.

[69] Case Leyla Sahin v. Turkey, complaint no. 44774/98. See: A. Grey, *Comparative Religious Freedom: The Right to Wear Religious Dress* in *The other people. Interdisciplinary perspectives on migration*, ed. M.W. Karraker (Palgrave Macmillan, 2013), 171; Overview of the European Court of Human Rights' case-law on freedom of religion, report prepared by the Research Division of the Court, updated on 31 October 2013. Report available on the website: http://www.echr.coe.int/Documents/Research_report_religion_ENG.pdf. Accessed 12.09.2017.

[70] Decision of the European Court of Human Rights on the inadmissibility of the complaint of 15.10.2001 in the case Dahlab v. Switzerland, complaint no. 42393/98. See: M. Kopalova, "European Courts' Case Law," in *Politics and Policies of Integration in Austria, Hungary, Czechia, Denmark and at EU level*, eds. R. Hokovsky, J. Kopal, League of Human Rights & European Values Think-Tank (Brno–Praga, 2013), 382.

where students come from different cultures and are of different nationalities. In the official statement of the government there was also an interesting argument, in accordance with which teachers perform an important role in society with regard to children, especially those attending a mandatory public school, in that children often identify with their teacher.

In its ruling the Court referred to the previous case-law,[71] emphasizing that in a democratic society, where there are often several religions functioning next to one another, it might be justifiable to introduce restrictions and limit religious freedom in order to protect the interests of different groups.[72] The Court ruled that in the case of Ms Dahlab, the Geneva authorities did not cross the margin of discretion and the means adopted by the authorities was adequate to the situation in which the students should be protected and a religious "harmony" should be preserved. In view of the above, the complaint was ruled to be inadmissible.

In a similar way, the inadmissibility of the complaint against a violation of Art. 9 ECHR was ruled by the Court in the case of Ebrahimian v. France.[73] The case concerned Ms Ebrahimian employed on a fixed-term contract in a state hospital at a psychiatric ward as a social worker. Shortly before the termination of her contract, Ms Ebrahimian was informed that her contract would not be renewed due to the fact that she wore an Islamic headgear, which caused complaints from the patients. Ms Ebrahimian took the matter to Court claiming that a violation of Art. 9 ECHR occurred on account of the lack of the possibility for her to manifest her faith. The Court ruled that a violation under Art. 9 did not occur and that the state, as the employer, had the right to apply the restriction on the manifesting of her faith during the performance of professional duties in order to maintain the principle of equal treatment of the patients.[74]

[71] Amongst others, to the case of Kokkinakis v. Greece, Judgement of the European Court of Human Rights of 25.05.1993, complaint no. 14307/88, further as judgement in the case of Kokkinakis v. Greece.

[72] See: sentence 11 of the judgement in the case Kokkinakis v. Greece.

[73] Judgement of the European Court of Human Rights of 26.11.2005 in the case Ebrahimian v. France, complaint no. 64846/11.

[74] The appropriateness of clothing in a public place and the connection between one's clothing and religion was also the subject of the cases: Barik Edidi v. Spain (Decision of the European Court of Human Rights on the inadmissibility of the complaint of 19.05.2016, complaint no. 21780/13) and Lachiri v. Belgium (complaint no. 3413/09). Both cases concerned the appropriateness of clothing in the courtroom. In the first case, a complaint was filed by a lawyer, who was asked to move to the part of the courtroom reserved for members of the public, on the ground that she was wearing an inappropriate headgear—a

One of the widely discussed cases concerning the wearing of religious clothing was that of Dogru v. France.[75] It concerned the pupils of a public secondary school who were Muslims and refused to remove their headscarves during their Physical Education lessons. The pupils were eventually expelled from the school and their parents brought an action to one of the national courts arguing that a violation under Art. 9 ECHR occurred.[76] The ECHR concluded that a violation under Art. 9 ECHR did not occur. The parents of the pupils in question had been informed about the school regulations when they enrolled their children in the school. The Court ruled in support of the national courts which had found that wearing a religious headscarf was inappropriate during Physical Education classes for safety and health reasons. In the opinion of the Court, the punishment of being expelled from school was a consequence of the violation of the school regulations and not an infringement of the right to freedom of religion, even more so in light of the fact that the pupils continued their education by way of correspondence.

Further, the case of Aktas v. France concerned a group of pupils expelled from the school on account of their refusal to remove the elements of religious clothing.[77] At the start of the school year some girls went to school wearing headscarves to cover their hair, while some boys wore the headgear typical of the Sikhs (the Sikh keski or under-turban). According to the French authorities, such behaviour was contrary to the law of 2004 prohibiting the wearing of all conspicuous signs of religious faith during lessons. According to the Court, no breach of the freedom of religion occurred as the prohibition was the implementation of the constitutional principle of secularism. Although some of the girls removed their headscarves and replaced them with bonnets, the Court ruled that the wearing of a bonnet instead of a headscarf was still a conspicuous manifestation of

hijab, whereas in accordance with the Court protocol a lawyer may appear in front of the Court only wearing the so-called biretta. The Court found the complaint under Art. 9 ECHR to be inadmissible on account of failure to exhaust domestic remedies. In the second case (complaint no. 3413/09) the applicant claimed that a violation under Art. 9 ECHR occurred on account of her exclusion from the courtroom as a result of her wearing a hijab.

[75] Judgement of the European Court of Human Rights of 4.12.2008 in the case Dogru v. France, complaint no. 27058/05.

[76] It is worth noting that the pupils proposed to the school authorities that they would wear hats instead of headscarves. Eventually, after being expelled from school, the girls continued their education by way of correspondence.

[77] Decision of the European Court of Human Rights on the inadmissibility of complaint of 30.06.2009 in the case Aktas v. France, complaint no. 43563/08.

religious feelings, whereas the act of 2004 did not allow for any actions with a view of circumventing the law. An extremely interesting ruling concerning participation in gymnastics lesson and fitting in with the Dogru case-law was that in the case of Osmanoglu and Kocabas v. Switzerland of 10.01.2017.[78] The case concerned two girls whose parents had both Swiss and Turkish citizenship and who refused to send their daughters to the mandatory swimming lessons in the school, claiming that their faith did not allow the girls to participate in coeducational swimming lessons. The parents were warned that they would have to pay a fine on account of their avoidance of the educational obligation. The school also attempted to mediate in this matter. The fine was eventually imposed, whereas the parents brought the case to Court claiming that a breach under Art. 9 ECHR occurred. The case was brought in front of the ECtHR. While examining the case, the Court found that the refusal to exempt the girls from the swimming lesson was aimed to protect foreign pupils from any potential form of social exclusion. In the opinion of the Court, school serves a special function in the integration process, whereas it is in the best interest of the child to fully participate in education and experience successful integration in accordance with the local custom. The interest of the child should take priority over the wish of the parents to exempt the child from the lessons. In the view of the Court, the objective of the swimming lessons was not only to learn to swim but primarily to take part in activities together with the other pupils, without making a distinction as to the child's country of origin, religion or the opinions of the child's parents. The Court emphasized that the school had been very flexible and offered the girls the possibility of wearing a hijab during swimming and the changing of clothes without the presence of boys. Thus, the Court ruled that by

[78] Judgement of the European Court of Human Rights of 10.01.2017 in the case Osmanoglu and Kocabas v. Switzerland, complaint no. 29086/12, further as the case of Osmanoglu and Kocabas v. Switzerland. What is interesting, in the judgement of 18 June 1993, the Swiss Federal Tribunal ruled that the refusal to participate in mixed-sex swimming classes insisted on by the Muslims lies within the scope of the protection under Art. 9 ECHR. However, in the judgement of 24.10.2008 the Federal Tribunal ruled that a refusal to dismiss Muslim children from mixed-sex swimming lessons does not violate the freedom of religion. As J. Krajczyński observes, referring to the text of the judgement, the change in the line of jurisprudence of the Swiss Tribunal was caused by the "important and urgent public interest relating to social integration," J. Krajczyński, "Wolność sumienia i wyznania w najnowszej jurysprudencji Trybunału Federalnego Szwajcarii. Kwestie z zakresu szkolnictwa publicznego," in *Aktualne problemy wolności myśli, sumienia i wyznania*, eds. P. Stanisz, A.M. Abramowicz, M. Czelny (Lublin, 2015), 162–164.

refusing to exempt the pupils from the swimming lessons the Swiss authorities held as a priority that children should participate in all lessons in the school and did not breach Art. 9 ECHR.

In 2011 France adopted the act 2010–1192 of 11.10.2010 prohibiting face coverings in public places. This law became the subject of a complaint brought in front of the ECtHR. The applicant, a Muslim, claimed that she could not fully manifest her religious identity by wearing the burqa, which covered her whole body with the exception of her eyes. The Court concluded that no breach under Art. 9 ECHR occurred (nor under Art. 8 ECHR, the examination of which was requested by the applicant).[79] On examining the law prohibiting any person from concealing their face in public implemented by the act, the Court concluded that the arguments of the government, in accordance with which such provisions are in the interest of protecting public safety, might be justifiable only when it was proven that there indeed existed a general threat to public safety. In the opinion of the Court, the French government failed to prove that the ban introduced by the act could be interpreted in this context. The Court stated that women were forced to abandon an element of their identity, which they found to be important, whereas it could have been introduced that each person had an obligation to reveal their face and be identified in case of a risk to public safety in each specific circumstance. In this meaning, the ban on concealing the face, according to the Court, was not necessary for protecting public safety in a democratic society.

Moving further, the Court observed that the prohibition of concealing the face might be considered as justifiable since it guarantees respect for the rights of others (the so-called *living together* principle).[80] The Court emphasized that the prohibition affected a small proportion of the Muslim society in France (around 1900 women), adding in passing, however, that the implementation of the new law in France had also led to an increase in Islamophobic attitudes. Nevertheless, what is important is that the act did not ban the wearing of any conspicuous religious symbols in public but merely prohibited the full-face covering, whereas the administrative fine for breaking the ban was established at a considerably low level (€ 150)

[79] Judgement of the European Court of Human Rights of 1.07.2014 in the case S.A.S. v. France, complaint no. 43835/11.

[80] See: I. Trispiotis, "Two Interpretations of "Living Together" in European Human Rights Law," *The Cambridge Law Journal*, vol. 75, issue 3 (2016): 580–607.

with a possibility that the Court might exchange the fine into participation in a civil course.

In the opinion of the Court, France, by introducing the act, wanted to protect the principle of interaction (civil coexistence) between the citizens, which, in the opinion of the government, was necessary for the functioning of pluralism, but also tolerance and broad outlook on life, without which democracy cannot exist. Eventually, the Court ruled that the restrictions in exercising the rights under Art. 9 ECHR were justified by the protection of the principle of *living together* as an element of the protection of the rights and freedoms of others. Such a restriction was, in the view of the Court necessary for the functioning of a democratic society.[81] Therefore, social and cultural integration is in some cases more important than the protection of particular cultural customs.

The ruling in question is very interesting because the Court in its argumentation oscillated between the issues of safety and the issues of culture. The French government introduced the said law primarily for safety reasons (as transpired from the justification). The problem of concealing the face is still a matter of debate in European states, which was mentioned by the Court in the justification of the judgement. A full-face covering is definitely not a part of European identity, in a similar way to other elements of clothing, which the Court referred to in its jurisprudence (headscarves, turbans). However, France is a specific country on account of its secularization and a clear separation of church and state. The Court found no grounds for ruling the lack of breach under Art. 9 ECHR with regard to safety issues but supported itself with an argument for the protection of pluralism in society. This is a questionable argument in so far as the French government intended to partly restrict this pluralism by the ban on wearing the burqas and niqabs. What is interesting, the ban affected in fact a very small community of radical Islamists. However, the ruling in the case of S.A.S. touches directly upon a very up-to-date problem, that is, the possibility of the functioning of diverse cultural signs in European countries.[82] In this respect, the cultural

[81] The discussion on the issue of the ban on face covering, which is postulated by representatives of European states, is increasingly becoming a pan-European debate. Suffice it to mention here the cases of Belkacemi and Oussar v. Belgium (complaint no. 37798/13) and Dakir v. Belgium (complaint no. 4619/12). The complaints concerned the full-face ban of a head covering (headscarf) introduced by the Belgian law, which according to the applicants (practising Muslims) violated their right to the freedom of religion.

[82] An interesting case, seemingly referring to the cultural safety of Europe was the case of Ouardiri v. Switzerland (Decision of the European Court of Court of Human Rights on the inadmissibility of the complaint of 8.07.2011, complaint no. 65840/09), in which the appli-

rights of certain groups, including groups of non-European roots, might be derogated for the purpose of the protection of other priority values, such as the principle of *living together*, as indicated by the Court.

In a similar way as in the case of S.A.S., the Court did not find a breach of Art. 9 ECHR in the Belgian cases: Dakir, as well as Belkacemi and Oussar v. Belgium.

In June 2008, Pepinster, Dison and Verviers municipalities adopted the law prohibiting the wearing of full-face coverings in public places. The applicant in this case was Ms Dakir, a national of Belgium, a Muslim, who brought action before Conseil d'État for withdrawing the said provisions since, according to her, they were in breach of the rights and liberties guaranteed under Art. 8 and 9 ECHR.[83] Referring to the ruling in the case of S.A.S., the Court observed that the choice whether a law, as in the case under discussion, would be in force is the choice of the given society. According to the Court, the aim of the introduced provisions was to protect the principle of *living together*, which was not in breach of the provisions of the Convention.

In the case of Belcacemi and Oussar the applicants were nationals of Belgium and Morocco, who claimed that the Belgian law adopted on 1 June 2011 prohibiting full-face coverings in public places violated their rights under the Convention.[84] Both applicants claimed that the prohibition of wearing the niqab was in breach of, amongst others, Art. 8 and 9 ECHR. Ms Oussar claimed that the introduced provisions forced her to stop leaving the house and as a result she could not participate in social life. Also in this case the Court referred to the ruling S.A.S., stating that the objective of the Belgian law was to protect public safety, gender equality and the principle of *living together*, whereas the question whether the wearing of the veil was to be accepted in Belgium was the choice of the

cants claimed that the constitutional ban on the building of minarets in the territory of Switzerland is in breach of their religious freedom. The Court found their complaint to be inadmissible (decision of 8.07.2011) arguing that the applicants were not able to demonstrate they factually had the status of victims and experienced a violation. In the opinion of the Court, their complaint had an *actio popularis* character. What is more, the Court decided that the Swiss Federal Constitutional Court in passing a ruling on the compatibility of the constitutional provisions with the Convention (judgement of 21.01.2010) ensured the possibility of Court control over the compatibility of future refusals to build minarets with the ECHR.

[83] Judgement of the European Court of Human Rights of 11.07.2017 in the case Dakir v. Belgium, complaint no. 4619/12.

[84] Judgement of the European Court of Human Rights of 11.07.2017 in the case Belcacemi and Oussar v. Belgium, complaint no. 37798/13.

society.[85] In this way, the Court held that in the case under discussion there was no violation of Art. 8 and 9 ECHR and there was no violation of the prohibition of discrimination.

Cultural matters were also at issue in the cases concerning entry into the territory of the European Union and border controls. An example of such a case is that of Phull.[86] The applicant was Suku Phull, a national of the United Kingdom, who was a practising Sikh.[87] During a journey from Luxembourg to the United Kingdom, he was asked to submit to a security check and remove his turban. The applicant claimed that there was no such need as he subjected to the scanning and hand-held metal detector. In examining the case, the Court focused on the question whether the restriction on the freedom of religion, as in the case of Mr Phull, is justifiable in a democratic society in order to protect public safety.

In the justification of its stance, the ECtHR referred to the case of X v. the United Kingdom,[88] in which the applicant was also a Sikh. Mr X was obligated to pay a fine on account of not wearing a helmet while riding a motorcycle. Despite Mr X's complaint that the law on road traffic violated his freedom of religion (since the religious rule of wearing a turban excluded wearing a helmet), the Commission ruled that the

[85] See also: Cultural Rights in the case-law of European Court of Human Rights, Council of Europe. European Court of Human Rights (2011): 21.

[86] Decision of the European Court of Human Rights on the inadmissibility of complaint of 11.01.2005 in the case Suku Phull v. France, complaint no. 35753/03. On the subject of the Sikh denomination, see: EASO Country of Origin Information Report, Pakistan Country Overview, August 2015, 94.

[87] The functioning of the Sikhs in the cultural sphere was also the subject of the judgement in the case of Mann Singh v. France, in which the applicant was trying to get a duplicate of a stolen driving licence. The applicant was refused the issuance of the document on two occasions since he supplied to the administrative bodies his photographs in a turban. In accordance with the guidelines, such photographs should show a person without a head covering and *en face*. The ECtHR ruled that the regulation concerning the document photograph did not violate the freedom of religion under Art. 9 ECHR. The aim of the regulation was to protect public safety. As the Court emphasized, Art. 9 does not protect each action motivated or inspired by religion or faith. What is more, Art. 9 does not always guarantee the possibility of behaviour according to one's faith. Decision of the European Court of Human Rights on the inadmissibility of complaint of 13.11.2008 in the case Mann Singh v. France, complaint no. 24479/07.

[88] Decision of the European Commission of Human Rights of 12.07.1978 in the case X v. the United Kingdom, complaint no. 7992/77.

obligation to wear a helmet is a necessary safety measure and it did not violate the freedom of religion. In a similar way, the Court argued in the case of Mr Phull, concluding that security checks at airports are a necessary measure for the protection of public safety and thus there was no violation of Art. 9 ECHR.

Moving further, in the case of El Morsli v. France the applicant was a Morocco national, who in 2001 married a French national.[89] Ms El Morsli was a Muslim and wore a headscarf. In March 2002 the applicant visited the French consulate in Marrakesh in order to obtain a visa and join her spouse. Ms El Morsli was refused entry into the consulate since she refused to remove her headgear for identification purposes. Next, the applicant applied for a visa by way of correspondence, but she was refused. A complaint against the refusal was filed on behalf of Ms El Morsli by her spouse. Ms El Morsli eventually brought the case before the ECtHR, claiming that in her case there was a violation of Art. 9 ECHR, even more so in view of the fact that she expressed willingness to undergo identity control but only in the presence of a woman. The Court ruled that in the case of Ms El Morsli no breach of the freedom of religion occurred, whereas the standard control was necessary for the protection of public safety, all the more so given the fact that the control the applicant was to be subjected to is usually very brief.

At this stage, it is worth mentioning the case of Perry v. Latvia.[90] The applicant was a national of the United States, a pastor belonging to an evangelical protestant federation Morning Star International, established in the United States. The applicant established a branch of his congregation named Morning Star. Mr Perry claimed that the Latvian authorities which granted him a residence permit at the same time prohibiting him from undertaking religious activity violated Art. 9 ECHR. The Court ruled that in the case of Mr Perry, a breach of Art. 9 occurred since the restriction imposed on him by the Latvian authorities was not provided for in any way in the national law. At the moment of issuing the decision on the residence permit there was no legal basis which would allow the

[89] Decision of the European Court of Human Rights on the inadmissibility of the complaint of 4.03.2008 in the case El Morsli v. France, complaint no. 15585/06, further also as the case of El Morsli v. France.

[90] Judgement of the European Court of Human Rights of 8.11.2007 in the case Perry v. Latvia, complaint no. 30273/03.

migration authorities to use the fact of extending the residence permit as a pretext for restricting a foreign national's activities of a religious character.

3.3 Right to Protection Against the Culture of the Country of Origin and the Guaranteed Scope of Protection

The cultural situation of third-country nationals arriving in the Member States is often complicated. On the one hand, they still have ties with the culture of their country of origin, which lies at the root of their primary identity. On the other hand, they embark on the building of cultural ties with the culture of the receiving country. With time, their right to cultural identity becomes a two-fold right, as they are under the influence of two cultural circles—the circle of their country of origin and the circle of their country of residence. The situation is further complicated when a foreign national's stay in the territory of the host country is of an irregular character and there is a risk of his expulsion to the country of origin. It often happens that the culture of the country of origin is of an oppressive nature, especially towards vulnerable groups, such as minors or single women.

In a situation when there are circumstances for the expulsion of a foreign national, to which he opposes, the Court examines the admissibility of the return, relying on the key principle of *non-refoulement*, in accordance with which a person cannot be returned to a country where he or she would be exposed to inhuman treatment under Art. 4 CFR (Art. 3 ECHR). Inhuman treatment is often based on persecution or other behaviours rooted in culture, of which probably the most drastic example is the so-called circumcision of women in African countries. Assuming that some behaviours, which are likely to occur in the migrant's country of origin, prevent the national authorities and international courts from issuing the return decision, one might propose a thesis of the existence of the right to protection against the culture of the country of origin. In my view, such a right exists within the framework of the guarantees of fundamental rights functioning within the so-called EU return and asylum law. This right should be exercised by migrants fearing for their life or fearing persecution on account of the cultural differences between their behaviour and the customary cultural patterns in their country of origin.[91] A confirmation of the functioning of this right is the rich case-law, primarily by the ECtHR. The Court referred to cultural customs on numerous occasions, as a circumstance which might prevent expulsion. The standards established by the ECtHR cited below constitute a reference point for the level of protection which should be guaranteed to immigrants who are subject to the norms of the EU's asylum and return law.

One of the circumstances of a cultural character raised by the ECtHR was the cultural differences in social life and a potential social exclusion which might be experienced by foreign nationals on account of their return to the country of origin. In the well-known case of N v. Sweden,[92] the applicant was an Afghan woman, who during her stay in Sweden was in a relationship with a Swede, while still remaining married according to Afghan law. The applicant claimed that on account of her extramarital relationship, in her country of origin she might face social exclusion, long prison sentence or even the death penalty. On the basis of the collected material on the situation in Afghanistan, the Court ruled that there was a risk of inhuman treatment.[93] A similar complaint was the subject of the case of W.H. v. Sweden,[94] in which the applicant was an Iraqi national, belonging to an ethnic and religious minority. The applicant claimed that in the case of expulsion, as a single, divorced woman she would be exposed to persecution, rape, forced conversion and forced marriage. Eventually, before the ECtHR examined the complaint, the applicant received the residence permit in Sweden.

Moving further, in the case of R.H. v. Sweden, the applicant was a Somali national, who claimed that in case of expulsion she might be

[91] As for the terminology, it seems that a fuller illustration of the object of protection might be rendered by the words: "protection against the culture of the country of origin"—for the sake of clarity, however, it should be added here that it is more common that an oppressive character can be attributed to specific elements of the given culture, and not culture understood *en masse*, with all its manifestations.

[92] Judgement of the European Court of Human Rights of 20.07.2010 in the case N v. Sweden, complaint no. 23505/09.

[93] In the justification the Court referred to mainly to the Afghan law of April 2009 in accordance with which women are not allowed to leave home without their husband's consent. Moreover, in accordance with reports examined by the ECtHR, over 80% of women experience domestic violence in Afghanistan.

[94] Judgement of the European Court of Human Rights of 8.04.2015 in the case W.H. v. Sweden, complaint no. 49341/10.

exposed to death from the side of her family members, whom she opposed by avoiding an arranged marriage or to another attempt to get her married against her will.[95] On examining the case, the Court confirmed that the situation of women in Somalia was extremely difficult but did not find the risk of violating Art. 3 on account of some inconsistencies in the evidence provided by the applicant and the eventual possibility of support offered to the applicant by her family.

It is also worth referring to the case of Hossein Kheel v. the Netherlands.[96] The applicant was a national of Afghanistan who was facing expulsion to the country of origin and separation from her husband and children. The Court applied interim measures in the case, deciding that there was a risk of violating Art. 3 in a situation when Ms Kheel as a single woman would return to her country of origin, where she would have no support from her family in order to protect her. Eventually, the Dutch authorities granted Ms Kheel a residence permit.

Another cultural circumstance often raised by foreign nationals trying to avoid expulsion is gender inequality and discrimination against women, as well as a lack of respect for women's rights. Such arguments were brought up, amongst others, in the case of V.F. v. France. The applicant claimed that if she were to return to Nigeria, she would be forced to return to prostitution and the Nigerian authorities would not be able to provide her protection. The Court found the complaint to be inadmissible, concluding that Nigeria had made progress in fighting against prostitution and crime network involved in such crimes.[97]

[95] Judgement of the European Court of Human Rights of 10.09.2015 in the case R.H. v. Sweden, complaint no. 4601/14.

[96] Decision of the European Court of Human Rights on the removal of the complaint of 16.12.2008 in the case Hossein Kheel v. the Netherlands, complaint no. 34583/08.

[97] Decision of the European Court of Human Rights on the inadmissibility of the complaint of 29.11.2011 in the case V.F. v France, complaint no. 7196/10. The complaint in the case of F.A. v. the United Kingdom concerned a similar situation, in which the applicant claimed that her return to Ghana would result in her getting into the hands of human traffickers who had forced her to prostitution. The Court decided that the complaint was inadmissible as the applicant did not exhaust all domestic remedies. See: Decision of the European Court of Human Rights on the inadmissibility of the complaint of 10.09.2013 in the case F.A. v. the United Kingdom, complaint no. 20658/11. A widely discussed problem of discrimination in the case-law also concerned the problem of discrimination on the grounds of sexual orientation. See: Judgement of the Court of Justice of 7.11.2013 in the case Minister

An important cultural circumstance is a threat that a foreign national might be subject to "honorary crime" in the country of origin. It was precisely this circumstance that was raised by the applicants in the cases of A.A. and others v. Switzerland (the applicants were a family—mother and five children who claimed that her expulsion to Yemen may result in an honorary crime, as she had left her country of origin against the will of her husband, showing him disobedience)[98] and R.D. v. France (the applicant was a national of Guinea who married a Christian and claimed that on account of that she might experience violence from her brothers and father who were Muslims).[99]

The concept of the protection against the country of origin also encompasses the problem of female genital mutilation. So far, the ECtHR has examined several cases of such nature, amongst others, the case of Collins and Akaziebie v. Sweden, in which the applicants were mother and daughter, who feared circumcision in case of being returned to Nigeria. The Court did not find in this case the risk of violating Art. 3 ECHR, arguing that even though the practice of female genital mutilation was then conducted in Nigeria, it was practised in some specific regions and not in the region where the applicants came from.[100] The risk of facing female genital mutilation was also raised by the applicants in the cases Izevbekhai v.

voor Immigratie en Asiel v. X and Y, and Z v. Minister voor Immigratie en Asiel, C 199/12, ECLI:EU:C:2013:720; Judgement of the European Court of Human Rights of 8.04.2015 in the case M.E. v. Sweden, complaint no. 71398/12 (the applicant was a national of Libya who was eventually granted a residence permit in Sweden); Decision of the European Court of Human Rights on the removal of the complaint of 10.07.2012 in the case A.S.B. v. the Netherlands, complaint no. 4854/12 (the applicant was a Jamaica national who was eventually granted asylum in the Netherlands).

[98] Judgement of the European Court of Human Rights of 28.06.2012 in the case A.A. and others v. Sweden, complaint no. 14499/09. The Court ruled that a threat of violating Art. 2 and 3 ECHR was not proven in that case.

[99] Judgement of the European Court of Human Rights of 16.06.2016 in the case R.D. v. France, complaint no. 34648/14. Similarly, the circumstance of honorary crime was raised by the applicant in the case of Jabari v. Turkey (Judgement of 11.07.2000, complaint no. 40035/98). The applicant was an Iran national, who feared that in case of her return to her country of origin she would be stoned on account of having committed adultery, which would be in accordance with the law of Islam. Thus, the Court ruled that the expulsion of the applicant to Iran would be in breach of Art. 3 ECHR.

[100] Decision of the European Court of Human Rights on the inadmissibility of the complaint of 8.03.2007 in the case Collins and Akaziebie v. Sweden, complaint no. 23944/05.

Ireland,[101] and Omeredo v. Austria.[102] In the latter case the applicant was a national of Nigeria, who had escaped her country in 2003 trying to avoid circumcision. She feared that in case of her return she might be forcefully submitted to the ritual or even killed by the inhabitants of her village. The Court ruled that in Nigeria there indeed existed the risk of women being subjected to female genital mutilation; however, the applicant's professional and educational experience should allow the applicant to start a new life in Nigeria without relying on family relations.

In a similar way, the Court ruled a lack of risk of a breach under Art. 3 in the case of Sow v. Belgium (the applicant was a national of Guinea).[103] Moving further, in the case of Bangura v. Belgium, the applicant was a national of Sierra Leone, who was eventually granted a residence permit in Belgium and the Court did not examine her case.[104] The ECtHR eventually did not find the risk of the violation of Art. 3 ECHR on the grounds of a risk of sexual violence, such as the female genital mutilation, in any of the above cases. The line of the jurisprudence of the ECtHR, which is hard to take issue with, seems to be at times a risky one, imposing on women the obligation to avoid the environments where they might encounter violence addressed at them and forcing women to choose to live in other regions of the country. The practice of circumcision, experienced by women in African countries, even though culturally motivated, cannot be accepted to any degree—it belongs within the dimension of a highly oppressive culture, against which any person deserves decisive protection.

In a similar way as in the case of Bangur, the proceedings in the case of Lunguli v. Sweden[105] also ended with a positive outcome for the applicant. In that case the applicant claimed that if she were to return to Tanzania, she would be exposed to the risk of female genital mutilation against her

[101] Decision of the European Court of Human Rights on the inadmissibility of the complaint of 17.05.2011 in the case Izevbekhai v. Ireland, complaint no. 43408/08. The applicants (mother and two daughters) claimed that as a result of the circumcision the eldest daughter of the family had died. The Court did not find a risk of the violation under Art. 3 ECHR.

[102] Decision of the European Court of Human Rights on the inadmissibility of the complaint of 20.09.2011 in the case Omeredo v. Austria, complaint no. 8969/10.

[103] Judgement of the European Court of Human Rights of 19.01.2016 in the case Sow v. Belgium, complaint no. 27081/13.

[104] Decision of the European Court of Human Rights on the removal of the complaint of 14.06.2014 in the case Bangura v. Belgium, complaint no. 52872/10.

[105] Decision of the European Court of Human Rights on the removal of the complaint of 1.07.2003 in the case Miriam Abraham Lunguli v. Sweden, complaint no. 33692/02.

will. As a result of the interim measures applied by the Court, the Swedish government decided to grant the applicant a residence permit.

A circumstance allowing to determine the risk of the violation of Art. 3 ECHR on the grounds of the customs of a cultural nature existing in the country of origin is also that of persecution on the grounds of religion,[106] including the followers of religions from the Christian circle. For instance, in the case F.H. v. Sweden,[107] the applicant referred to the risk of an infringement of Art. 2 and 3 ECHR in case of their deportation to Iraq on account of their following of the Christian faith (the Court did not find the risk of an infringement, allowing for the possibility of deportation). In a similar way, in the case F.G. v. Sweden, the applicant was a national of Iran who converted to Christianity[108] after he had left his country of origin. He claimed that he would be exposed to persecution if he were to be returned to the country of origin from Sweden. The Court ruled that the Swedish authorities did not assess the risk of returning the applicant to Iran and it implied a possible violation of Art. 2 and 3 ECHR in this regard (the assessment was conducted only with regard to the applicant's political activity). In its ruling, the Court concluded that the carrying out of an actual assessment is necessary for excluding the risk of an infringement.

The consequence of adopting the thesis of the existence of the right to protection against the culture of the country of origin, which might be oppressive and infringe the cultural identity of an individual, is the acknowledgement of the possibility that an individual should decide about their cultural identity. It often happens that an expulsion results in a two-fold infringement of cultural rights—on the one hand, a returning foreign national is exposed to cultural behaviours which he does not accept and which may, in extreme cases, pose a threat of inhuman treatment. On the other hand, the ties with the receiving country are severed and the process of integration is broken. A migrant's cultural identity is built based on the experience of acculturation and a forced return to the country of origin may entail an infringement of the right to identity through the damaging or the breaking of cultural ties with the host country. Good examples of

[106] The problem of the risk of persecution on the grounds of religion was also the subject of the above case of W.H. v. Sweden. The applicant was an Iranian national belonging to an ethnic and religious minority.

[107] Judgement of the European Court of Human Rights of 20.01.2009 in the case F.H. v. Sweden, complaint no. 32621/06.

[108] Judgement of the European Court of Human Rights of 23.03.2016 in the case F.G. v. Sweden, complaint no. 43611/11.

such a situation may be found among the selected rulings of the ECtHR, which partly illustrate the issue under discussion.[109]

In the case of Beldjoudi v. France, the applicant was a national of Algeria, born and living in France.[110] His wife was a French national. The applicant had a few criminal convictions and he had spent a total of more than seven years in prison. Eventually, he was issued a decision on expulsion on account of the fact that he posed a threat to public order. In those circumstances, he referred to Art. 8 ECHR claiming that his deportation would constitute a breach of the right to family life. The Court found his complaint to be valid arguing that Mr Beldjoudi had spent the whole of his life in France and had no connection with Algeria apart from his nationality. Additionally, in case of his expulsion, his wife, in order to preserve the unity of marriage, would also have to leave and probably would encounter considerable adaptation problems.[111]

Moving further, in the case of Uner v. the Netherlands, the applicant was a national of Turkey, living in the Netherlands since he was 12.[112] The applicant had a family in the Netherlands—a partner and two children. He was sentenced to seven years of imprisonment on account of his conviction of manslaughter and assault. As a consequence, his permanent residence permit was withdrawn and he was expelled to Turkey. The applicant claimed that his right to family life had been breached, but the Court did

[109] P. van Dijk enumerates the following criteria which allow to assess the connection of a foreign national with the host country: the fact of being born in the host country, the length of residence in the country, having received primary education in the host country, the knowledge of the language of the host country and the language of the country of origin, having (formerly) the citizenship of the host country or applying for such citizenship, remaining married to a national of the host country, having relatives in the host country, having close relatives living in the country of origin. See: P. van Dijk, "Protection of "Integrated" Aliens against Expulsion under the European Convention on Human Rights," in *Security of Residence and Expulsion. Protection of Aliens in Europe*, eds. E. Guild, P. Minderhoud (Nijhoff, 2001), 31–32.

[110] Judgement of the European Court of Human Rights of 26.03.1992 in the case Beldjoudi v. France, complaint no. 12083/86.

[111] A similar case to the above was that of Boultif v. Switzerland, where the applicant was a national of Algeria, who was issued a return decision. The Court ruled that in case of returning the applicant and separating the spouses an infringement of Art. 8 ECHR would occur. See: Judgement of the European Court of Human Rights of 2.08.2001 in the case Boultif v. Switzerland, complaint no. 54273/00.

[112] Judgement of the European Court of Human Rights of 18.10.2006 in the case Uner v. the Netherlands, complaint no. 46410/99. See: FRA Report: *Fundamental Rights of Migrants in Irregular Situation*, FRA 2011, 30.

not accept the arguments of the applicant (who relied on the lack of connection with the country of origin and the fact that his partner and children would experience adaptation problems, since they did not speak Turkish) and did not find a breach of Art. 8 ECHR.

In the case of Kaya v. Germany, the applicant was a Turkish national, who was born in Germany where he finished education. He was sentenced to imprisonment for, amongst others, attempting to traffic in human beings, driving under the influence of alcohol and possession of drugs.[113] On account of the applicant's rich criminal history, he was issued a deportation order to Turkey. In the proceedings, Mr Kaya argued that he spoke only colloquial Turkish and could not write in Turkish. The Court ruled that the deportation was in accordance with the law and necessary for ensuring public safety. Moreover, the ECtHR observed that the applicant was not able to integrate socially in Germany and what is more, did not apply for the process of naturalization in spite of meeting its requirements. Thus, the Court ruled that no breach of Art. 8 ECHR occurred.

Therefore, the right to the protection against the country of origin fits in within the concept of the protection "par ricochet," in accordance with which it is possible to "extend the scope of the application of certain rights with the areas which are not *expressis verbis* the subject of the provisions of the Convention,"[114] as is in the case of the application of Art. 3 ECHR to foreign nationals threatened by the risk of expulsion. Expulsion of a foreign national to a country where he would be exposed to the risk of inhuman treatment is the responsibility of the State which issues a return decision.[115] The protection standards of the right to protection against the culture of the country of origin are determined on the basis of the Strasburg case-law on account of the close relation between EU law and Convention laws with regard to the guarantees of the standards of treatment of foreign nationals threatened with expulsion. That is to say, during the realization of the return (and before, during qualification for protection) the Member States

[113] Judgement of the European Court of Human Rights of 28.06.2007 in the case Kaya v. Federal Republic of Germany, complaint no. 31753/02.

[114] J. Wojnowska-Radzińska, "Ochrona wydalanych cudzoziemców na podstawie art. 3 Konwencji o ochronie praw człowieka i podstawowych wolności," *Studia Europejskie*, issue 1 (2013): 10. See also: A. Szklanna, *Ochrona prawna cudzoziemca w świetle orzecznictwa Europejskiego Trybunału Praw Człowieka* (Warszawa, 2010), 222 et seq.

[115] J. Wojnowska-Radzińska, "Ochrona wydalanych cudzoziemców na podstawie art. 3," 112.

(being at the same time State Parties to the ECHR) apply EU secondary law, that is directives implemented into national law.

The situation is different than in the case of the threat of expulsion when entry into the EU Member State and reunification with family members constitutes a breach of social and cultural ties of a foreign national with the country of origin. Such a situation must be assessed by national courts. It remains an open question whether foreign nationals should have an autonomous right to decide about their cultural identity, as arbitrary decision of immigration authorities constitute an apparently forced imposition of cultural identity upon an individual.

This is what the ECtHR ruled, amongst others, in the case of Sen v. the Netherlands.[116] The applicants were parents, nationals of Turkey, who left their country for the Netherlands in 1986, leaving their three-year-old daughter under the care of their aunt. The Dutch authorities refused to grant the girl a residence permit, while the applicants claimed that there was a breach of Art. 8 ECtHR due to the lack of possibility for family reunification. The Court held that the girl had spent her entire life in Turkey, with which she was tied by culture and language. However, her family in the Netherlands (including her two siblings, who were born there) was in turn well integrated with the host country and would not be able to return to Turkey without problems so as to join the elder daughter. Therefore, the Court held there was a breach of Art. 8 ECHR by the national authorities.

In a similar vein, in the case of Osman v. Denmark,[117] the Court acknowledged an infringement of Art. 8 in the case where the applicant was a national of Somalia. The girl lived in Denmark since 7 until 15 years of age and then she was sent by her parents, against her will, to a refugee camp in Kenya in order to take care of her grandmother. When she wanted to return after two years, the Danish authorities refused to allow her to reunite with her family. The Court observed that the reason for refusal was in accordance with the national law and was aimed at discouraging immigrants from sending their children to their countries of origin in order to receive education in accordance with their ethnic roots. Nevertheless, in that case the Court acknowledged that the girl had spent most of her life

[116] Judgement of the European Court of Human Rights of 21.12.2001 in the case Sen v. the Netherlands, complaint no. 31465/02.

[117] Judgement of the European Court of Human Rights of 14.06.2011 in the case Osman v. Denmark, complaint no. 38058/09.

in Denmark and in that case the interest of the child was more important than migration control.

An opposite stance was taken by the Court in the case I.A.A. and others v. the United Kingdom.[118] A claim of a breach of Art. 8 ECHR was raised by young Somalis, who wanted to join their mother living in the United Kingdom with her second husband. In this case, the Court ruled that priority should be given to migration control and that the applicants, being already adults or teenagers were brought up in their country of origin and then in Ethiopia and it was with those countries that they had cultural and language ties.

Further, in the case of Berisha v. Switzerland, the Court did not find an infringement of Art. 8 ECHR in the case of the refusal to issue residence permits to the applicants' children.[119] The applicants were nationals of Kosovo, whereas their children aged 17 and 19 lived in Kosovo for an extended period of time (where they were raised and went to school), with which they did not lose family ties, in the opinion of the ECtHR.

The scope of the guarantees of the protection against the culture of the country of origin, in spite of being reconstructed on the basis of the case-law of the ECtHR, finds its application also within the EU's system of protection primarily due to the adoption of the concept of the equality of the scope of protection of the rights guaranteed under the CFR and under the Convention. The Convention standards should find their application especially in the process of qualification for protection and returns of third-country nationals to their countries of origin in EU law.

[118] Decision of the European Court of Human Rights on the inadmissibility of the complaint of 8.03.2016 in the case I.A.A. and others v. the United Kingdom, complaint no. 25960/13.

[119] Judgement of the European Court of Human Rights of 30.07.2013 in the case Berisha v. Switzerland, complaint no. 948/12. In a similar way, the Court did not recognize a breach of Art. 8 ECHR in an interesting case of Chbihi Loudoudi and others v. Belgium. The applicants were nationals of Morocco, who wanted to adopt their niece on the grounds of an agreement *kafala* with the girl's parents, which was in accordance with the law of Islam. Both, the national authorities as well as the Court took a stance that such an adoption would not be in the best interest of the child and that the status of the child would be different in Belgium (where the child would have adoptive parents) and different in Morocco. See: Judgement of the European Court of Human Rights of 16.12.2014 in the case Chbihi Loudoudi and others v. Belgium, complaint no. 52265/10.

3.4 Conclusions

As it transpires from the legal material analysed in the present chapter, the cultural rights of foreign nationals are the rights of a specific minority group, the guarantees of which might be to a large extent defined by, universal in their character, provisions of the Charter of Fundamental Rights. Despite the fact that the Charter *expressis verbis* does not guarantee cultural rights but merely the freedom of the arts and sciences (Art. 13 CFR), a comprehensive analysis of the provisions of the Charter allows for the confirmation of the thesis of the existence of the mechanisms protecting the rights and freedoms of a cultural character in the EU's legal system. One should mention here the rights analysed above in the present chapter: the right to respect for private and family life (Art. 7 CFR), the right to marry and the right to found a family (Art. 9 CFR), the freedom of thought, conscience and religion (Art. 10 CFR). A specific basis for the realization of the rights of a cultural character is Art. 21 CFR prohibiting discrimination as well as other provisions of Title III of the Charter, such as the guarantee of the protection of the rights of the child (Art. 24 CFR), the rights of the elderly (Art. 25 CFR) and the rights of persons with disabilities (Art. 26 CFR). The subjects of protection of those rights constitute groups of special needs and thus they will participate in cultural life in a special way. For instance, equal chances are especially required in the case of having access to the services of a cultural character or performing work in the professions within the culture sector by persons with disabilities. Cultural entitlements might also be interpreted on the grounds of Art 14 CFR (the right to education) or Art 12 CFR guaranteeing the right of assembly and of association.

The provisions of the Charter of Fundamental Rights of the European Union, in accordance with its Preamble, confirm the rights transpiring from the ECHR. The case-law of the ECtHR on the guarantees of respect for private and family life, the right to family life, the freedom of expression or the freedom of religion, parallel to the provision of the CFR, allows for the reconstruction of concrete standards of protection with regard to the specific group, such as third-country nationals.

As it can be seen on the basis of the analysed case-law of the ECtHR, it is justified to adopt a thesis on the existence of the right to the protection against the culture of the country of origin. This right protects an individual against the elements of an oppressive social culture, whose manifestations might lead to a risk of inhuman treatment in the case of a return of a foreign national to the country of origin. This right finds its justification under Art. 18 of the Charter of Fundamental Rights, guaranteeing the right to asylum and the qualification directive, whose provisions will be the subject of analysis further in the present study.

With regard to the proposed objective of the present study, which entails an in-depth analysis and evaluation of legal instruments regarding the guarantees of the cultural rights of third-country nationals in EU law and the determination of their borders, it is also necessary to attempt to try defining these boundaries based on the legal analysis conducted in the present chapter. In determining the boundaries of the cultural rights of third-country nationals, it will be useful to refer to the concept of limitation clauses (restricting)[120] and derogation clauses.

In the structure of limitation clauses, there are three basic elements—the addressee of the limitation, the indication of the necessity of restricting the right or freedoms and the reasons for the restriction, which, as B. Liżewski observes, are also based on values beyond the legal framework.[121] A general limitation clause can be found in Art. 52(1) of the Charter of Fundamental Rights in accordance with which:

> Any limitation on the exercise of the rights and freedoms recognised by this Charter must be provided for by law and respect the essence of those rights and freedoms. Subject to the principle of proportionality, limitations may be made only if they are necessary and genuinely meet objectives of general interest recognised by the Union or the need to protect the rights and freedoms of others.

On the other hand, in the ECHR limitations are indicated with regard to specific freedoms, as for instance in the case of the freedom of religion under Art. 9 ECHR.

In the cases referred to above in the present chapter, the limitations of the rights and freedoms allowing for the full realization of one's cultural

[120] The limitation clause is understood as a structure contained in a legal provision, allowing for the limitation of the rights and freedoms of a person. See: B. Liżewski, *Klauzule generalne i ich funkcje w Europejskiej Konwencji Praw Człowieka*, "Annales Universitatis Mariae Curie-Skłodowska, Lublin—Polonia" 2016, vol. LXIII, issue 2, 196.

[121] Ibidem, 197.

identity resulted primarily from the provisions with regard to public safety,[122] the protection of morality[123] and the rights of the child.[124]

Undoubtedly, an interesting, albeit controversial,[125] formula allowing for the justification of the limitation of the freedom of religion is the concept of *living together*, adopted by the European Court of Human Rights in the case of S.A.S. The formula of *living together* was criticized in the doctrine, amongst others, for the promotion of the preferences of the majority and putting them above the right of an individual, for the strengthening of cultural prejudices, but also for the deprecating of the right to identity, where this identity is not accepted by the majority of society. However, as I. Trispiotis observes, the principle of *living together* has also a positive resonance, as it allows for joining some minimal social values into a larger value which is democracy itself.[126] It also contributes to a mutual respect for differences and solidarity. As Trispiotis emphasizes, *living together* provides a specific guarantee for the joining of cultural belonging with democratic citizenship.[127] This principle may provide a specific remedy in finding solutions to cultural conflicts, providing that the limitations of the rights and liberties applied for the purpose of its realization do not prove too radical for individuals to accept. The adoption of the concept of *living together* with regard to the broadly understood cultural rights of third-country nationals seems to be a valuable solution, in as much as it supports dialogue between divergent groups.[128] Nonetheless, a discussion on the subject of the limitation of fundamental rights from the perspective of the best interest of a democratic society also constitutes an impulse for the strengthening of active involvement on the side of representatives of minorities, including third-country nationals, as members of local communities.

[122] As, for example, in the case of El Morsli v. France, Senger v. Federal Republic of Germany.

[123] As, for example, in the case of Z.H. and R.H. v. Switzerland and in the case of Janis Khan v. the United Kingdom.

[124] As, for example, in the case of Osmanoglu and Kocabas v. Switzerland.

[125] I. Trispiotis, *Two Interpretations of "Living Together,"* 581.

[126] Ibidem, 582.

[127] Ibidem, 606.

[128] On the subject of the principle of *living together*, see also: Freedom of religion and living together in a democratic society, Parliamentary Assembly Council of Europe, 30 September 2015, text of the resolution available on the website: http://assembly.coe.int/nw/xml/XRef/Xref%2D%2DXML2HTML-en.asp?fileid=22199&lang=en. Accessed 30.12.2017.

CHAPTER 4

Cultural Rights of Third-Country Nationals in the Migration Process: Entry and Return

4.1 Introductory Remarks

The rights of a cultural character of third-country nationals should be realized, in fact, at each level of the migration process—starting with the moment of applying for a visa, through entry into the territory of the Union (and the related border controls), stay and integration, until the return to the country of origin—voluntary or forced.

This chapter will focus on the regulations of European Union (EU) law which concern the issues of entry into the territory of the Union and return of foreign nationals into the countries of origin. Due to the thematic division of the study, the present chapter will include an analysis of the provisions with regard to the procedure of family reunification, as the instrument in question directly concerns the admission of foreigners, whereas the procedure of family reunification results in the entry of a third-country national into the territory of the Member State.

In order to provide the widest characteristic of the issues regarding the implementation of the provisions of the Union's law, together with the practical dimension of their functioning, for the illustration purposes, the selected provisions of the Polish law concerning the realization of the procedure of entry and return will be presented and analysed.

A. M. Kosińska, *Cultural Rights of Third-Country Nationals in EU Law*,
https://doi.org/10.1007/978-3-030-30154-5_4

4.2 Cultural Rights of Third-Country Nationals in View of the Procedure of Entry into the Territory of the European Union

4.2.1 Guarantees of a Cultural Character in the Schengen Borders Code

The basic act of EU law providing for the procedures with regard to the entry into the territory of the Union and border control is Regulation 2016/399—Schengen Borders Code,[1] which replaced Regulation 562/2006.[2] In accordance with Art. 3 of the Schengen Borders Code, it is applicable to any person crossing the internal or external borders of Member States, including persons applying for international protection.

An especially sensitive issue, with regard to cultural diversity of migrants crossing the external borders of the Union, is the procedure of performing border checks.[3] In accordance with Art. 7 Regulation 2016/399, the border guards during the performance of their duties should act in full respect for human dignity,[4] without discriminating against any person on the grounds of "sex, racial or ethnic origin, religion or belief, disability, age or sexual orientation."[5]

[1] Regulation (EU) 2016/399 of the European Parliament and of the Council of 9 March 2016 on a Union Code on the rules governing the movement of persons across borders (Schengen Borders Code), OJ L 77, 23.3.2016, 1, further also as Regulation 2016/399 or Schengen Borders Code.

[2] Regulation (EC) No. 562/2006 of the European Parliament and of the Council of 15 March 2006 establishing a Community Code on the rules governing the movement of persons across borders (Schengen Borders Code), OJ L 105, 13.4.2006, 1.

[3] This problem was the concern, for example, in the Judgement of the European Court of Human Rights of 11.01.2005 in the case Suku Phull v. France, Complaint No. 35753/03.

[4] See Judgement of the Court of Justice of 17.01.2013 in the case Mohamad Zakaria, C 23/12, ECLI:EU:C:2013:24.

[5] Art. 7(2) Regulation 2016/399. See also *Rights at airports: border checks at five international airports in the European Union*, FRA 2015, 54. Report available on the website www.fra.europa.eu. Accessed 12.09.2017. Interesting conclusions in the context of the respect for the cultural identity of third-country nationals are also to be found in the FRA report on the border checks at the land borders, for example, the report highlights that inappropriate food is served to foreign nationals—Muslims directed to control at the so-called second line (p. 25). The report also includes the conclusions addressed at the border guard officers of the Member States, who should pay special attention to cultural differences during their communication with the travelling persons (p. 27). See Fundamental rights at land borders: findings from selected European Union border crossing points, FRA 2014, www.fra.europa.eu. Accessed 12.09.2017.

In accordance with Art. 8(3) Regulation 2016/399, third-country nationals are subject to thorough checks on entry and exit. Such detailed checks should be conducted in a place allowing for full respect of a foreign national's privacy—the Code, however, states that border checks should be carried out in a private area, if such facilities exist at the border check (border crossing point) and if a foreign national agrees to a border check in a private area.

One of the essential elements facilitating the realization of the right to cultural identity is a person's clothing. What might be problematic is a situation when a person undergoing a border check comes from a different cultural circle (e.g., a Sikh in a turban or a woman wearing the Islamic headscarf) in a situation when there is a lack of facilities ensuring respect for privacy.

It is worth adding at this point that there are different, more rigorous criteria for border control during air travel and they are regulated by Regulation 185/2010 laying down detailed measures for the implementation of the common basic standards on aviation security,[6] replaced by Commission Implementing Regulation (EU) 2015/1998 of 5 November 2015 laying down detailed measures for the implementation of the common basic standards on aviation security.[7]

In accordance with Art. 4.1.1.1. Regulation 185/2010, passengers were subjected to a security check and were obligated to remove their coats and jackets, as well as other items at the request of a security officer. The security check might also involve a manual check or the use of metal detection equipment. Moreover, the equipment for screening persons might also be used. In such a case, passengers might ask to have the screening of their body analysed by a security officer of the chosen sex, which seems to be especially significant in certain cultural circles, where the honour of women is especially protected. Passengers also had the right to refuse being subjected to the screening control and then the security resorted to the given alternative methods.[8] At present, the issues of passenger control have been analogically regulated under Art. 4.1.1.

[6] Commission Regulation (EU) No. 185/2010 of 4 March 2010 laying down detailed measures for the implementation of the common basic standards on aviation security, OJ L 55, 5.3.2010, 1, further also as Regulation 185/2010.

[7] Commission Implementing Regulation (EU) 2015/1998 of 5 November 2015 laying down detailed measures for the implementation of the common basic standards on aviation security, OJ L 299, 14.11.2015, 1.

[8] Art. 4.1.1.10 let. e, 4.1.1.10 sent. 3 Regulation 185/2010.

of the new regulation. In accordance with its Art. 11.2.3.1., the staff carrying out passenger control have to undergo specialist trainings, which include competences such as "interpersonal skills, in particular how to deal with cultural differences and with potentially disruptive passengers."

A few years ago, in Poland, there was a much-publicized case of a Sikh, Shaminder Puri, a national of the United Kingdom, who was subjected to a security check at the Warsaw airport. The border guards (BG) asked him to remove his turban, which Mr Puri perceived as a violation of his rights and brought a claim against the BG seeking protection of his personal interests.[9] The Court of the first instance admitted that Mr Puri's interests had indeed been infringed, but held that the infringement was within the law. The Court of Appeal dismissed the complaint and finally the case was brought before the Supreme Court, which accepted the cassation complaint for examination.[10] However, the complaint was rejected by a judgement of 17 September 2014.[11] The Court ruled, affirming the findings of the Regional Court, that "the removal of the turban, which serves a symbolic function, especially in public, in the Sikh religion is treated as an offence, since the Sikhs do not perceive the turban as merely a head covering but as a part of one's clothing, the wearing of which is a fundamental manifestation of the practising of the Sikh religion." The Supreme Court also referred to the reasoning of the Court of Appeal, which held that the removal of the turban, even in a private area, was a violation of the freedom of religion, even though the behaviour of the

[9] See K. Rusiłowicz, "Shaminder Puri a Straż Graniczna. Przeszukanie na lotnisku a prawa człowieka." *Program Spraw Precedensowych. Biuletyn Informacyjny*, issue 1–2(44–45 2011): 1, Bulletin available on the Helsinki Foundation for Human Rights: www.hfhr.pl. Accessed 12.09.2017; D. Ferenc-Kopeć, "The limitation of religious freedom in regard to national security—deliberations on Shaminder Puri v Border Guard case," in *Human Rights between War and Peace*, eds. M. Sitek, G. Dammacco, M. Wójcicka (Olsztyn, 2014), 127–144. See Judgement of the Court of Appeal in Warsaw of 12 February 2013, I ACa 499/12. See also A. Partyk, *Poddanie człowieka wbrew jego woli praktykom religijnym lub działaniom sprzecznym z nakazami wyznawanej przez niego religii w kontekście naruszenia swobody sumienia i wyznania*, LEX/el. 2014, Publication No. 214137.

[10] See http://www.hfhr.pl/en/supreme-court-dismissed-complaint-in-sikhs-case/. Accessed 12.07.2019.

[11] Judgement of the Supreme Court of 17.09.2014 in the case S.P. v. the State Treasury—Commander-in-Chief of the Border Guard for the protection of personal interests, I CSK 439/13.

border guard officers was not illegal.[12] The Supreme Court, justifying the dismissal of the cassation complaint, referred to both its previous jurisprudence and the case-law of the European Court of Human Rights (ECtHR), amongst others, in the cases of other Sikhs, for example, Phull or Mann Singh (cited in Chap. 3, in the subchapter on the freedom of religion). Thus, in the opinion of the Supreme Court, even an intervention of a public officer which violates personal interests (including the freedom of religion), but remains within the bounds of legality, is justified.

Respect for cultural differences during the crossing of the border is indirectly guaranteed under Art. 15(3) of the Polish act on foreigners.[13] It says:

> A foreigner wearing a head covering in accordance with the principles of his/her religion may attach to the application a photograph showing him/her in such a head covering, as long as the image of his/her face is fully visible. In such a case the application shall be accompanied by the foreigner's statement confirming that he/she belongs to a religious community.

Additionally, in accordance with the Preamble of Regulation 2016/399, "Member States should ensure that control procedures at external borders do not constitute a major barrier to trade and social and cultural interchange. To that end, they should deploy appropriate numbers of staff and resources."[14]

Moreover, Annex No. I to Regulation 2016/399 determines the so-called supporting documents for the verification of the fulfilment of entry conditions. In the case of journeys undertaken in order to participate in cultural events, the travellers may be obligated by the officers of the border guards to produce invitations, entry tickets or programmes of events in which they are planning to participate. In a similar vein, such documents may be required of persons travelling for religious purposes. Cultural exchange with third countries impacts the quality and character of cultural life in the Member States. Third-country nationals, whose rights are analysed in the present study, are not only addressees of culture

[12] As the Supreme Court emphasized in the reasoning of the judgement, "The European law provides for, with regard to the Member States, only the framework requirements of the security control, allowing the national legislators a wide margin of discretion with regard to the regulating of the procedure of security control."

[13] Act on foreigners of 12 December 2013, uniform text, Journal of Laws of 2018, item 2094, as amended, further also as act on foreigners.

[14] Para. 17 of the Preamble to Regulation 2016/399.

in the territory of the EU, but also its creators. The Schengen Borders Code includes provisions facilitating artistic and cultural exchange, as well as the participation of foreign nationals in cultural events in the roles of both artistic creators and participants of cultural events.

4.2.2 Visa Law and Cultural Entitlements of Third-Country Nationals

Also in an indirect way the partial guarantees of cultural rights may be interpreted out of the provisions of the Community Code on Visas.[15] This regulation establishes the procedures and conditions for issuing visas for the purpose of transit or residence (for up to three months within the period of six months) to third-country nationals.[16] The Community Code on Visas in its Art. 16 introduces the obligation to pay a visa fee, which, however, might be waived in the circumstances listed under that provision. As one of the categories of the entities entitled to be exempt from the obligation to pay the fee the legislators listed "school pupils, students, postgraduate students and accompanying teachers who undertake stays for the purpose of study or educational training."[17] Without doubt, such an exemption facilitates the realization of the right to education, which is defined in its part as a cultural right. In spite of the fact that the right to education is not a right of a creative character, it still allows an individual to learn about a broadly understood "cultural heritage," including the acquisition of the knowledge on culture.[18] Apart from that, the regulation introduces an exemption from the payment of a visa fee for academics who are travelling for the purpose of doing research (thus contributing to the

[15] Regulation (EC) No. 810/2009 of the European Parliament and of the Council of 13 July 2009 establishing a Community Code on Visas (Visa Code), OJ L 243, 15.9.2009, 1, further also as the Community Code on Visas, Regulation 810/2009.

[16] The list of countries the nationals of which must apply for a visa was included in the Council Regulation (EC) No. 539/2001 of 15 March 2001 listing the third countries whose nationals must be in possession of visas when crossing the external borders and those whose nationals are exempt from that requirement, OJ L 81, 21.3.2001, 1. Now in force is Regulation (EU) 2018/1806 of the European Parliament and of the Council of 14 November 2018 listing the third countries whose nationals must be in possession of visas when crossing the external borders and those whose nationals are exempt from that requirement, OJ L 303, 28.11.2018, 39.

[17] Art. 16(4)(b) Regulation 810/2009.

[18] A.M. Kosińska, *Kulturalne prawa człowieka. Regulacje normatywne i ich realizacja* (Lublin, 2014), 220.

strengthening of the guarantees of the right to academic research and academic freedom).[19] The third group of foreign nationals which should be mentioned includes "participants aged 25 years or less in seminars, conferences, sports, cultural or educational events, organised by non-profit organisations"—thus, the Community Code on Visas introduces facilitations for the youth travelling from third countries for the purpose of participating in the events aimed at cultural exchange and cooperation.

In accordance with Art. 24 of Regulation 810/2009, a uniform visa may be issued for one, two or more entries for a period not exceeding five years. Multiple-entry visas might be issued with a period of validity between six months and five years, provided that the applicant proves the need to travel frequently and proves his or her integrity and reliability. Art. 24(2)(a) includes an open catalogue of cases justifying the issuing of a multiple-entry visa, including persons travelling for the purpose of educational training, seminars and conferences. What is significant is that this is not a closed catalogue and thus some other justified reasons, dictated by the needs of the conducted cultural activities, might also be taken into account by the authorities of the Member States.

The standards relating to the procedural requirements for the reception of visa applications are already listed in paragraph 6 of the Preamble to the Community Code on Visas. Accordingly, the reception of applications is carried out with due respect for human dignity, whereas the processing of applications is conducted in a professional and respectful manner. The determination of such standards is especially important in situations when the employees of the diplomatic missions of EU Member States have to deal with the applicants coming from the cultural centres which represent a different code of behaviour than in European culture. This was the

[19] This exemption was introduced with regard to the Recommendation of the European Parliament and of the Council of 28 September 2005 to facilitate the issue by the Member States of uniform short-stay visas for researchers from third countries travelling within the Community for the purpose of carrying out scientific research, OJ L 289, 3.11.2005, 23. As is emphasized in the Preamble of the Recommendation, the globalization of the economy requires an increase in the mobility of researchers and "For short stays, Member States should undertake to consider researchers from third countries, subject to a visa requirement under Regulation (EC) no. 539/2001 (5), as persons acting in good faith and extend to them the advantages provided for in the *acquis communautaire* for the purpose of the procedures for issuing short-stay visas" (para. 6 of the Preamble). In paragraph 3 of the document, the Member States are encouraged to promote the international mobility of researchers and to take into account the length of the research programmes in which the researchers are participating in the process of determining the period of validity of a visa.

situation in the case of El Morsli described above.[20] The clarification of the requirements concerning the conduct of the personnel in the performance of their duties regarding foreign nationals applying for visas is to be found under Art. 39 of the Community Code on Visas. In accordance with the Article, the applicants should be received courteously by consular staff, with due respect for human dignity and the measures applied should be proportionate to the objectives pursued. Additionally, all discrimination against persons on grounds of, amongst others, sex, but also racial or ethnic origin, or religion is prohibited. Such provisions make it possible for foreign nationals to have their procedural matters dealt with due respect to their cultural identity.

The existing case-law of the Court of Justice of the European Union (CJEU) with regard to the Schengen Borders Code and the Community Code on Visas has not concerned cultural rights in a direct way. However, it is worth mentioning here a recent judgement of the Court in the case of X and X v. État belge of 7 March 2017.[21] The national proceedings concerned a refusal to issue a humanitarian visa, which a married Syrian couple from Aleppo applied for. The Syrians submitted applications for visas with limited territorial validity at the Belgian Embassy in Beirut, before returning from Lebanon to Syria.

The applicants claimed that in their country of origin the situation is catastrophic and that they were experiencing persecutions on political and cultural grounds. This claim seems to be especially significant, as it touches upon the problem of guaranteeing protection against the culture of the country of origin. The Syrians claimed that on account of their religion—they belonged to the Orthodox Church—they were exposed to real persecutions in Syria.

The Belgian authorities refused to issue a visa to the Syrians, whereas the Office for Foreigners on examining the case held that "authorising the issue of an entry visa to the applicants in the main proceedings in order for them to be able to lodge an application for asylum in Belgium would amount to allowing such an application to be submitted to a diplomatic post,"[22] which was impossible in the light of the law. The applicants

[20] Decision of the European Court of Human Rights on the inadmissibility of the complaint of 4.03.2008 in the case El Morsli v. France, Complaint No. 15585/06.

[21] Judgement of the Court of Justice of 21.04.2017 in the case X and X v. État belge, C 638/16 PPU, ECLI:EU:C:2017:173, further as judgement in the case C 638/16.

[22] Para. 21, Judgement of the Court in the case C 638/16.

claimed that an infringement under Art. 18 of the Charter of Fundamental Rights occurred and the case was eventually brought before the CJEU. In the above case, the Court examined the possibility of applying Art. 25 of the Community Code on Visas, in accordance with which a visa with limited territorial validity might be issued, amongst others, in a situation "when the Member State concerned considers it necessary on humanitarian grounds, for reasons of national interest or because of international obligation." The applicants held that the concept of the reasons of national interest includes fundamental rights as guaranteed by the Charter of Fundamental Rights (CFR), especially those under Art. 4 and Art. 33 of the Geneva Convention. The Court of Justice held that the applications for the issuing of humanitarian visas are not covered by the scope of the application of the Community Code on Visas and the Belgian authorities should not examine such applications in light of Art. 25 of Regulation 810/2009. The Court supported the arguments of the Commission and of the Belgian government, which claimed that until then EU law had not adopted a legal act that would regulate the issuing of visas for humanitarian reasons. Thus, the Court ruled that the applications submitted by foreign nationals are not covered by the Union's law, but by the national law.

The said ruling has spurred a vivid discussion over the possibility of granting international protection to foreign nationals remaining outside the EU. What is interesting, the Advocate General in his opinion of 7 February 2017 stated that

> a Member State to which a third country national has applied for a visa with limited territorial validity on humanitarian grounds is required to issue such a visa if substantial grounds have been shown for believing that a refusal to issue such a document would have the direct consequence of exposing that national to treatment prohibited by Article 4 of the Charter, by depriving that person of a legal remedy to exercise his right to seek international protection in that Member State.[23]

[23] Opinion of Advocate General Mengozzi delivered on 7 February 2017 in the case X and X v. État belge, C 638/16 PPU, ECLI:EU:C:2017:93, further as Opinion of Advocate General in the case 638/16 PPU. See also E. Brouwer, AG Mengozzi's conclusion in X and X v. Belgium on the positive obligation to issue humanitarian visas. A legitimate plea to ensure safe journeys for refugees. *CEPS Policy Insights*, No. 9 (2017). https://www.ceps.eu/system/files/PI2017–09_EB_VisaCode.pdf; D. Moreno-Lax, *Asylum Visas as an Obligation under EU Law: Case PPU C-638/16 X, X v État belge (Part II)*, text available on the website http://eumigrationlawblog.eu/asylum-visas-as-an-obligation-under-eu-law%2D%2Dcase-ppu-c-63816-x-x-v-etat-belge-part-ii/. Accessed 12.09.2017.

What is more, according to Advocate General Mengozzi, in the process of examining applications and issuing visas the Member States are obligated to observe the Charter of Fundamental Rights. In his opinion, the Advocate General also referred to the question of persecutions on the grounds of religion, which might have been experienced by the applicants with regard to their beliefs. The reality of the prosecutions resulted from, amongst others, the fact of the applicants adhering to the Orthodox Church and baptizing children in the Orthodox ritual. In accordance with the reports prepared by international organizations and NGOs, Christians are exposed to real violence from armed groups in Syria.[24] The situation is similar in neighbouring countries, such as Lebanon or Jordan.[25] According to the Advocate General, the fact that the applicants belong to a religious minority is covered by the scope of the concept of humanitarian grounds under Art. 25 of the Community Code on Visas.[26]

The case X and X v. Belgium is an example of the proceedings in which formalism and legalism turned out to be non-rebuttable arguments in confrontation with the arguments relating to the priority of the protection of fundamental rights in the situation of a humanitarian disaster. In accordance with the judgement in the case of the Court of Justice (CJ) the principle *dura lex sed lex* applies in absolute terms, whereas the right to protection against the culture of the country of origin is not covered by guarantees in this case, even if it is an oppressive culture.

On the one hand, the refusal of a visa of a humanitarian character exposes families to persecution and inhuman treatment. On the other hand, such practice leads to a situation when such persons do not have the possibility of exercising their right to cultural identity. Obviously, it would be justifiable to ask a question about the possibilities of absorbing foreign nationals within the territory of the European Union and the answer would also be obvious, that is, that such possibilities are very limited. The Union is not, in principle, obligated to the protection of cultural rights, including the right to identity and the right to the protection against the invasive culture of the country of origin, outside its territory. However, one cannot avoid doubts whether the Union should possibly take some action in a situation when a practised culture, which is close to European culture or shares some of its elements with European culture, exposes

[24] See footnote 63 to the Opinion of Advocate General in the case 638/16 PPU.
[25] Para. 154 of the Opinion of Advocate General in the case 638/16 PPU.
[26] Para. 130 of the Opinion of Advocate General in the case 638/16 PPU.

persons to a risk of inhuman treatment. Such action might make it possible to avoid persecutions and apply for international protection, especially in a situation when the persecuted persons manage to get to the representative of the Member States. In the existing regulatory framework, there is no law on the responsibility for third-country nationals remaining in their country of origin and experiencing persecutions, also on the grounds of culture. However, from the moral perspective (especially taking into account the values on which the Union is based), such responsibility exists.

The said ruling should provide a starting point for further discussion on the effectiveness of the Union's actions in the area of civil protection and humanitarian aid, including the strengthening of the Union's presence in the third countries affected by military hostilities (especially those where there are camps for refugees and for persons internally relocated) and the creation, within the framework of this aid, of the possibility for the realization of cultural rights through access to education and the possibility of free expression of one's cultural identity. Examples of such actions carried out by the Union include the projects run by the Directorate of the European Commission—European Civil Protection and Humanitarian Aid Operations,[27] covering also educational activities.[28]

4.2.3 *Policy on Family Reunification*

A part of migration policy relating to the entry into the territory of the EU is the so-called policy on family reunification, which has been fuelling controversies for many years.[29] Initially, within the Community activities in

[27] http://ec.europa.eu/echo/what-we-do/humanitarian-aid/refugees-and-internally-displaced-persons_en. Accessed 12.09.2017.

[28] http://ec.europa.eu/echo/what/humanitarian-aid/education-emergencies_en. Accessed 12.09.2017.

[29] In accordance with the definition from the EMN Dictionary, family reunification denotes "the establishment of a family relationship which is either:

(a) the entry into and residence in a Member State, in accordance with Council Directive 2003/86/EC, by family members of a third-country national residing lawfully in that Member State ('sponsor') in order to preserve the family unit, whether the family relationship arose before or after the entry of the sponsor; or
(b) between an EU national and third-country national established outside the EU who then subsequently enters the EU." https://ec.europa.eu/home-affairs/what-we%2D%2Ddo/networks/european_migration_network/glossary/f_en. Accessed 12.09.2017.

support of the migrations of seasonal workers, the authorities, for example, of the Federal German Republic, were against family reunification.[30] Also, at present, the subject of family reunification is giving rise to numerous discussions, as it often happens that one foreign national's entry in the territory of the EU leads to the realization of his or her right to reunification with their numerous family. Undoubtedly, what seems to be one the most important elements in the discussion on the matter of the realizations of the rights and the functioning of integrative cultural obligations is the possibility of introducing integration tests by the Member States for the members of the reunited families, which will be discussed further in the study.

In EU law, the policy of family reunification was regulated by Directive 2003/86 on the right to family reunification.[31] In accordance with para. 4 of the Preamble, family reunification is a necessary instrument of making family life possible—thus, the right to family reunification serves the realization of the guarantees under Art. 7 CFR (and Art. 8 of the European Convention on Human Rights [ECHR][32]). What is significant is that in the Preamble it is emphasized that family reunification "helps to create sociocultural stability facilitating the integration of third country nationals

[30] As M. Szuniewicz observes, in the 1980s, most European countries had already introduced the provisions facilitating family reunification, M. Szuniewicz, *Łączenie rodzin cudzoziemców. Studium prawnomiędzynarodowe* (Gdynia, 2014), 234; S. Castles, M.J. Miller, *Migracje we współczesnym świecie* (Warszawa, 2011), 132. On the subject of the national policies on family reunification, see M.A.K. Klassen, *The right to family unification: between migration control and human rights*, 303–335. Doctoral thesis, Leiden University 2015, text available on the website http://hdl.handle.net/1887/36049. Accessed 12.07.2019.

[31] Council Directive 2003/86/EC of 22 September 2003 on the right to family reunification, OJ L 251 of 3.10.2003, 12, further also as Directive 2003/86, directive on the right to family reunification. See *EMN Synthesis Report for the EMN Focussed Study 2016 Family Reunification of Third-Country Nationals in the EU plus Norway: National Practices*. Report available on the website https://ec.europa.eu/homeaffairs/sites/homeaffairs/files/00_family_reunification_synthesis_report_final_en_print_ready_0.pdf. Accessed 12.09.2017. On the subject of the policy of family reunification, see also K. Eisele, *The External Dimension of the EU's Migration Policy. Different Legal Positions of Third Country Nationals in the EU: A Comparative Perspective* (Brill/Nijhoff, 2014), 283 et seq.

[32] On the subject of the case-law of the ECtHR, see M. Rohan, "Refugee Family Reunification Rights: A Basis in the European Court of Human Rights' Family Reunification Jurisprudence," *Chicago Journal of International Law*, vol. 15, no. 1 (2014): 359–361. Article available on the website http://chicagounbound.uchicago.edu/cjil/vol15/iss1/15. Accessed 12.09.2017.

in the Member State" and hence it has a direct impact on the character and cultural image of the Member States.[33]

The Union's policy on family reunification highlights the issue of integrative cultural responsibilities. The very directive in several places refers to the necessity of integrating the arriving members of families with the culture of the host country,[34] which, of course, is a condition for harmonious cultural coexistence. Generally, it seems that at present, despite some vivid discussions on the subject of the threats to European culture, very little space is devoted to the *stricte* integrative obligations of a cultural character—hardly any norms impose such cultural responsibilities on third-country nationals. In accordance with Art. 7(2) Directive 2003/86, "Member States may require third country nationals to comply with integration measures, in accordance with national law." This provision allows the Member States to impose a direct integrative obligation of a cultural character on foreign nationals. In essence, it refers to cultural integration, which is connected with learning about the culture and customs of the host country, followed by demonstrating respect for them. What is more, this provision facilitates verification of the realization of cultural obligation, as part of a test carried out by the Member States. As it transpires from the report by the European Migration Network (EMN) on the national practices with regard to family reunification,[35] most European countries do not impose integration measures on foreign nationals. Nevertheless, in countries such as Luxemburg, Norway, Finland or Ireland there is an ongoing discussion on introducing them. In the cases when the Member States do require submitting to the integration measures before entry into their territory, the measures include most often language tests at level A1 (in accordance with the report, such requirements are imposed by Austria, Germany and the Netherlands) and integrative tests introduced by the Netherlands. Obviously, national law provides for the

[33] Moreover, in para. 15 of the Preamble, it is emphasized that "(15) the integration of family members should be promoted. For that purpose, they should be granted a status independent of that of the sponsor, in particular in cases of breakup of marriages and partnerships, and access to education, employment and vocational training on the same terms as the person with whom they are reunited, under the relevant conditions."

[34] See also M. Szuniewicz, *Łączenie rodzin cudzoziemców*, 216–221.

[35] *EMN Synthesis Report for the EMN Focussed Study 2016 Family Reunification of Third-Country Nationals in the EU plus Norway: National Report*, European Migration Network, 17.04.2017, 26. Report available on the website http://emn.ie/cat_publication_detail.jsp?clog=1&itemID=3017&t=6. Accessed 12.07.2019.

possibility of exemption from the application of all the said forms of integration measures, for example, with regard to the members of families of the persons who received refugee status or subsidiary protection. The costs of the materials for the preparation for the integrative courses, as well as the course fees, must be covered by migrants themselves. More so, according to the report, the Netherlands and Austria impose on foreign nationals the obligation of passing a language examination on arrival (at level A2 or B2) whereas in other countries (e.g., in the United Kingdom) foreign nationals must pass an integration test. In Belgium and Germany, integration courses focus on issues such as the history of the host country and social values. Additionally, in Belgium and the Netherlands, foreign nationals are obligated to sign the so-called integration declaration.[36]

The Family Reunification Directive on the right to family reunification lists under Art. 4 the categories of family members who may apply for reunification. Difficult situations which are actually based in cultural differences occur when a foreign national is in a polygamous marriage. In such a case, European law allows for the reunification with only one of the spouses (Art. 4[5] Directive 2003/86), whereas further spouses are refused entry. Apart from that, the directive allows the Member States to set the minimal age requirement for the sponsor and his or her spouse—the aim of such a regulation is to better integrate foreign nationals and prevent forced marriages (Art. 4[5] Directive 2003/86).

In accordance with Art. 4(1)(d)(3) Directive 2003/86, for determining which members of the family are authorized to reunite with the sponsor, if a child is over 12 years of age and arrives independently from the rest of his

[36] EMN Synthesis Report for the EMN Focussed Study 2016 Family Reunification of Third-Country Nationals in the EU plus Norway, p. 27. See also K. Groenendijk, "Pre-departure Integration Strategies in the European Union: Integration or Immigration Policy?" *European Journal of Migration and Law*, vol. 13, issue 1 (2011): 1–30. The pre-integration tests were introduced in the Netherlands in 2006, while in Germany in 2007 (here, mostly as an instrument counteracting "forced marriages." In Germany the test has the form of a language exam and no knowledge on the functioning of the German society is required). As the author observes, language tests have been used in migration policy for a long time—suffice it to mention the "Natal diction test" used in South Africa since 1897 (dictation in the European language consisting of 50 words) or the "White Australia" test in Australia (ibidem, 4). At present, the Member States adopt various models of the tests—thus, for example, in France the language test passed before arrival is connected with the integration contract signed on arrival (ibidem, 10). What is important, however, is that most migrants arriving in France come from the French-speaking countries (Algeria, Morocco, Tunis, Mali and Senegal; ibidem, 16).

or her family, the Member State may verify whether the child meets the condition for integration provided for by the existing national law. Such activities should serve, on the one hand, the purpose of providing effective cultural integration in the Member State. On the other hand, if the child has strong ties with the culture of the country of his or her origin, the said activities should prevent the child's outrooting or his or her forced cultural unification, which might disturb the child's right to identity.[37]

The criteria for examining the applications for family reunification have been laid down in Art. 17 Directive 2003/86. In accordance with the provision, the Member States are obligated to take "due account" of the solidity of the person's family relationships, the duration of his or her residence in the Member State, as well as the existence of cultural and social ties with his or her country of origin. Such examination is especially important in the proceedings which end up with the rejection of the application or with the issuing of the decision to return. The regulation under Art. 17 of the directive is aimed at the protection of the foreign national's interests, especially in the area of cultural identity and the assessment of the possibility of returning the foreign national to his or her country of origin on the basis of cultural ties with the third country.

4.2.4 *Case-Law on Family Reunification*

The issues of family reunification in the context of the existence of certain cultural obligations have been present in the line of jurisprudence of the Court of Justice of the European Union.

The first ruling of the Court of Justice concerning the directive was the judgement of 27 June 2006 in the case of the European Parliament v. the Council of the European Union.[38] The Parliament requested the

[37] The ECtHR ruled in such cases—see, to that effect, Judgement of the European Court of Human Rights of 21.12.2001 in the case Sen v. the Netherlands, Complaint No. 31465/96, further also as judgement in the case Sen; Judgement of the European Court of Human Rights of 1.12.2005 in the case Tuquabo-Tekle and others v. the Netherlands, Complaint No. 60665/00; Judgement of the European Court of Human Rights of 30.07.2013 in the case Berisha v. Switzerland, Complaint No. 948/12. See A. Szklanna, *Ochrona prawna cudzoziemca w świetle orzecznictwa europejskiego trybunału praw człowieka* (Warszawa, 2010), 261.

[38] Judgement of the Court of Justice of 27.06.2006 in the case the European Parliament v. the Council of the European Union, C 540/03, ECLI:EU:C:2006:429, further as judgement in the case C 540/03.

annulment of Art. 4(1) Directive 2003/86 in the scope where it provided for the reunification of children aged over 12 years with the sponsor and Art. 4(6)[39] and Art. 8.[40] All the above Articles directly concern the process for the realization of the effective integration of foreign nationals. The European Parliament justified its complaint with the claim that the contested provisions infringe fundamental rights, especially the right to family life, guaranteed by the European Convention on Human Rights and the Charter of Fundamental Rights.[41] Moreover, in the opinion of the Parliament, the directive infringed the prohibition of discrimination on the grounds of age, guaranteed under Art. 21 CFR. Justifying the complaint, the Court referred broadly to the guarantees of human rights provided for in public international law.[42]

The Council of the EU in its stance emphasized that the right to family reunification does not equate with the right to family life, whereas the aim of Art. 4 Directive 2003/86 is to effectively integrate minor migrants. This aim may be achieved by encouraging the families of foreign nationals

[39] In accordance with the said Article, "By way of derogation, Member States may request that the applications concerning family reunification of minor children have to be submitted before the age of 15, as provided for by its existing legislation on the date of the implementation of this directive. If the application is submitted after the age of 15, the Member States which decide to apply this derogation shall authorise the entry and residence of such children on grounds other than family reunification."

[40] In accordance with the said Article, "Member States may require the sponsor to have stayed lawfully in their territory for a period not exceeding two years, before having his/her family members join him/her."

[41] Para. 31–32 of the judgement in the case 540/03.

[42] Justifying the complaint, the Court referred to the acts of international law. It cited "Article 24 of the International Covenant on Civil and Political Rights, adopted on 19 December 1966, which entered into force on 23 March 1976; the Convention on the Rights of the Child, adopted on 20 November 1989, which entered into force on 2 September 1990; the International Convention on the Protection of the Rights of All Migrant Workers and Members of their Families, adopted on 18 December 1990, which entered into force on 1 July 2003; and the Declaration of the Rights of the Child proclaimed by the General Assembly of the United Nations Organisation on 20 November 1959 (Resolution 1386(XIV)). The Parliament draws attention in addition to Recommendation no. R (94) 14 of the Committee of Ministers of the Council of Europe to Member States of 22 November 1994 on coherent and integrated family policies and Recommendation no. R (99) 23 of the Committee of Ministers to Member States of 15 December 1999 on family reunion for refugees and other persons in need of international protection. The Parliament invokes, finally, constitutions of several Member States of the European Union," para. 33 of the judgement in the case 540/03.

to bring children who are in the developmental age to the host Member States, where they have the greatest possibilities of social integration.[43]

Justifying the ruling, the Court referred to the case-law of the ECtHR, in accordance with which even if the ECHR "does not guarantee as a fundamental right the right of an alien to enter or to reside in a particular country, the removal of a person from a country where close members of his family are living may amount to an infringement of the right to respect for family life."[44]

The Court also extensively referred to the argumentation of the ECtHR in the case of Sen.[45] Further, the Court also referred to the Convention on the Rights of the Child[46] and Art. 24(2) CFR provided for taking into account the best interest of the child. However, the Court decided that those acts "do not create for the members of a family an individual right to be allowed to enter the territory of a State,"[47] whereas the contested fragment of Art. 4 cannot be regarded as being counter to the right to respect for family life.[48] With regard to the claim of discrimination on grounds of age, the CJEU supported the stance of the Council of the European Union in that the EU legislator rightly assumed that children aged over 12 years might not easily fulfil the aims of integration, whereas the aim of the integration process is to provide that all children should acquire a language competence facilitating their further education.[49]

In the proceedings under discussion, the Court also did not find incompatibilities in the other contested articles and eventually dismissed the complaint. In the doctrine, it is emphasized that this ruling allowed for the establishing of "elegant half-measures" in the area of protection of fundamental rights and at the same time allowed the Member States to preserve divergent integration policies.[50]

An interesting stance regarding the process of integration was presented by the Advocate General in her opinion on the case under

[43] Para. 47–48 of the judgement in the case 540/03.

[44] Para. 53 of the judgement in the case 540/03.

[45] Para. 54–56 of the judgement in the case 540/03. See also judgement in the case Sen.

[46] Convention on the Rights of the Child, adopted by General Assembly resolution 44/25 of 20 November 1989, Journal of Laws of 1991, no. 120, item 526.

[47] Para. 59 of the judgement in the case 540/03.

[48] Para. 62 of the judgement in the case 540/03.

[49] Para. 67–68 of the judgement in the case 540/03.

[50] C. Costello, *The Human Rights of Migrants and Refugees in European Law* (Oxford, 2016), 148.

discussion. In the opinion of J. Kokott, the stance of the Parliament that the concept of integration conditions does not leave a margin for taking into account the interest of the family is erroneous. In the opinion of the Advocate General:

> Such an integration test measures the extent to which an immigrant is, or is capable of being, integrated in the host State; it translates both the host State's interest in ensuring that immigrants are integrated into society and the individual immigrant's interest in not living in isolation. The family can be a relevant factor in both regards, particularly when a considerable number of well-integrated family members are already living in the host State.[51]

The Advocate General assumed that Art. 4 Directive 2003/86 can be interpreted in accordance with human rights.

The interpretation of the provision on family reunification of a cultural character under Art. 4(5) Directive 2003/86 was conducted by the Court of Justice in its judgement in the case of Marjan Noorzia v. Bundesministerin für Inneres.[52] In this case the Court examined the compatibility of the provision of Austrian law with the law of the Union. The Austrian provisions in question required that spouses in the procedure of family reunification should be over 21 years of age in order to be eligible for family reunification. On interpreting Art. 4(5) Directive 2003/86, the Court emphasized that the aim of the regulation is, on the one hand, to guarantee that a given person is of sufficient maturity to refuse a forced or arranged marriage. The second argument in support of this solution is that it is aimed at ensuring that a foreign national is mature enough to take a decision on the choice of the country of residence and undertake the process of integration.[53]

The connection between Art. 4(5) Directive 2003/86 with the protection of fundamental rights and most importantly with the protection of women's rights was emphasized in turn by the Advocate General, who pointed out that forced marriages are a hidden practice in Europe.[54]

[51] Opinion of Advocate General J. Kokott delivered on 8 September 2005 in the case the European Parliament v. the Council of the European Union, C 540/03, ECLI:EU:C:2005:517.

[52] Judgement of the Court of Justice of 17.07.2014 in the case Marjan Noorzia v. Bundesministerin für Inneres, 338/13, ECLI:EU:C:2014:2092, further as judgement in the case C 338/13.

[53] Para. 15 of the judgement in the case 338/13.

[54] Opinion of Advocate General Mengozzi delivered on 30 April 2014 in the case Marjan Noorzia v. Bundesministerin für Inneres, C 338/13, ECLI:EU:C:2014:288.

Nevertheless, the Advocate General pointed out that a prolonged separation in marriage (due to the fact that they did not reach the age provided for in the EU law) might have an adverse effect on the process of integration. Moreover, in the opinion of the Advocate General, the assessment of the integrative capabilities of the spouse with regard to age should in each case be carried out on the basis of an individual analysis,[55] and thus the provisions of the Austrian law are incompatible with Art. 4(5) Directive 2003/86. Eventually, the Court ruled that the provisions of the Austrian law are not incompatible with the provisions of the directive on family reunification.

Especially important for consideration in the present study is the interpretation of Art. 7 Directive 2003/86 concerning family reunification in the cases of Bibi Mohammad Imran v. Minister van Buitenlandse Zaken[56] and Minister van Buitenlandse Zaken v. K and A.[57]

The case of Bibi Mohammad Imran concerned a national of India, who wanted to enter into the territory of the Netherlands in order to join her husband and eight children. The Dutch authorities refused to give permission to her entry because she had not passed the integration examination, required by national law. In referring a question for a preliminary ruling, the national court wanted to clarify whether the obligation of taking integration examinations prior to entry does not constitute too restrictive a measure in the light of Art. 7 Directive 2003/86.[58] Finally, the proceedings were discontinued since the Dutch authorities issued Mrs Imran the permission to enter into the Dutch territory.

The second of the above cases concerned two foreign nationals who wanted to enter into the territory of the Netherlands in order to join their husbands. Mrs K was a national of Azerbaijan and applied for the permission to enter at the embassy in Ankara, where she produced a medical certificate to the effect that she could not take the integration examination outside the territory of the Netherlands. Mrs A, in turn, was a national of Nigeria, who, while applying for the permission to enter at the embassy in

[55] Para. 50 of the opinion of the Advocate General in the case C 338/13.

[56] Decision of the Court of Justice of 10.06.2011 in the case Bibi Mohammad Imran v. Minister van Buitenlandse Zaken, C-155/11 PPU, ECLI:EU:C:2011:387.

[57] I wrote about those cases in the article "Problematyka integracji migrantów z kulturą kraju przyjmującego w świetle aktualnego orzecznictwa Trybunału Sprawiedliwości Unii Europejskiej," in *Kulturalny wymiar integracji europejskiej. Kazus Ukrainy*, ed. E. Szczot, (Lublin, 2018).

[58] See also K. Groenendijk, *Pre-departure Integration Strategies*, 6.

Abuja, also produced a certificate to the effect that she was incapable of taking the integration examination on account of her mental problems.[59]

Since both foreign nationals were refused entry into the territory of the Netherlands, the case was brought before the national courts. In the proceedings there appeared doubts concerning the legality of the solution adopted in Dutch law, which rendered it possible to refuse entry and impeded family reunification merely on the grounds that a foreign national's spouse has not passed the integration test prior to entry. Therefore, the national courts referred a question for a preliminary ruling to the CJEU asking for the interpretation of Art. 7(2) Directive 2003/86 and an examination of the compatibility of the measures adopted in national law with this Article.

It is also worth providing a brief characteristic of the integration measures adopted in the Dutch system on the basis of Art. 7(2) Directive 2003/86. The so-called basic civil integration examination is carried out in an automatic way and this examination tests the knowledge of Dutch language and society. The language test is placed at level A1 and includes reading comprehension, listening and speaking tasks. At the exam, a foreign national also has to demonstrate basic knowledge of the history and geography of the Netherlands, the rights and obligations of its inhabitants and social rules.[60] The cost of the examination fee is €350, whereas the

[59] Judgement of the Court of Justice of 9.07.2015 in the case Minister van Buitenlandse Zaken v. K and A, C 153/14, ECLI:EU:C:2015:453, further as judgement in the case C 153/14. National law provided for the possibility of exemption from the obligation of taking the examination in a situation when a person would not be able to take it due to a mental or physical disability. See para. 19 of the judgement in the case C 153/14.

[60] In accordance with para. 26 of the judgement in the case C 153/14: "The spoken Dutch test consists of the following components: repeating sentences, answering short questions, giving opposites and retelling a short story twice. The required language level is level A1 of the Common European Framework of Reference for Languages. The part of the examination on knowledge of Netherlands society consists of questions concerning the film *To the Netherlands*, which the family member must view at home. The questions which may be asked concern, in particular, whether men and women have the same rights, where the Netherlands Government is located, whether there is a separation of Church and State in the Kingdom of the Netherlands, which country occupied the Netherlands during the Second World War, whether health insurance is compulsory and the age up to which education is compulsory. All the questions and answers can be studied at home with the help of a self-study pack. That pack is available in 18 languages and contains, inter alia, DVDs, a photograph album, an exercise book, audio CDs, a self-study textbook and practice papers. Since March 2011, the pack also contains a literacy module so that the reading comprehension test can be prepared for. That test assesses whether the family member is able to read Dutch at A1 level of the Common European Framework of Reference for Languages."

cost of the study materials (the self-study pack) is €110. Persons seeking entry into the territory of the Netherlands take their examination at the embassy or at the consulate general.

In interpreting Art. 7(2) Directive 2003/86, the Court of Justice emphasized that "the acquisition of knowledge of the language and society of the host Member State greatly facilitates communication between third country nationals and nationals of the Member State concerned and, moreover, encourages interaction and the development of social relations between them," which, in effect, should be useful for establishing ties between a foreign national and the receiving country.[61] However, in the opinion of the Court, integration measures should serve the facilitation of integration and not lead to a situation in which family reunification becomes impossible.

The Court also expressed its critical opinion on the issue of the fee for the integration examination, which must be covered entirely by the foreign national and must be repeated on each subsequent taking of the examination. Thus, in the opinion of the Court, the functioning of integration measures is, in principle, appropriate, but they must be regulated in such a way so as not to impede family reunification and not to impose an excessive financial burden on the foreign national.

The introduction of the obligation of taking integration tests by foreign nationals, which, in fact, is tantamount to imposing an obligation of a cultural character in the form of the necessity to acquire knowledge about the language and culture of the receiving country, should be evaluated as positive, in its essence. Some doubts might concern, however, the introduction of taking obligatory tests before arriving in the territory of the Member State, with whose culture a foreign national is to be integrated. In the doctrine, it is emphasized that such understanding of integration brings with itself a risk of exemption and discrimination.[62] What is more, the solution

[61] See para. 53 and 54 of the judgement in the case C 153/14.

[62] C. Costello, *The Human Rights of Migrants and Refugees in European Law*, 162. Moreover, some Member States exempt from integration requirements representatives of countries such as Canada, the United States, Japan or South Korea, ibidem, 6. In its report, the Human Rights Watch emphasized that integration tests introduced in the Netherlands and the accompanying fees might lead to an infringement of the right to protection of family life, see *The Netherlands: Discrimination in the Name of Integration Migrants' Rights under the Integration Abroad Act*, Human Rights Watch, 13 May 2008. Report available on the website https://www.hrw.org/report/2008/05/13/netherlands-discrimination%2D%2Dname-integration/migrants-rights-under-integration. Accessed 31.12.2017.

in which migrants are required to integrate with the Member State without prior stay in that country is increasingly deemed as irrational.[63] In order to strengthen European cultural identity, it would be justifiable to introduce at the level of the Union regulations delineating the requirements of the mandatory integration tests for foreign nationals who arrive into the territory of the Union with the intention of permanent settlement. However, it would be advisable to run such a test after a pre-determined period of time has elapsed, which would allow the foreign nationals to learn about and come to terms with the social and cultural aspects of the receiving country at least at a basic degree. The tests would also benefit from a case-to-case assessment of the integration progress. Such a solution, especially in the context of the present migration situation, would lie in the interest of the Member States and would to some extent guarantee harmonious cultural cooperation of the representatives of divergent cultural circles.

The legitimacy of the integration measures adopted by the Member States was emphasized in the opinion of Advocate General Kokott, who stated that

> learning the language of the country is an essential prerequisite for integration. Language proficiency not only improves the prospects of third-country nationals in the labour market, but also enables them to seek help in the host country independently in emergencies. Basic knowledge of a country also ensures that the person coming to join the family is familiar with important fundamental rules of co-existence, which can help to avoid misunderstandings and breaches of the law.[64]

4.2.5 *Right to Family Reunification of Citizens of Turkey in the Case-Law of the CJEU*

The right to family reunification of Turkish nationals was the concern of the cases of Naime Dogan v. Bundesrepublik Deutschland and Caner Genc v. Integrationsministeriet. Those cases were different in as much as

[63] C. Costello, *The Human Rights of Migrants and Refugees in European Law*, 162. The author refers to the study cited above by D. Kostakopoulou, "The Area of Freedom, Security and Justice and the Political Morality of Migration and Integration," in *A right to inclusion or exclusion? Normative fault lines of the EU's Area of freedom, security and justice*, ed. H. Lindahl (Hart Publishing, 2009), 204.

[64] Opinion of Advocate General Kokott delivered on 19 March 2015, in the case Minister van Buitenlandse Zaken v. K and A, C 153/14, ECLI:EU:C:2015:186. Para. 34 of the opinion of the Advocate General.

the legal basis of the EU-Turkey relations is the so-called Agreement establishing an association between the European Economic Community and Turkey—an international agreement signed in 1963.[65] The Agreement was supplemented in 1970 with the Protocol, including the so-called *standstill clause*—in accordance with Art. 41 of the Protocol: "The Contracting Parties shall refrain from introducing between themselves any new restrictions on the freedom of establishment and the freedom to provide services."[66]

In the first case in the national proceedings the party was Mrs Seydi Dogan, a national of Turkey, who filed an application for reunification with her husband, who had been living in Germany for many years and had a stable source of income there.[67] In accordance with the German law, a foreign national applying for family reunification must be able to communicate in German at least at a "basic level,"[68] unless he or she is ill or physically, mentally or intellectually disabled.

Lodging the application at the German embassy, Mrs Dogan attached to it a certificate from the Goethe Institute, confirming that she had passed an examination from the German language at level A1 with a satisfactory mark. The embassy personnel found that document to be unreliable—they considered Mrs Dogan to be illiterate and suspected that she had chosen answers in the test at random. Mrs Dogan filed a complaint against the refusal decision issued by the embassy and eventually the case was brought before the CJEU. The national court asked for the interpretation

[65] The Agreement establishing an association between the European Economic Community and Turkey and referring to the measures which must be undertaken for its implementation. The Agreement was signed on 12 September 1963 in Ankara by the Republic of Turkey as one party and the Member States of the European Economic Community as the other party. It was adopted, signed and ratified on behalf of the Community by the decision of the Council 64/732/EEC of 23 December 1963, OJ C 217 of 29.12.1964, 3685. Text published in OJ EC C 113 of 24.12.1973, 1.

[66] Additional Protocol signed on 23 November 1970 in Brussels and adopted, signed and ratified on behalf of the European Economic Community by the Decision of the Council (EEC) No. 2760/72 of 19 December 1972 regarding the signing of the Additional Protocol and Financial Protocol, signed on 23 November 1970, OJ L 293, 29.12.1972, 1. On the subject of the clause, see M.T. Karaygit, "Vive la Clause de Standstill: The Issue of First Admission of Turkish Nationals into the Territory of Member States within the Context of Economic Freedoms," *European Journal of Migration and Law*, vol. 13 (2011): 412.

[67] Judgement of the Court of Justice of 10.07.2014 in the case Naime Dogan v. Bundesrepublik Deutschland, C 138/13, ECLI:EU:C:2014:2066, further as judgement in the case C 138/13.

[68] See para. 15 of the judgement in the case C 138/13.

in the area of admissibility of the measures adopted by the directive on family reunification restricting the rights of Turkish nationals—the obligation to demonstrate the capability of communicating in German should be regarded as such a restrictive measure. Moreover, the national court asked for the interpretation in the area of the compatibility of an integration measure adopted in the national law, that is, the obligation of being able to communicate at least at a basic level in German with Art 7(2) of the directive on family reunification.

On examining the case, the Court found that the *standstill clause*, included in the Additional Protocol to the Association Agreement EEC (European Economic Community)-Turkey, is contrary to the national regulations, which imposed on Turkish nationals desiring to join their spouses under the right to family reunification the obligation to demonstrate the ability to communicate at least at a basic level in the official language of the Member State. In view of the answer provided to this question, the Court did not interpret Art 7(2) of the directive on family reunification.

As a result, in the case of Dogan we are dealing with a special situation, in which the priority turned out to be the right to exercise the freedom of entrepreneurship and the prohibition of its restriction introduced in the international agreement. On account of that, foreign nationals were exempted from the cultural integration obligation, which consisted of the demonstration of the basic linguistic skill that would facilitate their effective functioning in the cultural reality.[69] Despite the clear and unquestionable legal basis for the judgement it should be emphasized that such solutions should have a real dimension of *lex specialis*, since, when applied with regard to large groups of migrants, they may lead to their alienation and the creation of cultural ghettos.

The case illustrates also a different, difficult and often disregarded problem concerning cultural integration, namely that of illiteracy, which might not be the fault of the applicant herself, but rather result from the socio-cultural conditions in which she happened to be growing up.

[69] M. Sułkowski writes extensively on the subject of the cultural dimension of the functioning of migrants from Turkey: M. Sułkowski, *Pół wieku diaspory tureckiej w Niemczech. Społeczność turecka w Republice Federalnej Niemiec—procesy migracji i integracji po 1961 r.* (Warszawa, 2012), 205–225. The author refers to the research on the knowledge of German among the five largest migrant groups carried out in 2006, which demonstrated the lowest declared level of language proficiency among the Turks (only 62.3% answered that their knowledge of the language was good or very good).

Illiteracy, as if automatically, exempts such a person from the integration process. It is worth emphasizing that female migrants are often in a more difficult situation than men with regard to integration opportunities. If they come from typically patriarchal societies, their role mostly consists of taking care of the home and raising children. For such reasons their contacts with society might be limited, thus slowing or completely impeding their cultural and linguistic integration.[70]

Another case concerning a national of Turkey is that of Caner Genc v. Integrationsministeriet.[71] The applicant in the proceedings was a national of Turkey, born in 1991, whose father had been living in Denmark since 1997. The boy's parents were divorced and the parental authority was granted to the father, whereas the boy had remained in Turkey with his grandparents until the filing of the application for reuniting with his father in 2005. Caner Genc's two older brothers had been staying with their father in Denmark since 2003.

In accordance with Association Agreement EEC-Turkey cited in the case of Dogan (Art. 41[1] of the Additional Protocol) and decision 1/80,[72] the Member States are prohibited from introducing any restrictions aimed at impeding Turkish nationals and their families from having access to the job market (the so-called *standstill clause*).

In the Danish Law on aliens, which implemented the directive on family reunification, there is a regulation in accordance with which the issuing of the residence permit with regard to a child seeking reunification with his or her parent is possible "only if the applicant has, or has the possibility

[70] I. Koryś, *Kobiety—migrantki: warunki udanej integracji* (Warszawa: Instytut Spraw Publicznych, 2009), 10.

[71] Judgement of the Court of Justice of 12.04.2016 in the case Caner Genc v. Integrationsministeriet, C 561/14, ECLI:EU:C:2016:247, further also as judgement in the case C 561/14.

[72] Decision No. 1/80 of the Association Council of 19 September 1980 on the development of the Association (unpublished), attached to the Agreement establishing the Association between the European Economic Community and Turkey, signed on 12 September 1963 in Ankara by the Republic of Turkey as one party and the Member States of the European Economic Community as the other party. It was adopted, signed and ratified on behalf of the Community by the decision of the Council 64/732/EEC of 23 December 1963, OJ EC C 217 of 29.12.1964, 3685. An interesting interpretation of Decision 1/80 was carried out by the CJEU in the case Natthaya Dülger v. Wetteraukreis (Judgement of the Court of Justice of 1707.2012 C 451/11, ECLI:EU:C:2012:504). See also Judgement of the Court of Justice of 21.01.2010 in the case Bekleyen v. Land Berlin, C 462/08, ECLI:EU:C:2010:30.

of establishing, such ties with Denmark that there is a basis for successful integration in Denmark" (para. 9[13]).[73] Further, a deviation from this principle is possible only in the case when the overriding value is that of the preservation of family unity, the protection of the interest of the child or when a parent living in a third country is unable to properly take care of the child and when a parent living in Denmark would not be able to, on account of the state of health, return to his or her country of origin.[74] What is more, the application of the principle of assessing whether successful integration was enabled has no grounds in the case when the application for family reunification is filed before the period of two years has elapsed from the moment when a parent was granted the residence permit in the Member State.

Introducing the provision under para. 9(13) of the Danish Law on aliens, the Danish legislator explained that the provision is aimed to counteract situations when parents raise and educate their children in the system of values of the country of origin, which is frequently far from the values observed in the Danish society, only to apply for family reunification after the child has reached maturity. Thus, the above provision is aimed at protecting the Danish culture against values running contrary to the Danish standards. It is worth pointing out that the Danish legislator expressed intention in a straightforward manner, taking care in the first place of the interests of the receiving society and imposing on foreign nationals specific cultural obligations—if the parents who are foreign nationals want family reunification, they should apply for it early enough so as to give their children a chance to be raised in the values typical of the Danish culture, and, what follows, give them a chance for successful integration.

It is precisely on the grounds of para. 9(13) of the Danish Law on aliens that the application of Caner Genc was rejected. In justifying its opinion, the Ministry for Integration emphasized that the applicant did not speak Danish but only Turkish. He was never in Denmark and he received his whole education in Turkey and, what is significant, "has not been influenced by Danish standards and values to such a degree that he has or can establish sufficient ties to Denmark to enable him successfully to integrate."[75] The Ministry also had doubts as to the effectiveness of the integration of the father of the minor child and refused to re-examine the matter.

[73] Para. 10 of the judgement in the case C 561/14.
[74] Para. 13 of the judgement in the case C 561/14.
[75] Para. 20 of the judgement in the case C 561/14.

The first instance court where Caner Genc appealed to against the decision chose to override the complaint. The court of second instance had doubts as to the interpretation of the *standstill clause* carried out by the Court in the case of Dogan (especially in the historic context and as to the purpose of the association agreement) and decided to refer a question for a preliminary ruling to the CJEU. In the preliminary ruling reference, the national court asked a total of four extensive questions, which the Court reformed and decided to examine jointly.

The Court eventually examined whether the national measure, in accordance with which a reunification with a parent residing in the Member State is possible only on condition that the child has a chance for successful integration, constitutes a "new restriction," prohibited in the so-called *standstill clauses* of the Association Agreement EU-Turkey and decision 1/80,[76] and whether such a restriction is justified.

Answering the questions referred for a preliminary ruling, the Court emphasized that in the given case it should be examined whether the national regulation impeding family reunification might have an impact on the exercise of the freedom of entrepreneurship of Turkish citizens in the Member State. In the judgement in the case of Dogan, the Court held that the regulation impeding family reunification does constitute a "new restriction" within the meaning of the *standstill clause* and in the case of Genc the interpretation from the case of Dogan might be applied.

Additionally, the Court voiced its critical opinion on the subject of the regulation of the Danish law, in accordance with which the application for a reunification of a child and a parent should be filed within two years since the parent has been granted a residence permit in Denmark, as this provision does not take the child's personal situation into account and does not translate directly into the integrative capabilities of the child. In the opinion of the Court, the Advocate General's stance to the effect that the application of the time criterion causes the risk of discrimination against minor foreign nationals was a correct one.[77]

[76] The full version of the reformulated question referred for a preliminary ruling—para. 32 of the judgement in the case C 561/14.

[77] It is worth quoting here a fragment of the opinion of the Advocate General: "Let us imagine that Mr Genc obtained his permanent residence permit when his son was seven and a half years old, that his son has never stayed in Denmark, spent his whole childhood in Turkey and speaks only Turkish, as seems to be the case in the main proceedings. Then let us imagine that that child made his application when he was ten years old. Are those six additional months spent in Turkey such as to so change his likelihood of integration in Danish

The present ruling constitutes an interesting example of a case which includes the balancing of two interests—the protection of the culture of the country of origin against the inflow of foreign customs and the right to integration in the receiving country. As the Advocate General emphasized in his opinion, the provision under para. 9(13) of the Danish Law on aliens was based on a condition that in a situation of migration of third-country nationals we are dealing with the incompatibility of cultures. The Advocate General, however, raised several questions and voiced his doubts, concerning, first of all, the lack of definition of the "Danish values and standards" in the national law.[78] This concept has never been defined (not even in the implementing provisions), which constitutes a significant *lacuna iuris*. The introduction of provisions imposing on third-country nationals integrative cultural obligations requires precision as to their scope. What is more, such a legal definition would simultaneously contribute to the protection of the cultural identity of the Danes and would facilitate the elimination of potential behaviours that would be contrary to the culture of the receiving country. The Advocate General also presented his doubts as to the generalizing recognition that each third-country national, while raised in the country of origin, is brought up in a culture that is culturally very distinct from the Danish culture, and therefore there are no chances for successful integration.[79]

Obviously, the standards introduced by the Danish legislator are aimed at the protection of Danish culture, which restricts the right to integration of third-country nationals. Such a regulation fits well within the policy of the Member State and its aims. Nevertheless, the Advocate General rightly observes that the solution adopted under para. 9(13) is not exactly accurate in its assumption that there exists a correlation between an extended resi-

society that he can no longer demonstrate sufficient ties when, up to the age of nine and a half, he would probably have been granted a residence permit without it being possible to say that he had a closer link with Denmark?" para. 51 of the opinion of Advocate General Mengozzi delivered on 20 January 2016 in the case Genc v. Integrationsministeriet, C 561/14, ECLI:EU:C:2016:28, further as opinion of the Advocate General in the case C 561/14.

[78] Para. 48 of the opinion of the Advocate General in the case C 561/14.

[79] As the Advocate General emphasizes: "Assuming that the Law on aliens is applicable to American nationals, for example, would the Danish authorities view a 'late' application for reunification with the same strictness? Would they complain with the same steadfastness that the child was deliberately kept for as long as possible in its culture of origin, thereby negating any likelihood of integration?" para. 48 of the opinion of the Advocate General in the case C 561/14.

dence in a third country and the impossibility of integration.[80] Each case like that should be assessed on an individual basis, taking into account the goodwill of the foreign national and his or her willingness to learn about the social norms of the receiving country and their ability for integration.

4.3 Return Policy and Cultural Rights of Third-Country Nationals

4.3.1 Preliminary Observations

The law and return policy constitute a special branch of migration law, as they generally regulate the process of return of a third-country national to his or her country of origin.[81]

In the Charter of Fundamental Rights, the guarantees concerning returns are to be found under Art. 19, which prohibits collective expulsions and guarantees the observance of the principle of *non-refoulement*.[82] The present study has already addressed the problem of the qualification of the culture of the country of origin as an oppressive culture, which does not ensure protection of the cultural identity of a foreign national in the case of his or her return and exposes him or her to the risk of inhuman treatment. The principle of *non-refoulement* protects a foreign national against

[80] As the Advocate General observes in para. 49 of his opinion: "It should be borne in mind that the economic situation of those families often explains the absence of more frequent stays in Europe and that the choice of residence is determined not solely by a hypothetical cultural preference, but also, and perhaps above all, by real economic constraints," para. 49 of the opinion of the Advocate General in the case C 561/14.

[81] The priorities of the present return policy were laid down in the Communication adopted on 28.03.2014 in Brussels: Final Communication from the Commission to the Council and the European Parliament on EU Return Policy (com[2014] 199 final); Communication from the Commission of 9.09.2015 EU Action Plan on return (com [2015] 453 final); Communication of the Commission of 2.03.2017 adopted in Brussels—Communication from the Commission to the European Parliament and the Council on a More Effective Return Policy in the European Union—a Renewed Action Plan (com[2017] 200 final); Commission Recommendation of 27.09.2017 establishing a common "Return Handbook" to be used by Member States' competent authorities when carrying out return-related tasks, Brussels, 27.09.2017, C(2017) 6505.

[82] Art. 19 CFR is titled "Protection in the event of removal, expulsion or extradition." In accordance with the Article: "1. Collective expulsions are prohibited. 2. No one may be removed, expelled or extradited to a State where there is a serious risk that he or she would be subjected to the death penalty, torture or other inhuman or degrading treatment or punishment."

inhuman treatment (Art. 4 CFR),[83] simultaneously ensuring, if need be, the possibility of protection against the culture of the country of origin and preventing his or her expulsion.[84]

4.3.2 *Rights of a Cultural Character in the Return Procedure*

The most important legal act in the field of return law is the so-called Return Directive, that is, Directive 2008/115/EC of the European Parliament and of the Council of 16 December 2008 on common standards and procedures in Member States for returning illegally staying third-country nationals.[85] It should also be borne in mind that in the case of the return of foreign nationals, they fall under the provisions of the

[83] On the subject of the validity of the principle of *non-refoulement* in international law, see E. Hamdan, *The Principle of Non- Refoulement under the ECHR and the UN Convention against Torture and Other Cruel, Inhuman and Degrading Treatment and Punishment* (Brill/Nijhoff, 2016), 22 et seq.

[84] However, it is worth mentioning here a hypothetical possibility of a different situation, that is, a situation when a foreign national cannot be returned on account of the protection under *non-refoulement*, but he or she is not completely integrated with the host country. In such a situation, it is difficult to talk about the possibility of realizing the right to cultural identity. Such persons should be included into the integration process, taking into account their individual needs, so that their acculturation would be successful. Finally, the realization of the principle of *non-refoulement* also extends over the conducted sea operations and the saving of persons trying to reach the coasts of Europe. Such persons also come indirectly within the scope of the rights of a cultural character, as the very manner of conducting such operations and handling migrants in the process requires appropriate cultural sensitivity, so as not to violate the dignity of the saved persons. As part of the sea operations carried out by the Frontex Agency, the Code of Conduct is applied (for all persons participating in Frontex activity), which under its Art. 4 imposes upon the participants of the operation an obligation to protect the dignity and fundamental rights of other persons, without regard to their race, skin colour, ethnic origin, language, nationality, religion or faith; see Code of Conduct (for all persons participating in Frontex activity), adopted on 22 March 2011 r., available on the website http://frontex.europa.eu/assets/Publications/General/Code_of_Conduct_applicable_to_all_persons_participating_in_Frontex_operational_activities.pdf. Accessed 31.12.2017. See also R. Mungianu, *Frontex and Non-Refoulement. The International Responsibility of the EU* (Cambridge, 2016), 129 et seq.

[85] Directive 2008/115/EC of the European Parliament and of the Council of 16 December 2008 on common standards and procedures in Member States for returning illegally staying third-country nationals, OJ L 348, 24.12.2008, 98, further also as the Return Directive, Directive 2008/115. Moreover, the act of EU law concerning the return policy is the Council Decision 2004/573/EC of 29 April 2004 on the organization of joint flights for removals from the territory of two or more Member States, of third-country nationals who are subjects of individual removal orders, OJ L 261, 6.08.2004, 28.

Schengen Borders Code with regard to border checks—especially the provision under Art. 7, in accordance with which border checks should be carried out in full respect for human dignity and all forms of discrimination are prohibited. These guarantees also ensure the full respect for the cultural identity of the person undergoing the border check.

The Return Directive regulates, within the scope laid down under Art. 1, the procedures and standards for the realization of returns of third-country nationals, who have been illegally residing in the territory of the Member States.[86] Such returns are to be carried out in accordance with fundamental rights and the guarantees of human rights provided for in international law.[87] The provisions of Directive 2008/115 regulate the subsequent stages of the realization of the return of a foreign national to his or her country of origin. They are procedural guarantees, related to the issuing of the return decision, regulating the conditions for voluntary return and the realization of the expulsion, as well as determining the common standards for the application of detention measures.

At present, in the return procedure, it is a rule to grant a period for voluntary departure.[88] This instrument makes it possible for the foreign national concerned to individually depart for the country of origin and thus avoid a forced return. Generally, the period for voluntary return is between 7 and 30 days. However, under Art. 7(2) Directive 2008/115 it is provided that such a period might be extended on account of special circumstances, such as the attendance of school by the children or the

[86] On the subject of returns in the national law, see T. Gardocka, Ł. Majewski, "Wydalenie niepożądanego cudzoziemca," in *Uchodźcy w Polsce i Europie. Stan prawny i rzeczywistość*, eds. T. Gardocka, J. Sobczak (Toruń, 2010), 179 et seq.

[87] The guarantees for the protection of human rights in the return procedure are also articulated in the Preamble of the Directive 2008/115. Thus, in accordance with its para. 17: "Third-country nationals in detention should be treated in a humane and dignified manner with respect for their fundamental rights and in compliance with international and national law." In para. 21 of the Preamble, there is an anti-discriminatory clause. Accordingly, the Member States, in implementing the directive, cannot discriminate against anybody "on the basis of sex, race, colour, ethnic or social origin, genetic features, language, religion or belief, political or any other opinions, membership of a national minority, property, birth, disability, age or sexual orientation."

[88] In accordance with Art. 7(4) Directive 2008/115: "If there is a risk of absconding, or if an application for a legal stay has been dismissed as manifestly unfounded or fraudulent, or if the person concerned poses a risk to public policy, public security or national security, Member States may refrain from granting a period for voluntary departure, or may grant a period shorter than seven days."

existence of social relations with the host country. Thus, taking into account the open character of the special circumstances facilitating the extension of the period for voluntary return, the provision under Art. 7(2) Directive 2008/115 allows for the realization of certain entitlements of a partially cultural character—such as the right to education.[89] In a situation of preparation for the return, which is difficult for foreign nationals, especially minors, the right to education may constitute the only possibility of gaining cultural education, through contact with cultural values in the educational process.

At the procedural level, the directive guarantees the realization of foreign nationals' linguistic rights, through the translation carried out on demand of the main elements of the decision obligating a third-country national to return (Art. 12[2] Directive 2008/115).[90]

The realization of the return procedure also allows for the exercise of the forced expulsion in a situation when a foreign national does not conform to the granted period for voluntary departure or in the case of other circumstances provided for in the directive.[91] Art. 8 Directive 2008/115 determines the common standards for the Member States with regard to the expulsion of a third-country national. The expulsion carried out in convoy may in itself be a traumatic experience for a foreign national. Hence, the provision includes a clause imposing on the authorities of the Member States, which have to resort to enforcement measures, the obligation to act "in accordance with fundamental rights and with due respect for the dignity and physical integrity of the third-country national concerned." Such safeguards are especially significant for the respect of the

[89] Moreover, the right to continue education is provided for under Art. 14 Directive 2008/115, titled "Safeguards pending return." In accordance with the Article, the Member States are obligated to ensure that the minors are granted "access to the basic education system subject to the length of their stay" before the expiry of the period for voluntary return or before the expiry of the period for which the removal was postponed, under Art. 9 Directive 2008/115.

[90] Moreover, in accordance with Art. 12(3) Directive 2008/115, "Member States shall make available generalised information sheets explaining the main elements of the standard form in at least five of those languages which are most frequently used or understood by illegal migrants entering the Member State concerned." See also A. Kuś, "Selected issues relating to expulsion of foreigners in the judgments of Polish and European Union courts," in *Return Migration: Theory and Practice*, ed. T. Sieniow (Lublin, 2015), 205–207.

[91] See Art. 8(4) Directive 2008/115 on the subject of the application of the enforcement measures and Art. 7(4) Directive 2008/115 allowing the Member States to refrain from granting the period for voluntary departure.

right to cultural identity of a foreign national, which transpire from the principle of respect for each person's dignity. It is especially important in a situation when there are distinct cultural differences between the culture of the receiving country and the country of origin that a foreign national's return is to be carried out in a way that is respectful towards cultural customs and behaviour of the foreign national concerned. Obviously, such guarantees should not infringe the basic standards for the security of the return.

4.3.3 Cultural Rights and Detention of Migrants

A highly debated issue which often casts a long shadow over the humanitarian migration policy is the use of detention measures with regard to foreign nationals,[92] especially with regard to families with children.[93] It remains beyond doubt that resorting to detention, which means, in fact, depriving third-country nationals of their freedom, has an adverse effect on the possibility of exercising the rights and freedoms of a cultural character.

At present, within the framework of the Council of Europe, a code of rules regarding administrative detention to be applied with regard to foreign nationals is being prepared.[94] The document emphasizes the wide

[92] On this subject, see D. Wilsher, *Immigration Detention. Law, History, Politics* (Cambridge, 2012), 121 et seq.; G. Cornelisse, "A New Articulation of Human Rights, or Why the European Court of Human Rights Should Think Beyond Westphalian Sovereignty," in *Are Human Rights for Migrants? Critical Reflections on the Status of Irregular Migrants in Europe and the United States*, ed. M.B. Dembour, T. Kelly (Routledge, 2011), 100–105; D. Debono, "'Not our problem': why detention of irregular migrants is not considered a human rights issue in Malta," in *Are Human Rights for Migrants? Critical Reflections on the Status of Irregular Migrants in Europe and the United States*, eds. M.B. Dembour, T. Kelly (Routledge, 2011), 146–162; J. Białas, D. Cegiełka, A. Chmura, M. Górczyńska, E. Ostaszewska-Żuk, K. Rusiłowicz, K. Słubik, A. Trylińska, D. Witko, *Wciąż za kratami. Raport z monitoringu strzeżonych ośrodków dla cudzoziemców przeprowadzonego przez Helsińską Fundację Praw Człowieka i Stowarzyszenie Interwencji Prawnej pod redakcją Jacka Białasa i Witolda Klausa*, Helsińska Fundacja Praw Człowieka Stowarzyszenie Interwencji Prawnej (Warszawa, 2014).

[93] W. Klaus, A. Kunicka, Detencja dzieci cudzoziemców *Biuletyn RPO. Źródła*, no. 11 (2012): 53–61. See also *European legal policy framework on immigration detention of children*, FRA 2017, 7 et seq., Report available on the website www.fra.europa.eu. Accessed 12.09.2017.

[94] European Committee on Legal Cooperation, Codifying instrument of European rules on the administrative detention of migrants, 1st Draft. Draft text submitted to key stakehold-

cultural spectrum, relating, amongst others, to the regulations concerning the serving of meals to foreign nationals so that they cater for, as much as possible, the religious needs and cultural context (para. F9), as well as the necessity of possessing appropriate intercultural skills by the personnel working in the detention centres (para. J8). In the 20 guidelines adopted by the Committee of Ministers of the Council of Europe there are also guidelines concerning the use of detention measures with regard to foreign nationals.[95] In accordance with guideline 10.3, the personnel working in detention centres should have knowledge about the culture of the country of origin of migrants, as well as communicative skills facilitating the initiation of dialogue in a multicultural situation.[96] The United Nations High Commissioner for Refugees (UNHCR) also issued an important document on the subject of the conditions of using detention with regard to third-country nationals.[97] In accordance with guideline 8 (conditions of detention must be humane and dignified) para. VIII, there is a need to organize different types of cultural activities in detention centres, as well as to monitor the right of an individual to practise religion (para. IX). With reference to special needs of children, guideline 9.2. turns attention to the need of providing children with the right conditions for development in detention centres, with due respect for the ethnic, cultural, linguistic and religious background of the child.

The Return Directive provides for the general rules for applying detention measures, acknowledging, at the same time, that detention in a guarded centre should be a measure of the last resort, applied only in

ers and civil society for comment by Friday 30 June 2017 to the Secretariat of European Committee on Legal Co-operation (CDCJ), document available on the website https://www.coe.int/en/web/cdcj/european-committee-legal-cooperation/background. Accessed 12.09.2017.

95 Twenty Guidelines of the Committee of Ministers of Europe on Forced Return September 2005, http://www.coe.int/t/dg3/migration/archives/Source/MalagaRegConf/20_Guidelines_Forced_Return_en.pdf. Accessed 12.09.2017.

96 Special postulates have also been raised with regard to the situation of children remaining in detention centres. They should have their educational needs provided, especially if they have special needs of an ethnic or cultural character. See "Guideline 11. Children and families. Commentary," in *Twenty Guidelines of the Committee of Ministers of Europe on Forced Return*, September 2005. On the subject of communication in a multicultural situation, see M. Bosworth, *Inside Immigration Detention* (Oxford, 2014), 83.

97 Detention Guidelines. Guidelines on the Applicable Criteria and Standards relating to the Detention of Asylum Seekers and Alternatives to Detention, UNHCR 2012, document available on the website http://www.refworld.org/pdfid/503489533b8.pdf. Accessed 12.09.2017.

exceptional circumstances.[98] In accordance with Art. 16 Directive 2008/115, the Member States should detain foreign nationals in special centres and if it is not possible and detention is taking place in a prison, foreign nationals should be separated from regular inmates.[99] The directive guarantees the possibility of the realization, at least partially, of cultural needs, to the children remaining in the detention centres. In accordance with Art. 17 (which provides that unaccompanied minors and families with minors should only be detained for the shortest appropriate period of time) minors should be allowed to engage in "leisure activities, including play and recreational activities appropriate to their age." Apart from that, minors should be able to have access to education in the detention centre. In a similar way, access to education is ensured for minors in the Reception Directive.[100] However, as it transpires from the data gathered by the EU Fundamental Rights Agency, in nine European countries such access to education is not, in fact, provided.[101]

As was mentioned above, Directive 2008/115 determines the minimal standards for the realization of the return and the awaiting of the return, which should be implemented by the Member States. It does not contain any specific regulations on the organization of life in detention centres, which might be helpful in determining the existing guarantees for exercising cultural rights. Those safeguards may be subject to at least partial redefinition based on national law. Moreover, in September 2017, the European Commission published a common "Return Handbook," in

[98] In accordance with Art. 15(1) Directive 2008/115: "1. Unless other sufficient but less coercive measures can be applied effectively in a specific case, Member States may only keep in detention a third-country national who is the subject of return procedures in order to prepare the return and/or carry out the removal process, in particular when: (a) there is a risk of absconding or (b) the third-country national concerned avoids or hampers the preparation of return or the removal process."

[99] See Judgement of the Court of Justice of 17.07.2014 in the case Thi Ly Pham v. Stadt Schweinfurt, Amt für Meldewesen und Statistik, C 474/13, ECLI:EU:C:2014:2096; Judgement of the Court of Justice of 17.07.2014 in the case Adala Bero v. Regierungspräsidium Kassel and Ettayebi Bouzalmate v. Kreisverwaltung Kleve, C 473/13 and C 514/13, ECLI:EU:C:2014:2095.

[100] Art. 14 Directive 2013/33.

[101] The countries include Austria, Finland, France, Bulgaria (provides access to education for children in the procedure, but not to those awaiting the return), Denmark, Hungary, some of the German Federal States, Greece and Sweden. See *Current Migration Situation in the EU: Education*, May 2017, FRA, 6. Report available on the website www.fra.europa.eu. Accessed 12.09.2017.

accordance with which the personnel of detention centres should have knowledge on the subject of the countries of origin of migrants and cultural differences, whereas migrants themselves should have the possibility of realizing their cultural customs.[102] With reference to the case-law, the CJEU did not refer directly in the *acquis* on returns to the rights of a cultural character. However, it is worth remembering at this stage the ruling in the case of Thi Ly Pham,[103] in which the Court interpreted Art. 16 Directive 2008/115. In accordance with the Article, detention should not take place in a prison facility and if there is such a necessity due to the lack of separate detention facilities, foreign nationals should be kept separated from ordinary prisoners. The applicant in the national proceedings was a national of Vietnam Thi Ly Pham, who entered into the territory of Germany illegally and consequently she was issued a return decision. Ms Pham was placed in a detention centre and, what is interesting, she consented in writing to be placed with regular prisoners, as she wanted to remain in the surroundings of her compatriots—the Vietnamese who were serving a prison sentence. In this way, she wanted to maintain language contact with the culture of her country of origin in order not to feel alienated in the culture foreign to her. However, the Court held that the prohibition of placing regular inmates together with foreign nationals in a prison facility, when the prison also serves the function of a detention centre, is of an absolute character and does not leave any margin of discretion to the Member States. This view was shared by the Advocate General, who emphasized in his opinion that the lack of separation between foreign nationals and regular prisoners may lead to the criminalization of migrants in public opinion.[104] The Advocate General also had considerable doubts

[102] See ANNEX to the Commission Recommendation establishing a common "Return Handbook" to be used by Member States' competent authorities when carrying out return-related tasks, Brussels, 27.09.2017 C(2017) 6505, ANNEX 1.

[103] Judgement of the Court of Justice of 17.07.2014 in the case Thi Ly Pham v. Stadt Schweinfurt, Amt für Meldewesen und Statistik, C 474/13, ECLI:EU:C:2014:2096.

[104] Para. 99 of the opinion of Advocate General Y. Bot of 30.04.2014 in the joint cases C 473/13, 514/13, C 474/13, ECLI:EU:C:2014:336. Advocate General Bot emphasized that "[i]n turn, that requirement of separation directly contributes to respect for the human dignity and fundamental rights of one who has not committed any crime or even any offence. It makes it possible to ensure that, even within the prison facility, the detention of a migrant awaiting removal differs from the serving of a sentence. The requirement of separation also makes it possible to ensure that that detention takes place in conditions and under a regime appropriate to the legal situation of the migrant and proportionate to the purpose of the detention. Finally, it makes it possible to avert risks connected with the criminalisation of

whether the fact of placing Ms Pham in prison cells with other inmates indeed increased her chances for contact with her compatriots—in accordance with the data cited by the Advocate General in his opinion at the time of the apprehension of Ms Pham in the prison facilities for women in Bavaria there were merely three women of Vietnamese nationality and, therefore, the possibility of maintaining linguistic contact with her native language was considerably limited.

A summary of the policy of the Member States in the area of using detention with regard to foreign nationals can be found in the EMN report of 2014.[105] The data presented there indicates that all the Member States provide the detainees with access to all types of recreational and leisure activities, including libraries, television, the press and religious services.[106] It is worth pointing out here, for the sake of illustration, that Austria provides the detained foreigners with access to dancing lessons, while in Belgium, entertainment activities are organized with the help of educators. The Czech Republic offers music and visual arts workshops, Lithuania organizes activities on cultural awareness for various ethnic groups and the United Kingdom offers courses in arts and crafts.[107]

Due to the fact that detention centres house migrants from various countries, often culturally divergent from European culture, the Member States often resort to employing cultural mediators, in order to ensure that intercultural communication runs without conflicts.[108] Cultural mediation allows for the working out of the rules of peaceful coexistence between foreigners of various nationalities and, on the other hand, makes

certain migrants and to avoid the violence related to the prison environment that could affect the most vulnerable individuals."

[105] The use of detention and alternatives to detention in the context of immigration policies. *Synthesis Report for the EMN Focussed Study 2014*, Report available on the website European Migration Network: https://ec.europa.eu/home-affairs/sites/homeaffairs/files/what-wedo/networks/european_migration_network/reports/docs/emn-studies/ emn_study_detention_alternatives_to_detention_synthesis_report_en.pdf. Accessed 12.09.2017.

[106] The use of detention and alternatives to detention in the context of immigration policies, 33.

[107] Ibidem, see appendix A.3b to the report.

[108] See report: *At the limen. The implementation of the return directive in Italy, Cyprus and Spain*, EACEA—Education, Audiovisual and Culture Executive Agency, 2013, 32, Report available on the website http://www.mugak.eu/en/documentation/at-the%2D%2Dlimen-report-on-the-implementation-of-the-return-directive-in-spain-cyprus-and%2D%2Ditaly. Accessed 12.09.2017.

it possible to convince the very migrants to undertake specific activities, such as participation in medical examinations (the most sensitive issues involve the cultural differences in the understanding of the role of the sexes in society or the possibilities of cooperation with representatives of different sexes). It often happens that a similar role to that of cultural mediators is played by lawyers or interpreters.[109] Cultural mediation also strengthens social cohesion,[110] and therefore serves a specific integrative function—in as much as integration is not a priority activity in the process of detention, it remains invaluable in terms of, for example, mediations in educational processes. It is worth emphasizing here that there are cases when the expulsion of a foreign national turns out to be impossible and he or she is released from the detention centre (e.g., when the country of origin does not confirm the identity of the foreign national concerned). In such a case, the acculturation he or she experienced in the detention centre becomes an added value to his or her functioning outside of the detention reality.

A significant role in the realization of the guarantees of migrants' fundamental rights in the detention process is also played by the fact that they are ensured the possibility of having contact with representatives of NGOs. At present, highly specialized NGOs are functioning in the Member States. They possess skills and expertise in the area of migration and have extensive knowledge and practice in the field of multicultural issues (among Polish NGOs, it is worth mentioning the Helsinki Foundation for Human Rights, the Association for Legal Intervention or the Rule of Law Institute). Hence, the contacts between the detained persons and representatives of NGOs result in the initiation of an effective intercultural dialogue, facilitating the finding of solutions to the problems of migrants' functioning in the reality of detention. The Return Directive under Art. 16(4) provides for the possibility of visiting detention centres by NGOs and international organizations (such as the UNHCR). Such visitations may result in establishing and presenting recommendations, indicating the possibility for actions which might serve the strengthening of the guarantees of protection of fundamental rights of the persons detained in the

[109] R.F. Barsky, *Undocumented Immigrants in the Era of Arbitrary Law. The Flight and the Plight of People Deemed "Illegal"* (Routledge, 2016), 137–139.

[110] See M. Pawlak, M. Bieniecki, *Rozwiązania instytucjonalne stosowane w obszarze obsługi imigrantów w wybranych krajach Unii Europejskiej* (Warszawa: Instytut Spraw Publicznych, 2010), 13.

guarded centres.[111] Foreigners in the detention process, in accordance with Art. 16(5), may have the possibility of contacting NGOs—an example of the implementation of this provision into national law is the programmes of legal aid organized by NGOs, within which the detention centres are visited by lawyers who are also equipped with skills of effective cultural communication and information on the countries of origin of migrants.[112]

It is obvious that remaining in detention reduces the chances of an individual for the full realization of cultural needs and restricts the possibilities of the exercise of the rights of a cultural character. In the light of this thesis, an important postulate seems to be the use of alternatives to the detention of foreigners. It is worth emphasizing here that detention in EU law may be used with regard to migrants of an irregular status, awaiting return as well as the persons seeking international protection.[113] Directive 2008/115 does not list the measures alternative to detention, but under Art. 15 it is stated that the application of detention is a measure of the last resort and it should be applied "unless other sufficient but less coercive measures can be applied effectively in a specific case."[114] Broader regulations with regard to the application of the measures alternative to detention can be found in the so-called Reception Directive (Directive 2013/33).[115] In accordance with Art. 8(4) Directive 2013/33, "Member States shall ensure that the rules concerning alternatives to detention, such as regular reporting to the authorities, the deposit of a financial guarantee, or an obligation to stay at an assigned place, are laid down in national law." Therefore, in the Polish law, the types of alternatives to detention

[111] The effect of such activities was the report drawn by the Helsinki Foundation for Human Rights and the Association for Legal Intervention—J. Białas, D. Cegiełka, A. Chmura, M. Górczyńska, E. Ostaszewska-Żuk, K. Rusiłowicz, K. Słubik, A. Trylińska, D. Witko, *Wciąż za kratami. Raport z monitoringu strzeżonych ośrodków dla cudzoziemców.*

[112] An example of such a project was "Legal aid" realized by the Rule of Law Institute, providing assistance in the cases of migrants' obligations to return, which was co-financed by the National Asylum, Migration and Integration Fund and from the national budget.

[113] The basis for using alternatives to detention was listed in the report by the EU Agency for Fundamental Rights: *Alternatives to detention for asylum seekers and people in return procedures*, FRA 2015. See also T. Sieniow, *Stosowanie alternatyw do detencji cudzoziemców w Polsce w latach 2014–2015. Raport z monitoringu* (Lublin, 2016); *Stosowanie detencji wobec cudzoziemców. Raport z monitoringu i rekomendacje*, ed. T. Sieniow (Lublin, 2013), publications available on the website www.panstwoprawa.org. Accessed 12.09.2017.

[114] Art. 15(1) Directive 2008/115.

[115] Directive 2013/33.

that may be used by the national bodies are listed under Art. 317(1) of the Act on foreigners.[116] The measures include the following: reporting at specified intervals to the authority indicated in the ruling, paying a security deposit in an amount specified in the decision, no lower than twice the amount of the minimum wage stipulated by minimum wage regulations, leaving the travel document in the deposit, undertaking to reside in the place designated in the decision.[117] The application of such measures allows for a wider exercise of the rights and liberties provided for in the CFR and national law and thus a wider access to the rights of a cultural character. Suffice it to take into account here a generally unlimited access to the media (the press, the Internet, television), as well as access to the selected institutions of culture or religious services. Generally, alternatives to detention allow for the full realization of the educational obligation, especially with regard to minors.[118]

Detention also means a situation which pre-determines the way for the realization of cultural freedoms, including the freedom of artistic creativity. In as much as it cannot be definitively claimed that the realization of this freedom is impossible in detention, it still comes under significant restrictions resulting from, on the one hand, isolation of an individual from the outside world, and on the other hand, the restricted access to the artistic means of expression and the regulations adopted in the detention facility.

[116] See P. Dąbrowski, "Komentarz do art. 317 ustawy o cudzoziemcach," in *Ustawa o cudzoziemcach. Komentarz*, ed. J. Chlebny (Warszawa, 2015), 734.

[117] The EMN report on detention and alternatives to detention lists the types of alternative measures that are applied in different Member States—apart from those under Art. 317 Act on foreigners, the Member States also apply, amongst others, electronic monitoring, guarantees from a third person and release on the basis of a care plan. What is interesting is that the report also lists the programme of voluntary returns as an alternative measure. See the use of detention and alternatives to detention in the context of immigration policies. *Synthesis Report for the EMN Focussed Study 2014*, 33–34. The report on the subject of alternatives to detention was prepared by the European Migration Network and is available on the website https://ec.europa.eu/home-affairs/sites/homeaffairs/files/what-we-do/networks/european_migration_network/reports/docs/emn-studies/emn_study_detention_alternatives_to_detention_synthesis_report_en.pdf. Accessed 12.09.2017.

[118] P. de Bruycker, A. Bloomfield, E. Tsourdi, J. Pétin, *Alternatives to Immigration and Asylum Detention in the EU. Time for Implementation*, Odysseus Network 2015, 108. However, the authors also point out the problems that might be experienced by the persons using alternatives to detention; report available on the website http://odysseus-network.eu/wp-content/uploads/2015/02/FINAL-REPORT-Alternatives-to-detention-in-the-EU.pdf. Accessed 12.09.2017.

The scope of the application of alternatives to detention in the Member States varies, which transpires from the reports by the EMN and FRA.[119] Interesting conclusions on the applications of alternatives to detention in the selected Member States can also be found in the report drawn by the Odysseus Network. From the report it transpires that Lithuania applies alternatives to detention generally with regard to the migrants who have cultural, historical and language ties with the receiving country—in this way, instead of remaining in detention, the foreign nationals concerned may remain among the receiving society.[120]

The benefits resulting from the application of alternatives to detention as measures allowing for the exercise of one's economic, social and cultural rights were also pointed out by the International Detention Coalition in their report of 2015.[121]

4.3.4 *Voluntary Return and Cultural Rights*

A special instrument which indirectly strengthens the protection of the rights of a cultural character is the organization of voluntary returns of migrants to their countries of origin and supporting their reintegration in the community there.[122] Support for voluntary returns in the Member States was possible due to the financial resources from the European Return Fund.[123] In accordance with the decision establishing the Fund,

[119] Paper: "Alternatives to detention for asylum seekers and people in return procedures," FRA 2015. Document available on the website www.fra.europa.eu. Accessed 12.09.2017.

[120] P. de Bruycker, A. Bloomfield, E. Tsourdi, J. Pétin, *Alternatives to Immigration and Asylum Detention in the EU*, 89.

[121] There are alternatives. A handbook for preventing unnecessary immigration detention (revised version), International Detention Coalition (2015): III, 28. http://idcoalition.org/publication/view/there-are-alternatives-revised-edition/. Accessed 12.09.2017.

[122] In accordance with the definition presented in the *position paper* prepared by the IOM reintegration is a process which allows the returning person to once again participate in the social, cultural, economic and political life of the country of origin. *Reintegration. Effective approaches*, International Organization for Migration 2015, 13. See also Return Migration and Development Platform, European University Institute 2011, http://rsc.eui.eu/RDP/glossary-2/. Accessed 12.09.2017; L. Hammond, "'Voluntary' Repatriation and Reintegration," in *The Oxford Handbook of Refugee and Forced Migration Studies*, eds. E. Fiddian-Qasmiyeh, G. Loescher, K. Long, N. Sigona (Oxford, 2014), 595.

[123] Decision No. 575/2007/EC of the European Parliament and of the Council of 23 May 2007 establishing the European Return Fund for the period 2008 to 2013 as part of the General Programme Solidarity and Management of Migration Flows, OJ L 144, 6.06.2007, 45, further as Decision 575/2007. The Decision provides for the realization of activities in

within the instrument of the voluntary return, the reintegration in the country of origin should also be supported, in order to ensure that the return is effective.[124] It is a very significant postulate, since the foreign nationals residing in the territory of the European Union lose contact with the culture of their countries of origin for many years. In a situation when the country of origin is experiencing sometimes more or sometimes less dynamic cultural changes,[125] a foreign national loses his or her awareness of the current cultural codes and therefore may experience problems with a definitive determination of his or her cultural identity in the surrounding culture. It also happens that the returning persons are accompanied by their family, who (especially children) do not know the language of their country of origin and have never lived there.[126] In such circumstances, what is even more valuable are the initiatives facilitating the transfer from one cultural reality to the other, once familiar, but now changed or forgotten.[127] Psychological reintegration also plays an important role in the

support of returns with due respect for fundamental rights (Art. 2). The Preamble to the Decision also states that all the activities as laid down in the Decision should be carried out with due respect for fundamental rights guaranteed under international law (ECHR, the Geneva Convention) and CFR (para. 15 of the Preamble to the Decision). As part of the activities realized by the Polish organizations it is worth mentioning the projects implemented by the Helsinki Foundation for Human Rights (RETURNS. Legal aid and information for returning migrants) and the Halina Nieć Legal Aid Centre (Safe return—legal assistance and monitoring of the observance of human rights in returns of third-country nationals to their countries of origin). For more information on the subject of the financial resources used by Poland within the Fund, see https://fundusze.mswia.gov.pl/ue/fundusze/wdrazane/solid-program-ogolny-so/europejski-fundusz-pow/9084,Europejski-Fundusz-Powrotow-Imigrantow-EFPI.html. Accessed 12.09.2017.

[124] Para. 25 Decision 575/2007.

[125] On this subject, see *Comparative Research on the Assisted Voluntary Return and Reintegration of Migrants by Khalid Koser, Maastricht Graduate School of Governance and Katie Kuschminder, Maastricht Graduate School of Governance*, International Organization for Migration (IOM) 2015, 53, Report available on the website https://www.iom.int/files/live/sites/iom/files/What-We-Do/.../AVRR-Research-final.pdf. Accessed 12.07.2019.

[126] *Reintegration. Effective approaches*. International Organization for Migration 2015, 16, Report available on the website https://www.iom.int/reintegration-effective-approaches. Accessed 12.07.2019.

[127] In accordance with Art. 5(8) Decision 575/2007 as part of the eligible operation within the Fund, the Member States could realize activities directed at the reintegration of foreign nationals returning to third countries, entailing "cash incentives and other short term measures necessary to launch the progress of reintegration for the returnee's personal development such as training, placement and employment assistance, start-up support for economic activities and post-return assistance and counselling."

rebuilding of cultural identity and it is necessary with regard to the acceptance of differences in tradition, culture and roles assigned to the sexes in the given cultural circle.[128]

A definitively key role in the process of the realization of voluntary returns of foreign nationals to their countries of origin is played by the International Organization for Migration (IOM).[129] The Organization has been running a programme for assisting voluntary returns in Poland since 2006. The programme includes assistance in the organization of the return at the organizational level and its financing, including integration support on successful deportation. The Polish IOM projects were realized with substantial support from the European Return Fund. Reintegration programmes entail, apart from the strictly economic support, the facilitation of the realization of certain rights of a cultural character.[130] The AVENIR programme, as part of reintegration assistance, apart from satisfying the basic needs through financial help and through support of entrepreneurship, also entails the possibility of financing vocational trainings, as well as educational aid, directed primarily at minors.[131]

The permanence of a foreign national's return to the country of origin is a priority of the IOM. Hence, as part of the conducted AVENIR pro-

[128] *Reintegration. Effective approaches.* International Organization for Migration 2015, 16.

[129] It is worth mentioning that in Poland assistance in the voluntary return is also realized by the Head of the Office for Foreigners on the grounds of the Law of 13 June 2003 on granting protection to foreigners within the territory of the Republic of Poland, uniform text, Journal of Laws of 2018, item 1109, as amended.

[130] The term "reintegration" is often treated as synonymous to "re-inclusion" or "re-incorporation" of persons into a social group. The most frequently cited forms of reintegrative assistance include financial support, as well as assistance in finding a job and in continuing education. See European Migration Network (EMN) Common Template, EMN Focussed Study 2014 Final Version, 5 March 2014, Good Practices in the return and reintegration of irregular migrants: Member States' entry bans policy & use of readmission agreements between Member States and third countries, 7, report available on the website https://ec.europa.eu/home-affairs/sites/homeaffairs/files/what-we-do/networks/european_migration_network/reports/docs/emn-studies/05a.cyprus_rentry_bans_and_reintegration_study_final_en_version.pdf. Accessed 12.09.2017.

[131] A.M. Kosińska, P. Wojtasik, *Dobrowolny powrót jako priorytet polityki powrotowej Unii Europejskiej*, (Lublin, 2012), 42. From the report by the Comparative Research on the Assisted Voluntary Return and Reintegration of Migrants, it transpires that migrants, while receiving reintegration assistance, received the lowest level of cultural support in comparison with other types of assistance (e.g. drafting of business plans). Only 7% of the respondents admitted to having received assistance in increasing their cultural awareness, *Comparative Research on the Assisted Voluntary Return and Reintegration of Migrants*, 105.

grammes, the level of reintegration in its economic, cultural and security dimension is checked. As it transpires from the research findings presented by the IOM in its report on assisting returns and reintegration, 64% of the migrants returning to the country of origin felt reintegrated in the socio-cultural sphere (through the active participation in the life of the local community).[132] Cultural reintegration also includes participation in the events of religious character, as well as the ability to adjust to the norms of behaviour and values existing within society.[133]

4.3.5 *Undocumented Migrants and the Exercise of Cultural Rights in the "Grey Area"*

On the margin of the considerations regarding the returns of migrants to their countries of origin, one should mention the situation of a special group, such as migrants of an irregular status.[134] The term refers to the nationals of third countries staying within the territory of the Member States against the law.[135] As a rule, the law does not provide them with any

[132] *Comparative Research on the Assisted Voluntary Return and Reintegration of Migrants*, 9. From the research findings it transpires that the returnees willingly participated in local cultural events (79%), but only 21% of them were members of social organizations.

[133] *Comparative Research on the Assisted Voluntary Return and Reintegration of Migrants*, 80.

[134] The number of irregular migrants is difficult to estimate. A source which is often cited in this respect is the Clandestino project. The researchers, on the basis of the population data of the EU of 2005 estimated that then there might have been between 2 and 8 million persons of an irregular status. Simultaneously, in research projects the authors provide their own estimates, and, thus, in 2008 it was estimated that there were between 1.9 and 3.8 million persons within the territory of the EU. See Size and Development of Irregular Migration to the EU Clandestino Research Project, Counting the Uncountable: Data and Trends across Europe, Comparative Policy Brief—Size of Irregular Migration, October 2009, 4, document available on the website http://irregular-migration.net/fileadmin/irregularmigration/dateien/4.Background_Information/4.2.Policy_Briefs_EN/ComparativePolicyBrief_SizeOfIrregularMigration_Clandestino_Nov09_2.pdf. Accessed 12.09.2017.

[135] On the subject of the definition of irregular migration, see S. Valenti, P. Haywood, *Protecting the human rights of irregular migrants: the role of national human rights structures*, Joint European Union—Council of Europe Programme setting up an active network of independent non-judicial human rights structures, Workshop Debriefing Paper, 17–19 June 2008, Padua, University of Padua, 11, document available on the website https://rm.coe.int/16806f1543. Accessed 12.09.2017. As the main reasons of irregular stay one could list a situation when a third-country national legally entered into the territory of the EU, but exceeded the granted period of stay or undertook employment contrary to the provisions of the law; a situation when a person seeking refugee status was issued a negative decision and did not leave the Member State or cannot be returned; a situation when a foreign national

guarantees concerning their stay and, thus, they function in the so-called grey area.[136] As a result, it restricts the very possibility of active engagement of such persons in most of the spheres of life—among the problems signalled by the institutions of civil society one of the most serious ones is the lack of guaranteed access to medical services.[137]

An interesting concept which favours the extension of the legal protection over undocumented migrants is referred to by C. Costello in his work.[138] In accordance with the conception of the so-called social membership, that is, participation in social life, the social contacts established by migrants over an extended period of time (i.e., over the length of their stay in the host country) should legally guarantee an acknowledgement of the right to residence in the host country, even despite its initial illegal

did not appropriately extend his or her stay or was not granted a work permit; a situation when a foreign national illegally entered into the territory of the Union. See Study on the situation of third-country nationals pending return/removal in the EU Member States and the Schengen Associated Countries HOME/2010/RFXX/PR/1001, European Commission 2013, 15. Further, C. Morehouse and M. Blomfield enumerate eight ways for regulating one's status in the host country, C. Morehouse, M. Blomfield, *Irregular migration in Europe*, (Migration Policy Institute, December 2011), 4. As for the statistics regarding the number of persons detained with regard to their irregular stay, in 2014 there were 547,335 persons, out of which 64% were persons aged 18–34 years. See Irregular immigration in the EU: Facts and Figures EPRS | European Parliamentary Research Service; Author: Giulio Sabbati and Eva-Maria Poptcheva, Members' Research Service PE 554.202, April 2015, 3, document available on the website http://www.europarl.europa.eu/RegData/etudes/BRIE/2015/554202/EPRS_BRI(2015)554202_EN.pdf. Accessed 12.09.2017. In accordance with the Frontex Risk Analysis for 2017, in 2016, there were 511,371 illegal crossings of the border, there were issued 206,656 refusals to enter and there were over 2000 attempts to illegally cross the border at border crossings, *Risk Analysis for 2017*, European Border and Coast Guard Agency, report available on the website www.frontex.europa.eu. Accessed 12.09.2017.

[136] On the subject of the protection of irregular migrants' rights, see M. Merlino, J. Parin, Centre for European Policy Study (CEPS) REPORT Fundamental and Human Rights Framework: *Protecting Irregular Migrants in the EU*, report available on the website http://migration.etuc.org/en/docs_en/3%20Fundamental%20and%20Human%20Rights%20Framework_%20Protecting%20Irregular%20Migrants%20in%20the%20EU.pdf. Accessed 12.09.2017.

[137] On this subject, see FRA Report: *Cost of exclusion from healthcare. The case of migrants in an irregular situation, European Union Agency for Fundamental Rights 2015*, report available on the website www.fra.europa.eu. Accessed 12.07.2019. It is also worth pointing out that the very process of access to medical services is a culturally sensitive issue and there occur situations when the professed religion does not allow a foreign national to freely make use of the offered medical services.

[138] C. Costello, *The Human Rights of Migrants and Refugees in European Law*, 67.

character.[139] Social participation also equals acculturation—thus, in accordance with the above concept, an effective cultural integration might be a circumstance for the regularization of the foreign national's stay.

The functioning in the "grey area" has an impact on all the areas of the migrant's life, including the possibility of the realization of cultural rights. A natural consequence of the lack of the legalization of one's stay is the restriction of access to the cultural offer and to education. An interesting answer to this problem was the adoption by the Parliamentary Assembly of the Council of Europe of Resolution No. 1509 on human rights of irregular migrants (2206), in which it was emphasized that all children have the right to education, which should not affect their culture and language.[140] Also in the FRA report on the guarantees of fundamental rights for irregular migrants it is emphasized that education is of primary importance for minors and that there is a need to eliminate bureaucratic barriers in order to facilitate children's enrolment in schools.[141] R. Cholewiński postulates the introduction of intercultural education that would be available to all children, also those of irregular status. Such education, on the one hand, strengthens participation and integration and, on the other hand, guarantees the possibility of reintegration in case of the child's return to the country of origin.[142] However, as it transpires from the available statistical data, women and children comprise only 11–15% of irregular migrants and the group is dominated by adult men.[143]

[139] The author refers the selected case-law of the ECtHR in support of the thesis, amongst others, the case of Sisijeva v. Latvia—Judgement of European Court of Human Rights of 15.01.20017, Complaint No. 60654/00.

[140] Resolution 1509 (2006) Human rights of irregular migrants, Parliamentary Assembly COE, Origin—Assembly debate on 27 June 2006 (18th Sitting) (see Doc. 10924, report of the Committee on Migration, Refugees and Population, rapporteur: Mr van Thijn). Text adopted by the Assembly on 27 June 2006 (18th sitting), http://assembly.coe.int/nw/xml/XRef/Xref-XML2HTML-en.asp?fileid=17456. Accessed 12.09.2017. See also R. Cholewiński, *Study on obstacles to effective access of irregular migrants to minimum social rights*, Council of Europe Publishing (December 2005), 38. http://mighealth.net/eu/images/e/ec/Chol.pdf. Accessed 31.12.2017; Out of the shadows: a human rights perspective on irregular migration and development, Office of the High Commissioner for Human Rights (October 2012), 15. See *The Economic, Social and Cultural Rights of Migrants in an Irregular Situation*. United Nations Human Rights Office of the High Commissioner (New York and Geneva, 2014), 95.

[141] FRA Report*: Fundamental rights of migrants in irregular situation*, FRA 2011, 90.

[142] R. Cholewiński, *Study on obstacles to effective access of irregular migrants.*

[143] P.M. Orrenius, M. Zavodny, "Irregular Immigration in the European Union," *SIEPS*, Swedish Institute for European Policy Studies, European Policy Analysis, January (2016): 5.

Ensuring access to cultural goods to those groups lies within the positive obligation of neither the Member States nor the EU itself; however, depriving certain groups of the possibility of having access to cultural goods may lead to cultural exclusion and the deepening of the exclusion from social life in general. Obviously, in today's globalized reality, it is indeed hard to talk about a complete exclusion from cultural life, even less so in the case of culture mediated by the media. However, we should be aware of the fact that irregular migrants, especially those belonging to the so-called irremovable group,[144] will remain at least in part in the territory of the Union. Hence, it should be in the interest of the Member States to provide at least some limited form of cultural education, so as to counteract their social exclusion and the creation of cultural ghettos. It could also possibly be a first step towards regularization of migrants' stay with the help of newly acquired cultural competences.

Among the obstacles encountered by irregular migrants, the authors of the report titled "Protection and Delivering Fundamental Rights of Irregular Migrants at Local and Regional Levels in the European Union" enumerate four basic obstacles which impede the full realization of the economic and social rights,[145] but also have an impact on the weakening of the possibility for the realization of one's cultural rights, including the right to cultural identity. The first obstacle is the lack of the possibility of taking up legal employment. In the end, it causes social degradation, exclusion, often lower wages, longer working hours and, thus, a foreign national is deprived of the possibility of full participation in cultural life and has no access to the services from the sector of culture. The second of the articulated obstacles concerns migrants' lack of access to the health service. It is often accompanied, in a situation when a foreign national does get to use medical services, by the lack of qualified personnel who would understand cultural differences, which often prohibit the application of certain medical treatments carried out by the medical personnel of a different sex.[146] Such situations do not allow migrants to fully realize their cultural identity.

[144] D.J. Cantor, J. van Wijk, S. Singer, M.P. Bolhuis, "The Emperor's New Clothing: National Responses to 'Undesirable and Unreturnable' Aliens under Asylum and Immigration Law," *Refugee Survey Quarterly*, issue 36 (2017); *Picum Position Paper on EU Return Directive* (Brussels 2015), 23, document available on the website http://picum.org/picum.org/uploads/publication/Final_ReturnDirectiveEN.pdf. Accessed 12.09.2017.

[145] S. Carrera, J. Parkin, *Protecting and Delivering Fundamental Rights of Irregular Migrants at Local and Regional Levels in the European Union*, The Centre for European Policy Studies (2011), 11 et seq.

[146] *Fundamental rights of migrants in irregular situation*, FRA 2011, 78.

Another category includes the actual living conditions—as the authors of the report emphasize, referring to European research,[147] 52% of irregular migrants were not provided with secure living conditions.[148] The lack of such conditions deepens social exclusion, does not favour interaction with representatives of the receiving society and thus slows down integration, including cultural integration. Difficult living conditions can also contribute to exclusion from cultural life, for example, in situations which do not allow one to receive the mediated culture (through radio or television).

The last area of social life where infringements of fundamental rights might occur is education and therefore the problem of providing appropriate access to the system of education to the children of irregular migrants. R. Cholewiński points to similarly crucial areas where infringements of social rights might occur.[149] He also pays special attention to the necessity of realizing the guarantees counteracting racism and xenophobia.

On the margins of the analysis of cultural rights of third-country nationals in the return procedure, it is worth mentioning the right which had been shaped against the backdrop of cultural traditions and still functions, for example, in Germany. It is the so-called Church asylum, which has a long historical tradition and involves granting shelter in the church to persons seeking protection and who are fearing for their life due to a risk of being returned to the country in which they experienced persecutions. In Germany the Church asylum entered into the public sphere in 1983 when a Berlin parish offered shelter to three Palestinian families who feared being returned to Lebanon.[150] As it transpires from the data presented by the representatives of the Asyl in der Kirche Ökumenische Bundesarbeitsgemeinschaft[151] over 75% of the cases in which Church asylum was granted ended in success for the applicants and thus they avoided expulsion to the country of origin.[152]

In recent years, with regard to the increasingly vivid discussion on the subject of the realization of migration policy in the Member States, the

[147] Projekt "L'accès aux soins un droit non-respecté en Europe," website of the project http://www.ceras-projet.org/index.php?id=4079. Accessed 31.12.2017.

[148] S. Carrera, J. Parkin, *Protecting and Delivering Fundamental Rights*, 14.

[149] R. Cholewiński, *Study on obstacles to effective access of irregular migrants*, 31 et seq.

[150] B. Neufert, "Church Asylum," *Forced Migration Review*, vol. 48/XI (2014). http://www.fmreview.org/faith/neufert.html. Accessed 12.09.2017.

[151] http://www.kirchenasyl.de/. Accessed 12.09.2017.

[152] V. Mittermaier, "Experiences of more than 20 years' work in the field, relevance within the church, political framework," Article available on the website http://www.kirchenasyl.de/wp-content/uploads/2013/12/Church-asylum-in-Germany1.pdf. Accessed 12.09.2017.

subject of Church asylum in Germany has returned after the national authorities carried out a search in two churches in Rhineland-Palatinate. In those churches, the religious communities offered Church asylum to migrants. As a result of the search of the premises, a family from Egypt was placed in detention and next returned to the country of origin. The representatives of the religious communities addressed the national authorities with a statement in which they emphasized that offering shelter is a Christian obligation.[153]

4.4 Conclusions

The analysis in the present chapter concerned the guarantees of cultural rights for foreign nationals in the specific area of EU migration law, that is, the right concerning entry into the territory of the Union and the so-called return law.

Within the area of entry into the territory of the EU in the specific provisions of secondary law, the right to cultural identity and the right to behave in accordance with this identity are partially guaranteed. It is a derogable law, whereas the boundary for its realization is marked by the priority of protecting public policy and ensuring security in the migration process, especially in the transport by air. Additionally, it should be remembered that there are regulations which allow foreign nationals to exercise cultural mobility—that is, participate in cultural exchanges and cultural events. Such entitlements contribute to the strengthening of the guarantees of participation in cultural life and also at the supranational level.

A specific legal instrument, introduced within the policy of family reunification, is the one on so-called integration measures, which constitute the existence of so-called integrative cultural obligations. The realization of those obligations allows foreign nationals to establish cultural ties with the host country. The conditions concerning the admission of family members into the territory of the Union also indirectly delineate the boundaries of exercising cultural rights, including the realization of the right to one's own cultural identity and the right to cultural integration with the host country. The limits for the realization of those rights might be Europe's and each Member State's cultural traditions (as is in the case

[153] *Picum Bulletin*, 7 June 2017, http://picum.org/en/news/bulletins/56042/. Accessed 12.09.2017; *Picum Bulletin* 14 July 2017, http://picum.org/en/news/bulletins/56195/. Accessed 12.09.2017.

of Danish policy, protecting its own cultural norms). This is the situation, for example, in the case of the prohibition on the reuniting of polygamous marriages. The boundaries of exercising cultural rights, including the right to cultural integration, are also drawn by the real integrative possibilities of a foreign national, determined, for example, by the legal provisions introducing age limits with regard to the optimal chances of minors for a successful integration process.

Integration measures in the form of integration tests to be passed prior to arrival in the territory of the destination Member State are a controversial instrument. It seems that it often happens that migrants are deprived of the possibility of real cultural integration due to the lack of strictly theoretical knowledge on the culture of the country in which they want to enter. It would be advisable to introduce such tests after the arrival into the territory of the Union and make their passing the condition for further stay of a foreign national concerned within the territory of the Member State. Alternatively, the foreigner concerned could be obligated to successful integration through a system of incentives and the introduction of potential consequences in the case of his or her failing to fulfil such an obligation.

What requires special emphasis within the framework of the return policy is the right to the protection against the culture of the country of origin, which was discussed in the previous chapter and which has its roots in the principle of *non-refoulement*. In the return procedure, it is of special importance for the exercise of cultural rights of a foreign national that there is an instrument of granting a period for voluntary return, as well as the use of alternatives to detention of foreign nationals.

The limits to the exercise of cultural rights by migrants in the return procedure are also marked by the security reasons. In the case of detention, the possibilities of realizing one's cultural rights are necessarily restricted (e.g., freedom of the arts due to the limited availability of forms of artistic expression). However, return law to a minimal degree guarantees the rights of a cultural character, also during the stay in a detention facility—such as the right to the realization of one's religious needs, the right of access to cultural goods, such as the media, books, the right to participate in cultural events or the right to the realization of one's cultural identity. The boundary for the realization of the latter of the listed rights is respect for representatives of other cultures. Detention denotes a special situation and usually the community of migrants in a detention centre is very divergent culturally.

Not without significance for the analysis of the cultural rights of migrants in the return procedure are the rights with regard to the process of reintegration in the country of origin, including cultural reintegration, strengthened by the possibility of carrying out assisted voluntary returns.

Another restriction on the realization of foreign nationals' cultural rights is also their lack of legal status in the host country. As it transpires from the characteristics of the legal status of undocumented migrants, they also have restricted possibilities of participating in cultural life, primarily due to the exclusion from social life.

All foreign nationals who come within the scope of the analysed legal provisions remain in an extraordinary situation, which is far from the realities of everyday life. Therefore, the safeguards of cultural rights in those areas are also of a selective character. Nevertheless, it is an added value that such regulations exist and that they allow for the reconstructing in part of the model of the cultural rights of third-country nationals within the EU's legal system, which will be presented in the final conclusions of the present study.

CHAPTER 5

Possibilities of Protection and Exercise of the Cultural Rights of Third-Country Nationals Within the Framework of the Common European Asylum System

5.1 Introductory Remarks

Persons seeking international protection comprise a specific and exceptionally varied group of third-country nationals.[1] It often happens that those persons have very varied needs, as asylum seekers include persons such as adult men, families, single mothers or unaccompanied minors.[2] Both at the stage of the procedure and during stay in an open reception centre, as well as after being granted protection, their needs in the process of integration are very varied. This chapter will include an analysis of the provisions of the existing legal acts within the Common European Asylum System (CEAS) and the provisions provided for in the projects of new Regulations (Qualification, Procedures and Dublin IV) and the Reception Directive, which most

[1] As it was mentioned in Chap. 2, the legal framework for the Common European Asylum System consists of the following directives: Reception Directive, Qualification Directive and Procedural Directive, as well as the Regulation on the EURODAC system and Dublin III Regulation. See: 5th Annual Report on Migration and Asylum, Communication from the Commission to the European Parliament and the Council, Brussels, 22.05.2014 COM(2014) 288 final, 4. E. Haddad, *The Refugee in International Society, Between Sovereigns*, (Cambridge, 2008), 171 et seq.

[2] On the subject of the work with refugees' children, see D. Dunkerley, J. Scourfield, T. Maegusuku-Hewett, N. Smalley, "The Experiences of Frontline Staff Working with Children Seeking Asylum," in *Migration, Immigration and Social Policy*, ed. C.J. Finer (Blackwell Publishing, 2006), 81 et seq.

A. M. Kosińska, *Cultural Rights of Third-Country Nationals in EU Law*,
https://doi.org/10.1007/978-3-030-30154-5_5

probably will replace the existing legal instruments. The guarantees that will come under scrutiny will concern primarily persons seeking international protection, but also the beneficiaries of the protection, that is, persons who were granted refugee status and subsidiary protection in the territory of the Member States.

The legal *spectrum* of the cultural rights of persons seeking international protection is also broad—on the one hand, there are the needs of participation in the cultural life and having access to cultural goods, even books or the press, both at the stage of remaining in the centre and after the end of the procedures. The realization of such rights without the knowledge of cultural codes is difficult if a foreign national wants to have access to the cultural goods of the receiving country. Therefore, an extremely important role is played by the integration programmes and activities carried out in the reception centres for foreigners. On the other hand, foreign nationals want to remain in contact with the culture of the country of origin, which is not always easy. A very sensitive issue is the possibility of exercising a foreign national's right to cultural identity *in forum externum*, especially when in the reception centres there are persons from different countries of origin. In accordance with the European Asylum Support Office (EASO) data for 2016, the majority of asylum seekers came from Syria, then from Afghanistan, Iraq, Pakistan, Nigeria, Iran, Eritrea and Albania.[3]

The rights of a cultural character to a smaller or lesser degree are guaranteed by the provisions of European Union (EU) law and might be reconstructed on the basis of the legal acts comprising the CEAS framework. The basis for the CEAS can be found under Art. 78 Treaty on the Functioning of the European Union (TFEU) and Art. 18 of the Charter of Fundamental Rights guaranteeing the right to asylum.[4] Moreover, the guidelines for the realization of asylum policy were included in the multiannual programmes of the European Council, of which the first one was the

[3] Latest Asylum Trends Overview 2016, EASO, 1. The remaining countries of origin are, amongst others, Russia, Somalia, Bangladesh, Gambia, Guinea, Serbia, Morocco, Ukraine, Algeria, Ivory Coast, Kosovo, Turkey, Sudan, Senegal, Mali, Georgia, Ghana. Documents available on the website www.easo.europa.eu. Accessed 12.09.2017.

[4] A.M. Potyrała, "Komentarz do art. 18 Karty Praw Podstawowych," in *Karta Praw Podstawowych Unii Europejskiej. Komentarz*, ed. A. Wróbel (Warszawa, 2013), 652 et seq.

Tampere Programme.[5] An important stage for the integration of refugees, and thus for the possibility of the exercise of their cultural rights, at least partially, was the establishment of the European Asylum Fund, which was already mentioned in the Hague Programme.[6] Further, the Stockholm Programme, the last one of the multiannual programmes, included the guidelines for the procedure with regard to unaccompanied minors. In accordance with the recommendation contained in the document, with regard to minors who do not need protection, the undertaken actions should facilitate family reunification and ensure being raised in one's own cultural environment.[7]

The European Commission also took a stance on the subject of migrants' need for integration in the Communication: "A European Agenda on Migration," adopted in the face of the beginning of the migration crisis of 2015.[8] With the replacement of the European Refugee Fund (ERF) with a new complex financial instrument, that is, the Asylum, Migration and Integration Fund (AMIF), "the funds can support targeted initiatives to improve language and professional skills, improve access to services, promote access to the labour market, inclusive education, foster inter-cultural exchanges and promote awareness campaigns targeting both host communities and migrants."[9]

[5] A. Florczak, "Ochrona praw człowieka w systemie prawa wspólnotowego," in *Prawa Człowieka. Wybrane zagadnienia i problemy*, eds. L. Koba, W. Wacławczyk (Warszawa, 2009), 219.

[6] Council, The Hague Programme: Strengthening Freedom, Security and Justice in the European Union (2005/C 53/01), OJ C 53 of 3.03.2005, 1. Another document developing the priorities in the realization of the Union's asylum policy was the European Pact on Migration and Asylum adopted on 24.09.2008 (not published in the Official Journal). See also J. Balicki, *Imigranci i uchodźcy w Unii Europejskiej. Humanizacja polityki imigracyjnej i azylowej* (Warszawa, 2012), 173.

[7] The Stockholm Programme—an open and secure Europe serving and protecting the citizens, OJ C 115 of 4.05.2010, p. 1; part 6.1.7. Unaccompanied minors.

[8] Communication from the Commission to the European Parliament, the Council, the European Economic and Social Committee and the Committee of the Regions. A European Agenda on Migration, Brussels, 13.05.2015, COM(2015) 240 final.

[9] Ibidem, 19. The programme also establishes the basis for taking over the programme of resettlements. In accordance with the definition contained in the programme: "'Resettlement' means the transfer of individual displaced persons in clear need of international protection, on submission of the United Nations High Commissioner for Refugees and in agreement with the country of resettlement, from a third country to a Member State, where they will be admitted and granted the right to stay and any other rights comparable to those granted to a beneficiary of international protection" (ibidem, p. 22). In accordance with the FRA

5.2 Eligibility of Third-Country Nationals for International Protection: Qualification Provisions of a Cultural Nature

The legal act within the framework of the CEAS, which allows for the broadest reconstruction of the rights and freedoms of a cultural character of persons seeking international protection, is the Qualification Directive (at present, Directive 2011/95).[10] It lays down the standards for the qualification of persons for international protection. The directive is to be

report, on the basis of the legal instruments adopted in 2015 it was possible to resettle 14,000 persons to EU Member States until February 2017 (what is interesting, between January and the end of September 2016, 58,000 persons were resettled to the United States), see FRA Fundamental Rights Report 2017, 133. Report available on the website www.fra.europa.eu. Accessed 12.09.2017. The arrival in a new country often means a cultural shock for the resettled persons, especially if they come from a culture which is culturally divergent from European culture. In accordance with the handbook Paving the Way (Paving the Way, A Handbook on the Reception and Integration of Resettled Refugees, International Catholic Migration Commission Europe 2011, available on the website www.refworld.org/pdfid/543f83494.pdf; accessed 12.09.2017 r.), during the first stage of their stay in the host country, displaced persons should be ensured training with regard to cultural differences. Among the stages of integration with the new reality, the most difficult one is, most probably, the one coming after the so-called honeymoon, that is, the stage of hesitation, occurring four to six months after the arrival, when migrants feel lost in the new culture and need cultural training, as well as safeguards of their cultural needs (p. 42). At this stage, the sentiment for the culture of the country of origin is also very prominent. The authors of the report point out to the need of fighting against the negative stereotypes among the receiving society and to the need of increasing the cultural awareness among the inhabitants of local communities (p. 58). Cultural integration programmes are also of primary importance to the success of the resettlement programme. They should focus on the local customs and traditions in the receiving country and take into account migrants' identity characteristics, such as the country of origin, religion, age, sex and the level of education (p. 73). The environment where cultural differences are most conspicuous is school (which may easily lead to potential conflicts, p. 95). The factor facilitating integration, and, at the same time, allowing for the fuller realization of one's cultural identity is the knowledge of the local language—hence, participation of migrants in language courses is recommended (p. 97). On the subject of "pre-departure" training and the projects of cultural orientation, see Report: *Facilitating Integration Through Cultural Orientation*, IOM Mission in Netherlands 2011, 6–7.

[10] Directive 2011/95/EU of the European Parliament and of the Council of 13 December 2011 on standards for the qualification of third-country nationals or stateless persons as beneficiaries of international protection, for a uniform status for refugees or for persons eligible for subsidiary protection, and for the content of the protection granted (reformulated version), (in force since 21 December 2013), OJ L 337, 20.12.2011, 9, further also Directive 2011/95, Qualification Directive.

replaced by the regulation on the standards for qualifying third-country nationals or stateless persons as beneficiaries of international protection, a uniform status for refugees or for persons eligible for subsidiary protection and for the scope of the protection granted.[11] As was emphasized in the justification of the Proposal, the aim of the regulation is to eliminate the discrepancies in the procedures applied by the Member States and in the type of protection granted to third-country nationals, as well as to introduce coherent norms for the granting of protection.[12]

Under Art. 12(d), Directive 2011/95 defines a "refugee" as a

> third-country national who, owing to a well-founded fear of being persecuted for reasons of race, religion, nationality, political opinion or membership of a particular social group, is outside the country of nationality and is unable or, owing to such fear, is unwilling to avail himself or herself of the protection of that country, or a stateless person, who, being outside of the country of former habitual residence for the same reasons as mentioned above, is unable or, owing to such fear, unwilling to return to it, and to whom Article 12 does not apply.[13]

The definition of a "refugee" can also be found under Art. 2(3) of the Proposal for the Qualification Regulation.

Therefore, a refugee is a person who may be escaping from the country of origin due to the oppressive culture, which might be the source of persecution against other cultural attitudes. The reasons behind the escape might also be cultural, ethnic or religious conflicts. With the assumption of the effectiveness of international protection, a person who is a beneficiary of international protection may freely manifest his/her culture,

[11] Proposal of 13.07.2016 for a Regulation of the European Parliament and of the Council on standards for the qualification of third-country nationals or stateless persons as beneficiaries of international protection, for a uniform status for refugees or for persons eligible for subsidiary protection and for the content of the protection granted and amending Council Directive 2003/109/EC of 25 November 2003 concerning the status of third-country nationals who are long-term residents, COM/2016/0466 final—2016/0223 (COD), further also as the Qualification Regulation.

[12] As it transpires from the reasoning of the Qualification Regulation, "the set-up and application of country of origin information and safe country of origin lists, as well as the assessment of the credibility of the applicant during the examination of his or her well-founded fear of persecution or serious harm is noted as one of the main reasons behind the differences in recognition rates within the EU." Proposal for a Regulation of the European Parliament and of the Council on standards for the qualification of third-country nationals or stateless persons as beneficiaries of international protection.

[13] Art. 12 Directive 2011/95 concerns the possibility of exemption from international protection.

customs and religious beliefs, as opposed to the country of origin, and thus exercise one's right to cultural identity, not only internally, but also *in forum externum*.

The protection against the culture of the country of origin is ensured through the definition of the acts of persecution and the reasons for persecution under Art. 9 and 10 of the Qualification Directive[14] and analogously under Art. 9 and 10 of the Proposal for the Qualification Regulation. In accordance with Art. 10 of the Qualification Directive, when assessing the reasons for persecution of a given person, the national authorities should take into account, amongst others, membership of a particular ethnic group and the professed religious beliefs,[15] including participation in religious practices and forms of behaviour (individual or collective) based on religious belief. Moreover, nationality should also be determined on the grounds of cultural criteria. In accordance with Art. 10(1)(c) of the Qualification Directive, "the concept of nationality shall not be confined to citizenship or lack thereof but shall, in particular, include membership of a group determined by its cultural, ethnic, or linguistic identity, common geographical or political origins or its relationship with the population of another State."

[14] International protection, including protection on the grounds of persecution of a cultural character, is also possible in a situation when a well-founded fear of being persecuted appears with regard to the events which occur after foreign nationals leave their country of origin (Art. 5 Directive 2011/95). Such a situation may occur, in the light of the issues under discussion, when a third country is carrying out the so-called cultural revolution, such as Iran, where in 1979 an Islamic revolution took place, changing the cultural codes of behaviour and penalizing behaviours which had been acceptable before. In a situation when radical changes occur with regard to the cultural codes concerning the patterns of behaviour of entire groups (e.g., women) and their freedom to express culture or cultural identity, the granting of international protection is by all means justifiable.

[15] A significant ruling interpreting the conditions for qualifying for international protection on the grounds of religious persecution was the ruling of the Court of Justice in the case of Y and Z (see Judgement of the Court of Justice of 5.09.2012, Bundesrepublik Deutschland v. Y and Z, C 71/11 and C 99/11, ECLI:EU:C:2012:518). The significance of the ruling lies in the departure from the differentiation between the external and internal character of the freedom of religion. In the above case, the Court ruled that foreign nationals, parties to the proceedings, should have the right to publicly manifest their faith, and not merely restrict themselves to the sphere of private practice. See R. Bank, "Refugee Law Jurisprudence from Germany and Human Rights: Cutting Edge or Chilling Effect," in *Human Rights and the Refugee Definition. Comparative Legal Practice and Theory*, eds. B. Burson, D.J. Cantor, (Brill/Nijhoff, 2016), 164.

The consequence of protection against persecutions, including those of a cultural character (ethnic and religious), is the prohibition of returning persons seeking international protection to the countries, where they may experience inhuman treatment. The principle of *non-refoulement* is laid down under Art. 21 of the Qualification Directive and Art. 23 of the Proposal for the Qualification Regulation. As it transpires from the above data presented by the European Asylum Support Office (EASO), a large number of asylum seekers in the EU come from countries with oppressive cultures. Such cultures impede the manifestation and realization of cultural identity of broadly understood minorities or, alternatively, individuals are imposed the obligation to subordinate to the particular cultural customs.[16]

An invaluable source of information on the countries of origin, together with the oppressive character of their culture, are the reports on migrants' countries of origin prepared by the EASO. The data contained in the reports allows for a conscientious qualification of persons applying for international protection. For instance, for the sake of illustrating the point, it is worth mentioning the report on the situation in Nigeria. It focuses to a large degree on the situation of women and the cultural practice of the so-called ritual female circumcision. This practice is justified in the Nigerian culture with a belief that the contact of a child in birth with female genitals of the mother might be harmful to the newborn. Additionally, this practice is believed to increase fertility.[17] The risk of being threatened with the ritual is a circumstance raised by Nigerian women seeking international protection in European countries.[18]

[16] From the annual EASO report it transpires that in 2016, 26% of the applicants for international protection were Syrian nationals, then persons coming from Afghanistan and Iraq (15% and 10%). The other countries of the first ten were Pakistan (4%), Nigeria (4%), Iran (3%), Eritrea (3%), Albania (3%), Russia (2%), Somalia (2%). See Annual Report on the Situation of Asylum in the European Union 2016, EASO 2016, 12. Apart from the classical forms of asylum seeking, the report also points out to the problem of the IDPs, that is, internally displaced persons. In accordance with the reports by the Organization for Security and Cooperation in Europe (OSCE), the Crimean Tatars have been experiencing difficulties in practising their language, culture and religion (ibidem, 41).

[17] EASO Country of Origin Information Report, Nigeria Country Focus, European Asylum Support Office, June 2017, 39.

[18] See the case-law cited in Chap. 4 of the present study on the problem in question. Another cultural issue in Nigeria concerns the acceptance of violence against women (Nigeria Country Focus, 34). In Nigeria, there also occur problems in the case of marriages where spouses profess a different religion each (Nigeria Country Focus, 54).

Cultural customs also include polygamy, marriages between minors[19] and the forcing of women into marriages.[20] Among the countries which tightened the criteria for the reunification of migrants' families, in order to counteract forced marriages, were, amongst others, Denmark[21] and Italy.[22] Further, the countries of origin of persons seeking international protection with regard to being forced into marriage include Bangladesh, Nigeria, India, Indonesia, Iran and Ghana.[23]

Cultural problems are the domain of not only the inhabitants of countries distant from Europe but also the countries of the Russian Federation. Chechnya might serve as an example here, where single women find themselves in a very difficult situation socially,[24] and where there are still cases of

[19] EASO Country of Origin Information Report, Nigeria Country Focus, 43. A similarly difficult situation can be found in Pakistan, where arranged marriages, kidnappings or marriages of minors occur quite frequently. See EASO Country of Origin Information Report, Pakistan Country Overview, European Asylum Support Office, August 2015, 72. Extramarital relationships are also penalized—this crime is called *zina* and is punishable with stoning or 100 strokes of the whip (ibidem, 73). Similarly, the situation of women in Somalia is also hard, as women are forced to marry Al-Shabaab soldiers and if they are widowed they are coerced to marry soldiers of the same rank as their deceased husband—this phenomenon is called *dumaal*—the heritage of the widow; see EASO Country of Origin Information Report, South and Central Somalia Country Overview, European Asylum Support Office, August 2014, 110. Further, in Eritrea, women are forced to do military service—often the only way of avoiding drafting is to get married or become pregnant. See EASO Country of Origin Information Report, Eritrea Country Focus, European Asylum Support Office, May 2015, 34.

[20] On the subject of *forced marriages*, see C. Dauvergne, J. Millbank, "Forced Marriage as a Harm in Domestic and International Law," in *Human Rights and Refugee Law*. Vol. I, eds. J.C. Hathaway, Edward Elgar Publishing 2013, 227–258. See also *Addressing forced marriage in the EU: legal provisions and promising practices*, European Union Agency for Fundamental Rights, 2014, 12 et seq.

[21] D. Dauvergne, J. Millbank, *Forced Marriage as a Harm in Domestic and International Law*, 232.

[22] Misuse of the Right to Family Reunification. Marriages of convenience and false declarations of parenthood produced by the European Migration Network, June 2012, 14.

[23] D. Dauvergne, J. Millbank, "Forced Marriage as a Harm in Domestic and International Law," 238.

[24] EASO Country of Origin Information Report, Chechnya. Women, Marriage, Divorce and Child Custody, European Asylum Support Office, September 2014, 19. In Chechnya there were also unofficial attempts to introduce dress code for women (EASO Country of Origin Information Report, Chechnya, 15). See also E. Januszewska, "Problemy uchodźców z Czeczenii w ośrodkach dla imigrantów w Polsce. Na podstawie badan," in *Migracja, uchodźstwo, wielokulturowość. Zderzenie kultur we współczesnym świecie*, ed. D. Lalak, Warszawa 2007, 269 et seq.

the so-called honorary killings.[25] As B. Ibhawoh emphasizes, the procedures regarding the granting of a political asylum require a "'weak cultural relativism' in which understanding cultural practices is crucial, but those differences should not undermine positions on universal human rights."[26]

Among the most important cultural signs which constitute the cultural identity of individuals, one could list primarily religion (and clothing as a common element of demonstrating one's beliefs to the outside)[27] and language. The risk of persecution on the grounds of religion is one of the most frequent circumstances examined during the qualification procedure for international protection in EU law. As of now, the only ruling with regard to this matter rendered by the Court of Justice of the European Union (CJEU) was the one cited above in the case of X and Y.[28] An interesting ruling with regard to the risk of exposure to persecution on the grounds of religion in the case of return to Pakistan was the judgement of the European Court of Human Rights (ECtHR) in the case of Z and T, in which the Court ruled that the expulsion of the Christians to Pakistan would not constitute an infringement of Art. 9 of the European Convention on Human Rights (ECHR) and therefore the national authorities of the United Kingdom did not make a mistake in the procedure of qualification for protection.[29] As Costello observes, the said

[25] EASO Country of Origin Information Report, Chechnya, 17. The reasons for honorary killings are infidelity and the losing of virginity before marriage.

[26] C. Bohmer, A. Shuman, *Rejecting Refugees. Political Asylum in the 21st Century* (Routledge, 2008), 255. On the subject of honorary killings and other traditional practices, see also ibidem, 230.

[27] See D. Hollenbach, "Religion and Forced Migration," in *The Oxford Handbook of Refugee and Forced Migration Studies*, eds. E. Fiddian-Qasmiyeh, G. Loescher, K. Long, N. Sigona (Oxford, 2014), 447 et seq. See also K. Musalo, "Claims for Protection Based on Religion or Belief," in *Human Rights and Refugee Law*. Vol. I, eds. J.C. Hathaway (Edward Elgar Publishing, 2013), 286 et seq.

[28] Judgement to the Court of Justice of 5.09.2012 in the case Bundesrepublik Deutschland v. Y and Z, C 71/11 and C 99/11, ECLI:EU:C:2012:518.

[29] Judgement of the European Court of Human Rights of 28.02.2006 in the case Z and T v. the United Kingdom, Complaint No. 27034/05. The applicants in this case were nationals of Pakistan, Christians, who had been residing in the United Kingdom, where they filed applications for protection, which were answered in the negative. On the examination of the complaint, the Court confirmed that there had been attacks on Christian churches in Pakistan; however, the applicants had never been victims to direct violence, nor had they been forced to renounce their faith. The applicants claimed that they had received phone calls with threats and feared that they might become a target of attack due to their faith. Nevertheless, the Court held that the applicants did not demonstrate that there existed a risk of violation of the freedom of religion or that Christians should be perceived as a vulnerable group.

ruling was cited in the line of the jurisprudence of the CJEU and in the opinions of Advocate Generals, but it fortunately did not cause the tightening of eligibility criteria.[30]

5.3 Procedure for Granting Protection in View of Third-Country Nationals' Rights of a Cultural Nature

The Procedures Directive[31] establishes common standards of conduct within the Member States for the procedure of granting and withdrawing international protection. The directive is to be replaced by the Regulation establishing the common procedure for applying for international protection within the Union.[32]

Due to the fact that persons seeking refugee status often belong to doubly vulnerable groups (on account of the trauma of displacement and additional features such as single motherhood or illness) and additionally they usually come from a non-European culture background, it is important to ensure respect for their cultural rights at every stage of the refugee procedure, especially during interviews, and safeguard their language rights.

In accordance with Art. 10 of the Procedures Directive regarding the requirements for the examining of applications for protection, the Member States should ensure that "the personnel examining applications and taking decisions have the possibility to seek advice, whenever necessary, from experts on particular issues, such as medical, cultural, religious, child-related or gender issues."[33] Analogous regulations are to be found under Art. 33(3) of the Qualification Regulation, which adds to the concept of gender the adjective "socio-cultural," which points to the possibility of

[30] C. Costello, "The Search of the Outer Edges of Non-Refoulement in Europe: Exceptionality and Flagrant Breaches," in *Human Rights and Refugee Definition. Comparative Legal Practice and Theory*, ed. B. Burson, D.J. Cantor (Brill/Nijhoff, 2016), 201.

[31] Currently Directive 2013/32/EU of the European Parliament and of the Council of 26 June 2013 on common procedures for granting and withdrawing international protection, OJ L 180, 29.06.2013, 60, further also as Directive 2013/32, the Procedures Directive. It replaced Directive 2005/85.

[32] Proposal of 13.07.2016 for a Regulation of the European Parliament and of the Council establishing a common procedure for international protection in the Union and repealing Directive 2013/32/EU, COM/2016/0467 final—2016/0224 (COD), further also as the Procedures Regulation.

[33] Art. 10(3)(d) Directive 2013/32.

consultation in the area of divergent perceptions on the role of the sexes in various cultures.

Moreover, Art. 15 Directive 2013/32 introduces detailed guarantees with regard to conducting interviews of the applicants, with a view to protecting a foreign national's cultural identity and eliminating potential cultural differences, which might impede the giving of evidence. Therefore, the person conducting an interview should be equipped with competences to take account of "the personal and general circumstances surrounding the application, including the applicant's cultural origin."[34] Moreover, at the request of the applicant, the hearing should be conducted by an interviewer of the same sex[35] and translated by an interpreter of the same sex. What is more, the applicant indicates the preferred language of the interview.[36]

The understanding of cultural differences by the determining authorities is of crucial importance for the procedure of qualification for protection. Due to the fact that foreign nationals often come from cultural circles which are far from European culture, they often give account of their experiences in an entirely different manner than typical of a European narrative. The differences may lie in the depth of emotion embedded in their narrative, as well as in the choice of their vocabulary. It is the responsibility of the national authority to respect the ways of expression and vocabulary used by foreign nationals, which are a part of their own cultural identity.

The problems of the lack of understanding of foreign nationals' narratives and of cultural differences, which influence the manner of providing evidence (for instance, the avoiding of eye contact by women in certain cultures), are raised by lawyers in their accounts of their work with refugees.[37] Moreover, as V.C. Bickley observes, interpreters in the refugee pro-

[34] Art. 15(3)(a) Directive 2013/32; Art. 12(6) Proposal for the Procedures Regulation. Requirements concerning hearings, see Handbook on European Law Relating to Asylum, Borders and Immigration, Edition 2014, European Union Agency for Fundamental Rights, 2014, Council of Europe 2014, 102.

[35] Art. 15(3)(b) Directive 2013/32. In accordance with Art. 12(8)(2) of the Proposal for the Procedures Regulation, "Where requested by the applicant, the determining authority shall ensure that the interviewers and interpreters are of the same sex as the applicant provided that this is possible and the determining authority does not have reasons to believe that such a request is based on grounds which are not related to difficulties on the part of the applicant to present the grounds of his or her application in a comprehensive manner."

[36] Art. 15(3)(c) Directive 2013/32, Art. 12(8)(1) Proposal for the Procedures Regulation.

[37] C. Bohmer, A. Shuman, *Rejecting Refugees. Political Asylum in the 21st Century*, 148.

cedure not only facilitate communication between two persons speaking different languages, but are also mediators between cultures.[38] It often happens that the same words may have different denotations in different languages, for example, the word "brother" for refugees from Africa means not only brothers by blood but all members of the tribe.[39] Such misunderstandings resulting from the clash of cultures during interviews may have a huge impact on the final result of the qualification procedure, hence the need for maintaining appropriate concentration by the determining authorities of the Member States conducting the procedure.

In the Procedures Directive, there are also concepts of the safe country of origin and the safe third country. A safe third country is a country which meets the conditions listed under Art. 38 of the Procedures Directive. If a foreign national had entered into the territory of the EU from such a country and is applying for protection, it might be assumed that there is no risk of inhuman treatment in this third country and that the guarantees allowing for seeking international protection are ensured. In such a situation, the foreign national concerned might be returned to his or her third country in order to apply for international protection there. Among the criteria for accepting a country as a safe third country there are also conditions of treating a person concerned in such a way so that the person's life and freedom are not threatened on account of religion, race, nationality and membership of a particular social group and so as to ensure that there was no risk of sustaining serious harm by this person as defined in the Qualification Directive. Therefore, on the basis of the above criteria (as well as the other conditions listed under Art. 38 of the Procedures Directive), it might be assumed that a foreign national in a safe third country will have a chance to realize one's own cultural identity and will be protected against the culture of origin. The concept of the safe third country will also be included in the proposal for the new Procedures Regulation in its Art. 45.[40] Third countries will be designated as safe third

[38] W. Kalin, "Troubled Communication: Cross Cultural Misunderstandings in the Asylum Hearing," in *Human Rights and Refugee Law*, vol. II, ed. J.C. Hathaway (Edward Elgar Publishing, 2013), 612.

[39] Ibidem, 613–615.

[40] In accordance with Art. 45, a third country is designated as a safe third country provided that

> "(a) life and liberty are not threatened on account of race, religion, nationality, membership of a particular social group or political opinion; (b) there is no risk of serious harm as defined in Regulation (EU) No XXX/XXX; (c) the principle of non-refoulement in accordance with the Geneva Convention is respected; (d) the prohibition of

countries at the level of the Union in accordance with Art. 46 of the Proposal for the Regulation.

In accordance with Art. 37 Directive 2013/32, there is a possibility at the national level of designating a given third country as a safe country of origin and, indeed, the Member States introduce such national lists.[41] The criteria for designating a country as a safe country of origin can be found in the Annex to the Procedures Directive. Accordingly:

> A country is considered as a safe country of origin where, on the basis of the legal situation, the application of the law within a democratic system and the general political circumstances, it can be shown that there is generally and consistently no persecution as defined in Article 9 of Directive 2011/95/EU, no torture or inhuman or degrading treatment or punishment and no threat by reason of indiscriminate violence in situations of international or internal armed conflict.

While examining whether a given country can be designated as a safe one, the Member States should take into account whether in the given country there is sufficient level of protection against persecution or mistreatment.

The very concept of the safe country of origin is criticized both in the doctrine and by international organizations. It is hard not to agree with this criticism—it might always happen that in a given country there will appear a minority group experiencing persecutions.[42] However, generally, the concept of the safe country of origin allows for the assumption that the persons coming from such a country are not exposed to a risk of

removal, in violation of the right to freedom from torture and cruel, inhuman or degrading treatment as laid down in international law, is respected; (e) the possibility exists to receive protection in accordance with the substantive standards of the Geneva Convention or sufficient protection as referred to in Article 44(2), as appropriate."

[41] See H. Martenson, J. McCarthy, "'In General, No Serious Risk of Persecution': Safe Country of Origin Practices in Nine European States," *Journal of Refugee Studies*, No. 11/3 (1998): 304–325; C. Engelmann, "Convergence against the Odds: The Development of Safe Country of Origin Policies in EU Member States (1990–2013)," *European Journal of Migration and Law*, vol. 16, issue 2 (2014): 277–302. Article available on the website http://fasos.maastrichtuniversity.nl/profiles/Engelmann/Engelmann2014_Convergence.pdf. Accessed 12.09.2017.

[42] See J. van Selm, *Access to Procedures 'Safe Third Countries,' 'Safe Countries of Origin' and 'Time Limits,'* UNHCR 2001, http://www.unhcr.org/3b39a2403.pdf. Accessed 12.09.2017.

persecution, including persecution on religious, ethnic or cultural grounds, and may fully realize their cultural identity both *in forum internum* and *in forum externum*.

As a result of the migration crisis of 2015, the European Commission proposed the adoption of a regulation establishing a European list of safe countries of origin. This list included Albania, Bosnia and Herzegovina, Macedonia, Kosovo, Montenegro, Serbia and Turkey.[43] The inclusion of Turkey, especially in the context of the unstable internal situation and social conflicts, raised controversy. Similar reactions were evoked in the case of Albania.[44] The stance of the Commission holding that Turkey is a safe country of origin (hence, a place where it is possible to realize one's cultural rights, including the freedom of religion, without the risk of being exposed to persecutions) is contrary (at least in part) to the EASO report on the situation in Turkey. In accordance with the report, in Turkey there are instances of infringement of the freedom of speech and the Turkish media remain under pressure from the government.[45] The situation of the Kurds, Armenians and religion remains a sensitive issue in the media.[46] What is more, numerous minorities are not recognized by law. From the report it transpires that the Assyrians, Caferi, Yazidis or Roma cannot fully realize their cultural, religious or language rights there.[47]

At present, a new proposal of the regulation is being processed in the European Parliament, aimed at introducing a unified asylum procedure. In accordance with its Art. 47, a safe country of origin is a country in which there are no persecutions within the meaning of Art. 9 of the regulation on qualification (the project is also currently being drafted), there are no infringements of the prohibition of inhuman treatment and there is no threat of massive violence. Additionally, such a state must meet the require-

[43] Proposal for a Regulation of the European Parliament and of the Council establishing an EU common list of safe countries of origin for the purposes of Directive 2013/32/EU of the European Parliament and of the Council on common procedures for granting and withdrawing international protection, and amending Directive 2013/32/EU COM/2015/0452 final—2015/0211 (COD), http://eur-lex.europa.eu/legal-content/PL/TXT/HTML/?uri=CELEX:52015PC0452&from=en. Accessed 12.09.2017.

[44] See A.M. Kosińska, "Ewolucja koncepcji bezpiecznego kraju pochodzenia w dobie kryzysu migracyjnego," in *W obliczu kryzysu. Przyszłość polityki azylowej i migracyjnej Unii Europejskiej*, ed. A.M. Kosińska (Lublin, 2017), 159.

[45] *EASO Country of Origin Information Report Turkey Country Focus*, European Asylum Support Office, November 2016, 63. Information available on the website www.easo.europa.eu. Accessed 12.09.2017.

[46] Ibidem, 63.

[47] Ibidem, 66.

ments listed under Art. 47(3) of the above regulation concerning protection against persecution and mistreatment.[48] An interesting solution can be found under Art. 47(4) of the Proposal for the Procedures Regulation, in which a country designated as safe at a general level may be designated as a safe country of origin for a specific applicant, providing that the applicant concerned "has not submitted any serious grounds for considering the country not to be a safe country of origin in his or her particular circumstances."[49] The list of safe countries at the EU level will comprise an annex to the regulation and will be subject to regular verification by the European Commission.[50] In the case when there appears a situation excluding the possibility of designating a country as a safe one, the Commission will have an option to adopt a delegated act suspending the presence of a third country from the EU common list of safe countries of origin for a period of up to six months (Art. 49[1] Procedures Regulation) and to submit a proposal to remove that third country from the EU common list of safe countries of origin (Art. 49[3] Procedures Regulation). The Member States will be able to retain their lists of national designations for the period of five years from the moment of entry into force of the regulation.[51]

5.4 Reception of Persons Seeking International Protection in View of the Possibility of Protection of Cultural Rights

The Reception Directive (currently 2013/33)[52] establishes common standards for the Member States for the reception of applicants for international protection. The directive is to be replaced by a new Reception

[48] Among the requirements for qualification, the proposal lists the following: the functioning of laws and regulations of the country in the manner ensuring protection, the existence of relevant provisions of national law guaranteeing protection, observance by the given state of fundamental rights guaranteed in the ECHR, International Covenant on Civil and Political Rights (ICCPR) and other acts of international law prohibiting inhuman or degrading treatment, the observance of the principle of *non-refoulement* and the functioning of effective legal remedies.

[49] Art. 47(4)(c) Proposal for the Procedures Regulation.

[50] Art. 48(2) Proposal for the Procedures Regulation.

[51] Art. 50 Proposal for the Procedures Regulation.

[52] Directive 2013/33/EU of the European Parliament and of the Council of 26 June 2013 laying down standards for the reception of applicants for international protection (recast version), OJ L 180, 29.06.2013, 96, further also as Directive 2013/33, Reception Directive. It replaced Directive 2003/9.

Directive, which is currently in the process of being drafted.[53] Therefore, on the basis of legal provisions and their practical applications by the Member States it is possible to analyse the functioning of the guarantees of the rights of a cultural character in the reception procedure.

An especially difficult situation regarding the realization of the rights and fundamental freedoms is that of asylum seekers who are to be placed in detention by the national authorities.[54] Art. 10 of the Reception Directive lays down the minimal conditions in which the detained migrants should be staying—among them, there is, for example, access to open-air spaces. However, under Art. 10 one cannot find any guarantees regarding access to broadly understood cultural measures, even though in the guarded centres there might be families staying with children.[55] In accordance with Art. 10(4), representatives of NGOs also have access to detainees. Such contacts are not to be overestimated, as it is often possible to initiate intercultural dialogue and thus determine the needs of the applicant during such consultations. Analogous provisions can be found in the new version of the Reception Directive.

The right which is in part a cultural right is the right to education. In accordance with Art. 14 of the Reception Directive (similarly, Art. 14 of the proposal for a new directive), children of the applicants are ensured access to education, based on similar principles, as provided to citizens of the receiving country, until the enforcement of the return procedure against the applicant.[56]

The Member States may also organize appropriate preparatory courses and language courses in order to facilitate access to education. Minor children of the applicants are under special care. In accordance with Art. 23 of the Reception Directive (Art. 23 in the new version): "Member States shall ensure a standard of living adequate for the minor's physical, mental,

[53] Proposal of 13.07.2016 for a Directive of the European Parliament and of the Council laying down standards for the reception of applicants for international protection (recast version) COM(2016) 465, final 2016/0222(COD).

[54] See regulations concerning the detention of applicants—Art. 8 and 9 Directive 2013/33.

[55] See Art. 11 and 12 Directive 2013/33.

[56] The system of organization of reception facilities for foreigners seeking refugee status in Poland. The report was prepared by the National Contact Point of the European Migration network in Poland, October 2013, 49. In accordance with the data presented in the report "All children aged 7–18 are subject to compulsory education. Apart from support in enrolling children in school and in obtaining school materials, there are activities aimed at providing children with assistance from the so-called advisors on multiculturality."

spiritual, moral and social development." It is beyond doubt that the realization of the above guarantee also entails the creation of a possibility for exercising cultural rights, such as the right to one's individual cultural identity (which is realized by spiritual development and safeguards of the freedom of religion) or participation in cultural life, which is a condition of effective social acculturation and moral development.

Moreover, in accordance with Art. 16 Directive 2013/33, "Member States may allow applicants access to vocational training irrespective of whether they have access to the labour market."[57] On the one hand, vocational trainings indirectly fall within the realization of the right to education; on the other hand, they counteract social exclusion and strengthen integration. What is more, if foreign nationals are persons who work in the professions from the sector of culture, such professional training will facilitate their fuller engagement in the active realization of cultural rights.

A special role in the process of cultural adaptation of persons applying for international protection is played by reception centres for foreigners[58]—the minimal standards for the organization of the reception of foreign nationals in reception centres are laid down under Art. 18 of the Reception Directive. During stay in the reception centre for foreigners, considerable attention should be directed at persons from the so-called vulnerable groups[59]—such persons should be housed in special reception conditions, whose minimal norms are laid down in Chapter 4 of the Directive (Art. 21–25 Directive 2013/33, analogously, under the same Articles in the new Directive). Persons belonging to vulnerable groups, under Art. 21 (it includes an open catalogue of vulnerable subjects), include "minors, unaccompanied minors, disabled people, elderly people,

[57] A similar guarantee is to be found under Art. 16 of the Proposal for the New Reception Directive.

[58] In accordance with the directive, foreign nationals may resort to three forms of accommodation: "(a) premises used for the purpose of housing applicants during the examination of an application for international protection made at the border or in transit zones; (b) accommodation centres which guarantee an adequate standard of living; (c) private houses, flats, hotels or other premises adapted for housing applicants"—similar regulations are to be found in the Proposal for the new version of the directive. See also S. Łodziński, "Problemy osób oczekujących na nadanie statusu uchodźcy w Polsce w wybranych ośrodkach recepcyjnych," in *Kulturowe wymiary imigracji do Polski. Studia socjologiczne*, eds. E. Nowicka, S. Łodziński (Warszawa, 2006), 243 et seq.

[59] B. Mikołajczyk, "Obowiązki państwa w zakresie identyfikacji szczególnych potrzeb cudzoziemców ubiegających się o status uchodźcy," in *Uchodźcy w Polsce i Europie: stan prawny i rzeczywistość*, eds. R. Gardocka, J. Sobczak (Toruń 2010), 81.

pregnant women, single parents with minor children, victims of human trafficking, persons with serious illnesses, persons with mental disorders and persons who have been subjected to torture, rape or other serious forms of psychological, physical or sexual violence, such as victims of female genital mutilation." Victims of female genital mutilation listed in the last place under Art. 21 of the Reception Directive are in fact victims of the oppressive culture of the country of origin and cultural rituals unacceptable in European cultural circles. In accordance with Art. 25, the personnel working with such victims should have appropriate training, whereas the victims should be ensured psychological help.

Detailed data on the subject of reception practices of particular Member States can be found in the European Migration Network (EMN) report of 2014. One of the more interesting practices followed by the Member States is the way of relocating persons seeking refugee status in the territory of the host country. For instance, inasmuch as in France the applicants have the freedom to choose the region where they will stay,[60] in the United Kingdom, Portugal or Italy the relocation of asylum seekers is conditioned by the existence of the best options for integration. Hence, one of the decisive factors taken into account in allocation is the cultural match between the applicant's profile and the region, so as to avoid potential social tensions.[61]

The report also contains the results of research regarding the scope of cultural activities offered in the reception centres. Among the most frequently offered activities there are language courses and integration courses, but also cultural trips, sewing and cooking lessons (Belgium), access to books (the Czech Republic), television (with channels in English, Russian and French—Estonia), the Internet (Cyprus), arts-and-crafts workshops (the Czech Republic), cinema (Greece), art classes (Finland), music classes (Hungary), participation in theatre groups (Portugal).[62] As can be seen from the above, in spite of remaining in a specific social enclave, such as the reception facility, foreign nationals retain the possibility of actively participating in cultural activities. On the one hand, this offers them a possibility to maintain contact with the culture of their country of origin (mostly through the media and common religious prac-

[60] The Organisation of Reception Facilities for Asylum Seekers in Different Member States, European Migration Network Study 2014, 9.

[61] Ibidem.

[62] Ibidem, 52–59.

tices on the premises of the reception centre); on the other hand, they have a chance to be actively involved in the process of acculturation and to learn about the culture of the host country.

In Polish reception centres, it is ensured that foreigners have access to common rooms, TV rooms (due to cultural reasons, they are separated into rooms for men and for women), sports facilities, rooms designated for religious practices and computer rooms.[63] From the report of the Head of the Office for Foreigners it transpires that foreign nationals arriving at the reception centre have the possibility of participating in introductory meetings, where they are provided with the basic information regarding life in Poland, the existing norms, customs, traditions and rules of the functioning of the educational system.[64] In accordance with the data presented in the Polish report on reception, in reception centres foreign nationals receive meals in accordance with their professed cultural principles.[65]

In accordance with the report of the Polish Supreme Chamber of Control (NIK), "Social Security for Refugees. Information on the Control Findings," "Foreign nationals staying in reception centres had the opportunity to observe their customs, national and cultural traditions and perform religious practices (all reception centres had a prayer room)."[66] In the reception facilities there were also lessons on the Polish language,[67] but not

[63] Ibidem.

[64] Information by the Head of the Office for Foreigners on the application of the Act of 13 June 2003 on granting protection to foreigners within the territory of the Republic of Poland in 2016 (consolidated text Journal of Laws of 2016, item 1836) in terms of implementation of obligations of the Republic of Poland resulting from the Geneva Convention on the Status of Refugees and the New York Protocol relating to the status of refugees, Warsaw, March 2016, 21. Information available on the website https://udsc.gov.pl/statystyki/raporty-okresowe/raport-roczny-ochrona-miedzynarodowa/2016–2/. Accessed 12.09.2017. In the reception centres there are also available handbooks "First steps in Poland" on the basic aspects of social life in Poland, including holidays, customs and traditions.

[65] The system of organization of reception facilities for foreigners seeking refugee status in Poland. The report prepared by the National Contact Point of the European Migration Network in Poland, October 2013, 13, 30. See para. 10(3) regulation of the Minister of the Interior of 23 October 2015 on the rules of stay in the reception centre for foreigners, Journal of Laws of 2015, item 1828. See also M. Kochanowska, "Funkcje pracowników socjalnych w polskich ośrodkach dla uchodźców," in *Uchodźcy. Teoria i praktyka*, eds. I. Czerniejewska, I. Main (Poznań, 2008), 139 et seq.

[66] *Raport NIK: Pomoc społeczna dla uchodźców. Informacja o wynikach kontroli*, No. 159/2015/P/14/049/KPS, 2015, 31.

[67] Ibidem, 36.

in sufficient numbers concerning the needs of the refugees.[68] Language classes were also open to children, whereas language learning is carried out in every reception centre.[69] What is more, minors may participate in the language and culture classes of the country of their origin (with the same number of hours as in the case of extra lesson on the Polish language and compensatory classes), if they are subject to compulsory education.[70]

In accordance with the rules of stay in the reception centre, which is an annex to the ministerial regulation, "the reception centre shall provide the possibility of participating of minors in recreational activities and the possibility of organizing cultural, educational or sports activities with the involvement of institutions, organizations, associations and other bodies and natural persons."[71]

Animation activities conducted in reception centres and pre-integration assistance allow for the realization of cultural needs of the foreign nationals remaining in the procedure. In my view, participation in pre-integration activities should also be treated as a cultural obligation of foreign nationals. It would also be advisable if the period of acculturation ended with, at least, a partially official examination on the learned skills. If that were the case, the period of stay in the reception centre might be fully used by foreign nationals for absorbing new skills and would facilitate their functioning in society after leaving the reception centre.

5.5 Cultural Rights Guaranteed to the Beneficiaries of International Protection Within the Framework of the CEAS

The Qualification Directive determines the rights the beneficiaries of international protection are entitled to—refugee status ensures that third-country nationals in various walks of social life are treated at par with the original citizens of the host country. In a similar way, those issues were regulated in the Proposal for the Qualification Regulation. This is the case

[68] Ibidem, 41–42.

[69] Information by the Head of the Office for Foreigners on the application of the Act of 13 June 2003 on granting protection to foreigners within the territory of the Republic of Poland in 2016, 23.

[70] Ibidem.

[71] Para. 16 of the Regulation of the Minister of the Interior of 23 October 2015 on the rules of stay in the reception centre for foreigners.

regarding access to social benefits (Art. 29 Qualification Directive, Art. 34 Proposal for the Qualification Regulation) or health care (Art. 30 Qualification Directive, Art. 35 Proposal for the Qualification Regulation). Beneficiaries of international protection also have access to the job market (Art. 26 Qualification Directive, Art. 30 Proposal for the Qualification Regulation).

All the above guarantees contribute to the counteracting against social exclusion and strengthen the possibilities of integration, including cultural integration with the host society. The importance of support for social integration of beneficiaries of protection was emphasized in the project of the Regulation on qualification.[72]

The persons covered by refugee status are in fact fully fledged participants of private law framework[73] and social life—thus, they benefit from the right to have access to goods and services, as well as participate in the cultural life of the receiving country.

5.5.1 *Educational Rights*

In accordance with Art. 27 of the Qualification Directive, minors who benefit from international protection have access to education, subject to the same conditions as the nationals of the receiving country. Moreover, access to education (including the possibility of training and requalifying) is provided for adult beneficiaries of protection under the same principles as for third-country nationals, whose stay is of legal character in the host country.[74] An analogous regulation is to be found under Art. 31 of the Proposal for the Qualification Regulation. Art. 28 of the directive provides for equal treatment in the procedure of recognizing qualifications, including foreign diplomas and certificates.[75] This guarantee has also been included in Art. 32 of the Proposal for the Qualification Regulation.

[72] Para. 3 of the justification of the Qualification Regulation.

[73] See M. Kumela-Romańska, *Administracyjnoprawny status cudzoziemca w Polsce*, (Warszawa, 2017), 176.

[74] See ICRE Report: The Impact of the EU Qualification Directive on International Protection, October 2008, ELENA (European Legal Network for Asylum), 33. On the subject of classes in multicultural groups, see M. Bohosiewicz, I. Czerniejowska, T. Halik, J. Jurewicz, P. Kornacki, P. Kuspys, A. Marek, *Imigranci w mojej klasie* (Warszawa: Stowarzyszenie Vox Humana, 2014).

[75] In accordance with Art. 28 of the Qualification Directive: "Member States shall endeavour to facilitate full access for beneficiaries of international protection who cannot provide

The right to education, guaranteed under Art. 14 of the Charter of Fundamental Rights (CFR), is considered to be a right of a fundamental character in the system of international law, primarily in Art. 2 of Protocol No. 1 to the ECHR.[76] In accordance with the data presented in the FRA report, in 2016, as many as 600,000 children applied for international protection, including 100,000 unattended minors[77]—the Member States are obligated to ensure education to all those children.

Activities in favour of integration undertaken by the EU will be analysed in greater detail in the following chapter, which will be focused on legal migration into the EU. However, it is worth referring at this stage to the document entitled "Action Plan on the Integration of Third Country Nationals" in which it is emphasized that among the problems experienced by newly arrived migrants seeking international protection, one should also mention those regarding language and cultural barriers and fears of stigmatization in education.[78] It is an obligation of the Member

documentary evidence of their qualifications to appropriate schemes for the assessment, validation and accreditation of their prior learning. Any such measures shall comply with Articles 2(2) and 3(3) of Directive 2005/36/EC of the European Parliament and of the Council of 7 September 2005 on the recognition of professional qualifications." Communication from Commission: Brussels, 10.06.2016 COM(2016) 381, final Communication from the Commission to the European Parliament, the Council, the European Economic and Social Committee and the Committee of the Regions on a New Skills Agenda for Europe Working together to strengthen human capital, employability and competitiveness (SWD[2016] 195 final). The document entails the strengthening of the competences of migrants arriving in the EU, including refugees, on the job market, through support in language learning (p. 10).

[76] In its case-law, the ECtHR confirmed the necessity that children of foreign nationals have access to education. The Court ruled that an infringement of Art. 2 Protocol No. 1 occurred by Russia in the case of Timishev v. Russia (the case concerned Chechnyan children who could not exercise their right to education due to procedural obstacles). Judgement of the European Court of Human Rights of 13.12.2005, Complaint No. 55762/00 and 55974/00. See also *Handbook on European law relating to asylum, borders and immigration* 207 et seq. On the subject of the case-law of the ECtHR, see M.B. Dembour, *When humans become migrants. Study of the European Court of Human Rights with an Inter-American Counterpoint* (Oxford, 2015), 267; K. Łasak, *Prawa społeczne w orzecznictwie Europejskiego Trybunału Praw Człowieka* (Warszawa, 2013), 157–168.

[77] Current migration situation in the EU: Education, May 2017, European Union Agency for Fundamental Rights, 2.

[78] Communication from the Commission to the European Parliament, the Council, the European Economic and Social Committee and the Committee of the Regions, Action Plan on the Integration of Third Country Nationals, Brussels, 7.06.2016 COM(2016) 377 final, 4. https://ec.europa.eu/homeaffairs/sites/homeaffairs/files/what-we-do/policies/euro-

States to ensure that all migrants' children may continue education[79] and prepare local communities and teachers in such a way so as to avoid cultural segregation in educational institutions.[80] The effects of the activities conducted by the Member States for the purpose of genuine integration of migrants' children in the cultural, linguistic and educational aspects[81] often include a higher level of integration of children in comparison with their parents, who are more prone to experience cultural differences.[82]

5.5.2 *Integration Rights of the Beneficiaries of International Protection*[83]

The Qualification Directive in its Art. 34 guarantees the beneficiaries of international protection the right to participate in integration programmes,

pean-agenda-migration/proposal-implementation-package/docs/20160607/communication_action_plan_integration_third-country_nationals_en.pdf. Accessed 12.09.2017.

[79] On this subject in the system of Polish law, see *Prawne uwarunkowania integracji uchodźców w Polsce. Komentarz dla praktyków*, ed. W. Klaus (Warszawa: Stowarzyszenie Interwencji Prawnej, 2008), 54 et seq.

[80] Communication from the Commission to the European Parliament, the Council, the European Economic and Social Committee and the Committee of the Regions, Action Plan on the Integration of Third Country Nationals, p. 7. One of the planned activities is to prepare the possibility of learning a language online for the newly arrived refugees within the programme Erasmus plus—this activity provides for the issuing of 100,000 licences within three years (p. 8). It is worth noting that the Union's funds (including Erasmus plus) in the years 2014–2015 contributed to over 200 projects for the benefit of refugees, also within the area of integration (ibidem, 15). Data on the activities undertaken by the Member States within the scope of facilitating access to education for migrants' children arriving into the EU (including refugee children), through, amongst others, the introduction of preparatory classes preceding the joining of regular classes—Fundamental Rights Report FRA 2017, 138.

[81] On the subject of the programmes run by the Member States, see *Fundamental Rights Report,* FRA 2017, 135–140.

[82] A new beginning. Refugee integration in Europe, UNHCR, September 2013, Outcome of an EU-funded project on Refugee Integration Capacity and Evaluation (RICE), 105. Report available on the website www.refworld.org/docid/522980604.html. Accessed 12.09.2017.

[83] The instruments for the integration of third-country nationals implemented within the systems of EU law and migration policy will be analysed in greater detail in the following chapter of the current study on the rights of a cultural character of regular migrants. On the subject of integration instruments, see C. Bauloz, G. Ruiz, "Refugee Status and Subsidiary Protection: Towards a Uniform Content of International Protection," in *Reforming the Common European Asylum System. The New European Refugee Law*, eds. V. Chetail, P. De Bruycker, F. Maiani (Brill, 2016), 266; A. Balch, A. Geddes, "The development of the EU Migration and Asylum Regime," in *Migration and the new technological borders*, eds. H. Dijstelbloem, A. Meijer (Palgrave Macmillan, 2011), 30 et seq.

whose aim is to effectively integrate a migrant with the receiving country.[84] In comparison with the previous Directive 2004/83, there has been a significant change, since previously the beneficiaries of international protection could participate in integration programmes provided that the Member States established such programmes. It was a discretionary power of individual Member States.[85]

Those regulations were extended in the wording of Art. 38 of the Qualification Regulation, which is also to regulate access to integration measures. Contrary to Art. 34 of the Qualification Directive, the new provision enumerates examples of integration measures, such as language courses, programmes shaping European awareness, integration programmes and vocational trainings with regard to the needs of those people. The catalogue of the listed integration measures is of an open character.[86]

What is more, the Proposal for the Qualification Regulation provides for the possibility for the Member State to take a decision on the obligatory character of those measures (Art. 38[2]). However, as is emphasized in the justification of the Proposal for the Regulation, the Member States, in imposing on third-country nationals the obligation of participation in integration measures, must take account of the personal problems of the

[84] The criteria for the effectiveness of integration should remain at the centre of interest of the Member States while designing the syllabuses of integration classes. As A. Mińkowska observes, the process of cultural adaptation is closely intertwined with psychological adaptation, whereas a lack of the latter may lead to mental problems and depression. Foreign nationals may find support among a group of migrants from the same cultural or religious circle, but what is important is that "there is, however, a risk that when the values shared by a given group (religion) are contrary to the standards and patterns existing in the new, dominant environment, then the adaptation process of a migrant might be even further complicated." A. Mińkowska, "Rola buddyzmu dla uchodźców tybetańskich," in *Migracje. Religie i kościoły wobec migracji migrantów. Migracje i społeczeństwo*, vol. 14, ed. J.E. Zamojski (Warszawa, 2009), 196.

[85] C. Bauloz, G. Ruiz, "Refugee Status and Subsidiary Protection," 250.

[86] As emphasized in the Preamble of the Regulation: "In order to enhance the effective exercise of the rights and benefits laid down in this Regulation by beneficiaries of international protection, it is necessary to take into account their specific needs and the particular integration challenges with which they are confronted, and facilitate their access to integration related rights in particular as regards employment-related educational opportunities and vocational training and access to recognition procedures for foreign diplomas, certificates and other evidence of formal qualifications in particular due to the lack of documentary evidence and their inability to meet the costs related to the recognition procedures" (recital 49 of the Preamble).

person concerned, in accordance with the existing line of the jurisprudence of the CJEU.[87]

An effective integration of the beneficiaries of international protection is a condition for a harmonious coexistence of the receiving society and third-country nationals. The significance of this process was emphasized both in the justification of the Regulation and in its Preamble. In order to strengthen the process of integration, the Regulation provides for the possibility of applying the so-called integration incentives, due to which the Member States will be able to condition the access to certain social benefits on the effective participation in integration measures.[88] The basis for such a solution can be found under Art. 34 of the Proposal for the Qualification Regulation. An important element in the construction of this provision is the determination of the character of participation in integration measures. It is not enough for the participation to be active (with the foreigner's actual involvement), but it should also be effective. However, the provision does not provide for the means of verifying the level of its effectiveness, therefore leaving the Member States a margin of discretion in this regard.

The EMN report on the subject of the integration of beneficiaries of international protection on the job market lists the major obstacles which, according to the Member States, impede effective integration. They include primarily the lack of knowledge of the language and of cultural differences, discriminatory behaviours of the receiving society, lack of activity during the migrant's stay in the reception facility in the procedure and weak ties (social and cultural) with the receiving country.[89] In the report it is also emphasized that there is a necessity for activating women in the integration process, as due to their domestic obligations, which are culturally motivated, they might have difficulties in participation in integration activities.[90]

The learning of the language is deemed to be the key element of integration, at the pre-integration level during the migrants' stay in the

[87] Judgement of the Court of Justice of 4.06.2015 in the case P and S v. Commissie Sociale Zekerheid Breda and College van Burgemeester en Wethouders van de gemeente Amstelveen, C 579/13, ECLI:EU:C:2015:369.

[88] Recital 3 of the justification of the Proposal for the Qualification Regulation.

[89] *Integration of beneficiaries of international/humanitarian protection into the labour market: policies and good practices*. Synthesis Report for the EMN Focussed Study 2015, 15. On the subject of language courses, see ibidem, 23.

[90] Ibidem.

reception centre,[91] as well as after they have received protection. Language learning should be closely connected with cultural adaptation.[92]

An effective integration process conducted on the basis of a substantively coherent programme of support allows the beneficiaries of international protection to build their cultural identity in a new reality and thus facilitates a full realization of the rights of a cultural character. The very period of cultural adaptation is, however, much longer than the length of support programmes offered by the host countries. In fact, the shaping of a new cultural identity is a process which lasts many years. According to W. Tseng's concept, many of the socio-cultural differences are discerned by the migrants only at the third stage of their cultural adaptation (the middle one, between three and five years of their stay in the receiving country), when most of the initial difficulties have already been solved.[93] Only in the later stage, that is, 10–20 years after arrival in the host country, migrants begin to culturally identify with their new place of residence.[94]

The Member States retain their right to the autonomous creation of the programmes of integration activities. Nevertheless, as has been emphasized by the United Nations High Commissioner for Refugees in the report on the implementation of the Qualification Directive in 2007—they were so far of a limited character and focused primarily on language courses.[95] Moving further, Polish integration programmes (the so-called Individual Integration Programmes) are certainly too short—they span over one year, whereas it would be more valuable to have an activity facilitating supported acculturation for the period of two to three years.[96] In accordance with the regulation of the Minister of Labour and Social Policy on granting support to

[91] See A. Korniyczuk, *Nauka języka w integracji uchodźców—doświadczenia innych państw*, Instytut Spraw Publicznych (Warszawa, 2016), 14–15. What is interesting, as it transpires from the research conducted in the years 2012–2014 in the Polish reception facilities for the persons seeking international protection, the percentage of persons participating in language classes was relatively low at 15–17%. These classes are not obligatory.

[92] Ibidem, 27.

[93] M. Grzymała-Moszczyńska, "Klatka czy most? Rola religii w adaptacji kulturowej imigrantów," in *Migracje. Religie i kościoły wobec migracji migrantów. Migracje i społeczeństwo*, vol. 14, ed. J.E. Zamojski (Warszawa, 2009), 14.

[94] Ibidem.

[95] C. Murphy, *Immigration, Integration and the Law. The Intersection of Domestic, EU and International Legal Remedies* (Ashgate, 2013), 189.

[96] In Poland, the Individual Integration Programmes (IPIs) are run by the District Family Support Centres (the body responsible for the IPI is the Ministry of Labour, Family and Social Affairs). The programmes last 12 months. NIK Report: *Pomoc społeczna dla uchodźców. Informacja o wynikach kontroli*, No. 159/2015/P/14/049/KPS, 2015, 10.

foreigners,[97] the progress of integration should be evaluated quarterly and should include areas such as language education, work situation and social functioning ("especially in the area of establishing contact with the local environment and the level of participation in social, cultural and public life"[98]).

Participation in the integration programme should be considered as a cultural obligation imposed on a foreign national, who should fulfil this obligation with due diligence. Such possibilities will be provided for in the provisions of the new Qualification Regulations, which is currently being drafted. With regard to the offering of hospitality to foreign nationals in the receiving country, they should demonstrate goodwill and involvement in learning the cultural norms of the Member State so as to observe them in everyday life. Moreover, it would be advisable to complete integration programmes with an examination on cultural and social integration. In this way, it would be possible to realistically assess the effectiveness of the conducted activities. On the other hand, such an examination would provide an element of motivation for foreign nationals. Currently, in the Polish law there are no such regulations (assessment of integration progress is conducted, according to the regulation, in the form of face-to-face conversations with the foreign national concerned and it ends with an official note taken at the meeting), which has to be assessed in the negative and it is recommended that appropriate changes be introduced in this regard at the executive level.

5.6 Question of the Choice of the Place of Residence and Cultural Rights Within the Framework of the CEAS

An important aspect of cultural integration seems to be the possibility of the free choice of the place of residence in the receiving country,[99] so that the foreign national concerned could live in a region which would be

[97] The bases for providing integration support for beneficiaries of international protection in Poland are to be found under Art. 91 et seq. of the Act on social welfare of 12 March 2004, Journal of Laws of 2017, No. 1769, as amended and the Regulation of the Minister of Labour and Social Policy of 7 April 2015 on granting assistance to foreigners, uniform text, Journal of Laws of 2016 No. 1837. Additionally, on the grounds of Art. 92(2) of the Act on welfare there followed the Regulation of the Minister of Education of 18 February 2011 on the framework programme of the Polish language courses for foreigners, Journal of Laws of 2011 No. 61, item 306.

[98] *Raport NIK: Pomoc społeczna dla uchodźców. Informacja o wynikach kontroli*, 27.

[99] L. Hovil, *Local Integration The Oxford Handbook of Refugee and Forced Migration Studies*, eds. E. Fiddian-Qasmiyeh, G. Loescher, K. Long, N. Sigona (Oxford, 2014), 493. The Reception Directive also grants the freedom of movement to asylum seekers, which,

suitable for him or her culturally and where he or she would have the greatest chances for cultural integration. It is a specific right to the choice of cultural surroundings. The realization of such a right would certainly strengthen the integration possibilities of both persons seeking international protection and beneficiaries of such a protection.

With regard to beneficiaries of international protection the right to free choice of the place of residence is guaranteed under Art. 33 Directive 2011/95. Accordingly, "Member States shall allow freedom of movement within their territory to beneficiaries of international protection, under the same conditions and restrictions as those provided for other third-country nationals legally resident in their territories."

In this context, it is worth citing a Judgement of the Court of Justice of 1.03.2016 in the case of Kreis Warendorf v. Ibrahim Alo and Amira Osso v. Region Hannover,[100] in which the Court interpreted Art. 33 Directive 2011/95. The applicants in the national proceedings were the nationals of Syria—beneficiaries of international protection. German national law imposed on them the obligation of residence in the specific Land (in this case, it was the Hannover region, but what is interesting, with the exception of the capital of Lower Saxony), which was justified, amongst others, by integration reasons and was to

> help avert the concentration of welfare-dependent foreign nationals in specific areas and the associated emergence of points of social tensions with the negative effects which they have for the integration of foreign nationals. Such measures are also justified as a means of linking foreign nationals in particular need of integration to a specific place of residence so that they can avail themselves of the integration facilities available there.

In its answer to the question referred for a preliminary ruling, the Court held that Art. 33 Directive 2011/95 must be interpreted as not precluding

> a residence condition, such as the conditions at issue in the main proceedings, from being imposed on a beneficiary of subsidiary protection status, in receipt of certain specific social security benefits, with the objective of facilitating the integration of third-country nationals in the Member State that has granted that protection.

however, may be restricted on the grounds of public order, public interest or procedural questions (Art. 7[1][2] Directive 2013/33).

[100] Judgement of the Court of Justice of 1.03.2016 in the case Kreis Warendorf v. Ibrahim Alo and Amira Osso v. Region Hannover, C 443/14 and C 444/14, ECLI:EU:C:2016:127.

The Advocate General in his opinion on the above case observed that restrictions with regard to the place of residence help to avoid a concentration of migrants in a specific municipality or district and thus prevent social segregation.[101] However, according to the Advocate General, "[i]n the light of the weight of individual interest, and of the need to apply a strict level of scrutiny for assessing the principle of proportionality, abstract grounds connected to immigration and integration considerations cannot be enough to justify a measure such as the place of residence condition."[102]

In the current Proposal for the Qualification Regulation, an equivalent of Art. 33 Directive 2011/95 is Art. 28. In its para. 2 it provides for the possibility of imposing on a beneficiary of international protection the so-called residence conditions with regard to a person who receives certain social security or social assistance benefits. A circumstance allowing for the imposition of such "residence conditions" is a situation when such residence conditions are necessary for the facilitation of integration of the person concerned in the Member State that has granted the protection.[103] As it transpires from the justification of the proposal, the adding of paragraph 2 to Art. 28 was justified by the need to codify the case-law of the CJEU in the scope of the possibility of imposing on foreign nationals the conditions regarding the place of residence.

The Dublin III Regulation does not contain the provisions guaranteeing typical cultural rights; however, it is worth mentioning a few regulations which are characteristic of this law. The Dublin III Regulation establishes the mechanisms for determining the Member State responsible for examining an application for international protection[104] and, in principle, it is the country of first entry into the territory of the EU. The cri-

[101] Opinion of Advocate General P.C. Villalon of 6.10.2015 in the case C 4443/14 and C 444/14, ECLI:EU:C:2015:665 (para. 58 of the opinion), further also as opinion of the Advocate General in the case C 443/14.

[102] Para. 98 of the opinion of the Advocate General in the case C 443/14.

[103] Moreover, in accordance with Art. 29(1) of the project of the Qualification Regulation, "Beneficiaries of international protection shall not have the right to reside in Member States other than the one which granted protection. This is without prejudice to their right to apply and be admitted to reside in other Member States pursuant to relevant provisions of Union and national law and their right to move freely in accordance with the conditions of Article 21 of the Convention Implementing the Schengen Agreement."

[104] Regulation (EU) no. 604/2013 of the European Parliament and of the Council of 26 June 2013 establishing the criteria and mechanisms for determining the Member State responsible for examining an application for international protection lodged in one of the Member States by a third-country national or a stateless person, OJ L 180, 29.06.2013, 31,

teria are of an objective character and, as F. Maiani emphasizes, they are not based on the relations that an applicant may have with the Member State. Neither do they provide for the possibility of relocating migrants to the countries which would facilitate greater integration.[105] However, in accordance with Art. 17(2) Regulation 604/2013 (included in Chapter 4 entitled "Dependent Persons and Discretionary Clauses"):

> The Member State in which an application for international protection is made and which is carrying out the process of determining the Member State responsible, or the Member State responsible, may, at any time before a first decision regarding the substance is taken, request another Member State to take charge of an applicant in order to bring together any family relations, on humanitarian grounds based in particular on family or cultural considerations, even where that other Member State is not responsible under the criteria laid down in Articles 8 to 11 and 16. The persons concerned must express their consent in writing.

Therefore, in exceptional situations with regard to sensitive issues, the cultural aspects are treated with priority. This is what happened in the above-mentioned case C 245/11 K v. Bundesasylamt, in which the Court did interpret Art. 15 Regulation 343/2003(Dublin II); however, the case concerned a family reunification on cultural grounds, where the daughter-in-law was at a risk of exposure to violence from the male members of the family on account of the functioning of the tradition of returning honour to the family.[106] The Dublin III Regulation, as well as the other acts of the CEAS, also guarantees a broad access to language rights.[107]

further also as Regulation 604/2013, the Dublin III Regulation, Regulation 604/2013. This Regulation replaced previous Regulation 343/2003.

[105] F. Maiani, "The Dublin III Regulation: A New Legal Framework for a More Human System?" in *Reforming the Common European Asylum System. The New European Refugee Law, eds. V. Chetail. P. De Bruycker, F. Maiani,* (Brill 2016), 104.

[106] Judgement of the Court of Justice of 6.11.2012 in the case K v. Bundesasylamt, C 245/11, ECLI:EU:C:2012:685.

[107] Art. 4(2) Regulation 604/2013 guarantees the right to information in writing in the language understood for the foreigner, Art. 5(4) guarantees the right to have an interpreter during the interview with the applicant, Art. 26(3) guarantees that the basic information contained in the decision on the transfer should be issued in the language understood for the foreign national, Art. 27 guarantees access to legal and language assistance for foreign nationals.

In the proposal for a new Dublin IV Regulation, currently being processed, the discretionary clauses will be regulated under Art. 19 of the Regulation.[108] Nevertheless, in accordance with the adopted version of the act, family reunification will be able to take place without the need for humanitarian grounds based in family and cultural reasons.[109] This solution has been criticized by Amnesty International as one depriving the Member States of the discretionary assessment of individual needs of the applicants.[110]

The Proposal for the new Dublin IV Regulation also includes a new provision. The Regulation is to contain a new system, which will register all the proposals and will facilitate the monitoring of the participation of the Member States in the number of the applications. The rules for registering the applications in the system will be regulated under Art. 22 of the Regulation. The administering of the system will be the responsibility of eu-LISA.

The system also provides for a special mechanism, initiated in a situation of an increased migration inflow into one of the Member States—it will be the so-called corrective allocation mechanism. This mechanism is to be triggered automatically in a situation when "the number of applications for international protection for which a Member State is responsible exceeds 150% of the figure identified in the reference key."[111] In greater detail, the corrective allocation mechanism has been regulated in Chapter 7 of the Proposal for the Dublin IV Regulation. In accordance with Art. 34 of the Proposal, the purpose of the mechanism is to reduce the burden on the Member State that is faced with an unproportionate number of

[108] Proposal for a Regulation of the European Parliament and of the Council establishing the criteria and mechanisms for determining the Member State responsible for examining an application for international protection lodged in one of the Member States by a third-country national or a stateless person (recast), COM/2016/0270 final/2—2016/0133 (COD), further also as the Dublin IV Regulation.

[109] It is worth, nevertheless, noting that in the Preamble to the new Regulation there is a reference, missing from the currently in force Dublin III Regulation, concerning sibling reunification as a measure conducive to integration: "Reuniting siblings is of particular importance for improving the chances of integration of applicants and hence reducing secondary movements" (para. 19 of the Preamble).

[110] Position Paper. The Proposed Dublin Reform, Amnesty International European Institutions Office, 25 November 2016, 3.

[111] Para. 32 of the Preamble of the Proposal for the Dublin IV Regulation. The reference key is defined under Art. 35(2) of the Proposal and entails the consideration of two criteria: the total population and gross domestic product (GDP).

applications for international protection for which the Member State should take responsibility in light of the Regulation.

Doubts with regard to adopting this Regulation concern primarily the complete automatization of the process of distribution of applications, without taking account of the cultural *spectrum*. The regulation does not provide the possibility for beneficiaries to choose the country where they would be transferred and where, possibly, they would have greater chances for integration, due to the close proximity of the culture of the given Member State. Due to such distribution, as drafted in the Regulation under discussion, the potential resettlements might be unfavourable from the perspective of integration possibilities of third-country nationals seeking international protection. For instance, it might occur that foreign nationals will have no possibility of maintaining contact with local migration communities because quite simply in a given Member State there will be no such communities of foreigners coming from a specific cultural environment or country. It remains without doubt that an initial process of acculturation might be supported by third-country nationals who live there and are already well integrated in the given region. Therefore, their assistance might be crucial for newly arrived asylum seekers for understanding the cultural codes and customs of a given place. On the other hand, a positive aspect of the introduced procedure seems to be the maintenance of family unity during allocation under the guarantees of Art. 41(2).

The problem of the lack of possibility of indicating the preferred country for relocation was also raised by the United Nations High Commissioner for Refugees in his conclusions concerning the project of the Dublin IV Regulation. In the opinion of the UNHCR the foreign nationals subject to the corrective allocation mechanism should have the possibility of presenting their preferences with regard to objective criteria such as the residence of other family members in a given Member State, previous stay there or the possibility of continuing education there. Such a solution would certainly promote better integration.[112]

The right to choose the country of residence in accordance with the cultural preferences of the foreign national was also not provided for in the

[112] UNHCR Comments on the European Commission proposal for a Regulation of the European Parliament and of the Council establishing the criteria and mechanisms for determining the Member State responsible for examining an application for international protection lodged in one of the Member States by a third-country national or a stateless person (recast)—COM(2016) 270, December 2016, 34.

decision on relocation. The rights and obligations of applicants included in its Art. 6 included merely the protection of family unity, a special protection of the rights of the child and the right to information on the country of transfer.[113] It is worth pointing out that the CEAS supported the Member States in those solidarity activities through assistance in the choice of the appropriate receiving country, based on the existing language and cultural ties of the foreigner concerned with the said country.[114]

5.7 Other Legal Instruments Impactful in the Exercise of Cultural Rights by Persons Seeking International Protection

As it transpires from the analysed legal material, as well as from the process of the implementation of the Union's law into national law, persons seeking international protection can realize their cultural needs both while under the procedure and after receiving international protection.

Apart from the legal acts analysed in the present chapter, another regulation in the CEAS system currently in force is also the so-called Eurodac Regulation. This Regulation, due to its specificity, does not include any specific provisions with regard to the entitlements of a cultural character.[115] Regulation 603/2013 determines in its Art. 9 the method of taking fingertips (dactyloscopy) of the foreign national in order to place them in the Eurodac system. The problem which might appear during fingerprinting and which has already been pointed out by the Fundamental Rights

[113] Council Decision (EU) 2015/1601 of 22 September 2015 establishing provisional measures in the area of international protection for the benefit of Italy and Greece, OJ L 248, 24.09.2015, 80. Report from the Commission to the European Parliament, the European Council and the Council. Fifteenth report on relocation and resettlement, Brussels, 6.09.2017, COM(2017), 465, final.

[114] Annual Report on the Situation of Asylum in the European Union 2016, EASO 2016, 85.

[115] Regulation (EU) No. 603/2013 of the European Parliament and of the Council of 26 June 2013 on the establishment of "Eurodac" for the comparison of fingerprints for the effective application of Regulation (EU) No. 604/2013 establishing the criteria and mechanisms for determining the Member State responsible for examining an application for international protection lodged in one of the Member States by a third-country national or a stateless person and on requests for the comparison with Eurodac data by Member States' law enforcement authorities and Europol for law enforcement purposes, and amending Regulation (EU) No. 1077/2011 establishing a European Agency for the operational management of large-scale IT systems in the area of freedom, security and justice, OJ L 180, 29.06.2013, 1, further also as Regulation 603/2013.

Agency concerns cultural issues. Hence, the FRA recommends that foreign nationals should be informed about the reasons for the procedure of fingerprinting[116] in writing, in the language understood by the foreign national and in a culturally appropriate manner.[117] If a third-country national refuses to be fingerprinted, the application of detention with regard to the foreign national should be a measure of the last resort.

The EU's secondary law on migration also includes the so-called Temporary Protection Directive.[118] The directive provides for the possibility of adopting extraordinary measures in a situation when there is a risk of a mass influx of displaced persons from third countries and a risk that asylum systems will not manage to process all the applications for international protection.[119] Temporary protection is granted in principle for the period of one year.[120] So far, the mechanism of granting temporary protection has not been used by EU institutions and the Member States and thus remains a dead letter.[121] At the moment of the escalation of the migration crisis, the Union decided to adopt the mechanism of relocation and currently there is work in progress on the Dublin IV Regulation, whose provisions entail the introduction of the corrective allotment mechanism, characterized above. Directive 2001/55 still has a binding force and thus, at least hypothetically, its provisions may find a practical application. Directive 2001/55 enumerates the obligations of the Member States with regard to the beneficiaries of temporary protection. Among them one should list access to the educational system for persons below 18 years of

[116] Fundamental rights implications of the obligation to provide fingerprints for Eurodac, FRA Focus, 05/2015, European Union Agency for Fundamental Rights, 4. Document available on the website www.fra.europa.eu. Accessed 12.09.2017.

[117] Fundamental rights implications of the obligation to provide fingerprints for Eurodac, 2.

[118] Council Directive 2001/55/EC of 20 July 2001 on minimum standards for giving temporary protection in the event of a mass influx of displaced persons and on measures promoting a balance of efforts between Member States in receiving such persons and bearing the consequences thereof, OJ L 212, 7.08.2001, 12, further as Directive 2001/55.

[119] See Art. 1 Directive 2001/55.

[120] See Art. 4 and Art. 6 Directive 2001/55.

[121] M. Ineli-Ciger, "Has the Temporary Protection Directive Become Obsolete? An Examination of the Directive and its Lack of Implementation in View of the Recent Asylum Crisis in the Mediterranean," in *Seeking Asylum in the European Union. Selected Protection Issues Raised by the Second Phase of the Common European Asylum System*, eds. C. Bauloz, M. Ineli-Ciger, S. Singer, V. Stoyanova, (Brill/Nijhoff, 2015), 232 et seq. See also M. Ineli-Ciger, "Revisiting Temporary Protection as a Protection Option to Respond to Mass Influx Situations," in *Exploring Boundaries of Refugee Law. Current Protection Challenges*, eds. J.P. Gauci, M. Giuffré, E. Tsourdi (Brill/Nijhoff, 2015), 197–217.

age under the same rules as the nationals of the Member State. However, there is a possibility of limiting equal access only to public institutions.[122] Moreover, in accordance with Art. 14(2) Directive 2001/55, the Member States might facilitate access to education for adults. The activities listed in the directive, such as the creation of the conditions facilitating the undertaking of work by third-country nationals, access to medical services and social security, counteract the social exclusion of migrants and contribute to their acculturation in the host society.

An exceptionally valuable initiative, which supported integration activities for the benefit of refugees and persons under the procedure, was the establishment and functioning of the European Refugee Fund (ERF). The Fund was established in 2000 by the Council decision[123] and for the years to come its activity was prolonged by subsequent decisions. The last of them was Decision 573/2007/EC,[124] which facilitated the functioning of the programme in the years 2008–2013. Currently, integration activities for the benefit of the refugees are realized in the framework of the Asylum, Migration and Integration Fund (AMIF)[125] established for the years 2014–2020. M. Garlick expressed a critical opinion on the rules of functioning of the AMIF, observing that the distribution of funds based on the criterion of the number of persons seeking international protection in previous years placed in a favourable position those countries which already have highly developed asylum systems (such as Germany, Sweden or France).[126]

As eligible actions within the Fund Decision 573/2007 lists "actions enabling such persons to adapt to the society of the Member State in socio-cultural terms, and to share the values enshrined in the Charter of

[122] Art. 14(1) Directive 2001/55.

[123] Council Decision 2000/596/EC of 28 September 2000 establishing a European Refugee Fund, OJ L 252, 6.10.2000, 12.

[124] Decision No. 573/2007/EC of the European Parliament and of the Council of 23 May 2007 establishing the European Refugee Fund for the period 2008–2013 as part of the general programme "Solidarity and Management of Migration Flows" and repealing Council Decision 2004/904/EC, OJ L 144, 6.06.2007, 1.

[125] Regulation (EU) No. 516/2014 of the European Parliament and of the Council of 16 April 2014 establishing the Asylum, Migration and Integration Fund, amending Council Decision 2008/381/EC and repealing Decisions No. 573/2007/EC and No. 575/2007/EC of the European Parliament and of the Council and Council Decision 2007/435/EC, OJ L 150, 20.05.2014, 168.

[126] M. Garlick, "The Dublin System of Solidarity and Individual Rights," in *Reforming the Common European Asylum System. The New European Refugee Law*, eds. V. Chetail, P. De Bruycker, F. Maiani (Brill 2016), 190.

Fundamental Rights of the European Union" (Art. 3[3][b]), support for the durable and sustainable participation in cultural life of persons seeking protection and support for education and training (Art. 3[3][c,d]). Actions within the Fund supporting integration and pre-integration conducted by the Member States also contributed to the realization of the cultural needs of foreign nationals and to the building of their new, hybrid cultural identity.

It is also worth adding that within the ERF, NGOs, local administration bodies, but also public administration—the Border Guards and Office for Foreigners[127]—might apply for funding. Among the many projects of a cultural character currently in realization in Poland, one might mention the project "Szkoła różnorodności" (School of Variety) (Fundacja Dialog, No. of Project 17/8/EFU), which organized various seminars for teachers and classes with a multicultural group[128] or the project "Ośrodek samopomocy uchodźcom SINTAR" (SINTAR Support Centre for Refugees) (No. of Project 30/8/EFU), which focused on language courses, cultural animations or integration events. The partner of the latter project was the Caucasus Nations Culture Institute.[129] The fact-finding missions of the Office for Foreigners to Vietnam and Iran within the project "Fact-Finding Missions to the Countries of Origin" were also financed by the Fund.[130]

5.8 Conclusions

The current chapter included an analysis of the regulations of EU secondary law within the framework of the CEAS with regard to the guarantees of the rights of a cultural character both for persons seeking international protection and for beneficiaries of such protection. Within the Common European Asylum System, the rights of a cultural character concern both the process of qualification and the procedure of granting protection and reception of migrants into the host countries.

[127] The list of the programmes realized within the ERF in the years 2004–2007 in Poland can be found in the publication *Integracja uchodźców w Polsce w liczbach*, eds. A. Kosowicz, A. Maciejko (Polskie Forum Migracyjne, 2007), 103.

[128] General programme "Solidarity and Management in Migration Flows" SOLID 2007–2013, European Project Implementation Centre of the Ministry of the Interior, Warsaw 2015, 63.

[129] Ibidem, 67.

[130] Ibidem, 84.

A special regulation which facilitates for non-voluntary migrants the realization of their cultural identity and protection against the oppressive culture of the country of origin is the Qualification Directive (and the Qualification Regulation currently in the making), listing the conditions that must be met for granting international protection, including those which might be considered as circumstances of a cultural nature. Further, in the process of qualification for protection, the guarantees for protection of cultural differences and cultural identity are to be found in the provisions with regard to interviews.

What seems to be debatable from the perspective of protection of the rights of a cultural character is the conception, adopted in EU law, of the safe country of origin. In accordance with a presumption of safety, it should be assumed that a foreign national coming from such a country would have in his or her native country a full possibility to exercise his or her cultural identity both *in forum internum* and *in forum externum*. Nonetheless, assuming that a given state is a safe country for everyone seems to be a risky approach.

A broad interpretation of the rights of a cultural character can be conducted on the basis of the provisions of the Reception Directive. Such rights are guaranteed both in detention and in a situation when persons seeking international protection are staying in reception facilities. The actions undertaken by the Member States at the stage of pre-integration seem to be especially underestimated. It would also be advisable to strengthen the latter so as to fully use the time of the procedure for integration activities. What is significant, when in the reception centre, is that it is possible for foreign nationals to have contact with the culture of the country of origin, whereas for the duration of the whole procedure the applicants' children are provided with access to education.

The possibility for the realization of the right to cultural identity and effective and voluntary integration may also be impeded by the restriction in EU law on the choice of the place of residence by persons seeking protection and the lack of indication regarding which region would be the most suitable for them culturally. On the other hand, an instrument which contributes to the strengthening of the cultural rights for persons in the procedure and those with granted protection was the European Refugee Fund and the support programmes financed from its resources.

A specific boundary for the realization of cultural rights, including the right to cultural identity *in forum externum*, is the obligation of respect for the culture of the host country and therefore the very obligation to learn about the culture and customs of the receiving country in the process of integration of the beneficiaries of international protection, that is, the obligation for integration. However, cultural integration should be perceived as two-fold: both as an obligation and as the right to get to know the culture of the receiving country and active participation in cultural life. Thus, cultural integration obligations allow for the strengthening of European culture in the process of learning about and respecting it, which results in the lack of infringement of the traditional norms encoded in cultural norms and facilitates an effective use of migrants' potential in the process of development of vital elements of culture.[131] Culture should be understood as a value which is common to all the actors of the integration process.

Therefore, on the example of the rights of third-country nationals in the CEAS system, one could present the way of understanding the term "cultural security." As was mentioned in the previous chapters, cultural security is a value for the whole society in the scope within which it protects culture against degradation and strengthens the functioning of high culture. This aim translates into the obligation of the Member State to take care of the native culture by protecting and promoting it. The dimension of the functioning of cultural security should also be available to third-country nationals as the recipients of culture.

Cultural security also entails the safe functioning of the migrant concerned in the given culture of the host country. It is realized by the familiarity with cultural patterns and codes, which allow for the realization of individual cultural identity and reconcilement of divergent cultural norms. Cultural security understood in such a way is possible to be realized through the cultural education of the migrant conducted in a parallel way to his or her social integration. The above legal analysis confirms the existence of the catalogue of cultural rights with regard to persons seeking international protection, as well as beneficiaries of such protection.

[131] B. Togral, "Convergence of Securitization of Migration and 'New Racism' in Europe: Rise of Culturalism and Disappearance of Politics," in *Security, Insecurity and Migration in Europe*, ed. G. Lazaridis (Routledge 2016), 227 et seq.

CHAPTER 6

Cultural Rights of Third-Country Nationals: Regular Migrants

6.1 Introductory Remarks

The present chapter will include an analysis of the documents from the field of European Union (EU) integration policy and the legal acts regulating the conditions of stay of regular migrants (workers, students, academics).[1] The aim of the analysis is to assess the functioning of the regulations which allow migrants to realize their rights of a cultural character or which facilitate their access to cultural life and to cultural goods. Voluntary migrants consist of a very diverse group from the perspective of the purpose of their entry—they might be persons arriving for work (e.g., seasonal, highly specialized or scientific work), they might be members of the families of workers or persons continuing studies. The guarantees of the realization of the rights of a cultural character might be found in the acts of secondary law regulating the status of specific migrant groups. Those guarantees comprise a catalogue of the cultural rights of third-country nationals in EU law. The aim of the chapter is to isolate and provide a characteristic of those rights, as well as to delineate their boundaries, especially with regard to the existing regulations relating to the cultural integration obligations.

Moreover, the scope of the analysis conducted in the present chapter has been defined with a view to verifying the research thesis, assuming the

[1] C. Murphy, *Immigration, Integration and the Law. The Intersection of Domestic, EU and International Legal Remedies* (Ashgate, 2013), 169. See also Wewnątrzunijna mobilność obywateli państw trzecich. Raport przygotowany przez Krajowy Punkt Kontaktowy Europejskiej Sieci Migracyjnej w Polsce, May 2013, EMN, 13–25.

A. M. Kosińska, *Cultural Rights of Third-Country Nationals in EU Law*,
https://doi.org/10.1007/978-3-030-30154-5_6

existence of the right to cultural integration. As is emphasized in the doctrine, the integration of migrants in the receiving countries has become the subject of protection within the framework of the protection of human rights.[2] In accordance with the thesis proposed for the purpose of the legal analysis to be carried out in the current chapter, the right to cultural integration results from the specific regulation of EU secondary law and facilitates the realization of particular "integrative cultural rights" to an individual. This right is also a part of the catalogue of the cultural rights of third-country nationals in EU law.

Within the thesis proposed for the purpose of the analysis in the current chapter, it will be justifiable to investigate whether the right to cultural integration is essentially an individual right or whether it also assumes the character of collective third-generation rights. The rights of migrants as third-generation rights are identified in the doctrine by Y. Donders. She observes that third-generation rights[3] refer to the rights of collective entities *in se*, individuals as members of collective entities and the rights whose interest or subject is collective.[4] The International Convention on the Protection of the Rights of All Migrant Workers and Members of their Families[5] of 1990 provides an example of such a third-generation right, that is, the right of workers to manifest their religious beliefs either alone or in community with others,[6] as guaranteed in the Convention. As Donders observes, it is the right in which the subject is an individual, but an individual defined as a member of a particular group.[7] The analysis conducted in this chapter will aim at identifying the existence of the said rights.[8]

[2] R. Rubio-Marin, "Integration in Immigrant Europe: Human Rights at a Crossroad," in *Human Rights and Immigration*, ed. R. Rubio-Marin (Oxford, 2014), 100.

[3] The third-generation rights are also referred to as collective rights, peoples' rights, minority rights, group rights and community rights. Y. Donders, *Foundations of Collective Cultural Rights in International Human Rights Law* in *Cultural Rights as Collective Rights an International Law Perspective*, ed. A. Jakubowski (Leiden/Boston: 2016), 88. See also R. Baubock, *Cultural Minority Rights for Immigrants*, "The International Migration Review" 1996, vol. 30, no. 1, Special edition. *Ethics, Migration, and Global Stewardship*, 203–250.

[4] Y. Donders, *Foundations of Collective Cultural Rights*, 88.

[5] The International Convention on the Protection of the Rights of All Migrant Workers and Members of Their Families, adopted on 18 December 1990 by Resolution 45/158 of the General Assembly of the United Nations.

[6] Ibidem, Art. 12; Y. Donders, *Foundations of Collective Cultural Rights*, 89.

[7] Y. Donders, *Foundations of Collective Cultural Rights*, 89.

[8] What is interesting is that in her analysis Y. Donders holds that the third-generation rights include individual rights of a collective dimension—that is, the rights of individuals, the exercise of which is of a collective character, such as the right to participate in cultural life or the right to education. See ibidem, 90.

6.2 Significance of the Integration Process for the Exercise of Cultural Rights

Apart from asylum and return migration, the EU Member States experience a significant inflow of third-country nationals whose migration is of a regular character. Legal migration, and what follows, constant presence of third-country nationals in the territory of the Union result in the necessity of adopting integration policies both at the level of the EU and at the level of the Member States.[9] In accordance with the report prepared by the Organization for Economic Co-operation and Development (OECD) and the European Commission on the subject of migrants' integration, in 2013 within the territory of the EU there resided circa 20 million foreign nationals—among the most popular countries one should mention Germany, Spain, France and the United Kingdom.[10]

One of the aims of integration policy is to secure cultural rights of migrants and to facilitate their realization in a new cultural environment.[11] Access to the cultural rights of regular migrants is guaranteed in EU legal acts and documents, as well as in national law.

Culture is at present the focal point of discussions on migrants,[12] whereas cultural integration serves a key role for ensuring a peaceful process of migration and provides benefits for both migrants and the receiving country. With regard to the definitions of integration[13] presented in the above chapters, it should be emphasized that integration denotes participation—including par-

[9] See C. Murphy, *Immigration, Integration and the Law*, 54.

[10] Indicators of Immigrant Integration 2015. Settling In, OECD/European Union (2015), 304.

[11] The document *Handbook on integration for policy-makers and practitioners* (third edition April 2010, European Commission) points out to the role of cultural institutions in the process of integration, for example, that of libraries (p. 60). Moreover, an important role is played by the media (p. 28, 40).

[12] K. Romaniszyn, "Belonging or Not-Belonging: Migration as a Challenge to Guest and Host Identity," in *Culture and migration. The Cultural Implications of International Migrations in the Light of Fieldwork Evidence*, ed. K. Romaniszyn, (Kraków, 2008), 139.

[13] See A. Grzymała-Kozłowska, "Integracja—próba rekonstrukcji pojęcia," in *Problemy integracji imigrantów. Koncepcje, badania, polityki*, eds. A. Grzymała-Kozłowska, S. Łodziński (Warszawa, 2008), 23. In accordance with the definition cited by the author, integration denotes a situation when "divergent individuals or groups, while maintaining their cultural separateness, create a relatively permanent relations with the receiving society and participate in various areas of its life."

ticipation in culture, life and cultural practices.[14] The effectiveness of the integration process also entails the creation of cultural bonds between the migrant and the receiving society and the feeling of identity with the host country. The authors of the report titled "The Inclusion of Migrants and Refugees" use the term "power of culture" with reference to the possibilities of integrating with third-country nationals and learning about their culture in the integration process. This term points out to the significance of cultural integration[15] in a very accurate way.

The process of cultural integration involves the realization of various rights of a cultural character. The report titled "Human Rights in Culturally Diverse Societies,"[16] containing guidelines of the Council of Europe, enumerates particular rights of a cultural character which should be safeguarded and guaranteed in the integration process ("integrative cultural rights"). Among those rights one should point out the freedom of expression (including artistic expression), freedom of religion and the possibility to freely participate in religious practices, the right to education, the freedom of assembly (including the freedom of associations and migrant societies), participation in social and cultural life (including the promotion

[14] J. Fomina, "Czy migracja ma płeć? Analiza działalności organizacji pozarządowych wspierających migrantów w Polsce," in *W poszukiwaniu nowych wzorów integracji cudzoziemców, Wybór tekstów Polskiego Forum Integracyjnego*, ed. K. Grot (Warszawa, 2013), 66–72. See also A. Horolets, "Migrants' leisure and integration," in *W poszukiwaniu nowych wzorów integracji cudzoziemców. Wybór tekstów Polskiego Forum Integracyjnego*, ed. K. Grot (Warszawa, 2013), 81. The presence of migrants also means a richer cultural life for the receiving society.

[15] *The Inclusion of Migrants and Refugees: The Role of Cultural Organisations*, Maria Vlachou (coord.), Acesso Cultura, Associação Cultural 2017, 8. The report also highlights the role of art in the process of integration (p. 13). It is also worth referring to the definition of cultural integration, which should be understood as a "state or process based on the merging of specific features or elements of one or several cultures into a functional new whole." Entry: "Integracja kulturowa," in K. Olechnicki, P. Załęcki, *Słownik socjologiczny* (Toruń, 2002), 85, cited after: Ł. Łotocki, *Integracja i dyskryminacja. Krajobraz 2009*, Instytut Spraw Publicznych (Warszawa, 2009), 4. On the subject of the role of culture, see also *Cultural participation and inclusive societies. A thematic report based on the Indicator Framework on Culture and Democracy*, December 2016, Principal investigator: Helmut K. Anheier, Council of Europe 2017, 12. Report available on the website https://rm.coe.int/cultural-participation-and-inclusive-societies-a-thematic%2D%2Dreport-based/1680711283. Accessed 12.09.2017.

[16] See Human rights in culturally diverse societies. Guidelines adopted by the Committee of Ministers and Compilation of Council of Europe standards, Council of Europe 2016, 13 et seq., publication available on the website https://rm.coe.int/16806665fd. Accessed 12.09.2017.

of intercultural dialogue)[17] and the right to cultural identity. All the above rights can be exercised by migrants in accordance with the principle of *living together*.[18] The report also emphasizes the necessity of introducing legal guarantees, which will facilitate effective protection against discrimination and will eliminate cultural violence against women.[19]

The exercise of the right to cultural integration entails, of course, participation in culture, which should be defined in the broadest terms. It is worth pointing out here to the definition by the United Nations Educational, Scientific and Cultural Organization (UNESCO), in accordance with which, taking part in culture means "participation in any activity that, for individuals, represents a way of increasing their own cultural and informational capacity and capital, which helps define their identity, and/or allows for personal expression."[20] As the authors of the report titled "Cultural Participation and Inclusive Societies" observe, participation in culture may be of an active or passive character and may occur via divergent cultural channels, including the modern media.[21]

General conclusions on the subject of the process of integration of migrants in the host countries have also been presented in the report titled "Indicators of Immigrant Integration 2015. Settling In." However, in my view, they have distinct relevance for the possibilities of the realization of the rights of a cultural character in the integration process. Thus, with regard to the report data,[22] it should be pointed out that, generally, immigrants have a lower income than the nationals of the host country, which has a direct influence on the possibilities of their participation in the cultural offer. It might be added in passing that in accordance with A. Maslow's theory of the hierarchy of needs, an individual is able to satisfy one's spiritual needs as long as his or her basic needs, such as food or sleep, have been satisfied.[23] Only when the basic needs have been satisfied, it is possible to satisfy one's cultural needs. Thus, successful social integration and the fulfilment of migrants' social needs is, in a way, a condition

[17] Ibidem, 20.

[18] Ibidem, 12. On the subject of the principle of *living together*, see Chap. 3 of the current study as well as I. Trispiotis, "Two Interpretations of 'Living Together' in European Human Rights Law," *The Cambridge Law Journal*, vol. 75, issue 3 (2016): 580–607.

[19] Ibidem, 19.

[20] *Measuring Cultural Participation: 2009 Framework for Cultural Statistics Handbook no. 2*, UNESCO Institute for Statistics, Montreal 2012, 51.

[21] *Cultural participation and inclusive societies. A thematic report*, 11.

[22] *Indicators of Immigrant Integration 2015. Settling In*, 21 et seq.

[23] A.M. Kosińska, *Kulturalne prawa człowieka. Regulacje normatywne i ich realizacja* (Lublin, 2014), 78, cited after A. Maslow, *Motywacja i osobowość* (Warszawa, 2006), 62 et seq.

allowing for effective cultural integration, which is something that the Member States should take into account in their integration policies. In accordance with the report, integration, including cultural integration, is more effective the longer a migrant remains in the receiving country, whereas the best tool with regard to the integration of migrants' children is education.[24]

On the basis of the definitions of integration cited in the current study, which entail that integration is a two-way process, it might also be possible to propose a thesis that migrants and their presence have a real impact (albeit not always clearly visible due to migrants being a minority group[25]) on the cultural life of the host society.[26] Thus, migrants also contribute in some respects to the manner of realization of the cultural rights of the nationals of the host country. It is also conditioned by the cultural diffusion accompanying migration processes.[27]

Cultural integration of migrants should necessarily entail complete acculturation (i.e., it should encompass the acceptance of norms and values functioning in the host country[28]) or be at least the so-called designated acculturation, that is, "encompassing the adoption of such elements of culture which are beneficial for better adaptation, e.g. specific idioms in the language, slang language, customs in the workplace."[29] Further, acculturation strategies should not lead to separation or marginalization.[30]

[24] Indicators of Immigrant Integration 2015. Settling In, 23. On the subject of prejudices regarding the effectiveness of integration policy, see N. Finney, L. Simpson, *"Sleepwalking to segregation"? Challenging myths about race and migration* (Bristol, 2009), 73–87, 91–111. The authors dispel the popular myths on the subject of integration of third-country nationals, such as those that a large number of migrants cannot be effectively integrated or that migrants are unwilling to integrate.

[25] As D. Wadowski observes, "Minority culture is perceived by the whole society as something interesting and exotic, out of which some elements might be taken and introduced to the syncretic culture of the majority. … However, it creates a specific reaction on the side of minority groups, consciously emphasizing their cultural dimension. This is precisely the area in which minorities want to emphasize their difference, or to exert an influence on the whole society through their culture," D. Wadowski, "Więzi w grupach mniejszościowych a ich kultura," in *Kultura grup mniejszościowych i marginalnych*, ed. L. Dyczewski (Lublin, 2005), 25–26.

[26] Indicators of Immigrant Integration 2015. Settling In, 230.

[27] D. Niedźwiecki, *Migracje i tożsamość. Od teorii do analizy przypadku* (Kraków, 2010), 115.

[28] Ł. Łotocki, *Integracja i dyskryminacja*, 5.

[29] Ibidem, 4.

[30] Y. Algan, A. Bisin, T. Verdier, "Introduction: Perspectives on Cultural Integration of Immigrants," in *Cultural Integration of Immigrants in Europe*, eds. Y. Algan, A. Bisin, A. Manning, T. Verdier, Oxford 2012, 12 et seq. See also Ch. Harzig, D. Hoerder,

On the other hand, due to the two-sidedness of the integration process, it is worth remembering migrants' need to retain ties with the culture of their country of origin.[31] It is also a right of third-country nationals resulting from the right to integration. One of the sources of such a contact is the functioning of the Institutes of Culture, whose actions are regulated at the level of national law on the basis of bilateral agreements[32]; another is the possibility of establishing migrant societies.

The necessity for conducting effective integration activities has been very accurately summarized by G. Michałowska, who observes that

> the States experiencing massive migration influxes must in their policies acknowledge the stance and opinions of their own societies. On the one hand, they have to promote actions for the shaping of the attitudes of tolerance and solidarity ... on the other hand, they have to conduct an active policy of integration and of not leaving the newcomers to themselves. It should be a policy of counteracting migrants' enclosing within their own cultural environment and of preventing the emergence of parallel societies.[33]

6.3 Cultural Integration and Its Significance in Political and Strategic Documents of the European Union

The legal basis for the creation of migration policy of the Union in the area of migration is to be currently found in Art. 79 of the Treaty on the Functioning of the European Union. The current subchapter will include the most important political documents, which have become a basis for

D. Gabaccia, *What is migration history?* (Cambridge, 2009), 104. See also a model of migration and acculturation by D. Hoerder, "From Migrants to Ethnics: Acculturation in a Societal Framework," in *European Migrants. Global and Local Perspectives*, eds. D. Hoerder, L.P. Moch, Northeastern University Press 1996, 214.

[31] *INTERACT—Researching Third Country Nationals' Integration as a Three-Way Process—Immigrants, Countries of Emigration and Countries of Immigration as Actors of Integration. Maintaining national culture abroad. Countries of origin, culture and diaspora*, Sonia Gsir, Elsa Mescoli, INTERACT Research Report 2015/10, 10.

[32] A.M. Kosińska, *Kulturalne prawa człowieka*, 271–272; *INTERACT—Researching Third Country Nationals' Integration as a Three-way Process*, 19–23.

[33] G. Michałowska, *Ochrona praw człowieka w Radzie Europy i w Unii Europejskiej* (Warszawa, 2007), 240. On the subject of the necessary initiatives counteracting xenophobia, see Promoting respect and diversity. Combating intolerance and hate. Contribution to the Annual Colloquium on Fundamental Rights, European Union Agency for Fundamental Rights; document available on the website www.fra.europa.eu. Accessed 12.09.2017.

the cultural integration of third-country nationals,[34] carried out at the level of the EU and implemented by the Member States.

The placing of the characteristic and analysis of the strategic documents from the area of integration in this section of the study is justified by their significance for the interpretation of the scope of the "integrative cultural rights" (also as the rights of a collective character) and their impact on the entirety of guarantees of the rights of a cultural character with regard to third-country nationals within the territory of the European Union. The material presented in the following subchapter will also be useful in the interpretation of the "integration conditions" existing in the Member States and the integrative cultural obligations, which constitute one of the boundaries for the realization of cultural rights, resulting from them.

After the Treaty of Amsterdam had entered into force, the Area of Freedom, Security and Justice acquired the legal basis for its functioning.[35] In order to particularize the activities of the Union in this area the European Council adopted, beginning with 1999, multiannual programmes, out of which the last one was the Stockholm Programme.

In accordance with the Tampere Programme (adopted for the years 1999–2004), while ensuring fair treatment to third-country nationals, they should also be guaranteed the prohibition of discrimination in social and cultural life. Moreover, the policy of receiving migrants should take into account their ties with the country of origin—cultural as well as historical.[36] In accordance with para. 18 of the Programme, the Member States should aim at granting third-country nationals the rights and

[34] It is worth pointing out that the basis for the collection of data in the EU on the subject of integration was the so-called Zaragoza Declaration, adopted by the EU ministers responsible for integration and accepted by the Justice and Home Affairs Council on 3–4.06.2010. In the Declaration it is emphasized that for the assessment of migrants' integration in the EU it is important that migrants are not only integrated economically on the job market, but also through education, social integration and active civil life. See Together in the EU. Promoting the participation of migrants and their descendants, European Union Agency for Fundamental Rights 2017, 35. Report available on the website www.fra.europa.eu. Accessed 31.12.2017. See also Indicators of Immigration Integration, 300. On the subject of discussions on migration policies, see A. Favell, T*he Nation—State and Research on Immigrants in Western Europe* in *International Migration Research,* eds. M. Bommes, E. Morawska (Routledge, 2016), 47 et seq.

[35] See K.A. Morawska, "Migracja cyrkulacyjna w świetle polityki imigracyjnej Unii Europejskiej," *Studia Europejskie*, no. 3 (2013): 144.

[36] Tampere European Council 15 and 16 October 1999 Presidency Conclusions, http://www.europarl.europa.eu/summits/tam_en.htm. Accessed 12.09.2017.

obligations comparable to those of EU citizens—access to those rights should be realized through the instruments of integration policy.

The next programme of the European Council, the Hague Programme (2005–2009), includes a broad definition of integration, in accordance with which it is a continuous and two-way process, including both third-country nationals and the receiving society. Integration is also a process, in which the basic European values and fundamental rights are respected. In order to conduct integration policies, it is necessary to possess basic skills for living in society (a requirement which testifies to the fact that an individual's right to integration is also a collective right, as it entails an individual's engagement with a particular social group). What is more, integration "relies on frequent interaction and intercultural dialogue between all members of society within common forums and activities in order to improve mutual understanding."[37] An important element in the definition under discussion is the requirement of respecting European values and thus, indirectly, of respecting the traditions and European cultural heritage.

The last one of the adopted programmes so far, the Stockholm Programme (2010–2014), also included guidelines concerning third-country nationals' integration with the societies of the receiving countries. Among the priorities of the conducted integration there was a postulate of carrying out intercultural dialogue and delineating common integration practices, including preparatory courses and language courses.[38] In accordance with the definition contained in the Programme, "Integration is a dynamic, two-way process of mutual interaction, requiring not only efforts by national, regional and local authorities but also a greater commitment by the host community and immigrants."[39]

The key moment for the introduction of integration policy of third-country nationals in the European Union was the adoption by the EU Council in 2004 of the so-called Common Basic Principles on Integration, further also as Common Basic Principles.[40] The document highlighted that integration is a multidimensional process occurring at the level of an

[37] The Hague Programme: Strengthening Freedom, Security and Justice in the European Union, OJ C 53 of 3.03.2005, 1, para. 1.5.

[38] The Stockholm Programme—An open and secure Europe serving and protecting the citizens, OJ C 115 of 4.05.2010, 1 para. 6.1.5.

[39] Ibidem, para. 6.1.5.

[40] Common Basic Principles for Immigrant Integration Policy in the European Union. Council of the European Union, Conclusions, press release, 2618th Council Meeting Justice and Home Affairs, Brussels, 19 November 2004, further also as Common Basic Principles.

individual, as well as at the level of family life, local community and national level.

The Common Basic Principles constitute that integration is a two-way process (first principle)[41] and, what is crucial, it requires respect for the fundamental values of the European Union, among which one should mention the following: freedom, democracy, respect for human rights and the principle of the rule of law, as well as respect for the provisions of the Charter of Fundamental Rights.[42] Thus, one might propose a thesis that the very process of integration imposes certain cultural obligations on migrants, such as the obligation of familiarizing oneself with the history and heritage of Europe, followed by respect for the common values and cultural norms. Migrants should also possess an appropriate level of civil awareness and knowledge about the cultural norms and traditions of the so-called European culture. This requirement was clarified in the next integration guideline, in accordance with which the key element of integration is migrants' knowledge of the language and history of the receiving country.[43]

On the other hand, in order to effectively participate in the process of integration, the members of the receiving community should familiarize themselves with the basic information on the subject of the cultures of the countries of origin of migrants, which will be beneficial in terms of integration and cultural exchange at the level of an individual within the conducted intercultural dialogue. This was emphasized in one of the postulates entailing the need for frequent interaction between migrants and the nationals of the host country.[44]

In the guidelines, it is also emphasized that employment has key significance for the successful process of integration.[45] As it was mentioned in the preceding subchapter, the needs of a transcendental character, including

[41] Details on the subject of the integration programmes, already implemented or planned for the implementation, can be found in the FRA report: Together in the EU. Promoting the participation of migrants and their descendants, European Union Agency for Fundamental Rights 2017, 26–27.

[42] Common Basic Principles for Immigrant Integration Policy in the European Union. See Annex para. 1 and para. 2. In accordance with the integration guidelines, integration should ensure that migrants have the possibility of full participation in the economic, social, political as well as cultural life.

[43] Common Basic Principles for Immigrant Integration Policy in the European Union, para. 12. Common Basic Principle no. 4.

[44] Ibidem. Common Basic Principle No. 7.

[45] Ibidem, Annex para. 3. Common Basic Principle No. 3.

cultural needs, might be effectively safeguarded when an individual has his or her needs at the basic level satisfied. Employment entails broader possibilities of participation in cultural life and a broader social participation, which generally excludes marginalization.[46]

The guarantees of respect for cultural rights of third-country nationals are also to be found in the guidelines. According to the latter, the practising of cultural customs and religion is guaranteed in the Charter of Fundamental Rights and must be observed on condition that the said practices are not in conflict with other rights guaranteed by European and national law (especially regarding the rights of women, children and the freedom of practising or not practising religion).[47] Thus, the process of integration provides for respect for the cultural rights of third-country nationals.

A significant element facilitating integration is participation in education. In accordance with the guidelines, education facilitates not only the process of acquiring knowledge in a traditional sense, but also contributes to the transfer of norms and values existing and functioning in the host society.[48]

Another document which is important for the interpretation of the guarantees of the integrative cultural rights is the Communication from the Commission—A Common Agenda for Integration.[49] The Agenda provides for detailed activities which might be conducted at the national and EU level in accordance with the Common Basic Principles[50] of migrants' integration adopted in 2004. For instance, the fourth guideline: "Basic knowledge of the host society's language, history, and institutions is indispensable to integration; enabling immigrants to acquire this basic knowledge is essential to successful integration" should be realized by the Member States by means of introductory integration programmes—information packs, language courses or the so-called civil orientation in the

[46] See L. Dyczewski, "Grupy marginalne," in *Kultura grup mniejszościowych i marginalnych*, ed. L. Dyczewski (Lublin, 2005), 33.

[47] Common Basic Principles for Immigrant Integration Policy in the European Union, para. 16, Annex para. 8. Common Basic Principle No. 8.

[48] Common Basic Principles for Immigrant Integration Policy in the European Union, Annex para. 5. Common Basic Principle No. 5.

[49] Communication from the Commission to the Council, the European Parliament, the European Economic and Social Committee and the Committee of the Regions—A Common Agenda for Integration—Framework for the Integration of Third-Country Nationals in the European Union. Brussels. 1.09.2005, COM/2005/0389 final.

[50] P. Babis, "Wpływ Unii Europejskiej na budowę polskiej polityki integracyjnej," in *Praktyki integracji. Doświadczenia i perspektywy*, eds. M. Bieniecki, M. Pawlak (Warszawa, 2012), 119.

country of origin. Such activities should allow third-country nationals to acquire knowledge on the subject of the language, history, cultural life and respected values in the receiving country.[51]

In 2008, the European Council adopted the so-called European Pact on Immigration and Asylum. In the area of integration policy, it was pointed out that it should strike a balance between granting entitlements to foreign nationals and imposing obligations on them.[52] The European Parliament also voiced its opinion on the subject of integration, including cultural integration, in the resolution adopted in 2009. In the resolution, it was emphasized that integration strengthens cultural diversity in the European Union.[53]

In 2011 the European Commission adopted another communication in the area of integration—European programme for the integration of third-country nationals.[54] It held that integration through participation should be a priority in the integration process: "Integration requires the engagement by the receiving society in accommodating the migrants, respecting their rights and cultures and informing them about their obligations. At the same time, migrants need to show the willingness to integrate and to respect rules and values of the society in which they live."[55] The Communication postulates the necessity of undertaking activities which would make it easier for migrants to learn a language and effectively involve third-country nationals' children in the educational system. Moreover, the Communication points out to a very important issue, namely the necessity of conducting especially

[51] Communication from the Commission to the Council, the European Parliament, the European Economic and Social Committee and the Committee of the Regions—A Common Agenda for Integration—Framework for the Integration of Third-Country Nationals in the European Union, 7.

[52] European Pact on Immigration and Asylum of 24 September 2008 (not published in the Official Journal), available on the website http://register.consilium.europa.eu/doc/srv?l=PL&f=ST%2013440%202008%20INIT. Accessed 12.09.2017.

[53] A Common Immigration Policy for Europe. European Parliament resolution of 22 April 2009 on a Common Immigration Policy for Europe: Principles, actions and tools, P6_TA(2009)0257, (2008/2331[INI]), para. 28.

[54] Communication from the Commission to the European Parliament, the Council, the European Economic and Social Committee and the Committee of the Regions European Agenda for the Integration of Third-Country Nationals, 20.07.2011, COM/2011/0455 final.

[55] Communication from the Commission to the European Parliament, the Council, the European Economic and Social Committee and the Committee of the Regions European Agenda for the Integration of Third-Country Nationals, Part A.

intensive integration activities in cities which are threatened with poverty. The aim of such activities is to culturally activate migrants, which in turn should counteract the ghettoization of migrants and their exclusion from the social life of the receiving societies.[56]

A special moment for the European migration policy was the escalation of the migration crisis, which occurred in 2015. It was then that the Commission adopted the Communication European Agenda on Migration.[57] The Commission called upon the Member States to resort to the Asylum, Migration and Integration Fund in the face of the influx of migrants, especially within the programme for the displaced persons.[58] As was emphasized in the Communication: "The funds can support targeted initiatives to improve language and professional skills, improve access to services, promote access to the labour market, inclusive education, foster inter-cultural exchanges and promote awareness campaigns targeting both host communities and migrants."[59]

At the beginning of 2016 the European Parliament adopted an interesting resolution, emphasizing the role of intercultural dialogue, cultural diversity and education in promoting European values.[60] In the resolution it is emphasized that even though the intercultural dialogue is not a legal construct, it is still based on an international framework, whose aim is to protect human rights and cultural diversity.[61] Thus, one has to agree with the statement that the sources facilitating the construction of integrative cultural rights are also the so-called soft international law and international custom. The provisions of the Charter of Fundamental Rights are also of special importance for intercultural dialogue. They guarantee equality, prohibition of discrimination, cultural, religious and linguistic diversity, freedom of expression, freedom of movement, as well as civil

[56] Ibidem, Part B.1.

[57] Communication from the Commission to the European Parliament, the Council, the European Economic and Social Committee and the Committee of the Regions. A European Agenda on Migration, Brussels, 13.5.2015, COM(2015) 240 final.

[58] Communication from the Commission to the European Parliament, the Council, the European Economic and Social Committee and the Committee of the Regions. A European Agenda on Migration, 6, 19.

[59] Ibidem, 19.

[60] The role of intercultural dialogue, cultural diversity and education in promoting EU fundamental values. European Parliament resolution of 19 January 2016 on the role of intercultural dialogue, cultural diversity and education in promoting EU fundamental values (2015/2139(INI)), P8_TA(2016)0005.

[61] Ibidem, para. B.

rights to participate in economic and political life.[62] The Resolution also emphasizes that the Union is currently facing the phenomena of globalization, migration, religious and intercultural conflicts, as well as an increase in radical attitudes.[63] However, for the purpose of intercultural dialogue, it is crucial that the universal human rights and cultural rights are guaranteed.[64] With regard to the challenges of the intercultural dialogue, activities should be undertaken with a view to increasing the participation of migrants and refugees in cultural life.[65]

In the Communication adopted in 2016 titled "Action Plan on the Integration of Third Country Nationals,"[66] it is emphasized that migrants' integration needs are very individualized. On the one hand, highly qualified workers, with high cultural competences and knowledge of the language, enter the Union. On the other hand, the Union faces the problem of integrating persons seeking international protection, who are familiar neither with the language nor with the existing cultural codes.[67] Integration is defined as a dynamic and two-way process, which imposes obligations on immigrants (including cultural obligations) in the form of adopting and accepting fundamental values of the Union and the learning of the language. Integration also grants entitlements in the form of the possibility of participating in social life (as well as cultural life) of the host country.[68] As is emphasized in the document, "[a]ctively contributing and being allowed to contribute to the political, cultural and social life is at least as important to creating a sense of belonging and feeling fully anchored in the host society and to building socio-economically thriving societies."[69]

The Communication also enumerates the priorities of integration activities, among which it highlights the pre-arrival measures in the form of, for example, language courses for migrants or activities aimed at increasing the level of empathy and understanding in the host communities.[70]

[62] Ibidem, para. F.

[63] Ibidem, para. I.

[64] Ibidem, para. J.

[65] Ibidem, para. 25, 32.

[66] Communication from the Commission to the European Parliament, the Council, the European Economic and Social Committee and the Committee of the Regions, Action Plan on the integration of third-country nationals, 7.06.2016, COM(2016) 377 final.

[67] Action Plan on the integration of third-country nationals, 4.

[68] Ibidem, 5.

[69] Ibidem.

[70] Ibidem, 7.

Additionally, in the integration process emphasis should be placed on the learning of the language and education. Further, it should be ensured that access to education is provided to migrants' children, regardless of their cultural origin.[71] Migrants should also have access to vocational training[72] and actively participate in the life of the receiving community, also at the cultural level.[73]

Also the European Council in its Conclusions of December 2016 encouraged the Member States to undertake activities for the active participation of third-country nationals in social and cultural life, promotion of intercultural dialogue and mutual acceptance between third-country nationals and the host societies. Additionally, efforts should be made to promote European values through orientation programmes, as well as the promotion of immigrants' participation in cultural and sports events and through endowing them with cultural competences.[74]

Conclusions and recommendations with regard to the EU integration policy are to be found in the current FRA report "Together in the EU. Promoting the Participation."[75] The Agency pointed out to the need of engaging third-country nationals in social, political and cultural life.[76] Involvement in cultural life in practical terms entails the creation of access to cultural goods and the possibility of participation in cultural life *in se*, in accordance with the classical way of understanding cultural rights. Such involvement may be of an active as well as passive character and is usually guaranteed at the constitutional level with regard to the nationals of the given Member State or persons legally residing within its territory. Thus, the Union's activities in this area complement the policies of inclusion into cultural life, as realized at the level of national policies. Participation in cultural life of third-country nationals is, however, of a specific character, as they comprise a very special group—on the one hand, still of a marginal

[71] Ibidem, 8.

[72] Ibidem, 10.

[73] Ibidem, 14.

[74] Conclusions of the Council and the Representatives of the Governments of the Member States on the integration of third-country nationals legally residing in the EU—Council conclusions (9 December 2016), 5–6.

[75] Together in the EU. Promoting the participation of migrants and their descendants, European Union Agency for Fundamental Rights 2017. Report available on the website www.fra.europa.eu. Accessed 12.09.2017.

[76] Ibidem, 9. Moreover, according to the FRA, successful integration requires appropriate education, catering to the needs of third-country nationals' families and allowing for the access to teachers trained in the issues of multiculturality (p. 10).

character, but, on the other hand, a group that often relies on different cultural codes. Therefore, the inclusion of such groups into cultural life requires a different set of incentives and activities than the programmes realized with regard to the nationals of the Member States and the effectiveness of such measures depends to a large degree on the involvement of the local institutions of the Member States.

6.4 Cultural Rights with Regard to Third-Country Nationals' Stay in the Territory of the EU

Third-country nationals residing legally in the territory of the European Union may realize their cultural rights in the way provided for by national law and by the EU law at the universal level.[77] Moreover, depending on the character of the third-country national's stay in the Member State, he or she may be entitled to various cultural rights guaranteed in the provisions of the EU legal acts. Foreign nationals may be also obligated to realize specific integrative cultural obligations. The rights and integrative cultural obligations will be analysed on the basis of the specific legal acts regulating the rules of stay of third-country nationals in the Union—Directive 2003/109 on long-term residents, the new Directive 2016/801 regulating the stay of students and academics, the so-called Directive 2009/50 on the Blue Card (for highly qualified workers), the so-called Citizenship Directive 2004/38 and other legal acts.

6.4.1 *Long-Term Residents*

The directive on long-term residents (Directive 2003/109)[78] lays down the conditions for the granting of the long-term resident status to third-country nationals, together with the rights accompanying the status and the rules of stay in another Member State than the one which issued the decision on the long-term resident status.[79] The status of a long-term

[77] See Exploring the Connections Between Arts and Human Rights. Report of high-level expert meeting. Vienna, 29–30 May 2017, European Union Agency for Fundamental Rights 2017. Report available on the website www.fra.europa.eu. Accessed 31.12.2017.

[78] Council Directive 2003/109/EC of 25 November 2003 concerning the status of third-country nationals who are long-term residents, OJ L 16, 23.1.2004, 44, further also as Directive 2003/109.

[79] Art. 1 Directive 2003/109. The exemptions from the application of the provisions of the directive are listed under Art. 3. See K. Kruma, *EU Citizenship, Nationality and Migrant*

resident may be granted to a person who has resided legally and continuously within its territory for five years immediately prior to the submission of the application.[80] The condition for being granted the long-term resident status is that of having stable and regular resources which are sufficient to maintain the family without the need of resorting to the system of social welfare and having a full sickness insurance.[81] As I. Wróbel emphasizes:

> Directive 2003/109 is based on the well-established tradition in the Member States that the length of stay of a third-country national influences the scope of his/her rights. This interdependence is a significant element of integration with the receiving society of third-country nationals who intend to reside in the European Union for a longer period of time.[82]

The need for integration of third-country national having the status of a long-tern resident is articulated already in the Preamble of the Directive.[83] However, the most important provision regarding the integration of long-term residents which has spurred discussion in the doctrine is Art. 5(2) of Directive 2003/109. In accordance with the provision, "Member States may require third-country nationals to comply with integration conditions, in accordance with national law." This provision includes a norm allowing for the imposition of an obligation of a cultural character on third-country nationals by the Member States, which transpires from the process of integration. Participation in integration measures is aimed at the process of effective cultural integration and therefore this provision will be analysed in greater detail in the current subchapter. It remains without doubt that language competences and knowledge on the subject of values and culture of the receiving country are necessary conditions

Status. An Ongoing Challenge (Leiden/Boston, 2004), 253 et seq.; S. Peers, "Legislative Update EU Immigration and Asylum Law 2010: Extension of Long-term Residence Rights and Amending the Law on Trafficking in Human Beings," European *Journal of Migration and Law*, vol. 13, no. 2 (2011): 206–212.

[80] Art. 4 Directive 2003/109.

[81] Art. 5(1) Directive 2003/109.

[82] I. Wróbel, *Status prawny obywatela państwa trzeciego w Unii Europejskiej* (Warszawa, 2007), 261.

[83] In accordance with its recital 4: "The integration of third-country nationals who are long-term residents in the Member States is a key element in promoting economic and social cohesion, a fundamental objective of the Community stated in the Treaty."

allowing for integration and this was precisely the reason for introducing Art. 5(2) to the Directive.[84]

Wróbel points out that in the project of the directive instead of the term "integration conditions" there is a term "integration measures." As the author observes, the change in the terms used under Art. 5(2) is of significance importance for the practices of the Member States, as it allows for the possibility of imposing the costs of participation in integration measures on third-country nationals.[85] Moreover, the directive does not include the term "integration conditions," which results in the fact that "the interpretation and the actual scope of the conditions will be determined on the grounds of the divergent acts of national immigration law, political priorities and values preferred in particular Member States."[86] Apart from the lack of definition of the very terms of integration conditions, there is also a lack of limitations as to the potential size and character of the measures that may be applied.[87] As a result, as C. Murphy emphasizes, integration becomes in fact an instrument of exclusion and assimilation.[88] This argument is also repeated by J.M. Permoser, who points out that integration conditions are believed to constitute a disguised means for immigration control.[89]

[84] J.M. Permoser, "Civic Integration as Symbolic Politics: Insights from Austria," *European Journal of Migration and Law*, vol. 14, no. 2 (2012): 175.

[85] I. Wróbel, *Status prawny obywatela*, 254. See Ch. Joppke, "Immigrants and civic integration in Western Europe," in *Belonging? Diversity, Recognition and shared Citizenship in Canada*, eds. K. Banting, T.J. Courchene, F. Leslie Seidle (Institute for Research on Public Policy, 2007), 21, http://irpp.org/research/belonging-diversity-recognition-and%2D%2Dshare-citizenship-in-canada/. Accessed 12.09.2017. See also K. Groenendijk, "Legal Concepts of Integration in EU Migration Law," *European Journal of Migration and Law*, vol. 6, issue 2 (2004): 111–126.

[86] I. Wróbel, *Status prawny obywatela*, 254.

[87] A. Bocker, T. Strik, "Language and Knowledge Tests for Permanent Residence Rights: Help or Hindrance for Integration?" *European Journal of Migration and Law*, vol. 13, issue 2 (2011): 178.

[88] C. Murphy, *Immigration, Integration and the Law. The Intersection of Domestic, EU and International Legal Remedies* (Ashgate, 2013), 179. See also C. Costello, "Search of the Outer Edges of Non-refoulement in Europe," in *Human Rights and Refugee Definition. Comparative Legal Practice and Theory*, eds. B. Burson, D.J. Cantor (Brill/Nijhoff, 2016), 162. The author also points out to the practices at the domestic level, which might be considered discriminatory in a situation when integration requirements are not applicable to certain third-country nationals, such as the Japanese, Canadians or the nationals of the United States.

[89] J.M. Permoser, "Civic Integration as Symbolic Politics," 175.

The solution adopted under Art. 5(2) Directive 2003/109 is thus a point of criticism in the doctrine.[90] Apart from the above objections, attention has also been turned to the possibility of limiting the effectiveness of the provisions of Directive 2003/109[91] and high fees charged for enrolment in the courses and trainings,[92] which results in exclusion of persons with low income from integration.[93] Moreover, one of the frequently raised critiques of the provisions under Art. 5(2) Directive 2003/109 is the possibility of limiting the guarantees of migrants' rights (especially with regard to the prohibition of discrimination and the right to family life)[94] and a lack of respect for cultural diversity.[95] This argument is based on a claim that integration conditions result in the imposition of the culture and values respected by the majority of society on migrant minorities.[96] I cannot exactly endorse this statement. Obviously, the use of "cultural enforcement" should never be accepted. However, the application of integration tests in no way forces migrants to change the language or abandon the traditions and culture of the country of origin. The aim of the integration conditions is to acquire basic knowledge about the receiving country which will allow a third-country national to harmoniously engage in social and cultural life and counteract social and cultural exclusion. Integration as a

[90] Moreover, migrants themselves have mixed feelings about the effectiveness of the integration conditions. See R. van Oers, *Deserving Citizenship. Citizenship Tests in Germany, the Netherlands and the United Kingdom* (Leiden/Boston, 2014), 236.

[91] *EU Immigration and Asylum Law (Text and Commentary): Second Revised Edition, vol. 2, EU Immigration Law*, eds. S. Peers, E. Guild, D. Costa et al. (Leiden/Boston, 2012), 303. In the report on the implementation of Directive 2003/109 of 2001 the Commission pointed out that in the implementation of the directive (including its Art. 5[2]), the principle of effectiveness and proportionality should be observed, especially with regard to the level of knowledge required of third-country nationals (also in comparison to the level of knowledge of the receiving community), the costs of exams and availability of courses and tests (ibidem, 304). See *Report from the Commission to the European Parliament and the Council on the application of Directive 2003/109/EC concerning the status of third-country nationals who are long-term residents*, COM(2011) 585.

[92] *EU Immigration and Asylum Law (Text and Commentary): Second Revised Edition*, vol. 2, 303.

[93] J.M. Permoser, "Civic Integration as Symbolic Politics," 178. The author refers to the publication E. Guild, K. Groenendijk, S. Carrera, "Understanding the Contest of Community: Illiberal Practices in the EU?" in *Illiberal Liberal States: Immigration, Citizenship and Integration in the EU* (Ashgate, 2009), 1–28.

[94] J.M. Permoser, "Civic Integration as Symbolic Politics," 179.

[95] Ibidem, 175.

[96] Ibidem, 180.

two-way process requires respect for the cultures of migrants, but also requires migrants to respect the culture of the receiving country. The condition for respecting the norms of the host country is the knowledge of those norms. Positive aspects of introducing integration conditions are also highlighted by B. Mikołajczyk who observes that their aim is to promote migrants' integration in the new society. What is more, tests are supposed to strengthen the guarantees of fundamental rights in the area of preventing forced marriages and human trafficking.[97]

In light of the discussed issue, the problem of protecting the rights of women migrants seems to be debatable. Due to the fact that in many migrant societies there exist customary or religious laws from their country of origin, such women may experience exclusion from integration processes and remain on the margin of social life. Simultaneously, it might occur that despite the gender equality existing in EU law, the rights and freedoms of women migrants might be in fact violated. Such situations pose a challenge for the Member States, which require the knowledge of European cultural values of migrants, but they are not able to prevent the existing inequalities, which appear in migrant societies. The obligatory participation in integration and language courses might become an effective measure against the presented problem. It might contribute to increased literacy among the female migrants, strengthen their civil awareness and thus serve towards a more effective protection of their fundamental rights.[98]

The discussed provision of the directive allowed the Member States to introduce the integration conditions. This is what actually occurred, as is emphasized by the authors of a study titled "EU Immigration and Asylum Law." In 1999 only Germany required third-country nationals to pass a language examination in order to be granted a residence permit.[99] The effect of entering into force of Directive 2003/109 was the implementation

[97] B. Mikołajczyk, "Integracja obywateli państw trzecich w Unii Europejskiej—nowe tendencje i wyzwania," *Ruch Prawniczy, Ekonomiczny i Socjologiczny*, vol. LXXIII/2 (2011): 169.

[98] Ibidem.

[99] *EU Immigration and Asylum Law (Text and Commentary): Second Revised Edition*, vol. 2, 303. What is more, Germany was the first Member State which in 1999 introduced the obligation of taking language tests before entry into its territory. However, the requirement concerned only the youth aged 16–18 who wanted to enter Germany for the purpose of family reunification. See *The INTEC Project: Synthesis Report. Integration and Naturalisation tests: the new way to European Citizenship. A Comparative study in nine Member States on the national policies concerning integration and naturalisation tests and their effects on integration.* Financed by the European Integration Fund, Tineke Strik, Anita Bocker, Maaike Luiten and Ricky van Oers. Centre for Migration Law (Nimjegen, 2010), 11.

of the integration conditions in the majority of the Member States.[100] The Member States decided to introduce the so-called integration contract, obligatory language courses (level A1 to B2)[101] and tests checking the knowledge of culture and the rules of social functioning (amongst others, Denmark, France, Germany and the United Kingdom).[102] What is more, particular Member States decided to impose sanctions in a situation of non-compliance with integration conditions. The sanctions include primarily the refusal to grant long-term residence status, refusal to prolong the temporary residence permit, administrative measures or depriving migrants of social benefits.[103]

Detailed data on the subject of the integration conditions applied in the Member States can also be found in the report prepared within the INTEC project, realized by the Centre for Migration Law in Nijmegen and comprising data from eight Member States,[104] in the reports prepared by the ICMPD within the PROSINT project[105] and the report by the Fundamental

[100] A. Bocker, T. Strik, "Language and Knowledge Tests for Permanent Residence Rights," 156.

[101] Detailed data on the language integration of third-country nationals can be found in the report: *Linguistic Integration of Adult Migrants: Policy and Practice. Final Report on the 3rd Council of Europe Survey*, Language Policy Unit, Education Policy Division, Education Department, DGII, Council of Europe, Strasbourg 2014.

[102] A. Bocker, T. Strik, "Language and Knowledge Tests for Permanent Residence Rights," 162.

[103] Ibidem, 161.

[104] *The INTEC Project: Synthesis Report. Integration and Naturalisation tests: the new way to European Citizenship. A Comparative study in nine Member States on the national policies concerning integration and naturalisation tests and their effects on integration.* Financed by the European Integration Fund, Tineke Strik, Anita Bocker, Maaike Luiten and Ricky van Oers. Centre for Migration Law, Nijmegen 2010. See https://ec.europa.eu/migrant-integration/librarydoc/the-intec-project-integration-and-naturalisation%2D%2Dtests-the-new-way-to-european-citizenship. Accessed 12.09.2017.

[105] The ICMPD (International Centre for Migration Policy Development) is an organization conducting research on migration policies. As part of the PROSINT project (Promoting Sustainable Policies for Integration), which was implemented in the years 2009–2011, the thematic reports were prepared including, amongst others, a report on the relations between the policy of the admission of migrants and the policies of integration—A. Balch, A. Geddes, Connections between admission policies and integration policies at the EU level and given linkages with national policy-making, 2012; report on the implementation of the policies with regard to integration courses at the local level—M. Quirico et seq. *Study on the local implementation of integration/introduction courses for newcomers. Overview report*, 2012. All the publications are available on the website of the project http://research.icmpd.org/projects/integration-non-discrimination/prosint/. Accessed 31.12.2017.

Rights Agency "Together in the EU. Promoting the Participation of Migrants and Their Descendants." In the chapter on migrants' language learning and integration tests, a fourth condition from among the Common Basic Principles was cited, in accordance with which the basic knowledge of the language and history of the receiving society is an indispensable condition for integration. This priority is also worth referring to in the context of the criticism that integration tests pose a threat to cultural diversity. The respect for and knowledge of other cultures, including the dominant one, does not mean the elimination of the minority culture, but merely facilitates their coexistence. It is worth adding that through access to language and integration courses and through the acquired skills, migrants have the possibility of an easier and broader access (due to a potentially wider cultural offer) to cultural goods and active participation in cultural life. The report emphasizes that the majority of the Member States provide access to free-of-charge courses, except for Austria, Malta and the Netherlands.[106] Moreover, the FRA assessment has demonstrated that in 19 Member States there are no requirements of taking integration tests in order to acquire residence entitlements. The passing of such tests, however, is required of third-country nationals seeking residence status in Croatia, Malta, the Netherlands and the United Kingdom. Countries such as Austria, the Czech Republic, Hungary and Spain require the taking of tests only in the case of applying for citizenship.[107]

The provisions adopted by the Member States with regard to integration conditions and an assessment of their compliance with EU law was also the subject of the proceedings before the Court of Justice of the European Union (CJEU) in the case of P and S (C 579/13).[108] The appli-

[106] Together in the EU, 51.

[107] Ibidem, 52.

[108] Judgement of the Court of Justice of 4 June 2015 in the case P and S v. Commissie Sociale Zekerheid Breda and College van Burgemeester en Wethouders van de gemeente Amstelveen, Case C-579/13, ECLI:EU:C:2015:369, further as judgement in the case C 579/13. Interesting proceedings also took place before the national courts in the Netherlands, in which the applicants were nationals of Turkey. They claimed that on the basis of the Association Agreement they should be exempted from the integration conditions. The national courts in Rotterdam and Roermond held that the condition of participation in an integration course constitutes a limitation within the meaning of Decision 1/80 (Decision of the Association Council No. 1/80 of 19 September 1980 on the development of the Association, attached to the Agreement establishing an Association between the European Economic Community and Turkey). See N. Tezcan-Idriz, "Dutch Courts Safeguarding Rights under the EEC—Turkey Association Law. Case Note on District Court Rotterdam

cants at the national proceedings were two third-country nationals (the United States and New Zealand), who since 2007 and 2008 had the long-term residence status in the Netherlands. In the Netherlands integration policy was regulated by the national act on social integration, the so-called *Wi* (*Wet inburgering*), which entered into force in 2007. In accordance with its provisions, social integration concerns migrants who entered the Netherlands before 2007 as well as after 1 January 2007.[109] In the case of not taking an examination on integration or failing the examination, the act provided for, in principle, the imposing of an administrative fine on the third-country national concerned. The necessary circumstance for being granted long-term resident status for persons who entered the Netherlands after the act had entered into force was the passing of an integration exam. The applicants in the proceedings entered the Netherlands before 1 January 2007 but in accordance with the stance of the Dutch government, clarifying the wording of the provisions of the act, they were obliged to pass the integration examination, despite having resident status, on pain of a fine. What is significant is that such a fine could be re-imposed in each case when the third-country national concerned did not appear for the exam or whenever he or she failed the exam.

Due to the imposition of the obligation of integration on the two third-country nationals, they challenged the decision regarding the obligation of passing the integration exam, claiming that the decisions are contrary to Directive 2003/109. The national court decided to stay the proceedings and referred a question for a preliminary ruling to the CJEU, asking for an interpretation of Art. 5(2) Directive 2003/109 and whether national regulations are compliant with the said provisions.[110]

Judgments of 12 August 2010, and District Court Roermond Judgment of 1 October 2010," *European Journal of Migration and Law*, vol. 13, issue 2 (2011): 219–240.

[109] Para. 11 of the judgement in the case of C 579/13. The Act also includes provisions which exempt from the obligation of social integration, amongst others, persons aged over 65 and before 16 or persons who started residence in the Netherlands during the eight-year period of school education. What is more, "[p]ersons required to fulfil the civic integration obligation who have acquired a diploma, certificate or other document laid down by or in accordance with a general administrative order, showing that they have already acquired some of the knowledge and skills referred to in Article 7, are exempt from the obligation to acquire that part of the knowledge or skills and to pass the relevant part of the civic integration examination." For all the circumstances for exemption see para. 13 of the judgement in the case C 579/13.

[110] The first question referred for a preliminary ruling was the following: "Must the aim and scope of Directive 2003/109/EC, or of Article 5(2) and/or of Article 11(1) thereof, be

The Court decided to examine the questions jointly and distinctly emphasized that in the case of the applicants, their passing of the exam on integration was not a condition for granting them long-term resident status as they had been granted such status before.[111] Thus, the Court held that the obligation imposed on the applicants in the national procedure could not be deemed as a condition for integration within the meaning of Art 5(2) of the directive, but neither did it constitute an obstacle in adopting such integration measures in national law by the Member States.

In the case under discussion the Court also interpreted Art. 11 Directive 2003/109, granting long-term residents the right to equal treatment with nationals of the receiving country in the areas of social life listed in the Article. The Court held that the integration measure adopted in national law, which was imposed on the applicants, does not violate the principle of equal treatment. The Court based its interpretation on the stance that "the integration measures at issue consist, in essence, in the obligation to acquire and/or demonstrate oral and written proficiency in the Dutch language and knowledge of Netherlands society." The Court assumed that nationals of the Netherlands possess such knowledge and skills, whereas it was impossible to assume the same in the case of third-country nationals and the situations of the two groups were not comparable.[112]

In expressing its opinion on the subject of rules of the realization of integration measures by the Member States, the Court observed that they ensure "that the third-country nationals concerned acquire knowledge which is undeniably useful for establishing connections with the host Member State." Moreover, the Court emphasized that "it must be held that such an obligation does not, by itself, jeopardise the achievement of the objectives pursued by Directive 2003/109, but may on the contrary contribute to their achievement."[113] However, the Member States should take into account the specific guidelines in the process of implementing integration measures so that they are not contrary to the realization of the

interpreted as meaning that the imposition of the civic integration obligation, under national law, on third-country nationals who have acquired long-term resident status, with penalties in the form of a system of fines, cannot be reconciled therewith?" whereas the second question "In answering the first question, is it relevant whether the civic integration obligation was imposed before long-term resident status was granted?," para. 28 of the judgement in the case C 579/13.

[111] Para. 31 of the judgement in the case 579/13.

[112] See para. 42 and 43 of the judgement in the case C 579/13.

[113] Para. 48 of the judgement in the case C 579/13.

aims of the directive. Among the guidelines, under para. 49 of the judgement, the Court points out to the level of knowledge required to pass the civic integration examination, to the accessibility of the courses and material necessary to prepare for that examination, to the registration fees for the course, as well as to the consideration of the third-national's situation and his or her individual circumstances, such as age, illiteracy and education. The guidelines may be complemented by the Opinion of the Advocate General, in which he pointed out that the integration measures should remain compatible with the fundamental rights provided for in the Charter—the right to respect for private and family life (Art. 7 of the Charter of Fundamental Rights [CFR]), freedom of conscience and religion (Art. 10 CFR), the prohibition of discrimination (Art. 21 CFR), the rights of the child (Art. 24 CFR), the rights of the elderly (Art. 25 CFR) and the rights of persons with disabilities (Art. 26).[114]

Expressing its stance on the imposition of financial penalties, the Court held that, in principle, they are not contrary to the provisions of the directive. However, the imposition of large fines (amounting to EUR 100; the fine could be re-imposed), which might be imposed multiple times, together with the high costs of enrolling in the examination (EUR 230) might threaten the effectiveness of the directive.

The judgement under discussion, in which the Court conducted a comprehensive interpretation of Art. 5(2) Directive 2003/109, contains significant guidelines for the Member States with regard to the integration measures possible to be applied. Firstly, the Court took the stance that the imposition of integration exams even with regard to persons who already have long-term resident status is admissible. It is an important statement as it allows for the possibility of verifying the level of integration of third-country nationals. It is based on the assumption that through the period of a few years a person has learned both the language and social rules through everyday life. In such a case, passing an integration exam should not pose a problem. What is more, it should be an integrative cultural obligation, which would facilitate the verification of a person's knowledge on the culture and history of the host country. Such knowledge facilitates

[114] Para. 83 of the Opinion of the Advocate General in the case C 579/13. See Opinion of Advocate General Szpunar delivered on 28 January 2015. P and S v Commissie Sociale Zekerheid Breda and College van Burgemeester en Wethouders van de gemeente Amstelveen, 579/13, ECLI:EU:C:2015:39, further as Opinion of the Advocate General in the case C 579/13.

participation in the activities of the civil society and helps in building a new cultural identity of third-country nationals.[115] An important postulate for the Member States would be to exempt third-country nationals from registration fees for taking such exams and to ensure they have access to relevant materials (e.g., on Internet platforms). At the same time, attention should be paid to the consequent realization of such tests.[116]

A different stance was adopted by the Advocate General who in his Opinion points out that a person who had been living in the receiving society for an extensive period of time should have the possibility of an individual assessment of the integration progress—according to the Advocate General reliance merely on the results of the integration exam is a disproportionate measure "to the purpose of facilitating that person's further integration into society."[117] According to the Advocate General, the application of the integration measures with regard to long-term residents is also contrary to the above-mentioned Common Basic Principles adopted in 2004.[118] Obviously, the postulate of an individual assessment

[115] Also Advocate General M. Szpunar in his Opinion stated: "In my opinion, the imposition of integration measures on long-term residents is not contrary to the aims of Directive 2003/109, since those measures are intended solely to contribute towards the integration of the long-term resident into the economic and social life of the State of residence" (para. 49 of the Opinion of the Advocate General in the case C 579/13). The Advocate General also emphasized that "[w]here it is imposed on long-term residents, an integration obligation may not excessively impede the exercise of the rights associated with their status. That obligation may not impede the exercise of the right to employment and self-employed activity, education and vocational training. An essential matter here is access to evening courses. Account should also be taken of the cost of training and access to a system of material assistance" (para. 81 of the Opinion of the Advocate General in the case C 579/13).

[116] As a side note, it might be added that the Netherlands was also brought to Court by the European Commission under Art. 258 of the Treaty on the Functioning of the European Union (TFEU) with regard to the high fees for issuing third-country nationals residence documents. The fee for issuing the document confirming long-term residence status amounted to EUR 201 then, whereas the fee for the application for family reunification amounted to as much as EUR 803. In the judgement the Court held that the Kingdom of the Netherlands violated Directive 2003/109 by imposing excessive and unproportionally large fees, which might pose an obstacle in the exercise of the rights guaranteed in the directive. See Judgement of the Court of Justice of 26.04.2012 in the case the European Commission v. the Kingdom of the Netherlands, C 508/10, ECLI:EU:C:2012:243.

[117] Para. 92 of the Opinion of the Advocate General in the case C 579/13.

[118] Para. 93 of the Opinion of the Advocate General in the case C 579/13. In accordance with para. 94 of the Opinion: "The Common Principles define integration as a dynamic two-way process a key element of which is interaction, frequent contact between immigrants and citizens of a particular State and the promotion of inter-cultural dialogue. That document

of the level of cultural integration seems to be most accurate. However, a question remains concerning the actual realization of such an approach. The verification of knowledge of migrants about the receiving country should not be treated, in my view, as an oppressive measure, but rather as an opportunity for strengthening migrants' knowledge about the receiving country, which will be beneficial for further cultural integration. The form of an integration exam should not be the only manifestation of the activity of the State within the area of integration duties. However, if conducted properly, it might provide an incentive activating third-country nationals to verify their knowledge on the subject of the host country.

Another regulation allowing for the imposition of integration obligations on third-country nationals can be found under Art. 15 Directive 2003/109, which regulates the conditions of residence of a long-term resident in a different Member State than the one which issued the permission for the resident. In accordance with Art. 15(3), "Member States may require third-country nationals to comply with integration measures, in accordance with national law."

However, the law provides for the possibility of exemption from participation in integration measures if third-country nationals have already participated in such activities in connection with the issuing of long-term residence status in accordance with Art. 5(2) Directive 2003/109.[119] Nevertheless, in each case in order to obtain residence permit in a different Member State than the one which granted residence status, a third-country national may be obligated to participate in language courses.[120] As C. Murphy observes, the provision under Art. 15(3) of the directive may constitute a significant obstacle in the realization of the right to freedom of movement and generally puts third-country nationals with resident status in an unfavourable situation in comparison with citizens of the EU.[121] However, as A. Bocker and T. Strik point out, Art. 15(3) limits the possibilities of integration obligations of a cultural character which may be imposed on third-country nationals by the Member States by exclusion of

states that basic knowledge of the host society's language, history and institutions is indispensable to integration and enabling immigrants to acquire this basic knowledge is essential to successful integration. However, the various measures recommended for that purpose at national and EU level do not include integration exams or tests."

[119] Art. 15(3)(2) Directive 2003/109.

[120] Art. 15(3)(3) Directive 2003/109.

[121] C. Murphy, *Immigration, Integration and the Law*, 179.

exams, including language exams.[122] It is worth raising an argument which is often forgotten in the discussion on integration measures (voiced especially by the critics of their imposition as a specific type of obligations, often accompanied by a sanction) that all such activities should in fact work for the benefit of third-country nationals and contribute to the effectiveness of integration. It is difficult to instigate cooperation within the framework of the civil society if different groups rely on different cultural codes, which are mutually incomprehensible. Integration measures are aimed to level out the number of misunderstandings and support migrants in the integration process, even though they may be trying to avoid such integration.

Directive 2003/109 also ensures equal treatment of residents with citizens of the Member States[123] in such areas as access to the job market, access to education and vocational training, including academic scholarships,[124] recognition of qualifications, security and social welfare,[125] tax incentives, access to goods and services, freedom of association and membership in professional organizations and free access to the whole territory of the state (while preserving the limitations provided for by law for reasons of security).[126] As it transpires from the areas of social life listed under Art. 11 of the directive, a part of them concerns indirectly or directly the sphere of the realization of cultural rights and influences the possibility of guaranteeing cultural rights. Most certainly, what has an impact on the realization of cultural rights are the guarantees of equal treatment in the area of education and training, access to services, including the creative sector, the possibility of social activities of a cultural character in NGOs and associations of the creators of culture—if the

[122] A. Bocker, T. Strik, "Language and Knowledge Tests for Permanent Residence Rights," 179.

[123] In accordance with recital 12 of the Preamble of the Directive 2003/109, "In order to constitute a genuine instrument for the integration of long-term residents into society in which they live, long-term residents should enjoy equality of treatment with citizens of the Member State in a wide range of economic and social matters, under the relevant conditions defined by this Directive."

[124] In accordance with Art. 11(3)(b) Directive 2003/109, "Member States may require proof of appropriate language proficiency for access to education and training. Access to university may be subject to the fulfilment of specific educational prerequisites." On the subject of long-term residents' rights, see K. Kruma, *EU Citizenship, Nationality and Migrant Status*, 281.

[125] See *Migrant access to social security and healthcare: policies and practice. Synthesis report*, European Migration Network Study 2014.

[126] Art. 11 Directive 2003/109. See I. Wróbel, *Status prawny obywatela*, 256–257.

performed profession entails such specificity, as well as the possibility of free movement within the territory of the host country, which in itself facilitates free access to cultural goods.

The directive also provides for the protection against expulsion with regard to long-term residents. In accordance with Art. 12, a return decision may be issued with regard to a third-country national if he or she constitutes "an actual and sufficiently serious threat to public policy or public security." Such a decision cannot be based on economy and in the procedure preceding the issuing of the decision, account is taken of the length of stay of the third-country national concerned in the territory of the receiving country, his or her age, the consequences the issuing of the decision will have for private and family life of the third-country national concerned, the ties of the third-country national concerned with the country of residence and the lack of ties with the country of origin.[127] Such ties may be of a cultural character and should be examined in the return procedure, so the expulsion would not violate the fundamental rights of the third-country national concerned.

6.4.2 Cultural Rights of Other Groups of Third-Country Nationals Legally Residing in the Territory of the EU

EU law also regulates the legal situation of other groups of third-country nationals, other than long-term residents, whose stay in the territory of the European Union is of a regular character. Among them the most dominant groups are persons coming to the EU with the purpose of undertaking work. In their free time, such people also realize their cultural rights, in accordance with the framework of guarantees established in national law and EU primary law. The provisions of EU secondary law constitute in this situation a certain complementary element of the granted guarantees and contribute to the facilitation of the realization of the rights of a cultural character.

One of such legal acts is the so-called Blue Card Directive 2009/50.[128] The directive regulates the conditions of entry into the territory of the Union of third-country nationals in order to perform work in the profession requiring high qualifications, whereas the Blue Card is a permission

[127] Art. 12 Directive 2003/109. See P. van Dijk, *Protection of "Integrated" Aliens*, 36–39.

[128] Council Directive 2009/50/EC—Conditions of entry and residence of non-EU nationals for the purposes of highly qualified employment, OJ L 155 of 18.06.2009, 17, further also as Directive 2009/50.

allowing the third-country national concerned to stay and perform work in the Member State in accordance with the provisions of the directive.[129]

Directive 2009/50 allows for family reunification and on special conditions which constitute an exception with regard to the provisions of the directive on family reunification because in the case of the holders of the Blue Card there is no necessity to demonstrate that the third-country national concerned would receive the right of permanent residence. Directive 2009/50 provides for the possibility of applying the integration measures and conditions but only until the moment when the third-country national concerned is granted the right to family reunification.[130] Nevertheless, in accordance with recital 23 of the Preamble to the Directive, "[t]he derogation included in Article 15(3) of this Directive does not preclude Member States from maintaining or introducing integration conditions and measures, including language learning, for the members of the family of an EU Blue Card holder." Thus, the Member States may impose on third-country nationals the so-called cultural obligations, which should serve effective integration and the acquisition of knowledge on the culture of the receiving country.

Moreover, in a similar way as in the case of long-term residents, Directive 2009/50 provides for the equal treatment of the Blue Card holders with nationals of the Member States in the areas enumerated in its Art. 14. Among the latter, one should mention such areas of social life as access to education and vocational training, the freedom of association in workers' associations, recognition of diplomas and qualifications, access to goods and services and access to the whole territory of the country. These rights facilitate the realization of cultural rights, such as access to and participation in cultural goods (see *per analogiam* the situation of long-term residents described above).

A similarly equal treatment of third-country nationals is provided for in Directive 2011/98 on a single application procedure for a single permit for third-country nationals to reside and work in the territory of a Member State.[131]

[129] Art. 2(c) Directive 2009/50. See also *EU Immigration and Asylum Law (Text and Commentary): Second Revised Edition*, vol. 2, 47–69; C. Murphy, *Immigration, Integration and Law*, 184–185.

[130] Art. 15(3) Directive 2009/50.

[131] Directive 2011/98/EU of the European Parliament and of the Council of 13 December 2011 on a single application procedure for a single permit for third-country nationals to reside and work in the territory of a Member State and on a common set of rights for third-country workers legally residing in a Member State, OJ L 343, 23.12.2011, 1.

It often happens that a legal act provides for the minimal cultural entitlements, without which the exercise of one's cultural rights and the performance of the intended activity in the territory of the Member State would not be possible. This is the situation in the case of Directive 2014/36 which concerns seasonal workers. Generally, the only right facilitating the exercise of cultural rights that is possible to be reconstructed is precisely the principle of equal treatment with the nationals of the Member States in the areas listed under Art. 23.[132] Among the enumerated areas, the above-mentioned guarantees of access to goods and services and the territory of the Member States have an influence on extending the possibilities of exercising one's cultural rights.

6.4.3 *Cultural Entitlements of Members of Families of EU Citizens*

Certain cultural rights can also be partially reconstructed on the basis of the so-called Citizenship Directive, that is, Directive 2004/38, regulating the rights of the citizens of the Union and their families to free movement and residence in the Member States.[133] Such rights result from the citizenship of the Union. The rights provided for in the directive regard primarily the nationals of the Union, but also the members of their families, who might be third-country nationals. In the Preamble of the Directive there is an anti-discriminatory clause, in accordance with which the directive should be implemented together with the application of the prohibition of discrimination "on grounds such as sex, race, colour, ethnic or social origin, genetic characteristics, language, religion or beliefs, political or other opinion, membership of an ethnic minority, property, birth, disability, age or sexual orientation."[134]

[132] Directive 2014/36/EU of the European Parliament and of the Council of 26 February 2014 on the conditions of entry and stay of third-country nationals for the purpose of employment as seasonal workers, OJ L 94, 28.3.2014, 375.

[133] Directive 2004/38/EC of the European Parliament and of the Council of 29 April 2004 on the right of citizens of the Union and their family members to move and reside freely within the territory of the Member States amending Regulation (EEC) No. 1612/68 and repealing Directives 64/221/EEC, 68/360/EEC, 72/194/EEC, 73/148/EEC, 75/34/EEC, 75/35/EEC, 90/364/EEC, 90/365/EEC and 93/96/EEC (text with EEA relevance), OJ L 158, 30.04.2004, 77, further also as Citizenship Directive, Directive 2004/38. On the subject of the free movement, see B.K. Blitz, *Migration and Freedom. Mobility, Citizenship and Exclusion* (Edward Elgar Publishing, 2014), 46–47.

[134] Recital 31 of the Preamble to the Directive 2004/38.

Art. 12 Directive 2004/38 regulates the right of residence in the host Member State in the case of death or departure of a citizen of the Union. Thus, in accordance with Art. 12(3) in the case of departure or death of a citizen of the Union the right of residence is retained by his or her children and the parent who has actual custody of the children provided that the children are enrolled at an educational establishment. In such a case the children and the parent are entitled to the right of residence (irrespective of their nationality) until the completion of the children's studies.[135] Due to the safeguarded right of residence, third-country nationals and members of the family of a citizen of the Union may freely participate in the cultural life of the host country and exercise their universal guarantees of cultural rights, ensuring the freedom of creativity and the possibility of accessing cultural goods.

Indirectly, the Court interpreted the right to custody of children attending schools under Art. 12(3) in the case of Olaitan Ajoke Alarape and Olukayode Azeez Tijani v. Secretary of State for the Home Department.[136] In the proceedings, the Court focused directly on Art. 12 Regulation 1612/68,[137] which was replaced by Regulation (EU) No. 492/2011 of the European Parliament and of the Council of 5 April 2011 on freedom of movement for workers within the Union.[138] In accordance with the said Article:

> The children of a national of a Member State who is or has been employed in the territory of another Member State shall be admitted to that State's general educational, apprenticeship and vocational training courses under the same conditions as the nationals of that State, if such children are residing in its territory. Member States shall encourage all efforts to enable such children to attend these courses under the best possible conditions.

[135] The CJEU provided an interpretation of the above Article with regard citizen of the Union's children, who had the citizenship of the Union. See Judgement of the Court of Justice of 23.02.2010 in the case Maria Teixeira v. London Borough of Lambeth and Secretary of State for the Home Department, C 480/08, ECLI:EU:C:2010:83; Judgement of the Court of Justice of 23.02.2010 in the case London Borough of Harrow v. Nimco Hassan Ibrahim, Secretary of State for the Home Department, C 310/08, ECLI:EU:C:2010:80.

[136] Judgement of the Court of Justice of 8.05.2013 in the case Olaitan Ajoke Alarape and Olukayode Azeez Tijani v. Secretary of State for the Home Department, C 529/11, ECLI:EU:C:2013:290, further as judgement in the case C 529/11.

[137] Regulation (EEC) No. 1612/68 of the Council of 15 October 1968 on freedom of movement for workers within the Community, OJ L 257, 19.10.1968, 2.

[138] Regulation (EU) No. 492/2011 of the European Parliament and of the Council of 5 April 2011 on freedom of movement for workers within the Union, OJ L 141, 27.05.2011, 1.

The applicants in the proceedings were the nationals of Nigeria Mrs Olaitan Ajoke Alarape and her son O.A. Tijani. They settled in the United Kingdom in 2004 and in 2005 were granted residence permit—Mrs Olaitan as wife of a citizen of the Union and her son as a "descendant under the age of 21 or a dependant." O.A. Tijani studied in London and then was accepted at the University of Edinburgh in order to write his PhD thesis there. After the expiry of the residence permit of the applicants in 2009, the national authorities refused to extend it by a decision of 2010. On examining the complaint, the national court referred four questions for a preliminary ruling to the CJEU, which the Court decided to examine jointly and assess "what conditions must be met by a parent of a child who is more than 21 years old and who has obtained access to education on the basis of Article 12 of Regulation No 1612/68 if that parent is to continue to be entitled to a derived right of residence on the basis of that article."[139] The Court observed that if an adult child requires the custody of a parent in order to pursue education, the parent is unquestionably entitled to the right of residence.[140] The need to exert such care over the pupil/student may be assessed only by the national court, which should take into account circumstances such as "the age of the child, whether the child is residing in the family home or whether the child needs financial or emotional support from the parent in order to be able to continue and to complete his education."[141] In such a situation, the right of residence of the parent in a way guarantees the effectiveness of the right of a partially cultural character, which is the right to education, in this case the right to pursue university studies.

Moreover, the Citizenship Directive provides for the right to protection against expulsion. Before the issuing of the expulsion decision with regard to a citizen of the Union or the members of his or her family (who may be third-country nationals), the Member States take account of all significant information, such as the length of stay of the person in the territory of the host country, the level of social and cultural integration and the extent to which he or she is linked with the country of origin.[142] Thus,

[139] Para. 23 of the judgement in the case C 529/11.

[140] Para. 28 of the judgement in the case C 529/11.

[141] Para. 30 of the judgement in the case C 529/11.

[142] Art. 28 Directive 2004/38. See H. Oosterom-Staples, "Effective Rights of Third Country Nationals?" in *A right to inclusion or exclusion? Normative fault lines of the EU's Area of freedom, security and justice*, ed. H. Lindahl (Hart Publishing, 2009), 78–79.

the directive also protects, albeit indirectly, the right to cultural identity of the third-country national.

The process of integration of a third-country national with the host country may have its conclusion in the granting of nationality. Naturalization, that is, the process by which citizenship is granted to a foreign national, entails, on the one hand, complete integration and, on the other hand, ensures a wide spectrum of guarantees for the protection of human rights. They are not only first-generation rights, but also economic, social and, finally, cultural rights.[143] In the procedure of granting citizenship, many Member States apply tests confirming the knowledge of the culture and history of the receiving country.[144] The adoption of the policy with regard to the acquisition of citizenship belongs entirely within the competence of the Member States. However, it seems that the application of the integration condition with regard to migrants should entail in consequence that the persons who feel that they belong to a specific nation should also demonstrate the knowledge of its traditions, history and cultural codes. Even more so due to the fact that the consequence of acquiring the citizenship of a Member State is also that of acquiring the citizenship of the European Union.[145] As a side note, it is worth highlighting that the Polish law also does not provide for any verification tests (apart from the necessity of possessing documents confirming the knowledge of the Polish language), prior to the granting of citizenship.[146]

6.4.4 *Cultural Rights of Students and Academics*

Students and academics coming from the third countries comprise a specific group of third-country nationals, as their aim of entry into the Member States is clearly defined and, as if, it predestines the way in which

[143] C. Murphy, *Immigration, Integration and the Law*, 203 et seq.

[144] See R. van Oers, *Deserving Citizenship. Citizenship Tests in Germany, the Netherlands and the United Kingdom*, 41 et seq.

[145] K. Kruma, *EU Citizenship, Nationality and Migrant Status*, 119 et seq.

[146] See B. Wójcik, "Nadanie obywatelstwa polskiego," in *Nabywanie obywatelstwa polskiego*, ed. T. Sieniow (Lublin: Rule of Law Institute, 2013), 44. The Act of 2 April 2009 on Polish citizenship (uniform text, Journal of Laws of 2017, item 1462, as amended) provides that in the procedure of granting Polish citizenship by the President of the Republic of Poland, the foreign national should indicate in the application the knowledge of the Polish language and have an official document confirming the level of linguistic skill, for example, in the form of a language certificate. In the case of long-term residents, the way to citizenship is the procedure of acknowledging Polish citizenship, on the meeting of the provisions under Art. 30 of the Act.

they will exercise their rights of a cultural character. While studying and conducting research, they function within a specific environment of the academic sphere and university. A university is, on the one hand, a science-research unit and, on the other hand, a cultural institution, having a rich history and the tradition of functioning in European culture, dating back to the Middle Ages. A classical university but also many other institutions of higher education actively participate in the cultural sphere, organizing events of a cultural character, such as concerts, meetings, lectures, readings, conferences, artistic workshops or running libraries. Therefore, the academic community has a wider access to cultural goods and wider possibilities of participation in cultural life. Further, the activities organized by the university have a positive impact on the whole local community, which are usually the inhabitants of the city where the university is located.

In this way, university students or the academics carrying out research at the institutions of higher education exercise not only the freedom to conduct research and the right to education as partially cultural rights, but they also have the possibility of participating in the cultural life of the university, which allows for a special kind of participation in cultural life and conditions access to higher culture. Those entitlements are also exercised by third-country nationals coming to study in the European Union and academics conducting research at European universities. Hence, the right to university education and the right to conduct research of third-country nationals should be considered as specific cultural rights.

The following subchapter will include an analysis of those cultural rights which result from the realization of the educational and research processes. At present, the basic legal act in the system of EU law, regulating the access of third-country nationals to studies and the possibilities of arrival of academics from third countries, is Directive 2016/801,[147] which replaced Directive 2004/114 (on students)[148] and Directive 2005/71 (on admitting students conducting scientific research).[149]

[147] Directive (EU) 2016/801 of the European Parliament and of the Council of 11 May 2016 on the conditions of entry and residence of third-country nationals for the purposes of research, studies, training, voluntary service, pupil exchange schemes or educational projects and au pairing, OJ L 132, 21.05.2016, 21, further also as Directive 2016/801.

[148] Council Directive 2004/114/EC of 13 December 2004 on the conditions of admission of third-country nationals for the purposes of studies, pupil exchange, unremunerated training or voluntary service, OJ L 375, 23.12.2004, 12.

[149] Council Directive 2005/71/EC of 12 October 2005 on a specific procedure for admitting third-country nationals for the purposes of scientific research, OJ L 289 of 3.11.2005, 15.

6.4.4.1 *Foreign Students and Their Role in Building Academic Culture in EU Member States*

During the last few decades, the number of third-country nationals studying and interested in studying in the Member States of the European Union, as well as all over the world, has increased significantly. It is a consequence of an earlier process of the "massification" of higher education, which occurred in the 1940s.[150] As J. Bielecka-Prus emphasizes, based on the statistics of the OECD, in the years 1990–2005 the number of students who were third-country nationals doubled.[151] Further, in a publication titled *Studenci zagraniczni w Polsce* (foreign students in Poland) C. Żołędowski observes, on the basis of the International Organization for Migration (IOM)[152] data, that in the last 20 years the number of foreign students increased three times.[153] An especially high increase was experienced in 2012 by the Netherlands and Denmark (by 114% and 113%, respectively).[154]

The European Migration Network (EMN) report indicates that 190,000 third-country nationals entered the European Union in 2011.[155] In Great Britain in 2011 foreign students comprised 22% of all students.[156] For many countries of the European Union, the arrivals of foreign students are a way of alleviating the effects of demographic decline and the lack of domestic students at universities.[157] The research on the subject of international students is conducted by the OECD (in which the term

[150] S. Ruda, "Migracje edukacyjne—zasięg i znaczenie," in *Migracje edukacyjne. Studenci zagraniczni—dwie strony księżyca*, ed. Z. Kawczyńska-Butrym (Lublin, 2014), 24.

[151] J. Bielecka-Prus, "Strategie umiędzynarodowienia uniwersytetów w Polsce (Analiza zawartości stron internetowych wybranych szkół wyższych)," in *Migracje edukacyjne. Studenci zagraniczni—dwie strony księżyca*, ed. Z. Kawczyńska-Butrym (Lublin, 2014), 35. See: *Higher Education to 2030, vol. 1, Demography, OECD*, publication available on the website http://www.oecd.org/education/skills-beyond-school/highereducationto2030vol1demography.htm#2. Accessed 12.09.2017.

[152] See "Student mobility, internationalization of higher education and skilled migration," in *IOM World Migration Report 2008, Managing labour mobility in the evolving global economy*, International Organization of Migration, 105–126.

[153] C. Żołędowski, *Studenci zagraniczni w Polsce. Motywy przyjazdu, ocena pobytu, plany na przyszłość*, cooperation with M. Duszczyk, J. Godlewska, E. Jaroszewska, J. Łukaszewska, (Warszawa, 2010), 46.

[154] M. Okólski, "Nowa, krucha mapa europejskich migracji," *Studia Migracyjne—Przegląd Polonijny*, vol. 1/163 (2017): 19.

[155] *EMN Synthesis Report, Immigration of International Students to the EU*, European Migration Network Study 2012, 10.

[156] J. Bielecka-Prus, "Strategie umiędzynarodowienia uniwersytetów w Polsce," 35.

[157] *EMN Synthesis Report, Immigration of International Students to the EU*, European Migration Network Study 2012, 48.

international student means a person who is studying in a country different from the country of origin). In accordance with the report "Education at a Glance 2016," international students comprise 8% of the academic community at the level of the Union.[158]

International students in the Union also come from other continents, which strengthens cultural diversity at European universities—in accordance with the OECD data, the largest number of foreign students came from Asia (over 50%),[159] then from Europe and Africa.[160]

The Member States interested in the presence of foreign students undertake activities aimed at making the education process more attractive and facilitating the entry of third-country nationals into the European Union in order to commence studies. Among such activities, the EMN report on international students lists the development of joint study programmes, on the basis of which students take courses in two different countries and receive a double diploma (such practices can be found, e.g., in Austria, Bulgaria, the Czech Republic, Finland, France, Italy or Poland), the establishment of international campuses in third countries by European universities (Belgium, Sweden, the United Kingdom) and the creation of scientific or cultural institutes or higher education institutions in third countries (undertaken by Cyprus, Finland, France or Poland).[161] Nevertheless, such activities do not have a legal basis in EU law. Still, they are an example of a good practice strengthening participation in the academic and cultural life of universities.

Among the activities embedded in the Union's policy aimed at encouraging international students to arrive in the EU, one should mention the bilateral agreements signed with third countries (e.g., with Australia,

[158] *Education at a Glance 2016 OECD Indicator*, Published on 15 September 2016, 341, http://www.keepeek.com/Digital-Asset-Management/oecd/education/education-at-a-glance-2016_eag-2016-en#page341. Accessed 12.09.2017. See also S. Ruda, "Migracje edukacyjne—zasięg i znaczenie," 21.

[159] M. Okólski, *Nowa krucha mapa europejskich migracji*, s. 20. From the international perspective, the largest number of students came from China, Saudi Arabia and Vietnam.

[160] S. Ruda, "Migracje edukacyjne—zasięg i znaczenie," 22. Almost 12% of students came from Africa. However, as Ruda observes, Africa is experiencing brain drain: "it is estimated that since the beginning of the 1990s, 20 thousand people leave the African continent per year as part of the emigration of highly qualified workers. This loss comes at the cost amounting USD 4 billion," ibidem, p. 25. On the level of acceptance of cultural diversity, see Z. Kawczyńska-Butrym, "Inność Obcego—opis i emocje," in *Migracje edukacyjne. Studenci zagraniczni—dwie strony księżyca*, ed. Z. Kawczyńska-Butrym (Lublin, 2014), 121–138.

[161] *EMN Synthesis Report, Immigration of International Students to the EU*, 45.

Canada, India) or the programmes aimed at supporting the mobility of students (e.g., Maria Curie-Skłodowska Fellowship).[162] In the discussion on the presence of foreign students in the Union, it is also worth pointing out to the negative aspects of educational migrations, such as the overuse of student visas (in order to enter in the EU) and brain drain from the countries sending students abroad.[163]

6.4.4.2 Right of Third-Country Nationals to Participate in the Academic and Cultural Life

Through the possibility of undertaking studies at European universities and conducting research there, third-country nationals participate in scientific and academic life. The participation in university life is also connected with the possibility of active (or merely passive) participation in the academic cultural life. The condition for the full participation in university culture is the holding of student or researcher status, which will be characterized below.

The rights of third-country nationals to undertake studies at higher education institutions and to conduct scientific research are currently regulated by Directive 2016/801 on the conditions of entry and residence of third-country nationals for the purposes of research, studies, training, voluntary service, pupil exchange schemes or educational projects and au pairing.

The cultural dimension of educational migration is emphasized in recital 7 of its Preamble: "Migration for the purposes set out in this Directive should promote the generation and acquisition of knowledge and skills. It constitutes a form of mutual enrichment for the migrants concerned, their country of origin and the Member State concerned, while strengthening cultural links and enhancing cultural diversity."[164] The implementation of the directive and internationalization of education

[162] Ibidem, 15. In the report on international students in Poland the EMN points out to the possibility of following studies by third-country nationals, where apart from the regular fees, students can apply for scholarships granted by the Polish government or Polish universities (p. 20). The report also enumerates programmes of international cooperation realized by Poland. On the subject of international students in Poland, see also J. Bielecka-Prus, "Strategie umiędzynarodowienia uniwersytetów w Polsce," 35.

[163] M. Górczyńska, "Polityka Unii Europejskiej w stosunku do studentów z państw trzecich—obecny kształt i planowane kierunki zmian," in *Między wsparciem a ograniczaniem. Odpowiedzi na wyzwania migracji XXI wieku w wybranych krajach Europy*, eds. M. Fagasiński, M. Szczepanik (Warszawa, 2014), 64.

[164] See also L. Słodownik, "'Oczywistość' i 'nieoczywistość' kulturowa. Adaptacja do kultury polskiej oraz przemiany jej obrazu w doświadczeniach studentów zagranicznych," in

should also not encourage a brain drain from the sending countries, which in fact leads to the impoverishing of academic life in third countries.[165]

The provisions of Directive 2016/801 concern several groups of third-country nationals, out of which the most important ones for the purposes of the current study are students, scientists and pupils participating in educational projects.

The directive provides for the conditions of students' entry[166] into the territory of the Union.[167] They are general conditions provided for in Art. 7 of the directive and detailed conditions regarding only students under Art. 11. In accordance with the latter, the Member States may require of a student enrolled in a course of study a sufficient knowledge of the language of instruction.[168]

The interpretation of the provisions on admitting students was carried out by the CJEU on the basis of Directive 204/114, previously in force, which was replaced by Directive 2016/801.[169]

Kulturowe wymiary imigracji do Polski. Studia socjologiczne, eds. E. Nowicka, S. Łodziński (Warszawa, 2006), 24 et seq.

[165] Recital 13 Preamble to Directive 2016/801. In accordance with it "[i]mplementation of this Directive should not encourage a brain drain from emerging or developing countries. Measures to support researchers' reintegration into their countries of origin should be taken in partnership with the countries of origin with a view to establishing a comprehensive migration policy."

[166] In accordance with the directive, "'student' means a third-country national who has been accepted by a higher education institution and is admitted to the territory of a Member State to pursue as a main activity a full-time course of study leading to a higher education qualification recognised by that Member State, including diplomas, certificates or doctoral degrees in a higher education institution, which may cover a preparatory course prior to such education, in accordance with national law, or compulsory training." Art. 3(3) Directive 2016/801.

[167] Previously, those issues were regulated by the Council Directive 2004/114.

[168] Art. 11(1)(c) Directive 2016/801.

[169] See, for example, Judgement of the Court of Justice of 21.06.2012 in the case Leopold Sommer v. Landesgeschäftsstelle des Arbeitsmarktservice Wien, C 15/11, ECLI:EU:C:2012:371. The Court also interpreted the provisions regarding the rights of students—nationals of the EU in the cases such as Elodie Giersch, Benjamin Marco Stemper, Julien Taminiaux, Xavier Renaud Hodin, Joëlle Hodin przeciwko État du Grand-duché de Luxembourg, Judgement of the Court of Justice of 20.06.2013, C 20/12, ECLI:EU:C:2013:411; Judgement of the Court of Justice of 2.06.2016 in the case the European Commission v. the Kingdom of the Netherlands, C 233/14, ECLI:EU:C:2016:396; Judgement of the Court of Justice of 15.12.2016 in the case Noémie Depesme and others v. Ministre de l'Enseignement supérieur et de la recherche, joint cases C 401–403/15, ECLI:EU:C:2016:955; Judgement of the Court of Justice of 14.12.2016 in the case Maria do Céu Bragança Linares Verruga and others v. Ministre de

The Court interpreted Art. 6 and 7 Directive 2004/114 on the conditions of admitting third-country nationals in order to pursue studies in the case of Mohamed Ali Ben Alaya.[170] The proceedings before the national court concerned a national of Tunisia who was born in Germany but in 1995 left for Tunisia and continued his education there. In 2010 he began studies at a university in Tunis but he also applied for admission to a German university in Dortmund. His efforts ended with success. However, the German migration authorities refused to grant Mr Alaya a student visa "particularly in the light of the inadequacy of the grades previously obtained, his weak knowledge of German and the fact that there was no connection between his proposed course of study and his intended career,"[171] which, according to the authorities, testified to his lack of motivation to learn. The third-country national brought a complaint against that decision and the national court confirmed that Mr Alaya met all the conditions for being admitted as listed in the Student Directive. However, the national court had doubts with regard to the possibility of applying the discretionary measures by migration authorities in the case of issuing a decision on a student visa and referred a question for a preliminary ruling to the CJEU in order to determine whether Directive 2004/114 constitutes the grounds to make a claim for issuing a student visa in the case of meeting all the provisions for admittance under its Art. 6 and 7 and where there are no grounds for refusing to admit the student.[172]

In answering the above question, the Court emphasized that "[t]o allow a Member State to introduce, in relation to the admission of third-country nationals for study purposes, conditions additional to those laid down in Articles 6 and 7 of Directive 2004/114 would be contrary to the objective pursued by that directive of promoting the mobility of such

l'Enseignement supérieur et de la recherche, C 238/15, ECLI:EU:C:2016:949; Judgement of the Court of Justice of 18.11.2008 in the case Jacqueline Förster v. Hoofddirectie van de Informatie Beheer Groep, C 158/07, ECLI:EU:C:2008:630.

[170] Judgement of the Court of Justice of 10.09.2014 in the case Mohamed Ali Ben Alaya v. Bundesrepublik Deutschland, C 491/13, ECLI:EU:C:2014:2187, further as judgement in the case C 491/13.

[171] Para. 16 of the judgement in the case C 491/13.

[172] Para. 20 of the judgement in the case C 491/13. The Court decided to reformulate the question and in accordance with para. 21 of the judgement examine "whether Article 12 of Directive 2004/114 must be interpreted as meaning that the Member State concerned is obliged to admit to its territory a third-country national who wishes to stay more than three months in that territory for study purposes, where that person meets the conditions for admission laid down in Articles 6 and 7 of the directive."

nationals"[173] and because of that the Member States do not have the right to discretionary assessment; neither can they examine additional circumstances with regard to admission, such as the above-mentioned motivation for undertaking studies. In the judgement the Court held that the Member States have an obligation to admit a student into their territory if he or she meets the conditions provided for by the directive and there are no grounds for refusing to grant his or her the residence document.

The interpretation of the conditions for admitting students was also the concern of the judgement in the case of Sahar Fahimian.[174] The applicant in the home proceedings was a national of Iran, with a diploma in IT, who wanted to start postgraduate doctoral studies at the University of Darmstadt as part of the research programme carried out by the university. She annexed to her visa application all the required documents, including the description of the research project, which entailed "security of mobile systems, esp. intrusion detection on smartphones to security protocols."[175] Ms Fahimian was to conduct research in the area of designing security protocols for smartphones.

The application for issuing a visa was rejected two times, while the migration authorities as the grounds for refusal indicated the reasons of public security. The refusal decision pointed out to fears that the knowledge Ms Fahimian would gain during her doctoral studies might be used in her country of origin "for purposes of internal repression in Iran, or in connection with human rights violations more generally. The technologies that are the subject of Ms Fahimian's research project could be used by the Iranian authorities for surveillance of the population."[176]

The third-country national decided to complain against the refusal decision to the national court, which in turn decided to refer a question for a preliminary ruling to the CJEU asking for an interpretation of Art. 6 Directive 2004/114 within the scope of the existence of a wide

[173] Para. 30 of the judgement in the case C 491/13.

[174] Judgement of the Court of Justice of 4.04.2017 in the case Sahar Fahimian v. Bundesrepublik Deutschland, C 544/15, ECLI:EU:C:2017:255, further as the judgement in the case C 544/15.

[175] Para. 19 of the judgement in the case C 544/15.

[176] Para. 26 of the judgement in the case C 544/15. Moreover, the national authorities claimed that the applicant might still stay in touch with the persons at the university where she had previously studied (Sharif University of Technology, SUT), whereas the involvement of that institution in research for military purposes in Iran had been confirmed, amongst others, by the placing of the SUT on the list of entities subject to restrictive measures set out in Annex IX to Regulation no. 267/2012 (see: para. 24 of the judgement in the case C 544/15).

discretionary right for the Member States with regard to determining whether a third-country national poses a threat to the security of the state. Moreover, the national court asked the CJEU to examine whether the national authorities have the competence to refuse the granting of a visa in circumstances such as those in the case of Ms Fahimian.

In answering the question for a preliminary ruling, the Court referred to the ruling in the case of Sommer,[177] emphasizing that "the directive is intended to promote the mobility of students who are third country nationals to the European Union for the purpose of education, that mobility being intended to promote Europe as a world centre of excellence for studies and vocational training."[178] The Court also held that there exists a possibility of refusing to admit a student by a Member State in a situation when national authorities decide that the third-country national concerned poses a threat, even potentially, for public safety. What is more, national authorities should take into account the third-country national's individual behaviour as well as other circumstances, including those connected with his or her professional career.[179] The assessment of the threat, which can be created by a third-country national, also requires an examination of the situation in his or her country of origin, an assessment of the documents filed by the applicant and a prognosis of the foreign national's behaviour. Thus, the national authorities, in view of the Court, have at their disposal a wide scope of administrative discretion. The Court also held that the provisions of the Student Directive do not impede the issuing of a visa to a third-country national who holds a degree from a university subject to restrictive measures of the Union if he or she plans to conduct research in an area that is sensitive for public security of the receiving country and there exists a risk that the person concerned will use the acquired knowledge for purposes contrary to public security.[180]

As it transpires from the cited rulings, the right to pursue education at the university level is protected by EU law and the Court of Justice in as much as the person concerned does not violate the commonly accepted norms of functioning in European society.

In the scope of admitting scientists, Directive 2016/801 also includes detailed provisions in Art. 8. Moreover, in accordance with Art. 22 of the

[177] Judgement of the Court of Justice of 21.06.2012 in the case Leopold Sommer v. Landesgeschäftsstelle des Arbeitsmarktservice Wien, C 15/11, ECLI:EU:C:2012:371.

[178] Para. 35 of the judgement in the case C 544/15.

[179] Para. 40 of the judgement in the case C 544/15.

[180] See the sentence of the judgement in the case C 544/15.

directive, academics have the right to equal treatment with nationals of the receiving country, subject to the rules provided for under Art. 12 Directive 2011/98. The right to equal treatment thus covers the areas of social life listed in Art. 12 such as the conditions of work, freedom of association in workers' organizations, access to education and vocational trainings, recognition of qualifications and access to goods and services. In a similar way as in the case of other foreign nationals, the principle of equal treatment facilitates and broadens the possibilities of exercising the rights of a cultural character. Moreover, in accordance with Art. 23 Directive 2016/801, apart from research activities, scientists have the right to teach classes within the scope provided for by national law.

Directive 2016/801 also determines the rules of participation of students in exchanges and educational programmes. In accordance with Art. 3(12), "'educational project' means a set of educational actions developed by a Member State's education establishment in cooperation with similar establishments in a third country, with the purpose of sharing cultures and knowledge." Detailed conditions for admitting third-country nationals for participation in such types of programmes are provided for under Art. 12 Directive 2016/801. Activities such as participation in educational programmes with all certainty influence the strengthening of intercultural competences of the participants.

6.5 Financial Instruments Facilitating the Exercise of Integrative Cultural Rights

A special type of activities which has been provided in EU secondary law are the *stricte* integration activities. In the first phase they were realized within the programmes of the European Fund for the Integration (EFI) of third-country nationals, whereas at present within the Asylum, Migration and Integration Fund (AMIF).

The European Fund for the Integration of third-country nationals was established by the Council Decision of 25 June 2007 establishing the European Fund for the Integration of third-country nationals for the period 2007–2013 as part of the General Programme Solidarity and Management of Migration Flows.[181]

[181] Council Decision of 25 June 2007 establishing the European Fund for the Integration of third-country nationals for the period 2007 to 2013 as part of the General Programme

In the Preamble to Decision 2007/435, it is emphasized that integration of third-country nationals is a condition of economic and social coherence, whereas integration activities should be directed primarily towards the newly arrived migrants (which is emphasized in Art. 2 of the Decision).[182] The Decision in its Preamble also refers to the already discussed "Common Basic Principles for immigrant integration policy in the European Union" of 2004. Moreover, in accordance with recital 28 of the Preamble to the Decision, the promotion of the integration of third-country nationals cannot be achieved merely at the level of the Member States, but requires activities at the level of the Union, which will facilitate better results. Hence, it is possible to adopt common measures in accordance with the principle of subsidiarity as set out in Art. 5 of the Treaty on European Union.[183]

Art. 3 of Decision 2007/435, determining the purpose of the Fund, stated that integration is a dynamic and two-way process, which encompasses the nationals of the Member States and third-country nationals coming from "different economic, social, cultural, religious, linguistic and ethnic backgrounds" and entails mutual adjustment. The Fund had three specific objectives, laid down in Art. 3 of the Decision, whereas the eligible actions to be pursued within each of the objectives were characterized in the subsequent Articles, especially in Art. 4. Without analysing the specificity of the structure of the objectives of the Fund, which is not important for the issue under discussion, it should be pointed out that the eligible actions included, amongst others, the organization of information campaigns and the application of integration measures prior to arrival in the host country, such as "vocational training, information packages, comprehensive civic orientation courses and language tuition in the country of origin."[184] Such integration measures constitute the above-mentioned integrative cultural obligation, facilitating a more coherent and faster cultural integration. The natural consequence of the possibility of financing pre-integration measures by the AMIF was the fact that the Member States could realize

Solidarity and Management of Migration Flows (2007/435/EC), OJ L 168, 28.06.2007, 19, further as Decision 2007/435.

[182] Para. 3, Preamble to Decision 2007/435.

[183] The eligibility conditions of such actions were laid down in Art. 5 Decision 2007/435.

[184] Art. 4(1)(b,c) Decision 2007/435. Such activities could be realized as part of the objective: "facilitation of the development and implementation of admission procedures relevant to and supportive of the integration process of third-country nationals" (Art. 3[a] Decision 2007/435).

integration programmes to enable third-country nationals to acquire basic knowledge about "the host society's language, history, institutions, socio economic features, cultural life and the fundamental norms and values."[185] Moreover, within the activities encompassing the realization of integration measures, it was possible to address an individual offer to vulnerable groups (the elderly, women, children)[186] and young third-country nationals, who experience problems in determining their cultural identity.[187]

Among the eligible actions within the subsequent objectives of the Fund,[188] which have an impact on the realization of the integration rights of a cultural character, one should mention activities for increasing intercultural competences of the personnel providing intermediary services to third-country nationals,[189] actions for the strengthening of third-country nationals' linguistic rights (by improving access to interpretation and oral and written translation services)[190] as well as the implementation of instruments for managing multiculturality in social life.[191] A desirable action within the activities provided for by the Fund was also to be the promotion of a "durable and sustainable participation in civil and cultural life" of third-country nationals[192] and the creation of platforms for intercultural

[185] Art. 4(2)(a) Decision 2007/435.

[186] Art. 4(2)(c) Decision 2007/435. The Member States also had a possibility of introducing changes within the existing programmes in order to concentrate on increasing the civil awareness of third-country nationals. Another activity for improving the realization of integration measures could be the creation of modules facilitating their realization via the Internet so as to reconcile integration with educational or professional obligations (Art. 4[2][d]). Activities realized within the objective under Art. 3(b): "development and implementation of the integration process of newly-arrived third-country nationals in Member States."

[187] Art. 4(2)(e) Decision 2007/435. Activities realized within the objective under Art. 3(b): "The Fund shall contribute to ... development and implementation of the integration process of newly-arrived third-country nationals in Member States."

[188] Objective under Art. 3(c) Decision 2007/435: "The Fund shall contribute to ... increasing of the capacity of Member States to develop, implement, monitor and evaluate policies and measures for the integration of third-country nationals." Objective under Art. 3(d): "The Fund shall contribute to ... exchange of information, best practices and cooperation in and between Member States in developing, implementing, monitoring and evaluating policies and measures for the integration of third-country nationals."

[189] Art. 4(3)(a) Decision 2007/435. Including also "The Fund shall support actions in the Member States which ... develop and implement intercultural training, capacity building and diversity management, training of staff within public and private service providers, including educational institutions" (Art. 4[3][c]).

[190] Art. 4(3)(a) Decision 2007/435.

[191] Art. 4(3)(b,c) Decision 2007/435.

[192] Art. 4(3)(b) Decision 2007/435.

dialogue between religions, societies, third-country nationals and migration authorities.[193] An eligible action was also an activity for increasing acceptance for migrants within the receiving society and the organization of awareness-raising campaigns in the media.[194]

The expenses for the actions realized within the EFI were eligible until June 2015. Among the Polish examples of the realization of the projects strengthening integration of third-country nationals, including cultural integration, one should mention projects such as "Prawie jak u siebie" [Almost like at home], entailing language and cultural support for third-country nationals,[195] "Porozmawiajmy po polsku" [Let's speak Polish], which included an intercultural dialogue and classes in schools for foreigners (including Polish lessons) and lessons for Polish children on immigrant cultures.[196] The experiences gathered during the realization of the projects were collected in the work *Praktyki integracji. Doświadczenia i perspektywy* [Integration practices. Experiences and perspectives] as part of one of the projects realized within the Fund.[197]

After the end of the activities within the SOLID Programme, the Asylum, Migration and Integration Fund (AMIF)[198] was established by Regulation 516/2014. The AMIF, contrary to previous funds, encompasses

[193] Art. 4(3)(g) Decision 2007/435.

[194] Art. 4(3)(j) Decision 2007/435.

[195] Project "Prawie jak u siebie. Skuteczne wsparcie integracji poprzez działania edukacyjne," 1/1/EFI, realized by Stowarzyszenie Społeczno-Ekonomiczne ABSOLWENT in the years 2009–2011.

[196] Project "Porozmawiajmy po polsku," 40/8/EFI, realized by Stowarzyszenie Vox Humana. More on the subject of the projects realized within the Fund: General programme. Solidarity and Management in Migration Flows, SOLID 2007–2013, Centrum Obsługi Projektów Europejskich Ministerstwa Spraw Wewnętrznych, Warszawa 2015, 13–53. The full ranking list of the projects qualified for financing is available on the website: http://copemswia.gov.pl/fundusze-2007–2013/efi/wyniki%2D%2Dnaboru-wnioskow-efi/. Accessed 12.09.2017.

[197] See M. Bieniecki, M. Pawlak, "Praktyki integracji. Raport z analizy materiałów zastanych oraz wywiadów z realizatorami projektów EFI," in *Praktyki integracji. Doświadczenia i perspektywy*, eds. M. Bieniecki, M. Pawlak (Warszawa, 2012), 9–74. See also P. Babis, "Wpływ Unii Europejskiej na budowę polskiej polityki integracyjnej," in *Praktyki integracji. Doświadczenia i perspektywy*, eds. M. Bieniecki, M. Pawlak (Warszawa 2012), 126 et seq.

[198] Regulation (EU) no. 516/2014 of the European Parliament and of the Council of 16 April 2014 establishing the Asylum, Migration and Integration Fund, amending Council Decision 2008/381/EC and repealing Decisions No. 573/2007/EC and No. 575/2007/EC of the European Parliament and of the Council and Council Decision 2007/435/EC, OJ L 150, 20.5.2014, 168, further as Regulation 516/2014.

all actions for the purpose of the integration of third-country nationals—not only migrants of a regular status but also persons seeking international protection.[199] The detailed objective of the Fund, which concerns integration activities, is laid down in Art. 3(2)(b) of the regulation and entails support for legal migration in accordance with the needs of the Member States and promotion of the effective integration of migrants.

Chapter 3 of the regulation in a comprehensive way regulates the eligible integration actions with regard to third-country nationals which are acceptable within the Fund. Thus, the first of such measures is the organization of pre-integration activities such as information packages and campaigns promoting intercultural dialogue (including solutions via information technology)[200] and the running of language courses and courses increasing civil awareness of immigrants.[201] The Fund also provides for the possibility of supporting activities encompassing integration measures, such as the creation and development of integration strategies,[202] "actions introducing third-country nationals to the receiving society and actions enabling them to adapt to it, to inform them about their rights and obligations, to participate in civil and cultural life and to share the values enshrined in the Charter of Fundamental Rights of the European Union,"[203] and the organization of language courses.[204]

Other types of possible actions that can be financed within the integration funds also include the support for dialogue between third-country nationals and the receiving society, the facilitation of meaningful contacts between migrants and the local community and the strengthening of acceptance for migrants within the receiving society.[205] What is more, the Fund aims to support activities increasing equal access of third-country nationals

[199] The Fund joined all the previous actions conducted within the European Integration Fund, European Return Fund and European Refugee Fund. Hence, in accordance with Art. 3: "The general objective of the Fund shall be to contribute to the efficient management of migration flows and to the implementation, strengthening and development of the common policy on asylum, subsidiary protection and temporary protection and the common immigration policy, while fully respecting the rights and principles enshrined in the Charter of Fundamental Rights of the European Union."

[200] Art. 8(a) Regulation 516/2014.

[201] Art. 8(d) Regulation 516/2014.

[202] Art. 9(1)(a) Regulation 516/2014.

[203] Art. 9(1)(c) Regulation 516/2014.

[204] Art. 9(1)(d) Regulation 516/2014.

[205] Art. 9(1)(f) Regulation 516/2014.

to the services from the public and private sectors.[206] Such practice contributes to increased participation in broadly understood cultural life.

In a similar way as in the case of EFI, the AMIF also provides for the possibility of financing actions aimed at the strengthening of organizational structures for the management of diversity and integration and for the creation of platforms for intercultural and religious dialogue.[207]

The value of actions within the AMIF cannot be overestimated. The Fund provides coherent organization of integration activities, which have a real impact on the level of cultural integration of migrants in the Member States. What is more, such actions are carried out by local organizations, which are well-versed in integration problems. A wide array of supported activities facilitate the realization of integration activities with regard to the receiving society and third-country nationals. The regulations cited above seem to confirm the thesis that by the implementation of financial instruments, EU law strengthens the possibility of exercising the integration rights of a cultural character, which are essentially third-generation rights, as in accordance with the stance of Donders cited above, they are the rights of entities as collective subjects—the receiving society and the migration community. What is more, the interest of those groups, that is, the effective social integration, also within the cultural dimension, is also collective.

While characterizing the instruments facilitating the realization of the integrative cultural rights, one should also mention the project "Ariadne" realized between the years 2011 and 2012 within the Lifelong Learning Programme of the European Commission.[208] The aim of the project was to assess the role played by art and artistic activities in the process of the adaptation of migrants. One of the results of the project was the publication of a textbook titled *Art of Adaptation: Manual of Artistic Tools for Migrants*.[209]

[206] Art. 9(1)(g) Regulation 516/2014.

[207] Art. 10(e,f) Regulation 516/2014.

[208] The website of the project "Ariadne": http://www.ariadne4art.eu/page/ariadne-project/. Accessed 12.09.2017.

[209] Art of adaptation. Manual of artistic tools for migrants, red. V. Szabo, Ariadne Consortium 2012, publication available on the website https://issuu.com/artemisz/docs/ariadne_emanual_english. Accessed 12.09.2017. Other projects concerning cultural integration of migrants are realized, amongst others, within Creative Europe (actions directed at refugees). See *At a glance, Integration of refugees and migrants: Participation in cultural activities*, European Parliament, February 2017.

6.6 Conclusions

While summarizing the discussion presented in this chapter attention should be paid to the real dimension of the functioning of integrative cultural rights in EU migration policy.

Integration is a key process for ensuring coherent and harmonious social life in the countries which experience migration influxes. Effective integration encompasses all dimensions of social life including cultural life. It also has an impact on the possibility of realizing cultural rights understood in a classical way as the right of access to cultural goods and the right to participate in cultural life by third-country nationals. Further, third-country nationals' contribution to cultural life as a result of appropriately pursued integration is also valuable for the enrichment of the local cultural life and the strengthening of intercultural dialogue through active and perceivable presence of minority groups. It allows the members of the community to define their cultural identity—also the members of the dominant culture. Thus, the process of integration results in third-country nationals having the possibility of exercising cultural rights of both active and passive character.

However, it is not only the effects of the integration that are important but also the very process of integration. In accordance with the proposed thesis, EU law guarantees the right to cultural integration, which consists of the guarantees of particular integration rights, as discussed in the present chapter. They include, amongst others, the rights of a cultural character expressed in the Common Basic Principles and implemented in secondary law, the rights of an educational character, the rights to conduct research, the rights of access to cultural goods, the rights resulting from the application of integration measures allowing for acquiring the knowledge about culture, language and tradition of the receiving country or the rights conditioned by the actions carried out within the AMIF programmes, such as participation in intercultural dialogue or participation in civil life, including cultural life.[210]

The right to cultural integration has, on the one hand, an individual character, as it concerns a specific third-country national and the shaping of one's cultural identity. On the other hand, it is also of a collective

[210] As J. Mucha observes, migration always has an impact on the cultural situation of both the countries of origin and the receiving countries and it increases cultural diversity. See J. Mucha, "Migration and the transmission of cultural patterns. Introduction," in *Migration and the transmission of cultural patterns*, ed. J. Mucha (Kraków 2016), 5–6.

character as the interest within this right is, in fact, collective (social and cultural integration), whereas the rights of individuals are in fact the rights of entities as collective subjects—the migrant minority group and the receiving society.

It should also be explicitly underscored that integration entails not only rights but also integrative cultural obligations, such as that of acquiring knowledge about the culture of the receiving country, the acceptance of values the EU is based on and the learning of the language. The above constitute the boundary of exercising cultural rights by immigrants. Integration obligations also concern the receiving society and entail respect for other cultural traditions and prohibition of activities of a discriminatory and xenophobic character with regard to representatives of other cultures.

Apart from a broad outline and analysis of integrative rights of a cultural character, the present chapter includes an analysis of the specific legal acts determining the legal status of particular groups of immigrants. The analysis was carried out from the perspective of isolating specific entitlements of a cultural character or the instruments facilitating the exercise of classically understood cultural rights. The realization of such rights is also influenced by the political and strategic documents analysed above (described as "'soft' policy measures"[211]).

In the light of the lack of broader regulations guaranteeing the rights of a cultural character to immigrants arriving in the Member States, the principle of equal treatment acquires special importance. The principle of equal treatment finds its expression in the directive on long-term residents, as well as directive on the Blue Card, single permit or seasonal workers.

Moreover, an important entitlement is the right to participate in university scientific and cultural life—as reconstructed on the grounds of the provisions of the directive on students and academics and the rights they are entitled to and which result from the educational process or the specificity of academic work. The significance of financial instruments established for the actual implementation of integration policy within the scope of activities aimed at acculturation should also be appreciated.

On the basis of the above analysis, the boundaries of exercising the rights of a cultural character can also be delineated. The boundaries result primarily from the integrative cultural obligations, that is, the obligation to learn about and respect the culture of the receiving country. Migrants

[211] B. Mikołajczyk, "Integracja obywateli państw trzecich w Unii Europejskiej," 171.

are allowed to cultivate their cultural traditions in as much as they do not interfere with the common cultural norms existing in the host country. The boundary for exercising the rights of a cultural character is also provided by the principle of *living together*, analysed in the previous chapters. It entails the limiting of one's individual rights as an element of protection of the rights and freedoms of others, thus facilitating harmonious social coexistence within the framework of civil society. The boundaries of exercising cultural rights by immigrants are also determined by the obligation to meet the conditions of entry, connected with the obtaining of a specific migration status—for example, student status. Finally, the boundary for the realization of cultural rights is determined by the circumstances justifying the expulsion of a third-country national from the host country, that is, by the protection of public order and public security.

CHAPTER 7

Conclusion

On the basis of the analysis conducted in the current study, it transpires that there exists a catalogue of cultural rights of third-country nationals in the legal system of the European Union. The rights of a cultural character are protected to a sufficient level, while at the same time it is possible to define their limits on the grounds of the existing legal provisions.

The catalogue of the cultural rights of third-country nationals in the legal system of the European Union has been construed on the grounds of the existing norms of primary law, secondary law as well as the case-law of the Court of Justice of the European Union (CJEU) and the jurisprudential standards of the European Court of Human Rights (ECtHR) in the cases relating to foreign nationals or persons belonging to non-European cultural circles.[1] The cultural rights of third-country nationals include specific rights and entitlements guaranteed in numerous legal acts; thus, the catalogue consists of a multifarious collection of rights and remains of an open character.

[1] The fact which is especially important for the adopted catalogue of cultural rights of third-country nationals is that in the doctrine of fundamental rights of the European Union it is accepted that the Union is to protect the fundamental rights at the level no less than the one laid down by the ECtHR. Thus, the Convention and the convention *acquis*, consisting of the Strasbourg case-law, set a minimum level of a person's protection, in this respect in the area of the rights of a cultural character.

A. M. Kosińska, *Cultural Rights of Third-Country Nationals in EU Law*,
https://doi.org/10.1007/978-3-030-30154-5_7

7.1 The Scope of the Guaranteed Protection and the Structure of the Catalogue of the Cultural Rights of Third-Country Nationals

The structure of the prepared catalogue encompasses the cultural rights resulting from the norms of European Union (EU) primary law and laws of a cultural character resulting from the norms of secondary law. The fundamental cultural rights are guaranteed in the provisions of primary law (Charter of Fundamental Rights) and are essentially a type of metalaws in their character. Specific laws with regard to selected areas of migration processes are guaranteed in the acts of secondary law and concern specific groups of foreign nationals.

In the Charter of Fundamental Rights (CFR) there are guarantees of cultural diversity (Art. 22 CFR—on the basis of its provisions, third-country nationals have an individual right to respect for diversity of a passive character—they have the right to integrate with divergent cultures of the Union's regions), the right to freedom of art and sciences (Art. 13 CFR), the right to education (Art. 14 CFR), the right to respect for family life (Art. 7 CFR—this article also entails the language rights and the right to define one's identity and the right to cultivate one's customs and traditions), the right to found a family (Art. 9 CFR—interpreted also as the right to marry in accordance with the accepted cultural customs) and the right to religious freedom (Art. 10 CFR—the guarantee of religious freedom means for many foreign nationals also the guarantee to cultural identity). The grounds for protection of the cultural rights of third-country nationals can also be found in the principle of non-discrimination, as expressed in Art. 21 CFR.

One of the cultural rights of third-country nationals defined on the grounds of the standards of protection of fundamental rights, with regard to the protection against expulsion (non-refoulement) and qualification for international protection, is also the right to protection against the culture of the country of origin.

EU secondary law has been analysed in accordance with the division into thematic areas of the Area of Freedom, Security and Justice with reference to different types of migration processes.

In the area of the law regulating entry into the territory of the Union, the rights of a cultural character are guaranteed in the Schengen Borders Code (Regulation 2016/399) by ensuring respect for dignity and prohibition of discrimination in the procedure of border control—which also covers (to the extent it is not conflicting with the protection of security and public order) the right to protection of cultural identity. Moreover, the rights of a cultural character are guaranteed by the Community Code on Visas (Regulation 810/2009), which facilitates entry into the EU for the cultural and scientific purposes and provides respect for the dignity (and thus cultural identity) of a foreign national in the process of applying for a visa. A special right, also of a cultural character, is the right to family reunification (Directive 2003/86), which facilitates the creation of a socio-cultural stability and in this way assists integration. The policy of family reunification is also connected with integrative cultural responsibilities.

The rights of a cultural character are also guaranteed in such a special area of law as the so-called return law. Cultural rights are guaranteed in secondary law (Directive 2008/115) in the area of granting a period for voluntary departure (which might take into account the educational needs of the persons in the return procedure and thus facilitate the exercise of the right to education). Also the exit check or even (resorted to, as a rule, in exceptional situations) forced removal should be executed in full respect for the dignity of a foreign national, which also entails respect for their cultural identity, within the constraints dictated by security procedures. Special cultural rights are guaranteed to foreign nationals in the process of detention—respect for cultural rights in the detention procedure entails, amongst others, respect for cultural traditions and the creation of conditions for the exercise of cultural needs in free time. Specific norms in this area are regulated by national law, implementing Directive 2008/115. The use of alternatives to detention of foreign nationals also has an impact on the possibility of exercising by them their cultural rights, such as the right to participate in cultural life. From the guaranteed rights in the return law, it is also worth mentioning the assisted voluntary return, which allows for support of cultural reintegration of third-country nationals in the country of origin.

As part of the Common European Asylum System, we might distinguish several sub-areas within which the rights of a cultural character are guaranteed.

In the process of qualifying foreign nationals for international protection (Directive 2011/95), one of the provisions for granting protection is a well-founded fear of being persecuted, which might occur on cultural grounds and thus provide a circumstance to exercise the right for protection against the culture of the country of origin.

Within the framework of granting international protection (Directive 2013/32) there is a guarantee of respect for cultural differences by assuring the presence of, if need be, experts on cultural communication, as well as qualifying the personnel who receive applications so that they are sensitive to the issues of cultural differences in communication and thus could reliably receive evidence from the persons seeking protection. The protection of cultural rights of foreign nationals is also influenced by the concept of the safe country of origin (and a safe third country), according to which persons coming from such a country (or persons returned to a safe third country) are not exposed to any risk of persecution (including those on cultural grounds) and thus can fully exercise their cultural identity both *in forum internum* and *in forum externum*.

In the process of reception of foreign nationals (Directive 2013/33) who apply for international protection within the territory of the European Union, the educational rights are guaranteed and the reception centres generally facilitate access to cultural life through a range of activities of a cultural character. Additionally, an interesting practice of some of the Member States in the procedure of reception involves such placement of foreign nationals in the accommodation centres so that they are provided with the best options for integration and cultural adjustment of the region to the cultural profile of the foreign national.

Third-country nationals—beneficiaries of international protection are also entitled to educational rights—with regard to the granted international protection minors are guaranteed access to education; foreign nationals are also guaranteed the principle of equal treatment in the procedure for recognition of qualifications. Beneficiaries of international protection also enjoy the right to participate in integration programmes, facilitating cultural integration with the receiving society and inclusion in social and cultural life. Persons who were granted international protection, due to the regular character of their stay in the Member State, are also entitled to freely benefit from having access to cultural goods and to participate in the local cultural life.

The last one of the analysed areas of migration law includes the area regulating the stay of foreign nationals with a regular status. With regard to third-country nationals whose stay in the territory of the European Union has a documented character, it is a priority to conduct a successful integration process. During the course of research it has been demonstrated that within the legal system of the European Union there exists the right to cultural integration, which results from specific regulations of EU secondary law and facilitates the exercise of particular "integrative cultural rights" by an individual. In its character, this right also belongs to the third-generation collective rights. In the very process of integration, in order to make it effective, the following freedoms and rights should be guaranteed: the freedom of expression, religious freedom, the right to education, the right of association, the right to participate in civil and cultural life and the right to cultural identity.[2] Those rights should be exercised by migrants in accordance with the *living together* principle. In the process of the shaping of the right to cultural integration, the adopted political documents were important, especially the long-running programmes of the European Council, as well as the so-called *Common Basic Principles* (the Common Basic Principles for Immigrant Integration Policy in the EU).[3]

The cultural rights of third-country nationals with a regulated status might be divided into several groups. They include the rights of long-term residents (guaranteed in Directive 2003/109, e.g., the right to equal treatment in having access to education, including scientific scholarships) and their duties of an integrative character. The guaranteed right of equal treatment also entails equal access to services—including the services of the creative sector and the possibility of free movement within the territory of the host country, which in turn facilitates free access to cultural goods. Some partial cultural entitlements, such as the prohibition of discrimination or the right to remain in the Member State, are guaranteed by the so-called Citizenship Directive (2004/38). The right to equal treatment is also guaranteed in the Blue Card Directive (Directive 2009/50), as well as in the Single Permit Directive (Directive 2011/98).

Special cultural rights include the rights of students and scientists, which might be generally described as the right to participate in the scientific and cultural university life (regulated under the new Directive 2016/801). The directive also describes the rights of students to participate in educational projects, which facilitate cultural exchange between Member States and third countries.

[2] Human rights in culturally diverse societies. Guidelines adopted by the Committee of Ministers and Compilation of Council of Europe standards, Council of Europe 2016, 12. The publication is available at https://rm.coe.int/16806665fd. Accessed 12.09.2017.

[3] Council of the European Union, Conclusions, press release, 2618th Council Meeting Justice and Home Affairs, Brussels, November 19, 2004.

7.2 The Basic Features of the Catalogue

On the basis of the legal analysis conducted in the study it should be observed that the catalogue of cultural rights is of a dynamic character, in a similar way as in the case of the construct of fundamental rights as the general principles of Community law.[4] It is also justifiable to claim that *per analogiam* those laws are shaped in the process of implementing the law. Another argument confirming the above thesis is also the adopted concept of recognizing the Charter of Fundamental Rights as the so-called evolving instrument (*work in progress*)—thus the interpretation of fundamental rights of a cultural nature of third-country nationals, which transpire from the Charter, is shaped by the case-law of European courts—mostly by the CJEU.[5]

The structure of the catalogue and the guarantees of cultural rights of third-country nationals in the legal system of the European Union are also influenced by the changing structure and character of cultural rights in the globalized world, which is confirmed in the study by the conducted research analysis. Since the adoption of the International Covenant on Economic, Social and Cultural Rights (ICESCR), cultural rights in their structure have been dynamically evolving in order to address civilizational challenges with respect to the guarantees of those rights. At present, cultural rights entail not only the right to participate in cultural life, the right to have access to cultural goods, or the right to free artistic expression, but also the rights of minorities (defined as fourth-generation rights—e.g., the language rights, serving the purpose of preserving cultural identity), as well as third-generation rights, that is, solidarity rights (e.g., the right to have access to the world cultural heritage).

For the purpose of academic accuracy, it should be clearly emphasized that the whole body of the guarantees of the cultural rights of third-country nationals also includes the constitutional regulations of the national law, which guarantee the general principles of participation in cultural life, access to cultural goods, artistic freedom and the rights of minorities, together with guarantees at the international level. The latter include both

[4] E. Morawska, "Konstrukcja normatywna praw podstawowych Unii Europejskiej w Karcie praw podstawowych Unii Europejskiej," in: *Prawa podstawowe w prawie i praktyce Unii Europejskiej*, eds. C. Mik, K. Gałka (Toruń, 2009), 44.

[5] H. Izdebski, "Rola i miejsce Karty Praw Podstawowych w Unii Europejskiej w europejskiej filozofii praw człowieka," in: *5 lat Karty Praw Podstawowych UE*, ed. A. Gubrynowicz (Warszawa, 2006), 19.

international agreements adopted within the framework of international organizations (United Nations—including the United Nations Educational, Scientific and Cultural Organization [UNESCO] conventions, the Council of Europe or the Organization for Security and Co-operation in Europe [OSCE]), and, for instance, bilateral agreements on cultural cooperation with migrants' countries of origin. Finally, some of those guarantees of cultural rights are part of the legal system of the Union law. Even though they do not constitute the core of the guarantees of cultural rights due to the fact that cultural policies are largely left to the competence of Member States (Art. 167 of the Treaty on the Functioning of the European Union [TFEU] states that in the sphere of culture the Union has the competence for encouraging cooperation, support, and supplementing actions), yet, for the special group such as the immigrants to the Member States of the Union, the guarantees of cultural rights in the EU system are of key importance and determine to a large degree the quality of their stay in the host country, the extent to which they are allowed to exercise their right to cultural identity and the process of integration.

Another issue with regard to the functioning of the catalogue of cultural rights of third-country nationals concerns the recognition of the correctness of the assumption that foreign nationals with a regulated stay generally have the right to exercise their cultural rights guaranteed by the laws and policies of the Union, as analysed above in the current study. Their aim, in accordance with Art. 167 TFEU, is to popularize European culture and to preserve and protect the cultural heritage of a European character. Practical activities undertaken within programmes of the European Commission, such as *Creative Europe*, or other initiatives undertaken by the Education, Audiovisual and Culture Executive Agency (EACEA), allow for becoming familiar with the divergent European culture and increase the cultural offer in various Member States.

7.3 The Limits of Exercising Cultural Rights by Third-Country Nationals

The conducted analysis has demonstrated that it is possible to define limits of exercising cultural rights by third-country nationals. The general provision of the law in this area is Art. 52 of the Charter of Fundamental Rights, which provides a limitation clause, which is applicable to the rights guaranteed in the Charter, also those discussed in the current study, and which guarantees the rights of a cultural character to immigrants.

Additionally, the right to cultural expression and the exercise of broadly understood rights of a cultural character might be subject to limitations in the case of the need to protect the rights of a child or the protection of morality (in situations when there appears a conflict of cultural customs with those values), as well as due to the priority of safeguarding public order and security. With regard to the protection of the latter value, the exercise of cultural rights is reduced with regard to migrants remaining in detention, during border controls, as well as foreign nationals who have to be expelled and thus lose the possibility of exercising their cultural rights, together with contact with the culture of the host country.

From the conducted analysis of the case-law, it transpires that in the case of conflicting legal orders—the rights of the host country and customary or religious law—the priority here is given to the laws of the country and the domestic order and thus not all rights of a cultural character might be protected, especially when the cultural norms of migrants are contrary to the commonly accepted standards of behaviour in the host country.

A specific instrument which reduces the possibility of unconditional and free exercise of cultural rights includes the conditions for integration introduced by Member States under the provisions of the directive on family reunification, the reception directive and the directive on long-term residents. It happens as a result of the duty to learn about and respect the cultural tradition of Europe, and simultaneously the need to adjust one's behaviour on cultural grounds to the existing rules in the host society.

The limit of exercising the rights of a cultural character by an immigrant is also marked by the need to meet the conditions for entry (which define several areas, such as the foreign national's real potential for integration or the prohibition of entry for marriages of a polygamic character) and stay (in the case when a foreign national no longer fulfils the conditions of stay, he or she loses the possibility of further residence in a Member State and thus forfeits the guarantees to exercise cultural rights in the territory of the European Union).

A specific type of limitation to an unrestricted exercise of the rights of a cultural character is the lack of a full guarantee of an unrestricted choice of the place of residence, which would make it possible for a foreign national to choose a region which would be the most fitting from the perspective of culture and thus would increase the chances for their cultural identification (the so-called right to choose the cultural surroundings guaranteed currently in Qualification Directive 2011/95). Such guarantees are included neither in the Dublin Regulation nor in the regulation on qualification, both currently under procedure. They were also missing in the decision on relocation (2015/1601). A special rule interpreted in the case-law is the so-called concept of *living together*, which guarantees respect for the rights of all members of a given community, functioning in the public sphere and which might be the grounds for reducing the rights of a particular group. This principle provided the grounds for the rulings which stated that the implemented prohibition against face coverings does not violate the freedom of religious expression (decision of the ECtHR in the case S.A.S.). However, the application of the *living together* principle raises the risk of eliminating cultural signs from social life, as it restricts cultural expressions of both the home and foreign communities.

By examining the provisions facilitating a repeal of cultural rights of foreign nationals, it became possible to define the limits of exercising them. With regard to the third supporting thesis, the conducted analysis also leads to the conclusion that in the legal system of the Union and in the process of its application, it occurs more often that the cultural rights of foreign nationals become restricted rather than completely derogated. It happens especially in situations of an extraordinary character, such as return, detention or the procedure of applying for international protection.

However, it should be emphasized that the right of a cultural character, which is a non-derogable norm, is the right to protection against the culture of the country of origin, which is presented below, whereas its guarantees have their direct source in Art. 4 CFR and Art. 3 ECHR.

7.4 The Effectiveness of the Activities of the Union in the Area of Strengthening the Protection of Cultural Rights and the Protection of European Culture

On the basis of the analysis conducted for the current study, the supporting thesis to the effect that the European culture represents one of the values lying at the foundation and identity of the European Union can be confirmed. Despite the so-called competence for support, provided for in the cultural policies in EU primary and secondary law systems, there exist effective legal instruments facilitating the exercise of cultural policies and providing factual contribution to the improvement of the condition of European culture. The activities of the European Union conducted in the area of culture have their basis in Art. 167 of the TFEU. The guarantees under Art. 22 of the Charter of Fundamental Rights or the involvement of the EU in the preparation of the UNESCO convention on the protection and promotion of the diversity of cultural expressions of 2005 are also not without significance. The flagship activity of the Union in the area of promotion activities in the field of culture and cultural cooperation is the programme *Creative Europe* and the activities of the EACEA, as well as initiatives such as the European Capital of Culture or the European Heritage Days. Since the Lisbon Treaty, the case-law of the Court of Justice has been more focused on cultural life, whereas the cases pending before the Court of Justice concern the new dimensions of social life, such as digitization and preservation of Europe's cultural memory or the functioning of pop-culture icons in cultural industries. It seems justifiable to claim that the Court of Justice in its judicial activities protects cultural rights, despite the lack of Union's direct competences for autonomous cultural policy-making. The existing *acquis culturalis* concerns various areas of social and cultural life and reflects the phenomenon of diversity of the contemporary culture of the post-modern era.

7.5 The Essence and Significance of Integrative Cultural Responsibilities

The analysis conducted as part of the current study has also demonstrated that the integrative cultural duties of foreign nationals (understood as responsibilities of third-country nationals concerning specific activities relating to the necessity to learn and respect the basic social and cultural rules of the host country), whose implementation is facilitated by the existing norms of EU immigration law, allow for the actual protection and strengthening of European identity and culture. They also contribute to the real participation of third-country nationals in cultural life.

As it transpires from the analysis of secondary law (mostly from the directive on family reunification, directive on long-term residents, and Qualification Directive), as well as the case-law of the CJEU in this respect, the condition for effective implementation of integration policies is to learn and adopt the specific cultural patterns, which are accepted and used in a Member State. The conditions for integration are also strengthened by the guarantees of cultural rights, which may be exercised in keeping with the norms which form the basis of the legal and cultural system of the receiving country.

It is also justifiable to claim that cultural responsibilities of third-country nationals do not exempt the receiving society from the responsibility of familiarizing themselves with the information on the subject of migrants' country of origin, so that the process of integration is effective and conducted within the framework of intercultural dialogue. The compulsory education, which foreign nationals participate in, also entails a specific type of cultural responsibility, as the process of education facilitates an exchange of knowledge concerning the rules of functioning of the host society and the culture of the receiving country.

One cannot uphold the argument contained in the doctrine that integrative measures affect cultural diversity, as the knowledge of the cultural norms of the receiving country does not imply forced assimilation. Moreover, through the skills acquired during integration and language courses, migrants have a broader possibility of partaking in the cultural offer of the host country and a real opportunity to participate in cultural life.

Within the scope of the analysed material on the functioning of integrative cultural responsibilities, the following conclusions have been formulated. Firstly, it seems justifiable to postulate the introduction of a regulation at the EU level which would define the conditions for obligatory integrative tests for foreign nationals. Such a solution would serve the protection of cultural security within the meaning presented in the current study, that is, it would facilitate safe functioning of the very migrant within a given culture of the host country through the knowledge of cultural codes and patterns, allowing for the exercise of one's cultural identity and reconciliation of divergent cultural norms.

Secondly, integrative cultural responsibilities should be applicable to all categories of third-country nationals seeking to reside within the territory of the European Union. Thus, the existing measures of integration would constitute an effective system facilitating the process of integration by equipping migrants with concrete social tools, enabling them to function in a new cultural reality.

7.6 The Right to Protection Against the Culture of the Country of Origin

The legal analysis conducted in the current study also confirms the accuracy of the adopted supporting thesis, to the effect that in the legal system of the EU there exists the right to protection against the culture of the country of origin. This right protects a foreign national against the oppressive culture of the country of origin,[6] which prevents the exercise of their cultural identity. In a situation when foreign nationals were to experience persecution, within the meaning of asylum law, on account of their exercise of their cultural identity, or when they were to be exposed to inhuman treatment, they should be granted international protection and they should not be returned to the country of origin. The right to protection against the culture of the country of origin has its basis in the guarantees under Art. 4 CFR prohibiting inhuman treatment and in the principle of *non-refoulement*. Inhuman treatment may entail persecution and degrading treatment on cultural grounds, which is confirmed on the basis of the case-law of the CJEU and ECtHR analysed in the study. The right to protection against the culture of the country of origin should be relied on by the migrants fearing expulsion to the country of origin on the grounds of cultural differences between their behaviour and the customs in their country of origin. As a side note, it should be added that a large number of persons seeking international protection in the EU come from the countries with dominant oppressive cultures, exposing the representatives of minorities to repressions and making it impossible for them to manifest and exercise their cultural rights, as well as imposing on them the obligation to conform to specific cultural canons.

Among the indicators which might justify the decision to grant protection against the culture of the country of origin, one might, on the basis of the analysed case-law, list the risk of social exclusion (social ostracism) in the event of returning to the homeland, the lack of regard for women's rights and violence against women, the risk of being subject to honour crimes, inhuman cultural customs (such as, e.g., ritual circumcision of women in Nigeria) or persecution on religious grounds. The catalogue of indicators is of an open character.

In the adopted concept of protection against the culture of the country of origin, the consequence of the existence of guarantees of protection includes the acceptance of the right of individuals to decide about their cultural identity. What is significant is that the forced return of a migrant

[6] As has been emphasized in the study, as regard to the terminology, it seems that the term "protection against the culture of the country of origin" in a more substantial way refers to the substance of the protection. For the sake of clarity, however, it should be added here that it is usually the elements of a given culture that are of an oppressive nature, and not the culture understood *en masse*, with all its manifestations.

to the country of origin may constitute a violation of the right to identity through the breach or breaking of the existing cultural ties with the host country.

On the other hand, a reverse situation occurs when a foreign national's entry to a Member State and family reunification were to violate the existing cultural ties. However, it seems that foreign nationals should have the right to autonomously decide about their cultural identity, especially as arbitrary decisions of immigration authorities may amount to a forceful imposition of cultural identity on an individual.

To sum up, on the basis of the analysed legal material, it is justifiable to claim that the theses proposed in the current study are correct. In the legal system of the European Union there exists a catalogue of cultural rights and responsibilities of third-country nationals. Those rights are protected in a sufficient way, in order to provide immigrants with appropriate conditions for effective functioning in the cultural space of the receiving countries.

Selected Bibliography

Adamczyk, A., and G. Ilik. "Greek–Turkish Relations, UE and Migration Problem." *Yearbook of Polish European Studies*, vol. 19/2016.

Alexseev, M.A., *Immigration Phobia and the Security Dilemma. Russia, Europa and the United States*. Cambridge, 2006.

Algan Y., A. Bisin, and T. Verdier. "Introduction: Perspectives on Cultural Integration of Immigrants." In *Cultural Integration of Immigrants in Europe*, eds. Y. Algan, A. Bisin, A. Manning, T. Verdier. Oxford, 2012.

Andrzejczuk, R. *Prawa człowieka podstawą narodów do samostanowienia*. Lublin, 2004.

Andrzejczuk, R. *Prawa człowieka w'swietle uwarunkowań kulturowych i prawnych*. Lublin, 2011.

Andrzejewski, P.Ł.J. "Prawo człowieka do tożsamości kulturowej w Polsce." In *Prawa człowieka w społeczeństwie obywatelskim*, ed. A. Rzepliński. Warszawa, 1993.

Arden, M. *Human Rights and European Law. Building New legal orders*. Oxford, 2015.

Babiński, G. "Społeczne i etniczne konsekwencje migracji międzynarodowych." In *Polityka wielokulturowósci a migracje*, eds. M. Bieńkowska, A. Sadowski. Białystok, 2012.

Babis, P. "Wpływ Unii Europejskiej na budowę polskiej polityki integracyjnej." In *Praktyki integracji. Dóswiadczenia. Perspektywy*, eds. M. Bieniecki, M. Pawlak. Warszawa, 2012.

Balch, A., and A. Geddes. "The development of the EU Migration and Asylum Regime." In *Migration and the new technological borders*, eds. H. Dijstelbloem, A. Meijer. Palgrave Macmillan, 2011.

A. M. Kosińska, *Cultural Rights of Third-Country Nationals in EU Law*,
https://doi.org/10.1007/978-3-030-30154-5

Baldwin-Edwards, M. "The Sothern European "model of immigration". A sceptical view." In *European Immigration. Trends, Structures and Policy Implications*, ed. M. Okólski. Amsterdam University Press, 2012.

Balicki, J. "Imigranci islamscy w Wielkiej Brytanii. Brytyjczycy czy muzułmanie?" In *Integracja kulturowa migrantów. Wyzwania i dylematy*, ed. J. Balicki. Warszawa, 2007.

Bank, R. "Forced Migration in Europe" In *The Oxford Handbook of Refugee and Forced Migration Studies*, eds. E. Fiddian-Qasmiyeh, G. Loescher, K. Long, N. Sigona. Oxford, 2014.

Bank, R. "Refugee Law Jurisprudence from Germany and Human Rights: Cutting Edge or Chilling Effect." In *Human Rights and the Refugee Definition. Comparative Legal Practice and Theory*, eds. B. Burson, D.J. Cantor. Brill/Nijhoff, 2016.

La Barbera, M.C. "Identity and Migration. An Introduction." In *Identity and Migration in Europe: Multidisciplinary Perspectives*, ed. M.C. La Barbera. Springer, 2015.

Barsky, R.F. *Undocumented Immigrants in the Era of Arbitrary Law. The Flight and the Plight of People Deemed "Illegal"*. Routledge, 2016.

Bartoszewski, Wł. "Kultura – moje miejsce." In *Kultura i tożsamóść europejska. Duchowy fundament integracji naszego kontynentu*. Gliwice, 2001.

Bates, E. "History." In *International Human Rights Law*, Oxford 2010, eds. D. Moeckli, S. Shah, S. Sivakumaran. Oxford, 2010.

Baubock, R. "Cultural Minority Rights for Immigrants." *The International Migration Review* vol. 30, no. 1, Special Issue *Ethics, Migration, and Global Stewardship*, 1996.

Bauloz, C., and G. Ruiz. "Refugee Status and Subsidiary Protection: Towards a Uniform Content of International Protection." In *Reforming the Common European Asylum System. The New European Refugee Law*, eds. V. Chetail. P. De Bruycker, F. Maiani. Brill, 2016.

Bauman, Z. *Europa niedokończona przygoda*. Kraków, 2007.

Baumann, Z. *Obcy u naszych drzwi*. Warszawa, 2016.

Beitz, Ch. R. *The Idea of Human Rights*. Oxford, 2011.

Besselink, L.F.M. "Should the European Union ratify the European Convention on Human Rights? Some remarks on the relations between the European Court of Human Rights and the European Court of Justice." In *Constituting Europe. The European Court of Human Rights in a National, European and Global Context*, eds. A. Follesdal, B. Peters, G. Ulfstein. Cambridge, 2013.

Blanco Sio-Lopez, C., and P. Tedeschi. "Migrants and European Institutions. A study on the attempts to address the economic and social challenges of immigration in EU member states." In *The history of migration in Europe. Perspectives from economics, politics and sociology*, ed. F. Fauri. Routledge, 2015.

Blitz, B.K. *Migration and Freedom. Mobility, Citizenship and Exclusion*. Edward Elgar Publishing, 2014.
Bohmer, C., and A. Shuman. *Rejecting refugees. Political asylum in the 21st century*. Routledge, 2008.
Block, L., and S. Bonjour. "Fortress Europe or Europe of Rights? The Europeanisation of Family Migration Policies in France, Germany and Netherlands." *European Journal of Migration and Law*, vol. 15, 2/2013.
Bocker, A., and T. Strik. "Language and Knowledge Tests for Permanent Residence Rights: Help or Hindrance for Integration?" *European Journal of Migration and Law*, vol. 13, issue 2/2011
Bodnar, A. "Karta Praw Podstawowych: zróżnicowany charakter prawny postanowień Karty i ich skutki dla jednostek, sądów oraz ustawodawcy." In *Ochrona praw podstawowych w Unii Europejskiej*, ed. J. Barcz. Warszawa, 2008.
Bosworth, M. *Inside Immigration Detention*. Oxford, 2014.
Van Boven, T. "Categories of Rights in International Human Rights Law." In *International Human Rights Law*, eds. D. Moeckli, S. Shah, S. Sivakumaran. Oxford, 2010.
Cantor, D.J., J. Van Wijk, S. Singer, and M.P. Bolhuis. "The Emperor's New Clothing: National Responses to "Undesirable and Unreturnable" Aliens under Asylum and Immigration Law." *Refugee Survey Quarterly*, vol. 2017, issue 36.
Carrera, S., and J. Parkin. *Protecting and Delivering Fundamental Rights of Irregular Migrants at Local and Regional Levels in the European Union*. The Centre for European Policy Studies, 2011.
Castles, S., and J. Miller. *The Age of Migration. International population movements in the modern world*. Palgrave Macmillan, 2009.
Chalmerd, D., G. Davies, and G. Monti. *European Union Law, Second Edition*. Cambridge, 2011.
Cholewinski, R. *Study on obstacles to effective access of irregular migrants to minimum social rights*. Council of Europe Publishing, 2005.
Clayton, G. *Immigration and Asylum Law*. Oxford, 2016.
Cornelisse, G. "A new articulation of human rights, or why the European Court of Human Rights should think beyond Westphalian sovereignty." In *Are human rights for migrants? Critical reflections on the status of irregular migrants in Europe and the United States*, eds. M.B. Dembour, T. Kelly. Routledge, 2011.
Costello, C. *The Human Rights of Migrants and Refugees in European Law*. Oxford, 2016a.
Costello, C. "The Search of the Outer Edges of Non-refoulement in Europe: Exceptionality and Flagrant Breaches." In *Human Rights and Refugee Definition. Comparative Legal Practice and Theory*, eds. B. Burson, D.J. Cantor. Brill/Nijhoff, 2016b.

Dauvergne, C. *Making people illegal. What globalisation means for migration and law*. Cambridge University Press, 2011.

Dauvergne, C., and J. Millbank. "Forced Marriage as a Harm in Domestic and International Law." In *Human Rights and Refugee Law. Volume I*, ed. J. C. Hathaway. Edward Elgar Publishing, 2013.

Debono, D. "'Not our problem': why detention of irregular migrants is not considered a human rights issue in Malta." In *Are human rights for migrants? Critical reflections on the status of irregular migrants in Europe and the United States*, eds. M.B. Dembour, T. Kelly. Routledge, 2011.

Dembour, M.B. *When Humans Become Migrants. Study of the European Court of Human Rights with an Inter-American Counterpoint*. Oxford, 2015.

Van Dijk, P. Protection of "Integrated" Aliens against Expulsion under the European Convention on Human Rights." In *Security of Residence and Expulsion. Protection of Aliens in Europe*, eds. E. Guild, P. Minderhoud. Nijhoff, 2001.

Donders, I. "Foundations of Collective Cultural Rights in International Human Rights Law." In *Cultural Rights as Collective Rights an International Law Perspective*, ed. A. Jakubowski. Leiden/Boston, 2016.

Dunkerley, D., J. Scourfield, T. Maegusuku-Hewett, and N. Smalley. "The Experiences of Frontline Staff Working with Children Seeking Asylum." In *Migration, Immigration and Social Policy*, ed. C.J. Finer. Blackwell Publishing, 2006.

Eisele, K. *The External Dimension of the EU's Migration Policy. Different Legal Positions of Third Country Nationals in the EU: A Comparative Perspective*. Brill/Nijhoff, 2014.

Engelmann, C. "Convergence against the Odds: The Development of Safe Country of Origin Policies in EU Member States (1990–2013)." *European Journal of Migration and Law*, vol. 16, issue 2, 2014.

EU Immigration and Asylum Law (Text and Commentary): Second Revised Edition, vol.1: Visas and Borders Controls, eds. S. Peers, E. Guild, J. Tomkin. Leiden/Boston: Martinus Nijhoff Publishers, 2012.

EU Immigration and Asylum Law (Text and Commentary): Second Revised Edition, vol. 2: EU Immigration Law, eds. S. Peers, E. Guild, D. Costa et al. Leiden/Boston: Martinus Nijhoff Publishers, 2012.

Fabbrini, F. *Fundamental Rights in Europe. Challenges and Transformations in Comparative Perspective*. Oxford, 2014.

Fassmann, H., and U. Reeger. "Old Immigration Countries in Europe. The concept and empirical example." In *European Immigration. Trends, Structures and Policy Implications*, ed. M. Okólski. Amsterdam University Press, 2012.

Fauri, F. "European migrants after the Second World War." In *The history of Migration in Europe. Perspectives from economics, politics and sociology*, ed. F. Fauri. Routledge, 2015.

Finney N., and L. Simpson. *"Sleepwalking to segregation"? Challenging myths about race and migration*. Bristol, 2009.

Gammeltoft-Hansen T. *Access to asylum. International Refugee Law and the Globalisation of Migration Control.* Cambridge, 2013.

Garlick, M. "The Dublin System of Solidarity and Individual Rights." In *Reforming the Common European Asylum System. The New European Refugee Law*, eds. V. Chetail. P. De Bruycker, F. Maiani. Brill, 2016.

Geddes, A. "Borders, Territory, and Migration in the European Union: From the Politics of Migration in Europe to the European Politics of Migration." In *Of States, Rights, and Social Closure*, eds. O. Schmidtke, S. Ozcurumez. New York: Palgrave Macmillan, 2008a.

Geddes, A. *Immigration and European integration. Beyond the fortress Europe? Second edition, European Policy Research Unit Series.* Manchester University Press, 2008b.

Gijsberts, M., P. Scheepers, and M. Coenders. "Exclusion of Legal Migrants in Western Europe." In *Nationalism and Exclusion of Migrants. Cross – National Comparisons*, eds. M. Gijsberts, L. Hagendoorn, P. Scheepers. London and New York: Routledge, 2017.

Grey, A. "Comparative Religious Freedom: The Right to Wear Religious Dress." In *The other people. Interdisciplinary perspectives on migration*, ed. M. W. Karraker. Palgrave Macmillan, 2013.

Grey, C. *Justice and Authority in Immigration Law.* Oregon: Oxford and Portland, 2017.

Groenendijk, K. "Legal Concepts of Integration in EU Migration Law." *European Journal of Migration and Law*, vol. 6 issue 2/2004.

Groenendijk, K. "Pre-departure Integration Strategies in the European Union: Integration or Immigration Policy?" *European Journal of Migration and Law*, vol. 13 issue 1/2011.

Guild, E. "Who is an irregular migrant?" In *Irregular migration and Human Rights: Theoretical, European and International Perspectives*, eds. B. Bogusz, R. Cholewiński, A. Cygan, E. Szyszczak. Leiden: Brill/Nijhoff, 2004.

Guild, E., K. Groenendijk, and S. Carrera. "Understanding the Contest of Community: Illiberal Practices in the EU?" In *Illiberal Liberal States: Immigration, Citizenship and Integration in the EU.* Ashgate, 2009.

Haddad, E. *The Refugee in International Society, Between Sovereigns.* Cambridge, 2008.

Hamdan, E. *The Principle of Non-Refoulement under the ECHR and the UN Convention against Torture and Other Cruel, Inhuman and Degrading Treatment and Punishment.* Brill/Nijhoff, 2016.

Hammond, L. "'Voluntary' Repatriation and Reintegration." In *The Oxford Handbook of Refugee and Forced Migration Studies*, eds. E. Fiddian-Qasmiyeh, G. Loescher, K. Long, N. Sigona. Oxford, 2014.

Hartley, T.C. *The Foundations of European Union Law.* Oxford, 2010.

Harzig, Ch., D. Hoerder, and D. Gabaccia. *What is migration history?* Cambridge, 2009.

Den Hertog, L. "Fundamental Rights and the Extra-territorialization of EU Border Policy: A Contradiction in Terms?" In *Foreigners, refugees or minorities? Rethinking people in the context of border controls and visas*, eds. D. Bigo, S. Carrera, E. Guild. Ashgate, 2013.

Hoerder, D. "Migration in the Atlantic Economies: Regional European Origins and Worldwide Expansion." In *European Migrants. Global and Local Perspectives*, eds. D. Hoerder, L. P. Moch. Northeastern University Press, 1996.

Hollenbach, D. "Religion and Forced Migration." In *The Oxford Handbook of Refugee and Forced Migration Studies*, eds. E. Fiddian-Qasmiyeh, G. Loescher, K. Long, N. Sigona. Oxford, 2014.

Horspool, M., Humphreys, M. *European Union Law*. Oxford, 2010.

Joly, D. "Whose protection? European harmonisation on asylum policy." In *The Cambridge Survey of World Migration*, ed. R. Cohen. Cambridge, 2010.

Jovanović, M. "Cultural Rights as Collective Rights." In *Cultural Rights as Collective Rights. An International Law Perspective*, ed. A. Jakubowski. Leiden/Boston, 2016.

Jurkiewicz-Eckert, D. "Cultural Policy of the EU – How it Works in Practice." In *Introduction to European Studies: A New Approach to Uniting Europe*, eds. D. Milczarek, A. Adamczyk, K. Zajączkowski. Warszawa, 2013.

Kalin, W. "Troubled Communication: Cross Cultural Misunderstandings in the Asylum Hearing." In *Human Rights and Refugee Law*, vol. II, eds. J.C. Hathaway. Edward Elgar Publishing, 2013.

Karaygit, M.T. "Vive la Clause de Standstill: The Issue of First Admission of Turkish Nationals into the Territory of Member States within the Context of Economic Freedoms." *European Journal of Migration and Law*, issue 3/2011

Kay, D. "The resettlement of displaced persons in Europe." In *The Cambridge Survey of World Migration*, ed. R. Cohen. Cambridge, 2010.

Kerns, P. "Culture and EU Law: The Exploration of an Interface." In *Culture and European Union Law*, ed. R. C. Smith. Oxford, 2004.

Kneebone, S. "Refugees and displaced persons: the refugee definition and humanitarian protection." In *Research Handbook on International Human Rights Law*, eds. S. Joseph, A. Beth. Edgar Elgar, 2010.

Kostakopoulou, D. "The Area of Freedom, Security and Justice and the Political Morality of Migration and Integration." In *A right to inclusion or exclusion? Normative fault lines of the EU's Area of freedom, security and justice*, ed. H. Lindahl. Hart Publishing, 2009.

Kruma, K. *EU Citizenship, Nationality and Migrant Status. An Ongoing Challenge*. Leiden/Boston, 2004.

Lenzerini, F. "Suppressing and Remedying Offences against Culture." In *The Cultural Dimension of Human Rights*, ed. A.F. Vrdoljak. Oxford, 2013.

Linton, R. *Kulturowe podstawy osobowości*. Warszawa, 2000.

Loescher G., and J. Milner. "UNHCR and the Global Governance of Refugees." In *Human Rights and Refugee Law. volume I*, ed. J. C. Hathaway. Edward Elgar Publishing, 2013.

Loescher, G. "UNHCR and forced migration." In *The Oxford Handbook of Refugee and Forced Migration Studies*, eds. E. Fiddian-Qasmiyeh, G. Loescher, K. Long, N. Sigona. Oxford, 2014.

Maiani, F. "The Dublin III Regulation: A New Legal Framework for a More Human System?" In *Reforming the Common European Asylum System. The New European Refugee Law*, eds. V. Chetail. P. De Bruycker, F. Maiani. Brill, 2016.

Mantouvalou, V., and P. Voyatzis. "The Council of Europe and the protection of human Rights: a system in Reed of reform." In *Research handbook on International Human Rights Law*, eds. S. Joseph, A. McBeth. Edward Elgar Publishing, 2010.

Martenson, H., and J. McCarthy. "'In General, No Serious Risk of Persecution': Safe Country of Origin Practices in Nine European States." *Journal of Refugee Studies*, issue 11(3)/1998.

Martin, S. *International Migration. Evolving Trends from the Early Twentieth Century to the Present.* Cambridge, 2014.

Maslow, A. *Motywacja i osobowość.* Warszawa, 2006.

Młynarska-Sobaczewska, A. "Utopian Concept, Mixed Structure, Digital Extent and New Claims How to Take Seriously the Right to (Artistic) Culture?" *International Human Rights Law Review*, vol. 6, issue 2/2017.

Morehouse, C., and M. Blomfield. *Irregular migration in Europe.* Migration Policy Institute, December 2011.

Mucha, J. "Migration and the transmission of cultural patterns. Introduction." In *Migration and the transmission of cultural patterns*, ed. J. Mucha. Kraków, 2016.

Mungianu, R. "Frontex: Towards a Common Policy on External Border Control." *European Journal of Migration and Law*, vol. 15, issue 4/2013.

Murphy, C. *Immigration, Integration and the Law. The Intersection of Domestic, EU and International Legal Remedies.* Ashgate, 2013.

Musalo, K. "Claims for Protection Based on Religion or Belief." In *Human Rights and Refugee Law. Volume I*, ed. J. C. Hathaway. Edward Elgar Publishing, 2013.

Van Oers, R. *Deserving Citizenship. Citizenship Tests in Germany, the Netherlands and the United Kingdom.* Leiden/Boston, 2014.

Okólski, M. "Transition from emigration to immigration. Is it the destiny of modern European countries?" In *European Immigration. Trends, Structures and Policy Implications*, ed. M. Okólski. Amsterdam University Press, 2012.

Oosterom-Staples, H. "Effective Rights of Third Country Nationals?" In *A right to inclusion or exclusion? Normative fault lines of the EU's Area of freedom, security and justice*, ed. H. Lindahl. Hart Publishing, 2009.

Osiatyński, W. *Prawa człowieka i ich granice.* Kraków, 2011.

Van de Peer, P. "Negotiating the Second Generation of the Common European Asylum System Instruments: A Chronicle." In *Reforming the Common*

European Asylum System. The New European Refugee Law, eds. V. Chetail, P. De Bruycker, F. Maiani. Brill, 2016.

Peers, S. "Legislative Update EU Immigration and Asylum Law 2010: Extension of Long – term Residence Rights and Amending the Law on Trafficking in Human Beings." *European Journal of Migration and Law*, vol. 13, issue 2/2011.

Peixoto, J., J. Arango, and C. Bonifazi. "Immigrants, markets and policies in Southern Europe. The making of an immigration model?" In *European Immigration. Trends, Structures and Policy Implications*, ed. M. Okólski. Amsterdam University Press, 2012.

Permoser, J.M. "Civic Integration as Symbolic Politics: Insights from Austria." *European Journal of Migration and Law*, vol. 14, issue 2/2012.

Psychogiopoulou, E. "The European Union and Cultural Rights." In *The Cultural Dimension of Human Rights*. Oxford, 2013.

Ramcharan, B. *The Fundamental of International Human Rights Treaty Law*. Leiden/Boston, 2011.

Romaniszyn, K. "Belonging or Not-Belonging: Migration as a Challenge to Guest and Host Identity." In *Culture and migration. The Cultural Implications of International Migrations in the Light of Fieldwork Evidence*, ed. K. Romaniszyn. Kraków, 2008.

Rubio-Marin, R. "Integration in Immigrant Europe: Human Rights at a Crossroad." In *Human Rights and Immigration*, ed. R. Rubio-Marin. Oxford, 2014.

Smith, R.C. "The Development of Cultural Policy by European Community." In *Culture and European Union Law*, ed. R. C. Smith. Oxford, 2004.

Spengler, O. *Zmierzch Zachodu*. Warszawa, 2001.

Stamatopoulou, E. *Cultural Rights in International Law, Article 27 of the Universal Declaration of Human Rights and beyond*. Brill/Nijhoff, 2007.

Śledzińska-Simon A. "Is there a place for the Islamic veil in the workplace? Managerial prerogatives and the duty of reasonable accommodation in the EU anti discrimination governance." *Era FORUM*, vol. 17, issue 2/2016.

Ślusarczyk, M. "With us or Near us? Directions of Change and cultural integration of immigrants in Europe." In *Culture and migration. The Cultural Implications of International Migrations in the Light of Fieldwork Evidence*, ed. K. Romaniszyn. Kraków, 2008.

Tezcan-Idriz, N. "Dutch Courts Safeguarding Rights under the EEC – Turkey Association Law. Case Note on District Court Rotterdam Judgments of 12 August 2010, and District Court Roermond Judgment of 1 October 2010." *European Journal of Migration and Law*, vol. 13, issue 2/2011.

Togral, B. "Convergence of Securitization of Migration and "New Racism" in Europe: Rise of Culturalism and Disappearance of Politics." In *Security, Insecurity and Migration in Europe*, ed. G. Lazaridis. Routledge, 2016.

Trispiotis, I. "Two Interpretations of 'Living Together' in European Human Rights Law." *The Cambridge Law Journal*, vol. 75 issue 3/2016.

Tsourdi, E. "Qualifying for international protection in the EU. New understanding of the 1951 Convention and Beyond" In *Exploring Boundaries of Refugee Law. Current Protection Challenges*, eds. J.P. Gauci, M. Giuffre, E. Tsourdi. Brill/Nijhoff, 2015.

Wiessner, S. "Culture and the Rights of Indigenous People." In *The Cultural Dimension of Human Rights*, ed. A.F. Vrdoljak. Oxford, 2013.

Wilsher, D. *Immigration Detention. Law, History, Politics.* Cambridge, 2012.

Index[1]

[1] Note: Page numbers followed by 'n' refer to notes.

A. M. Kosińska, *Cultural Rights of Third-Country Nationals in EU Law*,
https://doi.org/10.1007/978-3-030-30154-5

CPSIA information can be obtained
at www.ICGtesting.com
Printed in the USA
LVHW081158151219
640572LV00015B/1018/P

9 783030 301538